STOPPING
WIFE ABUSE

A Guide to the Emotional, Psychological,
and Legal Implications . . . for the
abused woman and those helping her

Jennifer Baker Fleming

Anchor Books
Anchor Press/Doubleday
Garden City, New York   1979

The Anchor Books edition is the first publication of STOPPING WIFE ABUSE.
Anchor Books Edition: 1979

The author and publisher wish to thank the following sources for permission to reprint:

"She Leaves" and "The Woman in the Ordinary," from *To Be of Use*, by Marge Piercy. Copyright © 1969, 1971, 1973 by Doubleday & Company, Inc. Used by permission of the publisher.

Wifebeating: The Silent Crisis, by Roger Langley and Richard C. Levy. Copyright © 1977 by E. P. Dutton. Used by permission of the publisher.

Conjugal Crime, by Terry Davidson. Copyright © 1978 by Hawthorne Books, Inc. Used by permission of the publisher.

"For Shelter and Beyond," from *The Twelve-spoked Wheel Flashing*, by Marge Piercy. Copyright © 1978 by Alfred A. Knopf, Inc. Used by permission of the publisher.

Battered Women: A Psychosociological Study of Domestic Violence, edited by Maria Roy. Copyright © 1977 by Litton Educational Publishing, Inc. Reprinted by permission of Van Nostrand Reinhold Company.

Battered Wives, by Del Martin. Copyright © 1976 by New Glide Publications. Used by permission of the publisher.

"Alone," from *Oh Pray My Wings Are Gonna Fit Me Well*, by Maya Angelou. Copyright © 1975 by Random House, Inc. Used by permission of the publisher.

For Better, for Worse: A Feminist Handbook on Marriage and Other Options, by Jennifer Baker Fleming and Carolyn Kott Washburn. Copyright © 1977 by Charles Scribner's Sons. Used by permission of the publisher.

Women in Transition: A Feminist Handbook on Separation and Divorce, by Women in Transition, Inc. Copyright © 1975 by Charles Scribner's Sons. Used by permission of the publisher.

Material from *The Victimization of Women* (Vol. 3), Jane Roberts Chapman and Margaret Gates, eds. Copyright © 1978 by Sage Publications. Used by permission of the authors.

Material from *Victimology: An International Journal* (Vol. 2, 1977–78), Emilio Viano, ed. Copyright © 1978 by Visage Press, Inc. Reprinted by permission of the authors.

ACKNOWLEDGMENTS

This manual represents the monumental efforts of women across the country who have spearheaded recognition of the battered-woman problem and have pioneered, usually against great odds, in the development of the first sympathetic, caring effort in history to provide help to the thousands of women trapped by violent and abusive husbands. Without them and their work, this book would not have been possible.

I would like the following individuals to know that they have my heartfelt gratitude and appreciation for the efforts they have made in helping this manual become a reality: Eve Ann Schwartz, for gathering an impressive amount of data in an impossibly short time; Millie Pagelow, without whom we would not have had a research chapter; Bernice Brickland, who helped with Chapter IV and who really knows how to fill up a yellow legal pad; Carol Angell, for her important contributions to Chapter VIII; Bea Wiedener, for her creative artwork; Del Martin, for her wonderful Foreword; Muriel Fondi, for her outstanding contribution to Chapter II as well as her ongoing support, encouragement, and partnership; my agent, Ginger Barber, who never refused a phone call in spite of their number; my editor, Loretta Barrett, who never really cracked the whip, for which I will be eternally grateful; Joyce Bullock, for her many agonizing hours at the dining-room table, which resulted in vital contributions to many of the chapters; Casselle Trent and Ernestine Williams, for valuable typing help; Karen Lee, for going way beyond the call of duty by not only typing mountains of material through many long nights but by providing aid and sustenance during my periods of temporary insanity; Barbara Simon, who helped me whip the whole thing into shape and stuck it out until the bitter end; Linda Backiel, for the magnificent job she did on Chapter III; Carolyn Washburne, for her long-distance pep talks; Marge Gates, for her sound advice; Mary Peterson, for believing in me; my children, Robbie and Kathy, who are finally old enough to nurture and care for me; and finally, Schree Hicks, whose unqualified support and unflagging faith made the difference between success and failure.

CONTENTS

Structure • Legal Matters • Finances • Record
Keeping • Economic Development • Mail
Campaigns • Government Funds • Foundations
• Fund-raising Tips • Evaluation • Follow-up
• Organizing a Hotline • If You Are Within an
Existing Agency • Doctors, Nurses, Health
Paraprofessionals • Hospital Emergency
Rooms • Private Physicians and Clinics
• Company Medical and Counseling Departments
• Social Workers and Counselors • Welfare
Workers • Lawyers and Legal Workers
• Ministers, Priests, and Rabbis • Mandatory
Reporting • Accompaniment and Advocacy
• Hospital Protocol • Police Protocol • Relating
to Police and Hospital Personnel • Victim Relations
• Coalition Building • How to Establish a
Coalition

This book is dedicated to Kitty Genovese, who was murdered on the streets of Queens, New York, several years ago.

Although thirty-nine people heard her screams and cries, no one called the police.

Most explained that they had thought the murderer was her husband.

MOUNTAIN MOVING DAY

The mountain moving day is coming
I say so yet others doubt it
Only a while the mountain sleeps
In the past all mountains moved in fire
Yet you may not believe it
O man this alone believe
All sleeping women now awake and move
All sleeping women now awake and move.

Can you hear the river?
Canyons stretch above it
But if you listen you can hear it below
Grinding stones into sand
Yet you may not hear it
O man this alone hear
All silent women scream in rage
All silent women scream in rage.

The mountain moving day is coming
I say so yet others doubt it
Only a while the mountain sleeps

In the past all mountains moved in fire
Yet you may not believe it
O man this alone believe
All sleeping women now awake and move
All sleeping women now awake and move
All sleeping women now awake and move.

First verse: Yosano Akiko (1911)
Second verse and song: Naomi
Weisstein © 1972, written for
the Chicago Women's Liberation
Rock Band. "Mountain Moving
Day" (Rounder Records ⚡4001)
Reprinted in *Mountain Moving
Day: Poems by Women* (Ed.,
Elaine Gill).

AUTHOR'S NOTE

Approximately five years ago, while working at the Women in Transition program in Philadelphia, I answered the phone one day to hear a hysterical woman describe the physical abuse she suffered in her home. She told me that her husband would periodically closet himself in one of the rooms in their suburban home for hours at a time with their four sons, who ranged in age from six to seventeen. When they emerged, they would all beat her together. She told me that she had suffered permanent injuries from the repeated beatings, that she had had one nervous breakdown and feared she was about to have another.

Unfortunately, I didn't believe her. I was sure that the brutality she described was an exaggeration. After all, she lived in a nice home in the suburbs, and her husband was a respected, civic-minded member of the community.

But not only was Mrs. Brighton telling the truth, she was voicing a common experience. Gradually I came to realize that wife beating is a national pastime.

Later, after working with battered women for several years, I became convinced that it was time for us to begin to influence and change the systems with which battered women come into contact.

Hence, the development of the Women's Resource Network,* which provides training, consultation, and technical assistance to law-enforcement personnel, social-service practitioners, and family-violence programs. This book has emerged as a natural outgrowth of our work at the Women's Resource Network.

This manual is not designed to convince you that wife beating is a problem. We assume that if you are reading this book, you are already aware of the problem and are ready to move on to the next step.

Perhaps you have read Del Martin's landmark work *Battered Wives*. Perhaps you are a concerned individual, part of a group or agency that wants to provide or is already providing services to battered women. Or perhaps you are a battered woman in search of a way out of a violent relationship. Whatever your reason, this manual will not provide you with an exhaustive, in-depth analysis of the causes, nature, and extent of the problem. This has already been done and done well several times over. Our bibliography can provide you with adequate resources should you wish to focus on these factors.

What this book is designed to do is to provide you with the insight, information, skills, and knowledge you need if you are contemplating or are providing help to battered women.

As you read this book, keep in mind that things are moving very quickly within the community of concerned individuals who are at work on the problem. By the time you read this, some of the material will already be out of date. For updating, we suggest that you contact the National Coalition Against Domestic Violence, 6243 NE 19th St., Portland, OR 97211.

We also do not presume that what we have written is the final word on any of the subject areas covered. We have simply created

* The Women's Resource Network would like to extend its appreciation to the following for their support:
The Samuel S. Fels Fund
The Dolfinger-McMahon Foundation
The Philadelphia Foundation
The Ford Foundation
The Rockefeller Family Fund
The Law Enforcement Assistance Administration
The federal agency ACTION
The West Philadelphia Corporation.

a jumping-off place for persons interested in helping. We hope that what you read here will stimulate you to go far beyond what we have covered as you develop programs and services for abuse victims.

There are some issues we have not included. We had planned to discuss psychological abuse as well as physical, but space limitations dictated otherwise. Also, we were going to address the question of services for battered husbands, but after reading the literature on the subject, we have become convinced that this is a false issue and that there is an insufficient number of battered husbands to warrant such an effort (see Chapter VII). In addition, we had thought to explore battering within gay relationships but have since concluded that there is not (as of this writing) enough material available to allow us to address this issue satisfactorily.

Instead, we cover a number of other things: advice for battered women, legislative change, the legal system, and children; couple counseling; information on working with the abuser and with the victim; guidelines for establishing shelter and support services; and an overview of the research on wife abuse.

While our decision to write this book reflects our commitment to efforts that will alleviate the battered-woman problem, it is clear that the ultimate solution lies not in attempts at repairing existing damage but in preventing wife abuse from happening in the first place.

This will not occur, however, until we start doing things differently. We have to change the way we raise our children. We need to start teaching our boys to respect women and the feminine characteristics they possess, and we need to teach girls to respect and stand up for themselves. Once we begin, we will end up creating grown men and women capable of dealing with each other with equality and mutual respect. The solution to the problem of woman battering lies not in addressing the problem after the fact but in restructuring our society to eliminate inequality on account of sex.

JENNIFER BAKER FLEMING

Jennifer Baker Fleming is the founder and director of the Women's Resource Network, a national resource in response to family violence. Formerly she served as codirector of Philadelphia's Women in Transition program. She has coauthored two books: *Women in Transition, a Feminist Handbook on Separation and Divorce* and, with Carolyn Kott Washburne, *For Better, For Worse: a Feminist Handbook on Marriage and Other Options.* She has six years' experience in the field.

MURIEL FONDI

Muriel Fondi, M.S.W., has had twenty years of experience in all aspects of social work, including training, direct practice, supervision, and administration. She serves as director of training for the Women's Resource Network.

WOMEN'S RESOURCE NETWORK

The Women's Resource Network, 4025 Chestnut Street, Philadelphia, PA, 19104 is a private, non-profit corporation that provides technical assistance, training, and consultation to programs providing services in the area of family violence as well as to criminal-justice and mental-health personnel on coping with the domestic-violence problem. In existence since April of 1977, the organization is developing treatment models for working with abusive males, improved counseling techniques for battered women, a national police-training model, training programs for mental-health practitioners, and serves as a regional technical-assistance center on family violence. Chapters II and III contain information on the organization's training programs and support groups for abused women. The agency's therapy groups for abusive men are described in Chapter VI.

Introduction

THE MODERN MARRIAGE CONTRACT

If equality between men and women ever does become a reality, one institution that will have to undergo enormous change is marriage. In my previous book with Carolyn Kott Washburne, *For Better, for Worse,* I outlined the historical, cultural, and legal sanctions for wife beating.

While it is true that men no longer have the right to "chastise" their wives, the marriage and divorce laws in most states continue to relegate women to a subordinate role.

Even though married women can now own property and vote, they must face a legal system that continues to reinforce their submission and subservience to their husbands. The modern marriage contract still obliges the husband to render to his wife the basic necessities of food, clothing, and shelter, just as slave owners had to provide those necessities to their slaves under the southern "slave codes."

The wife is still required to render unpaid labor and sexual services, much as slaves were required to do. Should a husband choose to ignore his duty, most courts will do nothing as long as the parties are living together. In 1953, Mrs. Ruth McGuire petitioned a Nebraska court because she was living in a house with no toilet, no hot water, and no kitchen sink. The court refused to require her well-to-do husband to give her the fifty-dollars-a-month allowance she requested, on the grounds that, since the couple had been married thirty-three years and Mrs. McGuire had never petitioned the court before, there was no problem.

> The living standards of a family are a matter of concern to the household, and not for the courts to determine, even though the husband's attitude towards his wife according to his wealth and circumstances, leaves little to be said on his behalf. As long as the home is maintained it may be said that the husband is legally supporting his wife and the purpose of the marriage relation is being carried out. (McGuire v. McGuire, Neb. 226, 59 N.W. 2nd 336, 1953)

The rule is, if you live with him, take what he gives you and don't complain. If the marriage becomes a disaster, you are free to move out, assuming you have the means to do so and will not depend on him to support you during the separation.

In many states, another form of discrimination under the marriage laws centers around the definition of place of residence. Although married and single men and unmarried women have the right to establish domicile anywhere, married women do not have that right. A married woman is bound by law to reside with her husband. If she chooses not to do so, she can be charged with desertion. Consider the case of a woman who has been married for twenty-five years to a minister. When he was transferred to a new locality, she refused to go with him. Her husband was granted a divorce on the grounds of desertion. The court quoted the Old Testament as an accurate interpretation of Pennsylvania law: "For where you go, I go." The court recited, "It is the duty of the wife to live with her husband in a home provided by him. . . . Where there is a failure to comply with this duty, she is guilty of desertion." (Sachs v. Sachs, 200 Pa. Super. 223, 225) The fact that this wife had twenty years of service with the government and would lose all pension benefits if she went with her husband was irrelevant to the court.

In some states, a woman still cannot sue her husband if he breaches a contract to pay her for work she does in his business, nor can she sue him to enforce a partnership agreement. The assumption is that the wife owes her husband certain labor and is not entitled to financial compensation for that labor even if it goes above and beyond the call of duty.

> It is not the intention of the legislature to deprive the husband of his common law right to the earnings or services of his wife, rendered as wife, by her in or about either their domestic matters or his business affairs. For such services she has not legal recourse against him or his estate. (Standen *v.* Pennsylvania R. Co., 214 Pa. 189, 63 A. [1906]) *

Another interesting discrepancy occurs within the provisions regarding the age of consent to marry. In some states, women are allowed to marry without parental consent two or three years earlier than men. One of the underlying presumptions at work here is that since marriage is the most important goal of women, females should be encouraged to marry at an early age, while men should be encouraged to engage in more important pursuits, such as a career.

More damaging to many women is the assumption that rape does not exist within marriage. That of course, stems from the tradition that the wife is the property of the husband and it is his prerogative to do with her as he pleases. Within marriages that are physically abusive to the woman, rape usually occurs, and the abused wife finds that there is little, if any, recourse. Only now are some states considering legislation that would recognize the possibility of rape between spouses, particularly if they are separated.

Another issue is the question of how much control a wife has over her body. Although a U. S. Supreme Court decision clearly states that the decision to have an abortion belongs to the woman and her physician during the first three months of pregnancy, many hospitals and doctors will insist on having the husband's signature, fearing the possibility of suit. Some states now say consent of the spouse may not be required.

Most of the marriage laws are based on the presumption that

* A similar case is that of Yohey *v.* Yohey. 208 A. 2nd 902, 205 Pa. Super. 32 (1965).

the husband is the breadwinner and that the wife performs the support functions necessary to keep the family alive and well, such as cooking and cleaning. In fact the law says that no matter how much labor is performed by the wife, she is entitled only to bed and board, and as we have seen, the law stipulates that it is of no consequence what kind of bed and board; she is entitled to a roof over her head and subsistence-level food and clothing, nothing more. There are no protections under the law for a woman who has put all of her energy into working in the home, as she was encouraged and expected to do, only to find, twenty or thirty years later, that she can be discarded by her husband perhaps for a younger, sexier model, and left without income, job skills, security, or any means to pay the mortgage or bills. Her labor has gone unrecognized and uncompensated, in spite of the fact that recent studies indicate that it would cost the typical family $13,391.56 per year to replace the average housewife.† Once again, we see the ancient marriage myth at work, this time depriving women of the economic value of their work at home. The resulting economic dependence on the husband leaves many women incapable of providing for themselves or for their children, should the husband desert or refuse to pay.

If the marriage turns sour and the dependent wife decides to leave because her husband refuses to do so, she had better have an independent source of income to accomplish the move, or she becomes trapped with no resources to find a way out. She can't just pick up and move with three children. Where would she live? How would she pay the rent? What would she do with the children while she worked? What kind of job could she get?

The protections that many of us think exist within marriage simply are not there. There are thousands, perhaps millions, of women who believe that they would be protected by the law if their marriages didn't work and their husbands became abusive or hostile. Unfortunately, they are mistaken. It has been a heartbreaking experience to answer the telephones and listen to woman

† Margaret A. Sanborn and Caroline Bird, "The Big Giveaway: What Volunteer Work Is Worth," *Ms.*, Vol. 3, no. 8 (February 1975).

after woman describe the hopelessly unfair situations in which they find themselves. The economically dependent woman who wakes up one morning bruised and battered, to discover that her husband has cleaned out the bank account, refuses to give her any money, or refuses to leave the house while ordering her to leave if she doesn't like it, can do little or nothing.

I have talked with couples who have tried to write marriage contracts that eliminate the inequalities and role assumptions inherent in the traditional contract. These couples have found that although they are free to write, sign, and abide by such contracts, the state will in no way act to enforce them and will not permit either spouse to sue for breach of contract if the agreement is violated. Their reasoning: equal marriage contracts run contrary to the "nature" of marriage.

While many feminist groups are urging women to become economically independent, they are also pushing for more equitable marriage and divorce laws, insisting that the state begin to recognize the sexist nature of the laws and take steps to create a more fair and just system. In addition to these efforts, there is a large-scale campaign underway to ratify the federal Equal Rights Amendment, which would prohibit discrimination based on sex. How this legislation would affect marriage and divorce laws is not quite clear, but some states have passed state ERAs, and the limited litigation that has developed so far on the state level indicates that ERA legislation could eliminate discriminatory laws by extending to men some of the benefits currently given women only. On the other hand, some judges and courts are using ERA legislation to punish women. One example of this is burdening women with equal support responsibilities. This seems fine in theory, but until women are given equal pay for equal work, and equal educational and job opportunities, their earning capacity will remain much lower than that of men, and they will be unable to assume equal financial obligations. We are hopeful, however, that ERA legislation will eventually invalidate the legal presumption that the wife is subservient to and dependent upon the husband and will guarantee her adequate economic protection within marriage.

THE LAW IN THE FUTURE

In order for marriage to become the fifty-fifty proposition that we would like it to be, several things have to happen. First, ways must be found to compensate a wife for her contribution to the family's well-being and for her lack of marketable skills, if such is the case. Also, discriminatory forms of ownership and control of property must be done away with. It is clear that nothing short of a radical restructuring of the legal aspects of marriage can solve these problems. The historical assumptions about the nature of women and their obligations to provide servant labor to the family must be buried. Second, the judiciary must relinquish its pose of objective detachment and "dirty its hands" in domestic affairs when necessary to protect the rights of wives who are not given an equal voice in the management of family resources or who claim they or their children are abused by or not adequately supported by a husband with whom they live. More-drastic steps are necessary in the area of property law. Property ownership should be structured so that each spouse owns his or her share and can dispose of it at will. The presumption that any property purchased solely in the husband's name out of his earnings belongs to him alone (not applicable in community-property states) must be abolished until men and women have equal access to equally remunerative work, and equal responsibilities for housekeeping and child care.

As long as those circumstances do not exist, women must be specially compensated for the work they do in the home, either by a salary paid by the husband during the marriage or out of an escrow fund established by the husband to be used for the wife's benefit should the marriage dissolve or the husband die before her. Strong community-property laws should give whichever spouse is working in the home one half of the income brought in by the employed spouse. Until such measures are routinely established, women must have the right, upon separation or divorce, to be compensated for work previously performed in the home in the form of payments extending over a period of time to be determined by the husband and wife after consideration of the following factors: the length of the marriage, the time spent by each party doing housework and child care, and the educational and salary levels of the parties. If the husband is unable to compensate the wife adequately (or vice versa if the husband has been the homemaker), then ideally the state should provide the compensation, possibly through the Social Security system. Whatever the method, the goal should be economic independence for the dependent spouse. Wives who left college, discontinued job training, or otherwise interrupted an educational career in order to support their husbands' academic or professional training must be given the right to receive similar support from their husbands. Until housework becomes recognized as economically productive work, contributing both to the wealth of the individual family and to the gross national product, most married women will not be compensated for their labor either during or after marriage. And, until they are so compensated, married, separated, divorced, and widowed women will remain on the margins of the economy.

Until our society realizes that men and women are created equal human beings, we will continue to see laws that are based on the assumption of women's innate inferiority, laws that relegate women to a second-class position within the home and in society at large. When those laws are changed to reflect that child care, housekeeping, and careers must be shared responsibilities, depending on the needs, abilities, and inclinations of the spouses, rather than their sexes, we will have gone a long way toward ensuring for women their inalienable rights to life, liberty, and the pursuit of happiness.

FOREWORD

The problems that battered women face, and the needs they have, typify the situation of all women in today's society. The plight of the battered woman illustrates and clarifies the issues raised by the women's movement. For the battered woman magnifies what most women have experienced at some point in their lives.

According to Marya Grambs, clinical psychologist and a founder of La Casa de las Madres shelter for battered women, in San Francisco, any woman who doubts this need only ask herself these questions: Did you ever back down from an argument with a man because you felt intimidated? Did you feel that if you said anything more the situation might get out of hand? Have you ever felt threatened by a man's superior physical strength? Were you afraid that if he became any angrier he might strike you? Have you ever stayed in a relationship longer than you should have? Did you stay because you felt responsible for the other person? Were you afraid of loneliness? Did you stay because of the children? Did you have gnawing doubts that you could not make it on your own in the outside world? Were you fearful that you couldn't earn a decent living and manage the children by yourself?

"Get in touch with those feelings. Then you will know that you are no different from a battered woman," Grambs says.

The danger in dealing with victims of domestic violence and their assailants is to set them apart from other women and men as different or sick. The fact that researchers predict that one or more violent episodes will occur in the course of 50 per cent of American marriages indicates that it is folly to regard marital violence as a behavioral problem of particular individuals. It is a social problem of vast proportions, affecting millions of people. It has its roots in historical attitudes toward women, socialization of rigid life roles according to one's sex, and the power relationship of man over woman in marriage and in society at large. Women and men in violent relationships are the actors in the script we as a society have written for them. They accept and act out the traditional roles of dominant male and submissive female. In patriarchal society the husband is head of household. When he views his wife's behavior as a challenge to his authority, he believes he has valid reason to chastise her. Indeed, the husband did have that right legally until the end of the nineteenth century. The law was changed, but unfortunately social attitudes did not change with it. In an age of space travel and satellites, too many people still adhere to a horse-and-buggy-type marriage.

When I first began to research my book *Battered Wives,* in early 1975, there was a dearth of literature on violence in the home and a reluctance of people to admit that wife beating existed as a serious social problem. Since then, grass-roots women's groups and the media have played prominent roles in bringing the subject to the public's attention. The response—particularly from women—has been overwhelming. Task forces to provide supportive services and/or shelters for victims and their children have been established in both urban and rural areas across the country. Legislation has been enacted to tighten up loopholes in the law and to appropriate funds for services and research. Police departments have instituted crisis-intervention training. Where police are still reluctant to make arrests, class-action suits have been brought by women victims to force the police to change their policies and to take domestic crimes of violence more seriously. New techniques in counseling batterers and victims are being developed. But the battle to eradicate marital violence is far from won. We have only scratched the surface of the problem.

Jennifer Fleming's manual is a report of our progress. It shows the battered woman not only that there is help available where previously there was none, but also that she has options. She can make changes in her life and need not remain helpless in a dangerously violent situation. The manual also provides a summary of current theories and counseling techniques of value to the professional in recognizing and dealing with clients who are caught up in the battering syndrome. The book discusses candidly the differences that have developed over definition of the problem, service delivery models, research methodology, underlying assumptions about victims, causation, counseling techniques, keeping the family together, and treatment of offenders.

These conflicts—primarily between traditional professional agencies and grass-roots women's groups—need to be discussed openly and frankly if we are to effect social change and put a stop to the violence. As pointed out in the chapter "Working with the Victim," all women are victims of the sexist attitudes that pervade psychiatric thinking and the glorification of a man's use of force in popular fiction and the media. Traditional therapy is based upon theories of female masochism and victim precipitation, which shift responsibility from the batterer to his victim. To change the woman's behavior so that she is more compliant and less provocative in order to prevent further abuse and keep the marriage intact is only to further victimize her. Such an approach reinforces her helplessness.

Women's groups, who have taken the lead in providing services to battered women, see their role as one of advocacy. They believe that giving the woman the support she needs to retake control of her life is their primary function. They stress peer counseling and the value of interaction between women who have a common experience. Consciousness-raising groups enable the women to break down their isolation, validate each other's strengths, develop mutual support systems, help them to sort out personal responsibility from that imposed by society, and perceive a variety of possibilities for growth and self-determination.

Emphasis to date has been on the victim, primarily because she is the one in danger and in need of immediate crisis services. Emergency shelters and the "underground railway" by which women who are subject to continued harassment can be shipped from one state to another are the only real protections available. We are only in the beginning stages of learning how to deal with the batterer. Few seek help voluntarily, and counselors report a minimum of success when they do. Chapter VI, "Couple Counseling—Counseling the Abuser" describes some programs but warns that they are highly experimental and by no means can be seen as the panacea for the spouse-abuse problem. At best, therapy has effected a reduction in the violence, but not its elimination.

An assistant district attorney in Spokane suggested to me that probably the most effective means of stopping wife beating would be through peer pressure. "If men would stop making jokes about it and let the batterers know what wife beating is not acceptable male behavior, we would move a lot faster toward solving the problem," he said. Since then, in my travels and speaking engagements on the subject, I have challenged men to work with the batterers in much the same way as women are now working with victims. And I have learned that a network of men's groups have been established to help men understand how sexism victimizes them, too. Already there have been five national conferences on men and masculinity and a willingness expressed by some of the men involved to start peer counseling groups and support services for batterers.

Ms. Fleming's manual is not just theoretical in its approach. It offers valuable and practical advice to battered women and those professionals and paraprofessionals who wish to or do provide services. It is a "how to" guide through the legal system, on passing legislation, establishing shelters, and funding them. The chapter "Establishing Shelter and Support Services" describes various models, with their strengths and weaknesses. It details the problems encountered in day-to-day operation and gives constructive suggestions on staffing, training, house rules and philosophy, record keeping, children's services, community education, liaison with other agencies, and publicity.

This book is an excellent resource manual. It provides us with an update on what's happening in the field and tells those who are concerned how to plug in. In the Chapter "Children—Breaking the Cycle," it touches on prevention—recognition of violent response as learned behavior and the need to develop new role models. Sexism is deeply entrenched in our society. Until women are on a par with men in the home, on the job, in educational opportunity, and in politics, they will continue to be vulnerable to abuse by the men in their lives. That means drastic change in all our institutions and in our economy—a feat that will not be accomplished readily or rapidly. In the meantime, if we take advantage of the wealth of material in this manual by Jennifer Fleming, we may discover new pathways to resolve the battle of the sexes that plagues us all.

August 9, 1978
San Francisco, California

Del Martin
Author of *Battered Wives*
(San Francisco: New Glide Publications, 1976;
and New York: Pocket Books,
1977)

Coordinator, National Organization
for Women's Task Force on Battered
Women/Household Violence

"My minister told me to be tolerant and forgiving . . . ."

"I went to my doctor—he gave me pills to calm down . . . ."

"At the family agency, they told me I wanted to be beaten . . . ."

"I called the police—they would not do anything . . . ."

For Battered Women

Chapter I

FOR BATTERED WOMEN

THE WOMAN IN THE ORDINARY
The woman in the ordinary pudgy downcast girl
is crouching with eyes and muscles clenched.
Round and pebble smooth she effaces herself
under ripples of conversation and debate.
The woman in the block of ivory soap
has massive thighs that neigh,
great breasts that blare and strong arms that trumpet.
The woman of the golden fleece
laughs uproariously from the belly
inside the girl who imitates
a Christmas card virgin with glued hands,
who fishes for herself in other's eyes,
who stoops and creeps to make herself smaller.
In her bottled up is a woman peppery as curry,
a yam of a woman of butter and brass,
compounded of acid and sweet like a pineapple,
like a handgrenade set to explode,
like goldenrod ready to bloom.

Marge Piercy

JOAN

"What were your arguments mostly about?"
"Anything. If he didn't like the way you answered him or if he

didn't think you were answering him properly, he would start. Mostly about sex."

"You mean about whether you would or you wouldn't?"

"Who wants to go to bed with a drunk?

"I always had the feeling that he was a very sadistic person towards the end because he would come home and would like to start a fight—whether verbal, or whatever. And then after the fight was over, he would say, 'Let's go to bed.' We would fight over stupid stuff lots of times, and then when he got all his frustrations out, or whatever, then it was 'Let's go to bed.' "

IRENE

"And I never thought of going to a doctor and saying I think my jaw is broken or anything like that. I thought it was only bruised. Well, by the time I did go to the doctor, it was because my nose wouldn't stop bleeding, and the doctor really rattled me around. He said, 'You should have called me that night and I would have got a policeman, and we would have got him put away for good, because that just wasn't assault; that was actually attempted murder.' He says, 'If we had got him that night, he would be put away for years,' because they couldn't ever reset my jaw. I don't know, you can't notice it sometimes, but I've no cheekbone. It was pushed in, I've no cheekbone on this side, and the jawbone's out of line. I can't clench my teeth like other people, because, with me not going and getting it seen to, it healed up itself and it's healed up the wrong way. I still have no nerve endings on this lip; he punched me right from that eye down to here, in a triangle, and I didn't feel a thing. It's actually numb. I had no nerve endings, with the bones being broken and the nerves have all been cut."*

AMY

"To me it felt like, you know, ages and ages and ages cos† he just wouldn't stop. . . . I mean, whenever he hit me and I felt my head, you know, hitting the back of the lock of the door, I started to scream and I felt as if I'd been screaming for ages. When I came to,

* R. E. Dobash et al., "Wife Beating: The Victims Speak," *Victimology: An International Journal*, Vol. 2 (1977–78), Feb. 1978.
† Cos=because. ‡ Didnae=didn't. * Couldnae=couldn't. † Wasnae=wasn't.

he was pulling me up the stair by the hair; I mean, I think it was the pain of him pulling me up the stair by the hair that brought me around again. I can remember going up the stair, on my hands and knees, and the blood—I didnae‡ know where it was coming from—it was just dripping in front of my face and I was actually covered in blood. I just got to the kitchen door and he just walked straight to his bed. I just filled the sink with cold water, put a dish towel in it, and held it up to my face, and I remember I went through to the living room and I fell asleep and I woke up in the morning with this matted dish towel, and God, I couldnae* move. There wasn't a bit of me that wasnae† sore, you know."‡

Perhaps you turned to this book not because you are a professional in need of improved counseling skills, or a graduate student writing a paper—but because you are a battered woman in need of help. The purpose of this chapter is to provide a resource as you begin to analyze your situation in order to determine what you can do about it.

UNDERSTANDING YOUR FEELINGS

Often, you may find yourself experiencing a variety of emotions that can not only affect your ability to decide what is the best course of action but can get in the way of carrying out that decision. On the negative side, fear, guilt, embarrassment, anger, and feelings of helplessness and powerlessness do much to hold you back as you move to assert your right to a violence-free existence. On the positive side, perhaps reading this book or making a single phone call can represent the first step toward getting in touch with your own strength and taking steps to regain control of your existence.

You may be feeling strong and self-confident, ready to move and to avail yourself of whatever resources are at your disposal. Or you may be feeling terrified and convinced that any step toward independence can only lead to increased violence from your

‡ R. E. Dobash et al., op. cit.

husband or boyfriend. Perhaps you have tried to get help and have experienced a do-nothing attitude, lack of response, and an accusatory posture from traditional sources of help such as doctors, lawyers, ministers, or the police. If this is the case, finding nothing but closed doors has probably left you feeling incredibly frustrated and trapped. Whatever your state of mind, one thing must remain uppermost in your mind: YOU HAVE A RIGHT TO LIVE IN PEACE!

Often, we at the Women's Resource Network talk to battered women who feel guilty about being abused, as though they themselves might be responsible for their husbands' violence. Our belief is that traditional thinking about women has left behind a legacy of false guilt in battered women. Traditionally, women have been held responsible for the emotional well-being of their families, so that when their husbands become violent, many women feel guilty. Frequently, we hear battered women say, "If only I were a better wife and mother, maybe he wouldn't beat me." In a sense, what these women are really saying is that they must be failing to fulfill the *servant* functions of motherhood and the wifely role. Often, husbands beat their wives when they are dissatisfied with the way that the house is cleaned or the dinner is cooked. It has become apparent to us that the wifely role is frequently used as an excuse for violence by the battering male. An illustration of this is the common situation in which a man and woman live together without violence. They get married and, immediately afterward, violence begins. It is at this point that the husband feels that he "owns" his wife and has the right to beat her if she doesn't behave according to the customary legal and cultural "rules" surrounding wifely responsibilities. If you are a battered woman who has at times felt guilty about your husband's or boyfriend's violence, we urge you to bear in mind that the traditional rules about a wife's obligations are being seriously challenged by feminists, who argue that burdening the woman with primary responsibility for housework and child care is inherently unfair and sexist. It is the feminist position that husbands should share equally in household and child-rearing tasks. Whether or not these tasks are shared, there certainly is never any justification for the use of violence simply because a woman does not perform her "woman's work" according to the dictates of her husband.) It is also important to remember that it is a *crime* to assault physically, or threaten to assault, *anyone*—stranger, acquaintance, friend, enemy, or wife. It is also unjust for one person to feel that he is free to handle his frustrations by taking them out on another.

Perhaps you are not feeling any of the guilt feelings described above. Instead, you may have been made to feel guilty by individuals (some of whom may be well-meaning) who assume that you are behaving in such a way as to provoke your husband's violence, or that perhaps you even enjoy it. These assumptions will, we hope, make you feel angry rather than guilty. Anger can be a very healthy emotion. If you think about it, it makes more sense to get angry at someone who hurts you than to feel guilty about it. However, many women who have spent years feeling powerless develop a "victim's mentality"—a way of thinking and acting, of viewing themselves and others, that essentially says, "I deserve this. I am used to it and have no right to expect anything else." Getting appropriately angry at an outrageous situation can be the first step in breaking out of this pattern. It is also healthy to get angry at a society that rationalizes violence against women and condones wife beating.

Women are learning to challenge the notion that we are inherently inferior and masochistic and have a neurotic need to be abused. As far as provocation is concerned, it may be true that some battered women have verbal battles with their husbands or boyfriends that lead to battering, but engaging in a verbal battle or even saying hurtful, cruel things to your husband does not justify his use of violence. No matter how much he tells you that you "make him" hit you, such is not the case. If you had a fight with your girl friend and she beat you up, not many people would feel that she was justified, no matter what you said to her. Somehow, physical abuse is more easily understood and sometimes even encouraged when it involves husband and wife.

"This discussion we were having turned into an argument. I said quite a few bad things to him, because I was frustrated. My father —and I never will forgive this for the rest of my life—told him,

'You go beat that woman. Beat her. She's my daughter, but she deserves it.' So my husband jumped on me until my mother heard it. She was the one who pulled him off of me. She said she wasn't going to have this in her house, and he wasn't going to beat on her daughter like this."

Gerri

The important thing to remember is that it's *your husband* who has the problem, not you. Sometimes it can be difficult to hold onto that realization, but it is absolutely necessary if you are truly to understand the situation in which you find yourself. Feeling guilty will only serve to misdirect your energy and perpetuate the violence.

"The worst beating I ever got was when Bill got mad at me because the kitchen floor was dirty and dinner wasn't ready when he came home from work. After that, I thought that maybe if I kept the house spotless and dinner always served on time, then it would be alright. But no matter how hard I tried, he always found some excuse. Finally I realized that nothing I did was going to make any difference."

Sally

Depending on the severity of the abuse in your life and depending upon the amount of time it has been going on, fear can play a major role in your day-to-day existence. Living in an atmosphere of terror can do much to undermine your self-confidence and make you feel powerless.

Along with guilt and fear, you may be feeling some sense of shame and embarrassment. Perhaps it seems too humiliating to tell anyone that your husband or boyfriend is abusing you. Remember that it is *his* behavior that is shameful, not yours! It is often hard to stick to your guns when someone suggests that you try to be a better wife so you will not get beaten, but you can learn to do so. If someone tries to blame you for the situation, you would do well to say that you know you are not to blame, that it is impossible to keep your husband from beating you no matter how hard you try, that you have done nothing to deserve being physically assaulted, and that violence is not an acceptable method for solving problems. Feeling shame or embarrassment can prevent you from finding out things you need to know, such as what resources are available to help you in your situation.

A sense of powerlessness, the feeling that you don't have control over what happens to you and to your life, often builds up after several beatings. This can be a big factor in preventing you from making decisions on your own behalf. In trying to decide whether to leave or to stay with a man who abuses you, it may seem as if you're damned if you do and damned if you don't. Your family, friends, religious counselor, or doctor may suggest that it is your duty to stay. Other individuals may condemn you for not leaving. Your decision of whether to leave or to stay must be based on what is best for you and your children, not on what others think.

If you are in a severe battering situation, one that involves the use of weapons, for example, safety should be the determining factor in your decision. If you are viciously attacked on a regular basis, you may very well be courting homicide if you stay. Remember, 13 per cent of all homicides occur between husband and wife. Even if you should decide to return later, you cannot risk the possibility of yourself, your husband, or your child becoming one of these statistics. If the abuse is mild and infrequent, you have more of a choice about whether or not to leave, and certainly you have a greater amount of room to think and plan.

It is usually necessary for the battered wife to put distance between herself and her husband in order to stop the abuse. Often, the husband will refuse to seek any kind of help, in itself enough to dictate that the abuse will continue. If your husband is unwilling to get help, it will probably be necessary for you to leave at some point. We remind you again that the abuse will not go away by itself. In fact it will get worse. Facing this and taking the appropriate step is absolutely essential for your well-being.

If your husband is one of the rare abusers who is willing to be counseled, it is possible that he will become less abusive over time. Some domestic-violence programs are initiating couple and group counseling for battering men. For information, call your local wife-abuse program, mental-health center, or probation department (see Chapter VI).

Lately, some judges are requiring abusive men to undergo counseling as an alternative to incarceration. If you take your husband to court, mandatory counseling may be an outcome. Check on what happens to convicted batterers in your community.*

Be forewarned that obtaining therapeutic help does not necessarily mean that your husband will become nonviolent, especially if he is undergoing counseling because of a court order. Batterers who voluntarily undergo counseling stand a better chance than others of developing nonviolent problem-solving techniques, but even in this instance, a complete cessation of violence is by no means guaranteed.

Of course, the thought of leaving can be frightening. You may not be able to see any way out of your situation. If you have not worked outside the home before or don't have any job skills, you may worry about how to support yourself and your children. You may not know where to go, much less how to go about being on your own. You may be frightened of making your husband angry by leaving, and of the possibility that he will retaliate. On the other hand, there may be things about the relationship that you value. Indeed, you may wish to stay but wonder how to change things so that you can stay in safety and peace. Remember, however, that no matter how bad things may be now, you *can* learn more about your options. The worst feeling may be that you have no choice. We hope that as you read further in this chapter you will learn more about how to deal with your situation, and to realize that you can develop choices based not on fear but on what is best.

Your first step is to admit to yourself that you are a battered woman. This can be hard to do, but it is important to avoid the trap of making excuses for your husband, believing "He had a hard day at the office," or thinking "He doesn't really hit me that often" or "He doesn't really mean it; he's just upset right now."

---

* See Chapter III for further information on the criminal-justice system. Also see the section "Pressing Charges" in this chapter for the ins and outs of prosecuting your husband.

The fact is that two or three beatings should be enough to convince you that you are a battered woman. Failure to face this fact can leave you feeling trapped and resigned to a lifetime of misery you do not deserve. If and when you decide to seek help, try not to put yourself in a dangerous position. Don't feel guilty about keeping things from him. Making phone calls, reading this and other books, and talking to someone about your situation are important survival steps. If you have to do these things when he is not around, you are not being dishonest, you are responding to the position he has forced you into.

Occasionally we hear women say, "If my husband doesn't hit me, he doesn't love me." It is unfortunate that women have been taught that all we are worthy of is abuse and mistreatment. If you harbor these convictions, you are probably experiencing only mild abuse. Women who are seriously battered know very well that the abuse they suffer has nothing whatsoever to do with love. If you make the mistake now of thinking that abuse is a form of affection, you will realize only later, when the abuse escalates, that such is not the case.

YOUR CHILDREN

If you are a battered woman with children, you may feel particularly strained and upset. It can be difficult enough to figure out what to do for yourself, but you have the added responsibility of your children, which carries with it a whole other set of practical and emotional considerations.

Women who remain in bad marriages frequently feel they are doing it "for the children." They may mean this in all sincerity, because we have all been taught that the ideal living structure is the nuclear family: mother, father, and the children. However, we all know that in many cases this structure is far from ideal, and can be unsatisfying and destructive. Yet, it is difficult not to feel guilty for failing to provide your kids with this idealized family structure. Keep in mind that there are certain things that kids need to have in order grow up healthy and feeling good about themselves. Chief among these is an environment that is physically and emotionally safe. This environment can be provided in many different ways, and not necessarily within a traditional family structure. You may have believed all your life that this traditional family is the "only" way to bring up children. Perhaps this has been stressed within your religion, and perhaps everyone you know feels this way. It is important to know that many people are changing their feelings; in fact, close to one third of American children are currently growing up in single-parent families. Most of the studies done in this area clearly demonstrate that there is no damage done to children merely by growing up with only one parent. Experts in the field of child development tend to agree that it is the quality of a child's experience in growing up that is important, and that a child should feel loved, accepted, and safe.

Be aware that you are not doing your kids any favors by having them witness your being abused. The presence of violence in the home is detrimental to children. Kids need a sense of security, which they can't really have if they never know when violence will erupt. Adults who seem out of control terrify children, for they look to adults to provide the care and stability in their lives. Children won't comprehend why you are being beaten, which is understandable, since there is no valid reason and it is an expression of irrational behavior on your husband's part. But children need to make sense of the world around them, and they will probably come up with reasons in order to make their own lives less frightening. Frequently they will figure that you must have done something to deserve it; you may have done this yourself, so you can understand how they might think this. They may become very scared of their own behavior and feelings, thinking that they, too, are somehow "bad" and deserving of punishment. They may even feel that somehow it is their fault that you are being beaten. Children frequently feel very guilty about watching their mothers being harmed and not being able to do anything about it. They may feel that they should try to protect you even though this is not really in their power. They may have even tried, and themselves been beaten. Be aware that when a violent situation develops, children are often quick to sense the change, and they become very anxious. They may try to avert the violence by drawing fire to themselves, acting up so that you and/or your husband will get mad at them instead. This is another way that they may be taking on a responsibility that really isn't theirs. Seeing you getting hurt can make them very angry, and realizing their own powerlessness can make them even angrier and more frustrated. The ways in which children deal with their sense of powerlessness and frustration over your being hurt can be harmful to them and to the way in which they relate to you. One common reaction is known as "identification with the aggressor." This means that they see your husband as not only powerful but right in what he does, and try to be like him in order not to be so frightened of his power. They may then begin looking on you with scorn and treating you with a lack of respect, which you certainly don't deserve or need at this time.

On the other hand, some children, particularly girls, will identify more with the victim. They may see themselves as equally powerless and equally deserving of scorn, and begin seeing the world as a place where they have no control over what happens to them. Either reaction plays a strong part in continuing the cycle. The child who identifies with the aggressor usually grows up to be aggressive and violent, and probably an abuser in the next generation. The one who identifies with the victim may well become a victim and be drawn into an abusive situation in adult life. Children learn from experience and from what they see around them. They need to see people treating each other in honest, healthy ways in order to develop similar patterns themselves.

If you can, try to provide other resources for your kids to learn about people and how they behave. If they can have relationships with adults who do not treat each other violently, they will be exposed to alternative role models and may not get stuck in thinking that all marriages and all adult relationships have to be like yours.

It is possible that your husband is abusing your children as well as you. If he isn't, this remains a likely possibility, because you have already seen that violence is his way of handling his feelings and problems. This is frightening, and many women who have not been able to get out of abusive situations for themselves have done so at the point when their husbands began harming the children. The potential for this should not be taken lightly. You certainly wouldn't want your children subjected to the kind of violence that you have had to put up with. Child abuse can be critically dangerous, physically as well as emotionally. Even if you find it hard to think of doing something for yourself, you may be able to get mobilized for the sake of your children.

Perhaps you have found that you yourself are abusing your children. This is not easy to admit, but it is vitally important that you look at what you are doing. You know that it is harmful to the kids, but it can also make you feel even worse about yourself. It is understandable that when you are under such great stress, your kids' needs can make you feel overwhelmed and angry. It can seem hard enough to take care of yourself, without having them depend on you. Some women react to the frustration and rage of being beaten by taking it out on children, who can't fight back. If this is happening to you, remember that you can seriously hurt your child without wanting to. If it is your husband or boyfriend that you are really angry at, you're not going to solve anything by using the kids to vent your feelings. Violence never produces a healthy situation, nor will it solve your problems.

There are a growing number of organizations that have formed to deal with the problems of child abuse. Listen for spot ads on radio or TV, or contact a local social-service agency for information on how to contact one of these organizations. If you are concerned with how you are dealing with your kids, don't be afraid to contact these organizations. They are not there to judge you but to help you find better alternatives for controlling your emotions. As with wife abuse, child abuse doesn't go away by itself, but tends to get worse.

Frequently, abused women feel guilty for the effects their own abuse may have on their children. Remember that you are not responsible for your husband's violence and that you can't control it for your own sake or for theirs. However, there are specific things you can do for them to help them cope with the situation.

First, as we have seen, kids should not be made to feel responsible for you or for the situation, and you need to let them know this. Try to set up an arrangement so that they have someplace to go during a fight, to a neighbor's, friend's, or relative's home for instance, and let them know that this is OK. Tell them that they don't have to stay around to try to protect you, that it is not their job, and that you want them to leave, go to their rooms, or somehow remove themselves from the situation. Kids can also be made to feel overly involved and responsible when they are used as coconspirators. Don't saddle them with the job of lying for you or otherwise covering up. Avoid saying such things as "Don't tell Grandma how I got this black eye" or "Don't let Daddy know where I'm going." They should not be put in the middle or have to live in fear that if they say the wrong thing, you will get in trouble. Be clear that this is your problem to deal with, not theirs, and that although you don't like it, it will be your job to handle it. It can be immensely relieving to them to know that you do not, either directly or indirectly, expect them to handle something that is impossible for them.

This kind of approach may not always be possible, however. Occasions may arise when it becomes necessary, for your survival and perhaps that of the children, to instruct them to remain silent about certain matters. If you have stayed at a shelter the location of which is confidential, for example, and have returned home, your children should be told not to give their father the location or any other information about the shelter. Sometimes you may be trying to escape the house after a beating. Certainly you would tell the children not to let the father know where you are. Of course, the less information you give them, the less they will be able to reveal and the less guilty they will feel about helping to keep your secrets.

If you do blow up at your kids when you are upset, try to recognize this and admit to them when you have made a mistake, so that they are not left with the feeling that they are somehow at fault. Let them know that you realize you were unfair and that you are sorry. At the same time, try to avoid feeling overly guilty, apologizing too much or trying to make it up to the child. He or she will understand that you are human and can be wrong. Admit it, apologize, and be done with it. Otherwise, you may create a situation in which it is so gratifying to your child to get your attention in this way that she or he may try to anger you simply to enjoy the making up.

It may be difficult to talk comfortably with your children about your husband. Try not to "badmouth" him to them; they should not be put in the position of taking sides or of feeling guilty if they have some positive feelings toward their father. If you are angry at him, it isn't fair to try to get back at him by expressing your anger to your children. Keep in mind that as they grow up, they will be able to put things together for themselves and figure out who has been responsible for the violence in their lives. Trust that they will be able to form their own judgments, and try not to tell them what to think.

On the other hand, don't cover up for your husband either. Children need to know that what they are perceiving is true or they can become very confused and not be able to trust their own perceptions. If your husband hurts them or treats them unfairly or tries to get at you by punishing them, let them know that this is what is happening and that you realize it is wrong. One woman described an incident in which her husband became furious with her, provoked a fight, and then stormed out of the house just at the time when he had promised the kids he would take them to the circus. She was able to talk to the kids about what he had done and to let them know that they had a right to feel hurt and angry about it. In this way she could help them understand that what they felt was happening was in fact really happening, that their feelings were appropriate and acceptable, and that it was in no way their fault. Above all, try to be clear and matter-of-fact when talking with your kids.

SEPARATION

If you and your husband have separated, visitation can create problems. Exercising his right to see the children can provide the abusive man with a means of reentry into the home and the opportunity to recommence violent behavior. This possibility may justify your denying him visitation. If you do want your children to relate to their father, however, it may be necessary for you to initiate—either voluntarily or through a child-custody proceeding—methods for doing so that will ensure continued peace for you and your children. Arranging for your husband to pick up and drop off the kids in a neutral location, for example, is one way to accomplish this.

A word of caution: beware of your husband's snatching the kids and refusing to return them. Unless there is a court order specifying that you have custody, he has the legal right to do so. Many men make this move as a way of punishing their wives for ending the relationship.

If you think your children could benefit from counseling, read the portion on selecting a therapist, in the *Women in Transition Handbook*.† The points noted there are geared toward adults, yet many of them will help in the selection of a counselor for your children as well. Proceed with care. Neither mother nor children need the added oppressive experience of being ripped off by a "therapeutic" approach that views them as sick or inherently flawed or sees the basic task as helping them to accept and accommodate to their roles as victims. The trick is to find trained professionals who combine skill with warmth, caring, and humanistic or even feminist values to work with children who need more intensive and skilled help than even the most caring lay persons can offer. It is often useful to seek help through a child guidance center, as the staff has special training and expertise in working with children. Family therapy is another option, and often provides mothers and children with ways of working through their feelings about themselves and each other in order to establish more satisfying relationships.

Read the following adaptation of the *Women in Transition Handbook* section on "Mental Health Services for Children" to get more ideas about selecting a counselor for your children:

> The stress of a separation or having to live on a survival level can profoundly upset a child. Some of this is "normal" reaction to stressful situations and can only be resolved over time. Sometimes, however, a child's behavior seems essentially destructive and out of proportion to what she or he is going through, and it seems to be getting worse rather than better. It is very hard to draw the line between what is "normal" and what isn't. In addition, you are most likely confused about the power of your own emotions. It is hard enough for you to figure out if you need professional help for yourself, much less for your children.

† Women in Transition, Inc., *Women in Transition Handbook* (New York; Charles Scribner's Sons, 1975).

. . . Word-of-mouth referrals are especially helpful . . . in choosing a therapist. Try to find a children's therapist who is recommended by a friend or by a therapist you trust.

It is important that the therapist be trained in working with children, because there are specialized skills in that area.

Some therapists tell parents they are pushy or overbearing if they want to know what is going on between the therapist and the child. While we don't think a therapist should be expected to explain or justify everything she is doing, we would be suspicious if a therapist refused to talk with you about what she thinks is happening with your child, what progress is being made.

In many ways, we think family therapy, where the whole family is seen as a unit by the therapist, is a sensible approach. A child's problems aren't just hers or his, they are symptomatic of problems the whole family is having. A skilled family therapist can help children and parents talk in a more open way about the tensions within the family. The biggest drawback of family therapists is that they are trained and do their work in the same kinds of institutions as other therapists—those steeped in traditional notions about the way the world is. These notions are about what the family is and what women's role in it should be, how poor people behave, why black people are the way they are, etc. It is important to look for a family therapist who is trying to free herself or himself from these oppressive ideas.

A word about school guidance counselors: Most of us get pretty intimidated when a school counselor says that our child is having problems and tells us what we should do about them. Sometimes their observations are insightful; school counselors do pick up on things that we might overlook at home. But sometimes, especially if a school is very traditional, a child may be labeled a "problem child" just because she or he is different—by being aggressive or daydreaming or not mixing well with the other children. School counselors, especially those who aren't well trained, sometimes get carried away with themselves and the power they have. They are likely to misdiagnose problems or find problems when they aren't there. This is especially true for children of single-parent households; counselors are often so sure that a broken home is traumatic for children that they interpret everything in that light. Our best advice if a school counselor says your child is disturbed and you are uncomfortable with that is to get a second opinion from someone you trust. You can also talk with friends whose children have had similar problems.‡

Before an Attack

If you are living in an abusive situation, there are some practical measures you can take to protect yourself. It may seem strange to think in terms of preparing for an attack ahead of time, but that can be the very time that you are clearheaded, not upset, and capable of organizing some protective measures for yourself. First, let someone know what is going on. If a friendly neighbor is aware that your husband is abusing you, she or he may be able to call the police for you when you are unable to do so. Other friends, neighbors, or relatives may be able to provide shelter or transportation for you if you need to get out of the house, and if you talk with them ahead of time they can be prepared to help you when you need help the most. While you may feel isolated from other people, if you can begin to develop or reestablish contacts, you will gain not only sources of emotional support but very practical assistance as well. If you have the space in your home, select a room that can be locked from the inside in order to get away from an attack. Or, if you sense an attack coming, move closer to the door to avoid getting cornered and to help you get out of the house. Consider the things you could arrange to hide in order to help you during a crisis: extra money and/or a spare set of car keys can get you to safety. If you will need to get out of the house in a hurry, you may want quickly to get such things as food, extra clothing, diapers, extra glasses, medication, identification cards, medical insurance or welfare cards, important legal papers, and so on. Make a list of resources you might need, such as a shelter, a lawyer or legal center, hospital, and any other agency or person you might need to contact. If you have no safe place to keep these things, you may be able to store them with a friend or neighbor.

‡ Ibid.

During an Attack

During an attack, there is probably nothing you can say or do to make him stop. Because he is not in a rational state of mind, it is unlikely that you can reason with him. However, there are things to keep in mind that may help you. First, try not to panic or to lose your temper. While these reactions are understandable, they won't help you out of the situation. You will need to be clearheaded to think about what to do. Getting angry and insulting him may make him angrier, which will be worse for you. Save your anger for a time when you are safe from physical attack. There are varying opinions on whether to fight back. Some people feel that it is important to stand up for yourself and show that you won't be pushed around. Others claim that this may subject you to greater violence. Knowing your own strength and your husband's personality will tell you whether fighting back will benefit or harm you. The Milwaukee Task Force on Battered Women suggests the following things to do during an attack:

DEFEND AND PROTECT yourself, especially your head and stomach.

CALL FOR HELP. Scream, or if you can get away, run to the nearest person or home, say you are being hurt and that you need help.

CALL THE POLICE, or have someone else do it; they have a responsibility to protect you.

GET AWAY. If it is unsafe to stay at home, call a neighbor, friend or a cab. Find shelter and take your children with you.*

In terms of leaving the house, the *Legal Handbook for Battered Women*† provides some valuable information, which we have adapted:

If you leave your children home, you may have problems later in obtaining legal custody of them, should your husband decide to

---

* Milwaukee Task Force on Battered Women, *Battered Women: Handbook for Survival*, Rev. Edition, 1978.
† *Legal Handbook for Battered Women: How to Use the Law*. Legal Help for Battered Women, Cambridge, Mass., 1978.

challenge your right to custody. However, a court will take into account the fact that you were escaping a violent husband. The sooner you return to get your children the better your case will be.

Some women have found that anything that works to calm down their husbands is best to try and then leave the next day, when he's gone. Only you can be the judge of what will be most effective in your situation, and you should follow your instincts.

A common threat used to intimidate women who leave home is that they will be prosecuted for "desertion." In most states, to prove this in a court proceeding a husband must show that you left the marital home without cause. If you or your children are being threatened or beaten, you have sufficient legal cause to leave without adverse consequences.

A practical problem in leaving is that your husband may make it difficult for you to get any property you may have left behind. Even if you leave with nothing but the shirt on your back, you can request police assistance to accompany you as you return for your personal belongings (or, for that matter, for your children). In some states, after you leave you can obtain an eviction or vacate order from the courts, forcing your husband to leave the marital home. See section on civil remedies in this chapter. You may also be able to enjoin your husband from destroying or disposing of your property. Usually an attorney will be needed.

If at all possible, try to take important family documents with you, such as your own and your children's birth certificates, your marriage certificate, your lease or deed to the house, your husband's most recent pay stub or your previous tax returns, your immigration papers, if any, and bankbooks. You may need these documents in future legal proceedings, to obtain welfare or unemployment, an independent visa or citizenship status, etc.

Your personal safety and the welfare of your children are the most important things; you can deal with property and custody issues after you leave; without adverse consequences. If you are unable to plan your departure beforehand or gather the information and personal property mentioned above, don't worry about it. You can usually obtain emergency food, shelter, and clothing if necessary.

In *A Handbook for Beaten Women,* published by the Brooklyn Legal Services Corporation, Marjory Fields and Elyse Lehman point out that if you stay with someone temporarily, make sure that it's a woman friend or relative. Do not stay with a man who lives alone unless he is your brother, father, or some other close relative. It might appear that you are committing adultery, which could cause a custody fight and you could stand to lose alimony if it exists in your state.

The Milwaukee Task Force also notes the following about the legal implications of leaving your children at home: "As a practical matter, it is always best to take your children with you. If you are married, both you and your husband have an equal 'right' to the children. Temporary custody can be awarded to either parent through the courts. . . . You have a better chance of receiving custody if the children are already in your care.

"If you must leave without them, get the children back into your care as soon as possible. You may use any method short of exerting physical violence against your husband or property."‡

They suggest that you contact the local child-welfare agency if you do not have your children and are afraid they are being ill-treated or badly cared for. This unit has the power to conduct an investigation into the children's situation and to commence court proceedings to have them removed from the home.

After an Attack

Immediately after an attack, it is important to get medical help, for two reasons. First and foremost, you may have suffered physical damage you are not aware of, such as internal injuries or concussions. Second, by being seen in a hospital emergency room, you are establishing a permanent medical record of the assault, which can provide valuable evidence should you decide to take further legal action. Save any torn or bloody clothing, and if you can, get someone to take pictures (preferably in color) of your injuries. These can also serve as important evidence in convincing people that your situation is *serious*. A friend or relative who can go with you to the hospital can provide moral support and often help you settle yourself and get your story straight. It can also be helpful to line up any possible witnesses to the attack to confirm your story. The *Legal Handbook for Battered Women* has some suggestions regarding your speaking with a hospital social worker, either at your own request or by referral from hospital personnel:

‡ Milwaukee Task Force, op. cit.

It may be helpful for you to have someone to talk to about being battered. Social workers are sometimes able to furnish other kinds of assistance, such as legal, housing and public-assistance referrals. However, some women have found that *some* social workers and counselors contribute to their feelings of guilt or shame. Remember that you do not have to see a counselor or social worker even if a hospital recommends it—it is *your* decision. Hospitals are not legally allowed to give a husband information as to your whereabouts.

If you do have contact with a sympathetic social worker or other hospital staff members, take advantage of it to express how you are feeling and to ask questions. Remember that you are in need of help and entitled to it.

Calling the Police

Dealing with the police can be a frightening or frustrating experience, but keep in mind at all times that as a victim of criminal assault you are entitled to their protection. It is also important to remember the following:

You should call the police during or immediately after the attack or threat *if you want the man who beat you arrested.*

Whether or not you are legally married to the man, if you are physically hurt you may go to the police and ask the police to arrest him.

If the police refuse to arrest him, you have the right to make the arrest yourself. This is called a "citizen's arrest." The police must assist you in taking the man to the police station and filling out the arrest forms.

If the police say they cannot help you because the man is your husband or the father of your children, write down the officers' names and badge numbers. Let them see you do this. Then report them to their commanding officer.*

There are many things to keep in mind in dealing with the police:

In Massachusetts, as in every state, it is a crime to physically attack another person or to threaten to attack or harm another person.

* Legal Help for Battered Women, op. cit.

However, when the assailant is married to, living with, or somehow "involved" with the victim, the police (and the courts) respond differently from the way they do to assaults involving strangers.

Be aware of this difference and be firm in your dealings with the police. Always keep in mind that you are the victim of a crime and you have a right to seek their protection. If police officers are uncooperative, find out their names and badge numbers. You can call and complain about their conduct later. Also, just asking for the information may force them to take you more seriously. Another tactic is to ask to speak to someone with more authority; for example, ask to speak to the police officer's immediate supervisor or superior officer on duty.

One of the first problems you may face when you call the police is getting them to respond. Many police stations have a formal or informal policy of screening calls; the first calls usually screened out are the "family" cases. Some women have been forced by police inaction to call the police and say some man or burglar is breaking into their house; others have pretended to be a neighbor and reported a disturbance or fight. Emergency calls to the police station are either tape-recorded or recorded in a police log by the person taking the call. These records can be useful later in legal proceedings, so it's advisable to be clear over the phone about what is actually happening. When you or others call the police, say there is a crime in progress or that you think there is a weapon involved, because only in these cases will they think it's worth their time to respond and can legally make an arrest. If you have any temporary restraining orders, tell them that, too. If you already have a Vacate Order, your husband is not only in contempt of court, he is also trespassing. You can report that crime or say that some man is breaking and entering. Another approach is to have your neighbor telephone the police saying there is a fight next door and it is disturbing the peace. If there is a witness present during the assault, their call to the police could be important, as would their presence when the police arrive.

What the police can legally do when they arrive depends on whether the crime committed against you is classified as a *felony* or a *misdemeanor*. The police generally view their function as one of conciliation ("kiss and make up") rather than arrest—often at your expense. Police officers invariably tell a woman that she must go to the Probate (Family) Court or get a lawyer to have the man removed, or that she must go to the District Court to file a criminal complaint. They say that they can't arrest or remove your attacker. This is partially correct. *An officer may arrest a man without a warrant if a) he believes a felony has been committed or b) if a misdemeanor has been committed in front of the officer.* Essentially, felonies are assault with weapons, and particularly deadly-force weapons. In addition, felonies can be assault with a certain intent. Any object not used for the purpose for which it was intended could be a deadly weapon; for example, a cigarette or a boot. A witness who has seen the assault could help convince the police that a felony has been committed.

An officer cannot arrest a man if the crime he has committed is in the misdemeanor category unless it is committed in the officer's presence. For example, if your husband punches you with his fist before the police arrive, this is usually considered a misdemeanor. If your husband held a gun to your head and threatened you, this would be a felony and they can legally arrest him when they arrive.

When the police arrive, try to be as specific as possible under the circumstances. If your attacker picked up the phone, nearly strangled you with the cord and said that he was going to kill you, SAY ALL OF THAT AND DEMAND THAT HE BE ARRESTED FOR ASSAULT AND BATTERY WITH INTENT TO MURDER. Some women have found that the police are more likely to take a man into "protective custody" if he has been drinking. . . . You might consider using that opportunity to leave the house. If you want to do so, you can ask them to stand by while you pack a few things to leave. *Be aware that if the police come and your attacker senses that nothing is going to happen to him, you may be in additional danger.* Therefore, having him out of the house immediately may not be the major priority—worry about it after you are out of danger.

If your attacker is your former husband, or you have been separated from him, or is someone you have been living with, the police are more likely to take stronger action. Show the officers any legal papers granting you a Divorce or Separation, or ordering him not to interfere with your liberty. If it is your apartment or house and he has entered against your will, show them the lease, deed, or canceled rent checks; demand that they remove him. Should the police not take action, demand that they make a report and get their badge numbers. Again, this may force them to take you more seriously. You may also use the information in later legal proceedings.

Instead of calling the police, some women go directly to the station. Reporting the assault this way is also good. The police will usually keep a record of it and also have the equipment to take photographs of your injuries; you may request that they do so. You may also request that they return to your home with you so that you may get your things or kids.

If the police do not cooperate, a call from your attorney, if you have one, may also be effective. Any reports to the police or subsequently filing formal charges, are extremely useful in pursuing legal action against the man who beats you.

Although it is not always the case, be prepared for a "there's nothing we can do" attitude. This stems at least in part from the fact that the police simply do not know how to cope with domestic violence. FBI statistics indicate that more police officers are killed each year responding to domestic violence than to all other crimes combined. It also stems from a general unwillingness to accept the seriousness of the problem, because women's concerns in general are not taken seriously in a society whose laws are made to protect men's rights. Police officers are usually men who believe strongly in society's view of the traditional roles of men and women; man is the boss and woman is the one who serves. Similarly, many of these officials share society's view that the home is a private castle and that a man is free to do as he pleases within the privacy of "his" home.

TRY NOT TO BE INTIMIDATED BY THIS ATTITUDE AND REMIND THE POLICE THERE IS PLENTY THEY CAN DO TO PROTECT YOU AND YOUR CHILDREN AND THAT IT IS THEIR SWORN DUTY TO DO SO.†

It is not hard to feel intimidated when dealing with police officers who are not sympathetic or receptive to your difficulties. Often they want to get things quieted down and get out; they may suggest that you forgive and forget, or may even blame you for the attack. Keep in mind that this method of blaming the victim has served to keep women from complaining or demanding their rights, and that *you* are not the one who has committed a crime. The Milwaukee Task Force on Battered Women notes that if your husband or boyfriend is arrested, he may be released or be freed on bail in a matter of hours, possibly to come home even angrier than before. They therefore suggest that you either leave home or arrange to have someone come and stay with you.

† Ibid.

If you are a minority woman, you will probably find the police particularly unsympathetic and perhaps outright hostile. Many policemen believe the myth that wife beating occurs only in low-income or ghetto communities (even though some of them may be beating their own wives). The prevailing attitude is "Well, this is how these people live. They like it that way and why should we do anything to change it?"

If you are a middle-class, suburban woman, you may find that the police are reluctant to believe that you are being abused unless they find you bleeding or covered with bruises. If your husband is known and respected in the community, chances are you will be perceived as a hysterical wife out to get "Mr. Nice Guy."

For rural women, calling the police can be even more useless than it is for suburban or urban women. Sometimes only the state police are available, and if the assault occurs in the middle of the night, they may not even arrive until the next morning, thinking it isn't anything serious. As experience shows, police in general don't take wife assault seriously.

If you are in any of these situations, all we can do is reemphasize that you be assertive. Demand your rights. Copy badge numbers. Call commanding officers. Visit the police station. Get assistance from friends, family, lawyers, social workers.

Although these measures will help, by no means will they solve the problem. Not until our police forces are retrained and encouraged to change their beliefs about wife assault will we see any significant improvement in their attitudes and procedures regarding battered women.

Pressing Charges

Attempting to seek justice by prosecuting your husband is usually time-consuming, frustrating, dangerous (if you are living with him), fraught with red tape, and, in the end, relatively ineffective. We do not point this out to discourage you; we want you to know that the system is not geared to work in your behalf. Although our laws no longer permit men to beat their wives, getting those laws enforced is another story. In all states, assault and battery is a crime, including assault between husband and wife; but the major thrust of those working with district attorneys and magistrates involves screening out domestic complaints, rather than moving to build a case. The prevailing attitude is that domestic violence is a social, rather than a legal, issue, and negative assumptions about the abused wife are the rule and not the exception.

Criminal-justice personnel fail to see that the system is extremely cumbersome and unproductive, leaving the victim vulnerable to further attack from her spouse during the prosecution process. They assume that battered women often fail to follow through with prosecution, due to "innate" masochism or because the problem is not really serious.

Once a complaint is filed, it can be many months before things are settled, and even then, it is unlikely that your assailant will receive any kind of real penalty. Upon conviction, short-term, nonreporting probations are generally the rule. Unless you are staying in a shelter or at some other undisclosed location, you will have no protection as you proceed. If you live in a rural area, utilizing the criminal-justice system is even more difficult and frustrating. Frequently, one must wait for a traveling judge to file a complaint, and long delays before court appearances are the norm (see Chapter VIII for more information on rural women).

The tendency to blame you for your own victimization permeates the entire process. You may meet with hostility, lack of sympathy, and even outright contempt as you try to get your rights enforced. Racist attitudes make the process doubly humiliating and difficult for minority women.

What does all this mean? We mention these cautions not to warn you against having your grievances redressed. We feel, though, that it is important for you to be aware of what you're up against should you decide to prosecute. You need to assess your motivation and ability to cope with the stress and possible danger involved and make a decision that will work in your own best interest.

One consideration in deciding whether or not to prosecute is your husband. If he is the type of person who would be intimidated by being charged with a crime, then you may be able to use the prosecution process as a lever in getting him to reduce his use of violence. If, however, he is aware of the ineffectiveness of the courts, and particularly if he has been prosecuted before, he knows that the most he will receive is a slap on the wrist. (Such ineffectiveness by the courts serves to signal the abuser that his violence is not taken seriously and is in fact condoned by the very system that should be telling him in no uncertain terms that wife beating is unacceptable behavior.) Unless it's his third or fourth appearance before the court, he really has very little to worry about. If he knows this, you cannot expect the prosecution process to effect any positive change in his behavior. In fact, just the opposite can occur. He may become even more enraged and respond with increased violence. When considering prosecution, bear in mind that you will be a lot safer, and it will be easier to follow through, if you are not living with him.

Of course, the system will not improve until women start to fight back and demand that their rights be enforced. You have the right to live a violence-free existence, and the criminal-justice system should be one tool among many at your disposal as you move to gain control over your life. Some women's programs provide advocacy and court accompaniment for battered women who prosecute. If such is the case in your community, your chances of achieving a more sympathetic and effective response are much greater. In addition, if there is a civil remedy available in your state, pursuing it in conjunction with filing a complaint may make for more effective use of legal measures (see following section).

The courts cannot provide answers to the problem, however. Often, battered women turn to the criminal-justice system not because they want their husbands jailed but simply because they don't know where else to turn. Occasionally we speak with abused women who want to take their husbands to court primarily for revenge. Although we find such a desire to be completely understandable and although we sympathize, we feel that this is misdirected energy. If you have such feelings, it would be better if you dealt with them in a supportive group or in one-to-one counseling, and put your energy into constructive measures designed to enable you to rebuild your life.

If you are economically dependent on your spouse, incarceration could jeopardize your means of support. But if you think that taking your husband to court will be an effective measure in curbing his violence, we must inform you that this possibility is small. If you lack the necessary support from others to see you through the ordeal, or if you feel shaky about whether or not you can follow through, or if you would prefer to seek non-legal remedies to your dilemma, we suggest you read the resource-development section of this chapter for other avenues of help and assistance.

In the event that you do decide to prosecute, read on:

PROCEDURES FOR PROSECUTION

Procedures vary from state to state, so you must determine exactly what they are in your area. Legal counseling or contact with a women's group can be helpful. What follows is general information that probably applies in your state.

Arrest

As mentioned before, the police may make an arrest if the abuse is severe and they determine that a felony has been committed. They may also arrest if a misdemeanor has been committed in their presence. In some states, if the police do not make an arrest, a warrant for arrest can be issued by the district attorney, magistrate, clerk of the district court, or other appropriate official, if you file a private criminal complaint within a few days of the assault.

Filing the Complaint

Frequently when the police respond to a domestic-disturbance call, they will advise you to visit the appropriate office to file a complaint against your assailant. When you arrive, you will be interviewed by an assistant district attorney, clerk, or other official. The interview will determine whether or not the state will take up your case. It is not your decision. If the interview results in a decision to prosecute, either a warrant or a summons will be issued.

Some states provide a variety of options for the district attorney besides issuing a warrant or summons, such as sending your husband a letter telling him to stay out of trouble, ordering him to appear with you at a review hearing for further investigation into the incident; drawing up a formal complaint that you must sign to go on record, or "continuing" (postponing) the case for a few months. In this instance, your husband will be warned that if he beats you again before the continuance date, he will definitely be prosecuted for assault and battery. (This procedure can be appealed.)

Once the warrant is issued, there is no guarantee that your husband will be arrested. Often, the police don't look too diligently for him, and even when they do, abusive men have been known to elude them and avoid arrest for long periods of time.

Arraignment and Preliminary Hearings

Your husband will be arraigned shortly after his arrest or on receiving his summons. In addition, a number of preliminary, grand-jury, review, or show-cause hearings can take place before the actual trial. Often these cases don't reach the trial stage, since almost all the intermediate steps are designed to screen the matter out of the criminal-justice system. In the event that a felony has been committed, a trial is more likely to occur, and you will probably have to appear at a grand-jury hearing. At the arraignment, your husband will be advised of the charges against him and of his legal rights. If he cannot afford a lawyer, the court will appoint one, either from a list of local practicing attorneys that donate their time or from a public defender's office. Bail will be set, and the judge may decide the terms of release from arrest.

Sometimes informal review hearings are held to determine whether there is enough evidence of assault and battery for a complaint to be issued. Frequently, more-formal preliminary hearings take place at which decisions are made as to whether the case is to be terminated or proceed to trial. Sometimes the preliminary hearing is held shortly after the arraignment or the issuance of a summons; other times several weeks can go by before a hearing takes place. It is often at this juncture that cases are dismissed or the charges are dropped.

The Trial

Most likely the trial will take place a few months after the preliminary hearings or reviews have been completed. During this time your husband will be free. He will choose whether to have a jury trial or a bench trial (before a judge only), and will decide whether to plead guilty, not guilty, or stand mute. If he stands mute, an automatic not-guilty plea will be entered in his behalf. If a jury trial is chosen by the defendant, frequently the jury will be selected the morning of the trial.

In some areas a felony trial will be heard by a jury of twelve, but a misdemeanor trial will be heard by a jury of six. Mindy Resnick, in her counselor training manual, points out that it is quite probable that one or more postponements will take place due to overloaded court dockets and requests by the defense attorney for more time to prepare the case.‡ Often, the underlying reason for such requests is that the defense attorney hopes the case will eventually be dropped by the complaining witness and that other witnesses won't be available by the time the case comes to trial.

The prosecutor will be a district attorney assigned to your case. Your husband will be the defendant. Both attorneys will make opening statements to the jury. They will explain what they intend to prove to the jury, what witnesses will be called, and why they think the jury should agree with their position. You should expect to be called to the stand, perhaps more than once, to testify about the incident. You will be questioned by both the district attorney and your husband's lawyer (cross-examination). Your testimony will be given under oath. The DA will question you about who you are, where you live, the time, place, and type of assault, what was said by you and your husband, how you felt, what your injuries were like, what you did after the beating, etc.

Witnesses will probably be sequestered outside the courtroom during the testimony of others so that they will not be influenced by what is said. After their testimony, they are permitted to remain in the courtroom. Your husband may testify but is not required to do so.

After all testimony has been heard, the attorneys will summarize their cases and remind the jury of what they think the verdict should be.

In some locations, the verdict must be unanimous; in others, a

‡ Mindy Resnick, *Counselor Training Manual #1,* Domestic Violence Project—Ann Arbor NOW, 1976.

verdict can be reached by a ten-to-two decision or other, similar ratio. If the defendant is found guilty, he may appeal to a higher court.

Plea Bargaining

Sometimes a case never comes to trial, since the matter is settled through plea bargaining:

The defense and prosecuting attorneys meet and decide if the case can be settled without going to court. A typical case might involve a man charged with felonious assault. The defense lawyer has heard the evidence and the witnesses and feels sure that his client will most likely be convicted. He will ask the prosecutor if he will accept a guilty plea to a misdemeanor and save the bother and expense of going through a trial. If the prosecutor is agreeable and the defendant agrees, such a deal will be made. The prosecutor may agree to ask for a suspended sentence in return for the guilty plea. The victim is not usually present or consulted during plea bargaining. It is not necessary to consult her, since it is the government that is prosecuting the case and not her. She is a witness to her own assault. Sometimes the lawyers don't even bother to notify her. It's not uncommon for a battered wife to call the prosecutor's office to find out some information about her case and be told that the matter has been settled.*

Sentencing

If an assailant is found guilty, the usual penalty is probation and/or a fine, according to Mindy Resnick. If the assault is particularly severe or if it's his second or third conviction, he may spend some time in jail and receive a suspended sentence. Often, the judge will make it a condition of the probation or suspended sentence that he maintain distance from you and stop beating you. Sometimes mandatory counseling is decreed. None of these measures, however, insures that future violence will not occur. Many men on probation beat and even kill their wives. The *Handbook for Battered Women* advises that if a wife beater is free on a suspended sentence or on probation, the authorities should be in-

* Roger Langley and Richard C. Levy, *Wifebeating: the Silent Crisis.* (New York: E. P. Dutton, 1977).

formed immediately of any further violence. You are advised to file a complaint and report any violence to the probation officer. The court may end his probation or suspended sentence and send him to jail until his sentence has run out.

Diversion

Some communities have instituted diversion programs, which use mediation procedures, instead of a trial, to divert wife-battery cases to a dispute center for possible resolution. Usually the concerned parties meet with counselors and try to resolve the problem. (More information on dispute centers is contained in Chapter III.)

Peace Bonds and Restraining Orders

One possible legal step is the obtaining of a peace bond or a restraining order that orders your husband to cease and desist from assaulting, molesting, threatening, or physically abusing you.

We do not recommend that you take such action, because we have found that these documents are universally worthless. In fact, some communities no longer issue them, since they do so little good. Generally, the police won't enforce them even though violation of the bond is a misdemeanor under the law. The policy within district attorneys' offices is generally one of non-arrest, and the police will usually advise you to call your attorney if a bond is violated.

Making the Process Work

When you decide to file a private criminal complaint against your husband, you should anticipate attempts by the authorities to discourage you from prosecuting. Throughout the criminal process, it will be necessary for you to be assertive and maintain your determination to exercise your rights. It is important that you not let others discourage you from utilizing the criminal process or talk you into dropping any charges or signing any agreements that you do not feel good about. Remember that at every step along the way the pressure will be there to screen you out.

This, however, is a generalization and may not be universally true. In some areas, improvements are beginning to be made through pressure exerted by women's groups. In Philadelphia, the District Attorney's Office has established a separate Domestic Violence Unit, which has made space for counseling of battered women by the local shelter group in its offices. In those communities that have victim/witness assistance programs, victim advocacy may be more prevalent within the criminal-justice system. Still, the majority of battered women who try to utilize the criminal-justice system find it necessary to employ a variety of survival tactics and pressure techniques in order to achieve any measure of success.

When you visit the District Attorney's Office to file a complaint, the first obstacle you face is convincing them to prosecute your case. You must, however, visit the office as soon as possible after the abusive incident. The longer you wait, the more difficult it will be to get them to take action. If you have visible bruises, it helps. Bring photographs if you have them.

The *Handbook for Battered Women* points out:

> The Clerk may try to persuade you not to file a complaint as soon as he (and he is seldom a she) realizes it is a "family matter." . . . The Clerk may suggest that you go to the Probate Court instead of filing a criminal complaint (Probate Courts handle divorce matters, etc.). Firmly remind the Clerk that crimes are the business of the District Court and not the Probate Court.
>
> A Clerk may also try to convince you not to file because the criminal process is so long and trying. Tell the Clerk you know that, but stress to him that you are serious about following through on the complaint. Repeat as many times as possible that you are in fear of your life and the welfare of your children. Bring in witnesses and your medical records. If you called the police earlier, bring in a copy of their report or ask the officer with whom you spoke to be at the District Court when you file.†

Although it is important to be assertive, you also want to make sure that you are cooperative. Give as much information as possible during the interview. If drug use and/or alcohol abuse are in-

† *Legal Help for Battered Women.*

volved, make sure you mention it as well as any mental illness. You are not required, however, to give out any intimate or personal details about your relationship.

Be careful about the tendency of the interviewer to reduce the charges contained in the complaint. If you were assaulted, the charge should not be harassment. If you were beaten, the charge should not be threats.

If court dates are set during the interview, try to get them scheduled at your convenience.

If the interviewer refuses to take your complaint, try getting help from the victim/witness assistance program if there is one, or call your local wife-abuse group. It may be possible in your locality to appeal the decision to a judge.

From the *Handbook for Battered Women:*

> The more appeals that are brought, the more likely it is that clerks will begin to take these complaints seriously.
>
> There are no further steps to take if the judge doesn't act, unless you have a lawyer who is willing to sue the District Court for not doing its duty. The only legal reason the Clerk or the judge has for not issuing a complaint or scheduling a show-cause hearing is that he does not believe that you were battered by your husband. That is why it is extremely important to prepare carefully beforehand— know dates, times, places—to be thorough in telling the story and in complete detail. If you have filed before, dropped charges, and are questioned about this, state honestly why (for example, you were afraid or had no money to leave).

If you do not want to reveal your address, tell the clerk your reasons. Should he insist, request that it be kept confidential.

One of the most important things you can do for yourself, when filing a complaint and at all stages of the prosecution process, is to have an advocate accompany you to the DA's office and to court. An ongoing source of support can mean the difference between feeling isolated, afraid, and uncertain, and feeling strong, confident, and capable. You may be able to find an advocate through a local abuse program, women's group, or close friend or relative.

If your husband is being arraigned, it is not necessary that you attend, but it is probably a good idea to do so, as it will keep you up to date and informed about the case.

In many instances, the preliminary hearing can be almost as important as the trial, since this is the point at which the charges can be dropped. Sometimes the defendant can waive the preliminary hearing, although usually he will choose not to do so. You don't need a lawyer of your own either for the hearing or the trial, as the prosecuting attorney is on your side, although technically he is representing the state and not you. You must appear at the hearing or the case will be dropped and your husband will be released. In many ways, the preliminary hearing is sort of a "minitrial." The victim and witnesses must appear. The witnesses—including yourself—can be called to testify under oath and can be cross-examined by the defense attorney and the judge. If anyone lies, he or she can be prosecuted for perjury. Make sure that you are well prepared for the hearing, especially if you have any mixed feelings about following through with the prosecution. It is probable that you will be given the opportunity to drop the charges at this hearing.

You might be asked, "If he promises to leave you alone, will you drop the charges?" If you agree, then most likely you will both sign an agreement stipulating that he will not assault or harass you. Your husband will probably be told that if the agreement is violated, sterner measures will be taken. Unfortunately, these agreements are not worth much, and we urge you not to sign if you want any real results from prosecuting your husband.

A Handbook for Battered Women gives the following advice regarding the preliminary hearings:

> It is important that you present your case well. Do not shout, but speak loudly, slowly, and clearly. Practice with a friend. Tell what the man did to you. Tell of your injuries and fear. Show pictures of your injuries. Tell how the beating upset your children. Make it a *short* story.
>
> Answer the judge's questions briefly. Do *not* show anger with what the judge asks or says. If you get upset, you can cry.
>
> Talk only to the judge. The man who hurt you will tell his side of

what happened. Do not get angry with him. Do not fight with him or interrupt him, no matter what he says. When he is done, the judge will let you talk again.‡

Others stress that you prepare carefully for your appearance:

She should get the sequence of events straight in her mind, noting the time and location of the event she is describing and how long each event took. She should expect the repeated questions about precise details of her story.

She should avoid appearing uncertain about what happened when. She should speak in a firm, positive way and avoid using phrases such as "I think" when describing the crime. She must convince others that she is certain about what she is saying and at the same time avoid appearing as if she rehearsed her testimony. She must be careful not to change details on the stand.

When she is cross-examined by her husband's lawyer, she should answer only what she is asked and avoid volunteering any additional information. She should avoid answering any question too quickly. She should pause before speaking, perhaps mentally count up to seven before saying anything. This slight delay gives her attorney a chance to object to a question he feels is improper.*

Periodically you may begin to have doubts about putting your husband in jail. Try to remember that you are the victim of a crime and that the system was established for victims to seek justice. It is important not to let doubt or guilt feelings get control over you. Having an advocate or friend in court with you will help you to get beyond any negative feelings that may crop up. Sometimes the judge will clear the courtroom before the hearing. If there is someone with you whom you'd like to remain with you, be sure to tell the prosecutor, so that he can pass the information on to the judge.

Make sure that you bring any supportive documents to the hearing such as medical records, etc. If you are worried that your husband will follow you when you leave, you should request that he be detained until after you have left. Have your advocate or

‡ Fields and Lehman, op. cit.
* Langley and Levy, op. cit.

friend take notes. They can be helpful later, when preparing for the trial.

After a trial has been scheduled (anywhere from two months to a year after the preliminary hearing), you will be notified of the date by the court. Bear in mind, however, that several postponements are likely.

When preparing for the trial, refer to any notes that your friend or advocate has taken either about the beating or the preliminary hearing. If you don't have any notes, you may be able to get a copy of the transcript of the hearing through the court. As in the hearing, all details should be gone over so that you have the sequence of events straight. Mindy Resnick points out that many victims are intimidated by defense attorneys who insist on a step-by-step, movement-by-movement account of the incident.† Remember that the defense attorney will try to make it look as though you are lying or that you did something to cause the incident. In addition to this preparation, "It is generally reassuring for the victim to understand court procedures, the setting, where to sit and stand, the sequence of events in a trial, who will be present, etc. The best way to accomplish this is to attend another trial."‡

Most likely, you will not have the same prosecutor at the trial that you had at the hearing. While this is unfortunate, there are a number of things you can do to increase your chances of getting good results from the trial. First, make sure that you always appear when scheduled to do so, even if you are fairly certain that the proceedings will be postponed. Convince the prosecutor of your ability and determination to follow through. The *Handbook for Battered Women* points out that the prosecutor may be unsympathetic or overworked and may not have time to prepare your case sufficiently. Therefore, "You or your advocates can offer to help the District Attorney/Police Prosecutor collect evidence, interview witnesses and generally prepare the case. It is important to offer assistance and to encourage him to vigorously prosecute the case. Make sure he has all the information, documents and name(s) of witnesses he needs to handle your case."

† Resnick, op. cit.
‡ Ibid.

Sometimes witnesses to the assault will not want to get involved. If this is the case, you can have a summons issued to be sure that they show up in court.

The *Handbook* gives some final advice regarding the trial: "Testifying at a trial is very difficult. It is important to have emotional and legal support before and at the trial. A District Attorney or Police Prosecutor should review your testimony before the trial, telling you what questions he will ask. . . . It is a good idea to arrive early so you can get your bearings before your case is called. . . . In addition to information about yourself (who you are, where you live, etc.) you will have to remember the place, time, type of assault, what was said by you and your husband, how you felt, what your injuries were like, what you did after the beating, etc. . . . Your story must be very clear and accurate. If you are married to your attacker or separated, any motive you may have in bringing criminal procedings will be highlighted. In particular, if there is a pending probate (divorce, etc.) proceeding and you are asking for money in that proceeding, the defense attorney may try to show that the purpose of the criminal complaint is to squeeze more money out of the husband."

Honesty is the best and only policy when under oath. If you are unsure of an answer, it is better to say, "I don't know," rather than say something that could later be used to confuse or discredit you. Honesty, though, should not be confused with openness: you should talk to no one about the case except the prosecutor, friends, and/or advocates while in the court building.* Clever defense attorneys can convince unsuspecting witnesses to tell them about the incident, and later use the information against them.

As with the hearing, you may request that your address be kept confidential.

The *Handbook for Battered Women* discusses the difficulties involved in obtaining a conviction: "Like all criminal cases, woman-abuse must be proved 'beyond a reasonable doubt.' This is not an easy thing to do; it requires more than your word against your husband's/lover's. The 'burden of proof,' that is, responsibility for showing the court that your version of the beating is

* These suggestions are from Resnick, op. cit.

true 'beyond a reasonable doubt' is on *you,* the charging party. You need to be more convincing than your husband."

A *Handbook for Battered Women* reminds us that while some judges are very sympathetic to battered women, some blame the victims for causing their own assault. "This is the gamble whenever you go to court."

If your husband is found guilty, he may be assigned to undergo counseling either through the court's own counseling program or through some other facility. Often, the wife is encouraged to participate. Remember that you are not required to do so. Likewise, if your case was diverted to a mediation or dispute center, you are not required to participate in mediation procedures if you don't want to.

Recently, some judges have begun to assign wives as their husbands' probation officers. The reasoning behind this is that the husband will be less inclined to assault his wife if he knows that she has the authority to put him in jail. If your husband has been convicted and you think such an arrangement might be useful, you could ask the prosecutor to suggest to the judge that he follow this procedure.

Be sure to keep copies of any documents that have accumulated during the legal process. It is important to have these on hand to show the police if necessary. If they know that you have taken serious legal action against your husband, they will be more willing to intervene.

Langley and Levy note that a battered wife whose husband has been convicted of criminal assault may be eligible for compensation as a victim of crime in states where such laws exist. You can check through an attorney or local victim/witness assistance program. Our research shows that this is unlikely, but it's still worth checking out.

You should watch out for attempts at plea bargaining by the prosecutor and defense attorney. Inquire if any such negotiations are underway periodically as the trial approaches. If you are opposed to plea bargaining, emphatically urge the prosecuting attorney not to make any deals, and impress upon him your capability and intention of following through.

Civil Remedies

Several states have recently enacted spouse-abuse legislation that provides that orders of protection and/or eviction can be issued in domestic-violence situations. These orders generally specify that an abusive spouse must refrain from further violence. If the abuse is severe, the abuser may be ordered to vacate the home for a period of a few months to a year, after which time it is usually possible to renew the order. The order may include provisions for support, custody, and visitation.

The order does not affect title to the property, and the abuser can be evicted even if the dwelling is jointly owned and sometimes if it is in his name only. The evicted spouse does not lose any rights to the property, however. The abuser may be ordered to make either the rent or mortgage payments. The petition for a protective order can be brought after the battered spouse has left the home if she has been forced to do so. In some states, the order applies to couples living together as well as to those who are married, and in some states the legislation applies to child abuse as well as to spouse abuse.

The procedure for obtaining a protective order usually consists of filing a petition with family court. Legal representation is generally necessary, but recently in Pennsylvania battered women have been filing their own petitions. This is particularly important when the battered woman cannot afford a private attorney and does not qualify for legal services. When a petition is filed, a hearing will be scheduled and you should be represented by an attorney.

Your husband may or may not be represented. If the situation is an emergency, often a temporary eviction order can be issued until the hearing takes place, usually within a day or two. Sometimes these temporary eviction orders can be issued without the abuser's being present. At the hearing, all the same things apply that were described earlier in the chapter under "Pressing Charges." Once again, it is necessary for you to file the petition as soon after the abuse as possible. Usually, there is a filing fee, sometimes as much as twenty-five dollars. There may be provisions for getting the fee waived if you are indigent.

After the order is issued, you will be given a copy. In some states, a copy is filed with the police. If this is not the case in your area, keep your own copy hidden in a safe place so that you can show it to the police if your husband violates the order. The police are responsible for enforcing the protective order. How effectively they accomplish enforcement varies from state to state. In some areas, the police cannot arrest your husband if he violates the order unless they catch him at it. In these instances it will be necessary for you to return to family court to file a contempt petition. Your husband may or may not be detained until the contempt hearing is held. If he is found to be in violation of the order at the hearing, he may be fined or sent to jail. Recent amendments to the Pennsylvania Protection from Abuse Act enable police to make arrests for violations without witnessing them, and if family court is closed, the abuser can be arraigned in criminal court and sentenced to six months or more and/or fined up to one thousand dollars. After the order is issued, showing a copy to your landlord or to the public housing authority may get your husband's name crossed off the lease.

The major difference between filing for a protective order and pressing charges against your husband is that the civil process (protective order) does not involve the criminal courts. The abuser gets no criminal record and spends no time in jail unless the order is violated. You may want to consider using both the criminal and the civil processes at the same time. This can be advantageous. It is possible that where one may not completely do the job, the other may help. Neither of these proceedings will have any effect on your divorce should one be pending.

Another difference between the two is the length of time required for processing. A protective order may be issued immediately, while a criminal case can drag on for months, and during that time the abuser will be out of jail (see Chapter IV for more information on legislation pertaining to spouse assaults, and Chapter III for additional information on civil and criminal remedies).

Utilizing Resources

Even if you do not want to leave your home yet, you may at some point want to consider possible alternatives. The single most important step you can take is to get connected with other women. Even though we are all used to looking to the "experts" to tell us what to think and how to see ourselves, remember that women are the real experts on problems and concerns of women. We need each other's support, respect, and caring if women are to break the cycle of powerlessness in which they have been kept.

Begin looking into resources for a place to go should you decide to leave your home, and for other possible sources of help. Explore the possibility of staying with friends or relatives. A local group working with abused women, or the local chapter of the National Coalition Against Domestic Violence, may sponsor an emergency shelter for abused women in your area. Also ask about hotlines, which you can call for emergency advice. Look in the phone book under "Women" for names of other women's organizations. Betsy Warrior, who has done a great deal of work in the area of wife abuse, publishes a list of most of the known women's groups and individuals working on the problem all over the country. This list is frequently updated, and you can get a copy by writing to her at 46 Pleasant Street, Cambridge, MA 02139. Also, see the listing of resources done by the Center for Women Policy Studies, which is in the back of the book. Be sure you know how to contact local social-service agencies, which may be able to provide concrete aid such as emergency food, shelter, clothing, or money. Check out services available through your church or community organizations, such as Catholic Charities and the Salvation Army. If your husband has a drinking problem or if alcohol is playing a part in your fights, consider calling Alcoholics Anonymous—or Al-Anon, which provides help for families of alcoholics. Take a look at Chapter VIII for more information on women's shelters—what they are all about and how they might be of help to you.

WELFARE

Welfare might be an important and necessary source of financial support for you if you are thinking about moving out on your own. It can be difficult to utilize the welfare system to your advantage, due to the fact that you cannot get on welfare until you have left and you may not have the money to leave. If you can arrange for a temporary place to stay, you may be able to get the welfare system to provide you with some money immediately. There are two distinct categories of clients needing welfare, as explained by the Marital Abuse Project of Delaware County (Pennsylvania): "1. If a woman, with or without children, has no money, no home, no food and no resources, this is an 'emergency.' 2. If a woman, with or without children, has a roof over her head, a little money, food, and nearby parents who can help temporarily, this is not an 'emergency.'" However, even if your situation does not constitute an emergency, you can apply for welfare once you are out of the home, either for yourself or for you and your children. It is pretty well known that dealing with the welfare system may not be a particularly pleasant experience, particularly for minority women. If you were never on welfare before, you may be uncomfortable about the possibility, having heard the myths about "welfare cheaters" and perhaps feeling that being on welfare is somehow disgraceful. Keep in mind that it is the function of any society to provide for the well-being of its citizens by allowing access to education, training, and jobs. When these are not available or when people are held back from taking advantage of them, such people still have right to a decent standard of living. It is important for you to feel justified in getting any kind of assistance you need to survive, although welfare grants cannot by any stretch of the imagination be considered to provide decent living standards.

Because in many ways the welfare system is deliberately designed to discourage people, you will need to be very clear about your needs and your rights. If you can, take someone with you when you apply, preferably someone who knows the system well. Remember that many welfare workers reflect society's biases and myths about welfare recipients, and that you may find yourself treated in ways that make you feel demeaned. Be sure to stand up for your rights; try to find out what you are entitled to, and insist that you get it. If you feel that the social worker who takes your application is treating you unfairly, ask to speak to the supervisor, and insist on doing so. Stay calm, even if the social worker is being unreasonable, and try to stick to the issues. If you continue to be treated unfairly or if you have questions about your rights, call the Welfare Rights Organization (WRO) or some other, local advocacy group, or get in touch with a women's group in your area, to find out what you should do.

Often, women are told that they must take their husbands to support court before they can be eligible to apply for welfare. It is *illegal* for the welfare board to force women to file for support from their husbands. You should be aware of this before you apply. If the welfare authorities wish to take your husband to court, they have the right to do so, but they can't force you to do it.

For more information, see the Resources list.

Utilizing Legal Services

When you decide to take legal action, it is almost always advantageous to have representation. If you cannot afford a private attorney representation may be obtained through community legal services or the local legal-aid program. If you're on welfare, you automatically qualify for free legal services. If you are not on welfare, your eligibility will be determined by the standard set by the local legal-aid or community-services program. An ironic Catch-22 ensnares many battered women who seek legal representation. Frequently, legal service programs determine a female applicant's eligibility not on the basis of *her* income but on that of her husband. You may be declared ineligible even if you haven't got a dime of your own. If you do not qualify for legal aid, we suggest that you contact one of the women's groups in your area that deals with problems of battered women. They will be able to help you find adequate legal representation at reasonable cost.

Finding a competent, reasonably priced private attorney can be difficult. It has been our experience that unscrupulous lawyers often rip off vulnerable female clients, fail to provide adequate representation, and behave in a patronizing and condescending manner. When dealing with lawyers, it is almost always imperative that you know the law and your rights.†

† The book, *Women in Transition,* includes a section on "What to Look for in a Lawyer." It is a valuable guide for obtaining effective representation.

Getting Him Out

There is no legal way to force an abusive spouse out of his home. Sometimes, however, if you file criminal charges, he will agree to leave under the condition that the criminal charges be dropped. If he does agree to leave, you must make sure that he signs the house over to you or that the lease is rewritten in your name only. If you fail to do this, he can return at any time and demand access. A lawyer will be helpful here. You must examine what leverage you have and use it in bargaining with the abusive spouse to leave. Sometimes bargains can be struck over rights to property or support.

Mental-illness Commitment

In some states, a person who endangers or threatens to endanger his or her own life or the life of another and has done so because he or she is mentally ill can be committed, for evaluation, to a mental-health facility. The procedure in such a case is to call your local mental-health officer, whose name can be obtained through the local mental-health/mental-retardation unit. The abuser will be evaluated and a hearing will be held to determine whether further inpatient treatment is necessary because of the psychiatric disease and the violence resulting from it. This option should be exercised only when it is clear that *mental illness* exists.

COUNSELING

If you are currently living in an abusive situation, you may be feeling some of the things mentioned earlier in the chapter: guilt, shame, embarrassment, powerlessness, fear, isolation. Even if you have found a way out, it will probably take time for you to recover from living in a violent atmosphere. If you feel the need for some help, it does not mean you are sick or have anything wrong with you. It is a rare person indeed who can walk away undamaged after having been victimized, especially if the victimization has occurred over a period of time. Sympathetic counseling, particularly in a women's group, can play an important part in helping you to gain control of your life.

There is no doubt that the counseling programs and approaches developed by the women's groups working on the wife-abuse problem are the most effective and helpful. We urge you to make every effort to get in touch with one of these groups. Most likely, they will be able to provide you with some initial emotional support over the phone, and there may be a rap group that you can join. Meeting with other women who have experienced situations similar to yours will help to make you aware that you are not alone, that you are not sick or crazy, that your situation is not hopeless and that you are a valuable human being, who does not deserve to be treated abusively. Former battered women who have participated in these groups often report that the experience is extremely positive. Frequently, it can make the difference in being able to successfully break the cycle of violence.

If there is no women's group in your area that provides services to battered women, you may be able to join a regular consciousness-raising group through calling your local women's center. For it is not uncommon to find abused women in such groups, as well as a warm, supportive atmosphere.

Although many battered women eventually find it necessary to leave their husbands, you are not pressured to do so if you call a women's group. The first priority of these women is to provide you with what you feel you need, not to pass judgment or make decisions that only you can make. Their approach will be to help you develop your emotional and economic independence, so that your decisions—whatever they may be—will be made out of strength and confidence, rather than fear or desperation.

You may want to try your community mental-health center or family service agency for individual counseling or to see if they sponsor any women's groups. Many of these institutions are becoming more aware of women's issues and have initiated special programs for women.

If it is not possible for you to find a women's group, the next-best thing is to locate a private feminist therapist. Historically members of the therapeutic community have approached their work with women clients based on the traditional concepts surrounding the female role. Unfortunately this often resulted in therapy that served to rechannel women into what was considered acceptable feminine activity or back into unhappy marriages, rather than into roles or activity that promoted their independence and well-being (see Chapter II). Happily, this is beginning to change; many therapists (mostly females, but also some males) are rethinking the traditional approach and developing therapeutic models that reinforce women's strengths and build their self-esteem.

It is imperative, if you are a minority woman and your therapist is not, to check out your potential therapist for any indication of racism, before entering into a counseling relationship. Be clear about how the therapist perceives you before beginning to counsel with her or him. Since the best intentions *cannot* counterbalance deeply felt prejudices along racial lines, a therapist with racist perceptions is a therapist you must steer clear of.

There may be a feminist therapy collective in your area. Your local women's center or NOW group may keep a list of therapists that they have screened and can recommend. If none of these resources is available in your community and you have to find a therapist on your own, read the tips from *Women in Transition*‡ about selecting a therapist. This section will serve as a useful tool as you search for the kind of counseling that is in your best interests.

If you are already involved in individual therapy, joining a women's group will probably not conflict with the help you are currently getting. In fact, participation in a women's rap group frequently augments and enhances the therapeutic process.

You may prefer to seek couple counseling. If so, traditional service agencies and private therapists may be your only recourse. Beware of choosing someone unfamiliar with counseling abused women and abusers. Competent couple counselors are not necessarily competent *violent*-couple counselors (see Chapter VI).

Other Resources

There are several additional pieces of information that you may need if you decide to take concrete action:

‡ *Supra.*

Self-Defense
Separation
Divorce
Support
Child Custody
Child Care
Property
Public Housing
Employment
Continuing Education
Job Training
Common Law Marriage
Finding and Choosing Lawyers and Therapists
Living on Welfare

This information is covered in the *Women in Transition* book, mentioned earlier. In addition the Women's Resource Network has a resource kit containing this information which is available upon request.

THE FUTURE

Whether or not you have separated from your husband, you may at some point consider moving in with another man or getting married again. See Chapter VI for a personality profile of the abusive man if this is the case. Having information of this sort can help you avoid another abusive relationship. The most useful thing to do at this point, however, is to stop and think, and to remember that you have plenty of time to consider such a decision. Sometimes, by making too hasty a decision, women get themselves into another unsatisfying or abusive situation and end up feeling even more helpless and trapped. This can result from continually looking for someone to rescue one from a bad situation, which always puts one at someone else's mercy. It is certainly understandable if the stresses and fears of being on your own tempt you into wanting someone to take care of you, but you will be cheating yourself if you feel that the only way to survive is to be dependent upon a man. In fact, the basis for any healthy, satisfying relationship is strength, not weakness, and the more capable and independent you feel, the less likely you will be to allow yourself to be abused again. You may be feeling scared and lonely, but you *can* get through it. It is always a bad idea to make an important decision or a long-range commitment when feeling panicky. Give yourself a chance to calm down, to sort out what you have been through, to learn to enjoy your friends, your children, yourself. Women have historically been made to feel like failures if they are not with a man, and you may experience pressure, not only from yourself but from other people, to "find" someone. Don't let this attitude influence you. Remember that you are important in your own right, as a whole person, with or without a man.

In the event that you do remarry, you can and should have a clause put into the marriage vows specifically forbidding the use of any physical force. You may also want to draw up a marriage contract specifying the rights and obligations of both parties, including the stipulation that there will be no violence or physical abuse.*

Frequently, battered women find that once they have left the abusive relationship, obtained some sort of regular income, and relocated, they are relatively isolated. Often loneliness sets in, particularly when it has been necessary to leave the old neighborhood to escape a violent husband. If you are a low-income or minority woman, you may find that moving out of your community leaves you especially cut off from many people and things near and dear to you. If such is the case, you will need to make an extra effort to keep in touch with those who have supported you and helped you to get reestablished. You may feel extremely vulnerable to returning to the marriage, especially if your husband has found you and is pressuring you to return. Continued contact with your support system (women's group, friends, advocates, etc.) is very important. If you have stayed at a shelter, you may want to return periodically for emotional support and concrete help.

---

* For further information on how to do this and how to achieve a marriage that is an equal partnership see Jennifer Baker Fleming and Carolyn Kott Washburne, *For Better, For Worse: A Feminist Handbook on Marriage and Other Options,* (New York: Charles Scribner's Sons, 1977). Also, *Women in Transition, a Feminist Handbook on Separation and Divorce, supra,* which contains extensive information on everything from welfare to buying insurance to obtaining adequate health care.

One possibility to consider is moving in with other women who can provide consistent and continuing encouragement and aid. In England, this type of communal housing has been established for women who have stayed at shelters. These support systems don't exist here yet, but that doesn't mean that you can't develop your own.

Finally . . .

Although it may seem that you face almost insurmountable hurdles, we want you to know that there are many women who care about what happens to you. We are determined that society recognize and respond to your victimization. We are demanding that the blame for someone else's inability to cope does not fall on you, that shelters and services be developed to meet your needs, that future generations of boys and girls be raised to treat each other as equals, with mutual respect and caring. And we are demanding that your right to live a life free from violence be ensured.

But, in the end, only you can make the decisions and take the steps that will set you free. The Milwaukee Task Force puts it best: "You have both the freedom and the responsibility to care about yourself. You have the right to think and feel and make choices and changes. Consider thinking about yourself in new ways:

I am not to blame for being beaten and abused.
I am not the cause of another's violent behavior.
I do not like it or want it.
I do not have to take it.
I am an important human being.
I am a worthwhile woman.
I deserve to be treated with respect.
I do have power over my own life.
I can use my power to take good care of myself.
I can decide for myself what is best for me.
I can make changes in my life if I want to.
I am not alone. I can ask others to help me.
I am worth working for and changing for.
I deserve to make my own life safe and happy.

In this chapter, we have tried to provide you with useful tools as you move to change your life. Although you face immense difficulties, you have the unqualified support and encouragement of thousands of individuals. Remember the autobiographical words of Andrea Dworkin:

> The clarity of the survivor is chilling. Once she breaks out of the prison of terror and violence in which she has been nearly destroyed, a process that takes years, it is very difficult to lie to her or to manipulate her. She sees through the social strategies that have controlled her as a woman, the sexual strategies that have reduced her to a shadow of her own, native possibilities. She knows that her life depends on never being taken in by romantic illusion or sexual hallucination.
>
> The emotional severity of the survivor appears to others, even those closest to her, to be cold and unyielding, ruthless in its intensity. She knows too much about suffering to try to measure it when it is real, but she despises self-pity. She is self-protective, not out of arrogance, but because she has been ruined by her own fragility. . . . She knows that some of her own emotions have been killed and she distrusts those who are infatuated with suffering—as if it were a source of life, not death.
>
> In her heart she is a mourner for those who have not survived.
>
> In her soul she is a warrior for those who are now as she was then.
>
> In her life she is both celebrant and proof of women's capacity and will to survive, to become, to act, to change self and society. And each year, she is stronger and there are more of her.†

DO YOU KNOW A BATTERED WOMAN?

You may have a friend, relative, neighbor, or acquaintance who is being abused by her husband or boyfriend and doesn't seem able to do anything about it. Your support and involvement may be the most important thing she has, and you can play a vital part in helping her.

Any abusive situation can be dangerous, and you don't want to

† Andrea Dworkin, "The Bruise That Doesn't Heal," *Mother Jones,* July 1978.

involve yourself in ways that could harm you or make things worse for your friend. On the other hand, don't be unduly reluctant to help.

Don't try to reason with the man; you already know that he's unreasonable, and he could turn on you or become angrier at her for bringing you into the situation. Most abusers are jealous and possessive. They don't like "their" women to have outside contacts, they don't want other people knowing "their" business, and they don't want to look bad in the eyes of others. You may be able to find convenient times to talk to her: when he's at work or when she is free to come over to see you. If you are present during an attack, consider whether trying to defend her will do any good or make things worse. If he becomes threatening toward you, let him know in no uncertain terms that you will bring charges against him. If it seems unwise to interfere, you can still help by getting out of the house and calling the police. (Check first to be sure she would want to have the police called.) You can also serve an important role as a witness, backing up her story and reporting exactly what you saw to the police, a lawyer, or a judge. As upset as you may be, try to keep your feelings out of it —you want to be listened to and don't want to look as though you're prejudiced or carrying a grudge against her husband.

You can be helpful by concentrating on what you can do for your friend. Share with her what you have learned, or give her this book. Be available to talk and to offer emotional support. Talk to her about her options. Remind her that she is an important person and that you don't want to see her mistreated.

If the situation in her home is too dangerous, stay away, and arrange to see her when you can. You may be able to provide transportation if she needs to get away, or to provide her with a temporary place to stay, lend her money, food, or other things she may need in an emergency. Perhaps you are in a position to take care of her children if she has no place to leave them.

Talk to her about getting together an emergency supply of money, food, clothing, and other items mentioned earlier in this chapter. If she has no safe place to keep them, you may have room in your home where she can store them. Share with her any information you have such as where to apply for welfare; names

of lawyers, counselors, or other people you may know and have
personally found helpful; how to contact a local women's shelter
or other women's group. She probably feels scared and helpless,
and may need your support to make contacts. Your belief in her
ability to do so can bolster her morale and help her feel more
confident.

It is important that you be as nonjudgmental as possible. It
won't be very helpful if you become frustrated or annoyed with
her paralysis or apparent inability to take meaningful action if
such is the case. Read on to Chapter II for an understanding of
the psychological effects of abuse.

She leaves

Someone you fell in love with
when you were virgin and succulent,
soft and sticky in strong hands.

How you twined over him, rampant
and flowing, a trumpet vine.
How you flourished in the warm weather
and died down to your roots
in the cold, when that regularly came.

Then slowly you began to discover
you might grow on your own spine.
You might dare to make wood.

What a damp persistent guilt comes down
from ceasing to need.
Every day you fight free,
every morning you wake tied
with that gossamer web,
bound to him sleeping with open
vulnerable face and closed eyes
stuck to your side.

You meet others open while awake:
you leap to them. The pain
in his face trips you.

You serve him platters of cold gratitude.
They poison you and he thrives.

What a long soft dying this is between you.
Drown that whining guilt
in laughter and polemics. You were trained
like a dog in obedience school
and you served for years in bed, kitchen, laundryroom.
You loved him as his mother always told him
he deserved to be loved.
Now love yourself.

                                    Marge Piercy
                              From *To Be of Use.*

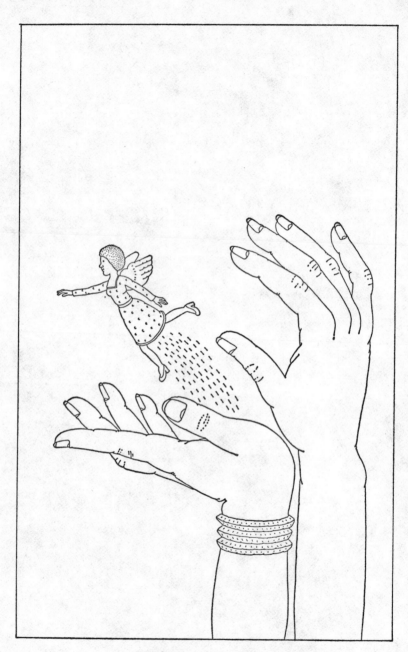

Working with the Victim

Chapter II

WORKING WITH THE VICTIM

the chains are still here
laying on this body strange
no metal – no clang

chains laying strange
chains laying light-weight
chains laying funny
chains laying different
chains laying dyke
chains laying bull-dagger
chains laying pervert
chains laying no jobs
chains laying more taxes
chains laying beatings
chains laying stares
chains laying myths
chains laying fear
chains laying revulsion

chains laying strange
strange laying chains
　　　chains

how do i break these chains

the chains are here
no metal – no clang
chains of ignorance & fear
chains here – causing pain

how do i break these chains
to whom or what
    do i direct pain
    black – white
    mother – father
    sister – brother
    straight – gay

how do i break these chains
how do i stop the pain
who do i ask – to see
what must i do – to be free

sisters – how do i break your chains
brothers – how do i break your chains
mothers – how do i break your chains
fathers – how do i break your chains

    i don't want to kill –
    i don't want to cause pain –

how –
how else do i break – your chains.

                Pat Parker

I have decided there's nothing I can't do after living through this period of abuse. There's no more devastating a failure than allowing another human being to invade your physical body.

I'm a battered wife; he's a very sick man. My children are anybody's guess at this point. Who knows what the long-term effects on them are going to be? And they, too, have been physically abused, only to a lesser degree than I. . . . For I am still considered RESPONSIBLE for HIS anger, HIS loss of control, HIS drunken behavior, and HIS need to physically assault someone else. Consider me his EXCUSE.

So I begin to contact resources. I'm convinced there's someone smarter and more powerful than I. But I'm wrong again. I have no money, no negotiating skills, no wherewithal when it comes to getting resources together. Everyone seems strangely bound up with their own internal problems. Lawyers need money. Police need witnesses. Social services can't provide services for THIS kind of thing. These problems and lack of services become another proof that I am stuck with my lot. Maybe, I think, I do deserve this after all. Didn't the therapist say, "How do you make him mad?" Didn't the social-service director say, "Haven't you tried to even get a job?" Didn't the police say, "What you've told us is hearsay and we need witnesses"? And even when I'm finally, at the point of a knife, brutally raped and injured, didn't I hear them say there's no law that provides for the rape of a wife by a husband? By now I've reached my limit once again. There are no more straws to grasp. My back is broken, though not literally. My psychological bank is empty due to excessive withdrawals with no deposits. I've now heard of battered women who were killed, hospitalized for mental illness, or even committed suicide when reaching the end of their ropes.*

I can't involve my friends or family, for they are powerless, scared, and threatened now too. I am beaten for talking on the phone, to anyone, even a salesman who calls by mistake this number of mine. I have been beaten, burned, fractured, and thrown down steps. Later, I find others have experienced even worse. There can't be much more I can experience now that will hurt me. Death sticks out in my mind as a blessing. But there are the children to consider; and I don't DESERVE to die. I keep telling myself that. And I keep experiencing the hurts of being abused. It doesn't get any easier. It's a constant battle to keep myself getting up each day.

I am desperate now to do something about my life. But where will I get the money for a lawyer? And why don't the police arrest him when my neighbors call them to stop our fighting next door? And where will I get a job, with no skills and no experience? Who has the power to help me change this terrible life I'm leading? What kind of people are my children going to become, seeing us or hearing us live this way? Will my son abuse his wife or girl friend as he's seen his father do? Will my daughter live in fear and dread of every man she meets? For THEM, if not for me, I've got to do something. But instead, I stay, and stay, and stay for what seems like an eternal hell. I

* From *Introduction to Battered Women: One Testimony*. Southwest Community Mental Health Center, Columbus, Ohio.

can't see my way out. I'm fearful of losing family respect for my failed marriage, afraid of censure about my religious convictions, fearful of a terrible reputation with my own friends (the few who are left). Finally, I become obsessed with a fear of losing my respect for myself, and for my sanity—what's left of it.†

"Women are like the masses in wanting to be mastered and ruled."‡
                                                            Sigmund Freud

PSYCHIATRIC ATTITUDES

Throughout history, as male dominance became more deeply entrenched, a variety of means were developed to ensure the subordination of women to men. The advent of monogamy and marriage institutionally insured the dominance of the individual male over the individual female. Various legal codes and schools of thought developed that served the established order with a rationale and tools for maintaining control of the female population.

Ruby Rohrlich-Leavitt, speaking at the Tribunal on Crimes Against Women in New York, pointed out that the first known written laws (the Code of Hammurabi, 1750 B.C.) included a "reform" measure denying women the right to have two husbands. The code stipulated that the punishment if a woman violated that law was death by stoning. It was also decreed that a woman who talked back to her husband was to have her name engraved on a brick, which would be used to bash her teeth out.

In her article "What Did You Do to Provoke Him?" Mary Metzger reminds us that, during the Middle Ages, violence against women was not only condoned but openly encouraged by the Catholic Church. Men were urged from the pulpit to beat their wives, and women were urged to kiss the rod that beat them. Later, as the influence of the Church waned, the psychiatric profession emerged as the most powerful institution in the lives of women. Psychiatric thought became the basis of public policy and a means of social control.

Ms. Metzger points out that, with the development of Freud-

† Ibid.
‡ Sigmund Freud, *Three Essays on the Theory of Sexuality.*

ianism, "male violence against women, while no longer justified by Biblical scripture or legally sanctioned by statute, was still not perceived as a problem, but rather as the natural, masculine, aggressive response to 'women's innate masochism.' It formed the 'natural' relationship between the sexes."*

One might think that the past few decades would have seen a departure from this analysis of the "natural" constructs of the male-female relationship. However, such is not the case. A striking illustration of the mischaracterization of the battered woman and the battering relationship is contained in a 1964 article, on wifebeaters and their wives. The authors imply that battered wives are aggressive, efficient, masculine, and sexually frigid. Then they go on to make a classic misjudgment of the battering relationship: "The periods of violent behavior by the husband served to release him momentarily from his anxiety about his effectiveness as a man, while, at the same time, giving his wife apparent masochistic gratification and helping probably to deal with the guilt arising from the intensity expressed in her controlling, castrating behavior.† This report clearly illustrates the sexist attitudes that pervade traditional psychiatric thinking; the assumptions that aggressiveness and efficiency are characteristics that should belong exclusively to men; that women who are not passive and weak are neurotic; that wife beating might not be all that bad since it gives a man the chance to feel better about his masculinity; that women are inherently masochistic.

Since the article appeared in 1964, one could argue that the authors had not yet been exposed to the reasonable feminist concept that men and women are created equal. No such possibility exists, however, for an article by Menachim Amir, published as recently as 1971: "The underlying idea of the psychoanalytic school of thought is the tendency for victimization as a universal condition of every woman. . . . Reflected in women is the tendency for passivity and masochism, and a universal desire to be possessed and aggressively handled by men."‡

* *State and Mind,* Fall, 1977.
† John E. Snell, Richard J. Rosenwald, and Ames Robey, "The Wifebeater's Wife," *Archives of General Psychiatry,* Vol. 11, Aug. 1964.
‡ Menachim Amir, *Patterns in Forcible Rape* (Chicago: University of Chicago, 1971).

From Freud, who held that the right of possession over a woman is the essence of monogamy, to Deutsch, who believed that "masochism is the most elemental power in female life,"* to modern clinicians such as John R. Lion, of the University of Maryland, who writes of wives gaining sustenance from masochistic involvement in violent relationships,† we find theoretical and professional sanctions for male violence against women. The traditional analysis of female psychology thus serves as one of the important underpinnings of the male-dominated society and ensures that those in the helping professions will do their part to perpetuate the established social order.

Although numerous hypotheses have been presented that fit the data of women's lives far more closely than does the masochism theory (see Bibliography), and in spite of the fact that literally hundreds of grass-roots groups working with battered women uniformly report the absence of masochism as part of the profile of the abused woman, the tendency to blame the victim remains deeply entrenched within traditional psychiatric circles. Mildred Pagelow, in her paper "Blaming the Victim,"‡ mentions numerous writers who still point an accusatory finger at the female victim. Beverly Nichols, in her article "The Abused Wife Problem,"* points our that "the position caseworkers take often supports a belief that the wife encourages, provokes or even enjoys abusive treatment."

Ms. Metzger recalls a former social-services consultant who recently told her: "It's a masochistic situation. You can't believe what these women do to provoke getting beaten."† She also discusses the tendency of therapists, particularly male therapists, to mistakenly enmesh the sexual qualities of sadomasochism with the decidedly nonerotic situation in which women are beaten.

Natalie Shainess, in a recent article, "Psychological Aspects of

* Helene Deutsch, *The Psychology of Women* (New York: Grune & Stratton, 1944).
† John R. Lion, "Clinical Aspects of Wife Battering," University of Maryland School of Medicine, Baltimore, MD. Unpublished paper, 1976.
‡ Paper presented at the annual meeting of the Society for the Study of Social Problems, September 1977, Chicago, IL.
* Beverly B. Nichols, "The Abused Wife Problem," *Social Casework*, January 1976.
† Op. cit.

Wifebeating," writes: "It may come as a surprise that the wife almost inevitably plays a part in her own assault." Although she says that she does not mean to assess blame, the message is clear: "People pick mates in response to their own (unrecognized) neurotic needs."‡

The inevitability of a wife's playing a part in her own assault is directly challenged by Lenore Walker's viewpoint, which allows plenty of room for accidental and situational elements as explanatory forces: "It is entirely possible that any woman may find herself in a battering relationship by accident. My interviews with such women indicate that they do not like being beaten; they are not masochistic; and they do not leave because of complex psychosocial reasons. Many stay because of economics, dependency, children, terror, fears and often they have no safe place to go. Their victimization often provides them with compelling psychological factors which bind them to their symbiotic relationships. Both the men and the women are frightened that they cannot survive alone."*

Dr. Lion, in his paper "Clinical Aspects of Wife Battering," says that "the victim plays a crucial role." He states that there is usually no immediate or satisfactory response when battered women are asked why they have put up with abuses."

If such is the case, then his client population differs dramatically from the thousands of battered women encountered daily by those staffing shelters and hotlines. These victims do indeed have a variety of "immediate and satisfactory responses," which we explore in depth later in this chapter.

The belief that abused women provoke their assaults goes hand in hand with the masochism myth. The assumption is that the victim will "ask for" the abuse, if it is not already forthcoming, in order to achieve satisfaction. Ms. Pagelow points out that this belief is reinforced, perhaps unintentionally, by some of the recently emerging victimology theory in which it is suggested that victims

‡ Natalie Shainess, "Psychological Aspects of Wifebeating." In Maria Roy, ed., *Battered Women: A Psychosociological Study of Domestic Violence* (New York: Van Nostrand Reinhold, 1977).
* Lenore Walker, "Battered Women and Learned Helplessness," *Victimology: An International Journal*, Vol. 2 (1977–78), Feb. 1978. See also Lenore Walker, *The Battered Woman* (New York: Harper & Row, 1979).

of violent crimes are often negligent, take precipitative action, or provoke the criminal behavior of another.

While such may be the case with some forms of crime, wife beating is not one of them. As one battered wife stated emphatically: "No one has to provoke a wife beater. He will strike out when he is ready, and for whatever reason he has at the moment. I may be his excuse, but I have never been the reason."†

Although many beatings are preceded by verbal arguments, and while it may be true that women in general have more verbal skills and can, therefore, get the best of an argument or say particularly hurtful things, this does not justify violence. If two men have an argument in a bar and one wins with words, does that give the other the right to use violence? We don't think so. While many assaults occur during verbal battles, many more occur unexpectedly, with no warning. The most frequent reasons given by battered women for beatings concern such things as the dinner not being cooked on time or the house being dirty. Quite often, victims are assaulted in their sleep. In fact, many battered women say that one of the most debilitating aspects of their situations is the fact that they must live in constant terror, afraid of going to sleep and never knowing when or where the next attack will take place. Raising the question of provocation actually shifts the responsibility from the dominator to the dominated, as pointed out by Ms. Metzger. She notes, "As an explanation for the phenomenon in question, such 'provocation' tells us more about the therapist than the patient."

The rationalization of wife beating by psychiatrists and others in the mental-health field has profoundly negative effects on the battered woman. Members of the judiciary, law-enforcement personnel, medical doctors, and others with whom the abuse victim is likely to come in contact all tend to adopt those explanations for behavior put forth by the psychiatric establishment. As a result, psychotherapists', psychologists', and social workers' negative assumptions about the victim serve to maintain the pattern of abuse rather than treat it. This results in a consistent lack of sympathy for the woman's situation and systematic efforts to rechannel her

† Del Martin, *Battered Wives* (San Francisco: New Glide Publications, 1976).

back into the marriage, since it is assumed that she asks for the abuse and perhaps enjoys it. This can not only be psychologically damaging for her and her children, it can be dangerous as well if the abuse is severe and is escalating to the point of homicide.

Society in general also reflects psychiatry's attitudes and beliefs, and the abused woman usually finds little sympathy or support from family members, friends, neighbors, co-workers, or the person in the street. Cultural norms legitimizing wife beating abound. Barbara Cooper, of the Domestic Violence Project of Ann Arbor NOW, writes in her *Counselor Training Manual ✗2:* "Movie heroes 'discipline' their leading ladies generally after the women become a bit too independent, and the happy couple often walk off together into the sunset in the end. Violence against women is promoted in pornography as a terrific prelude to sex. Sadomasochistic behavior seems to be encouraged or at least condoned by such popular magazines as *Playboy* and *Viva,* and not discouraged by society as a whole.

"A man's use of force against a woman is often glorified in popular fiction and in the media. Those cases in real life in which the 'discipline' turns bloody, resulting in aborted pregnancies, broken bones, disfiguration, and even death, are embarrassing mainly because of the lack of restraint involved."‡

Ms. Cooper also points out that wife beating is perceived as more of a joke than a problem. "Have some fun—Beat your wife tonight," reads an ad for a bowling alley. And we all remember the old joke "When are you going to stop beating your wife?"

Like the rape victim, the abused woman finds herself assaulted twice, once by her assailant and again by the system to which she turns for help. Lenore Walker writes: "Battered women have related stories of being treated as though they engaged in 'crazy' behavior. Many have been institutionalized involuntarily. In some cases, they were given so many shock treatments that their memories were impaired permanently. These women were diagnosed as paranoid, evidenced by their suspiciousness and lack of trust of people they feared might say the wrong thing to their batterers. . . . Many battered women's coping techniques,

‡ Barbara Cooper, Domestic Violence Project—Ann Arbor NOW. *Counselor Training Manual ✗2,* 1976

learned to protect themselves from further harm, have been viewed as evidence of severe intrapsychic personality disorders. My pilot research project has yielded data indicating that battered women suffer from situationally imposed emotional problems due to their victimization. They do not choose to be battered because of some personality deficit but develop behavioral disturbances because of the battering."*

The recognition of this distinction is crucial to the diagnostic process. The counselor or therapist must be able to distinguish between preexisting psychopathology and pathology that is induced by the battering. Dr. Lion's paper illustrates the failure of traditional practitioners to make such a distinction. With references to the "pathological relationships between paranoid women and dependent men" and the "unconscious needs which propel them [battered women] to seek abusive men," Dr. Lion not only fails to perceive the true psychology of the battered woman but comes to conclusions that serve to reinforce and perpetuate the "blame the victim" syndrome: "It is my feeling that probably a majority of wife-battering cases involve some overt or covert participation of the victim or wife. . . . The wife was seen with the husband during which time she appeared as a rather hostile and castrating individual . . . certain wives may gain psychological satisfaction from beatings and batterings."† These blatantly biased perceptions and conclusions should have been dismissed long ago from clinical analysis of female behavior. This is not to say that battered women do not adopt a "victim mentality" or that there is *never* any masochism present. What we are challenging is the use of such arguments to explain generally the battered-woman syndrome and the resulting shift of responsibility from the batterer to his victim.

Clearly, the need is for women's perspectives to be presented. As Suzanne Prescott and Carolyn Letko point out, "What men see as aggressiveness in females, women see as asserting their personal integrity; what men automatically see as masculinity in fe-

* Lenore Walker, "Treatment Alternatives for Battered Women." In Jane Roberts Chapman and Margaret Gates, eds., *The Victimization of Women*, Vol. 3 (Beverly Hills, CA: Sage Publications, 1978).
† Lion, op. cit.

males, women sense as their own competence. What some men may see as frigidity, appears to women to be a natural lack of sexual responsiveness to their violent husbands. And what men see as masochism, women see as the sense of being trapped in their marriages."‡

In the course of this chapter, we hope to provide professionals and peer counselors with an appropriate profile of the battered woman as well as with a variety of skills and techniques that will enable the practitioner to work in the best interests of this particular client population.

WHY SHE STAYS

Battered women experience a wide range of emotional reactions. An awareness of the most common of them is an important tool for those working with the victim.

Guilt: In addition to the indirect negative effects that psychiatry has on the battered woman through its influence on almost every sphere of our society, she herself tends to internalize the prevailing sexist assumptions regarding her psychological makeup. She often assumes the blame for her own victimization and spends useless energy trying to determine how to avoid provoking her husband. She will go to great lengths to avoid a confrontation only to discover that while he may beat her one night for putting the kids to bed too late, he may very well turn around and beat her the next for putting them to bed too early.

Ms. Metzger makes an astute comment on the abused woman's tendency to assume culturally assigned guilt: "For many battered women the ideology, which has branded them inferior as women, maintained their position as their husband's property, and mandated their subordination to their husbands' wills, has been internalized to the degree that they often accept being beaten as their 'just' due. Not only men, but women also accept that women should be, or deserve to be, or even need to be beaten, and that

‡ Suzanne Prescott and Carolyn Letko, "Battered Women: A Social-Psychological Perspective." In Maria Roy, ed., *Battered Women: A Psychosociological Study of Domestic Violence* (New York: Van Nostrand Reinhold, 1977).

husbands have the right to do so. In a study done by Gelles, there were statements from women such as 'I asked for it,' and 'I deserved it.' One woman said: 'I kept thinking it must be my fault . . . what did I do to provoke him? Then one night I was in bed asleep and he came in and started hitting me, and I said, Boy, I didn't provoke this.' The battered wife often sees herself as a failure in those primary roles by which the male society defines her (wife, mate and mother) and thus believes that it is somehow her fault that she is being beaten. Herein lies the true efficacy of the ideology."*

Another contributing factor to the self-blame syndrome is the fact that society holds women responsible for the emotional well-being of family members. Many women assume that their husband's violence is a result of the women's failure to meet the men's emotional needs. Of course, it is well documented that men often batter for reasons that are virtually unrelated to the behavior of their wives but, rather, because of an inability to handle frustration or because they attempt to use violence as a problem-solving device. Unfortunately, the majority of battered women lack this information and therefore have no way of knowing that they are not responsible for their husbands' behavior.

Emotional Dependence: The extent to which the battered woman has been socialized according to traditional sex roles is related to how effectively she is able to respond to her situation. If she has been significantly programmed for dependency, passivity, and docility, she is less likely to behave in an assertive manner. Prescott and Letko point out: "Traditional women's roles have confined sources of self-respect to appropriate performance of traditional sex-role prescriptions and have placed heavy emphasis on the husband as the exclusive source of approval and reward."† Patricia Ball and Elizabeth Wyman, in their article "Battered Wives and Powerlessness: What Can Counselors Do?" make a similar point: ". . . the battered wife is a victim of oversocialization into a stereotypical feminine role. She has learned to be docile, submissive, humble, ingratiating, nonassertive, dependent, quiet, comforting and selfless. Her identity is founded on being

* Metzger, op. cit.
† Prescott and Letko, op. cit.

pleasing to others, being responsible for others, being nurturant to others, but not to herself. Her dilemma has its origin in the passivity and dependence which define the traditional feminine role. Having learned all her life to be dependent on others to meet her basic needs, she feels incapable of 'making it on her own,' even in the face of spending a lifetime with an abusive husband. She has no experience in independent decision making or in being responsible for herself. Furthermore, she has no expectation of success if she were to try to take control."‡ Ms. Cooper adds: "If a woman believes that she is weak and unable to make positive changes in her life, she will tend to respond with resignation or despair to assault."*

Economic Dependence: Although most of the material in this chapter deals with the psychology of the battered woman, it should be well understood that, regardless of the emotional state of the victim, the degree to which she is economically dependent upon her husband is the ultimate determinant in whether or not she will achieve an independent existence. While it may be true that some victims who have the financial wherewithal to survive independently of their husbands choose not to utilize it, it is also true that the vast majority of assault victims, are dependent upon their husbands for their survival and consequently are locked into violent relationships regardless of how strong, confident, independent, or capable they may feel. In the end, a positive attitude can mean very little without the means to live independently.

Why does she stay? The answer is quite simple. If she has children but no money and no place to go, she has no choice. The fact that shelters for battered women are swamped from the moment they open testifies to the enormous numbers of women who would choose to leave the battering relationship if there were a way out and if resources were available.

In violent marriages, the husband invariably controls the family finances—usually with an iron hand. It is the rare victim who has

‡ Patricia Ball and Elizabeth Wyman, "Battered Wives and Powerlessness: What Can Counselors Do?" *Victimology: An International Journal,* Vol. 2, 1977–78. Feb. 1978.
* Cooper, op. cit.

more than a few dollars she can call her own. Most battered women consider themselves lucky if they are allowed enough money to shop at the supermarket once a week. (For that matter, many consider themselves lucky if they are allowed to go to the supermarket once a week.) We are told of one abused woman who finally managed to save enough money to put herself and her two children on an out-of-town bus. The fare was $5.60. It took her two years to accumulate it, due to the fact that she had been virtually imprisoned in her own home.

The long-term unfamiliarity with the day-to-day skills necessary for her survival, such as basic money management, leaves her particularly crippled when it comes to even the most minimal level of independent functioning. Having been denied the opportunity to learn, many battered women do not know how to write a check, take a crosstown bus, or file an insurance claim.

Generally, the abused woman has no knowledge of the family finances and frequently she finds that her husband has put any property, stocks, bonds, etc. in his name only. If he has incurred debts, however, they will be in both names, which means that she can be held responsible by their creditors should he default. And sometimes he does.

It is most commonly during middle age that abusive men decide to take off for greener pastures, either to "start all over again" or to be with a younger woman. Imagine the bewilderment and terror of the middle-aged victim severely lacking in self-esteem and self-confidence as she discovers that she is alone, in debt, impoverished, and completely unequipped psychologically or practically to deal with any of it. Surely some of the fears that served to keep her in the battering relationship were not totally unjustified, since it appears that the worst of them have come true.

One battered woman described her husband's last abusive act. Aware of the fact that he was terminally ill, he spent his last few months calculating and planning to ensure that his wife would receive virtually nothing from his estate. He was relatively successful. It appears that some men continue to batter their wives even from the grave.

Learned Behavior, Low Self-esteem: Ms. Cooper reminds us of the mixed and conflicting messages that society sends regarding whether or not a woman has the right to be free from physical assault in her own home. She mentions the inadequate and discriminatory definitions of assault between men and women and between marital partners in particular: "The issue of a man's *right* to use physical violence against a woman is assumed. . . . The message is that a good master disciplines fairly and with moderation. . . . Many women are not socialized to expect or to demand freedom from physical assault within their own homes."† They are taught that it is part of the wifely role to accept a certain amount of abuse, that it's part of the "worse" of the "for better or for worse" in the marriage ceremony. Often, they have witnessed their mothers and grandmothers before them tolerate abuse over long periods of time. They have come to regard such abuse as a normal part of marital relations. Richard Gelles notes that women tend to stay in violent situations if they experience significant violence during childhood.‡

Perceiving themselves as their husbands' property, financially dependent and almost totally lacking in resources, many women never question their husbands' use of violence as long as it doesn't get "out of hand." Often, women are conditioned to believe that if their husbands don't hit them, they don't love them. Needless to say, it would be impossible for anyone with a positive self-image to embrace such a belief. Unfortunately, women develop negative self-images early in life as the culturally assigned messages about "innate inferiority" become internalized. The extremely low levels of self-esteem found among many battered women allow them to conclude that although they may not be worthy of much, at least they merit the attention of a beating. This phenomenon parallels the child who prefers violent attention to no attention at all. Although each beating serves to reinforce the abused woman's negative self-image, she may also feel that she has succeeded in at least one of her assigned tasks as wife. She has provided her husband with the opportunity to reaffirm his "manhood" and has fed and boosted his ego. In that sense, she may feel that she is "succeeding" on one level, albeit a painful and terrifying one. A related

† Ibid.
‡ Richard J. Gelles, "Abused Wives: Why Do They Stay?" *Journal of Marriage and the Family*, 1976.

phenomenon occurs in the woman who sees her husband's violence as evidence of his need for her nurturance and care. She may feel unloved and unwanted, but repeated violent outbursts indicate to her that he has serious problems and that by providing help she can serve some purpose. This enables her to feel that the relationship is not a total loss. It is a perceived function frequently reinforced by members of her husband's family who tell her that she is his only hope and without her he would be destroyed.

Concern for her children's well-being works to the advantage of the battered woman when and if the husband's violence spills over onto them, a not uncommon occurrence. Although reluctant to seek help for herself (she's not important enough), she will take action once it is apparent that her children are becoming targets of abuse or if they show signs of being adversely affected by her being beaten.

Traditional Value Systems: One factor that motivates the abused woman to remain in the violent home is the belief that her children will be seriously damaged by growing up in a single-parent household: "A bad father is better than no father at all." Although common sense would indicate that continued exposure to parental violence is extremely dangerous and that there are untold numbers of healthy and happy children in single-parent homes, the traditional values frequently held by the battered woman make it difficult for her to realize that it is the current situation that is harmful and that her children would undoubtedly be better off in a violence-free environment no matter what the living situation otherwise.

Traditional socialization often precludes separation and divorce as reasonable alternatives for many battered women, particularly those with strong religious convictions, and the stigma attached to becoming a welfare recipient (most often the only income option available) often serves as a deterrent to change.

Anger: Mindy Resnick, of the Ann Arbor NOW Domestic Violence Project, discusses the anger experienced by battered women in her *Counselor Training Manual #1:** "All victims will be ex-

* Resnick, op. cit.

periencing anger at some level about their situation. Some victims will be able to express their anger directly on or at the assailant but others will not. The victim may well internalize the anger, getting angry at herself instead of the assailant, thus leading to feelings of guilt and self-blame. At other times, the victim may ventilate the anger towards police, medical, social-service personnel or at the counselor." Ball and Wyman point out: "Others [battered women] who have totally internalized the stereotyped feminine role may be out of touch with feelings of anger. In such cases the anger may be disguised as depression or as various somatic symptoms."† Prescott and Letko write: "Depression is accompanied by low emotional energy at a time when women may need this resource in order to deal with violence in their marriages. Depression can affect how frequently or how persistently women seek help directly from community agencies or other helping groups."‡ In their article "Sixty Battered Women," Elaine Hilberman and Kit Munson make the following observations about battered women and anger:

> Like rape victims, battered women rarely expressed their anger directly, although their stories elicited anguish and outrage in the listener. . . . It is likely, however, that the constellation of passivity, panic, guilt, intense fear of the unexpected and violent nightmares reflect not only fear of another assault, but also a constant struggle with the self to contain and control aggressive impulses.*

Isolation: Ms. Cooper writes: "A wife assault victim may be quite isolated. Her husband may actively work at keeping her that way. She probably has few friends or sources of support. If she does have friends, she may never have told them of her home situation. She may have no positive links to rewarding work, assistance with child care, educational or recreational opportunities. Access to other sources of reinforcement for self-worth and per-

---

† Patricia G. Ball and Elizabeth Wyman, "Battered Wives and Powerlessness: What Can Counselors Do?" *Victimology: An International Journal*, Vol. 2, 1977–78, Feb. 1978.

‡ Prescott and Letko, op. cit.

* Elaine Hilberman and Kit Munson, "Sixty Battered Women," *Victimology: An International Journal*, Vol. 2, 1977–78, Feb. 1978.

sonal growth may be lacking. The more isolated a woman is in her own home, the more dependent she is upon her mate for any input about her value as a person."†

Fear: Hilberman and Munson describe the role that fear plays in the battered woman's life: "The women were a study in paralysing terror which is reminiscent of the rape trauma syndrome except that the stress was unending and the threat of the next assault ever-present. . . . Agitation and anxiety bordering on panic were almost always present: 'I feel like screaming and hollering, but I hold it in.' 'I feel like a pressure cooker ready to explode.' They talked about being tense and nervous by which they meant 'going to pieces' at any unexpected noise, voice, or happening. Events even remotely connected with violence, whether sirens, thunder, people arguing or a door slamming, elicited intense fear. . . . There was chronic apprehension of imminent doom, of something terrible always about to happen. . . . Sleep, when it came, brought no relief. Nightmares were universal."‡

Ms. Resnick notes that "Tremendous fear may result and/or a sort of emotional paralysis so that the victim feels passive and experiences all that happens around her as being done *to* her."*

Ambivalence: Ms. Cooper addresses the mixed feelings of many battered women who contemplate leaving the abusive relationship: "The assault victim may be ambivalent about leaving her husband or boyfriend. Change represents radical and frightening independence and even loneliness. She may not believe in her ability to care for herself and/or her children. Perhaps she has threatened divorce or leaving in the past. She may have left the home before, and after a short while returned, frightened at the thought of loneliness and financial insecurity. Her inability to sustain these resolutions may have resulted in more self-blame and lowered her self-esteem.†

These mixed feelings about leaving correspond with the mixed realities—social, economic, and psychological—that attend leaving. Elizabeth Waites has summarized the welter of conflicting

† Cooper, op. cit.
‡ Hilberman and Munson, op. cit.
* Resnick, op. cit.
† Cooper, op. cit.

risks that confront a woman who considers leaving the abusive relationship:

1. Identity versus identity loss— It has been noted that, while man achieves an identity, woman marries one. Whatever her other roles and goals, the role of wife is likely to remain a cornerstone of identity. This development is in part a function of the relation between "women's work" and self-esteem. As Laws . . . has pointed out, the jobs available to women are the least motivating ones and, it may be inferred, the jobs least likely to raise a woman's self-esteem. The popular contrast between career woman and homemaker has never reflected the real options available to most women. In consequence of existing sex role stereotypes, many women are socialized to define the role of wife as a submissive one. And, to the extent that authoritarian attitudes are an expectable concomitant of a traditionally "feminine" identity, we might expect any autonomously assertive act to threaten the submissive wife with identity loss. Thus, even choosing to leave may be threatening.

2. Social approval versus stigmatization— Marriage is not only the traditional route to female identity—or, as Sheehy . . . has suggested, the traditional substitute for female identity; it is also the surest route to social approval as far as many women are concerned. Singleness, particularly for women, has often been stigmatized in American culture, the epithets "old maid" and "gay divorcee" being pervasive cultural stereotypes. A woman may view her ability to get or keep a man as the major dimension along which she is evaluated by others. And, in addition to feeling that she is a failure if she leaves her husband, she may share the social tendency to stigmatize the "broken home" as a cause of all sorts of social ills, ranging from the maladjustment of children to the downfall of Western civilization. The stigma attached to the "broken home" is especially likely to fall on women. . . . Since they typically obtain child custody following divorce, they often come under the scrutiny of sociologists, mental health professionals, and the courts who employ such pejorative labeling. . . .

3. Economic support versus economic deprivation and downward social mobility— Although there is no real evidence that wife abuse is a lower-class phenomenon or that the abused wife is economically disadvantaged while living with her husband, the economic deprivation of the separated or divorced woman has been clearly established. In 1969, single women between the ages of 25 and 44 who

had children had a median income of four thousand dollars a year. . . . A study of divorced mothers and their children in treatment at a psychiatric hospital . . . reported a drastic reduction in family income as a major cause of stress in single-parent families.

The factors contributing to the economic deprivation of the woman who leaves her spouse include those which affect women generally: the low pay associated with women's jobs, lack of training, discriminatory hiring practices, etc. In addition to these, the woman with young children is faced with the prospect of supporting them should she leave her husband. Practically speaking, this often means providing child care for them while she works or seeking welfare assistance. Either way, it may be difficult to rise above the poverty level following a separation from her husband.

The assumption that fathers provide support following marital dissolution, particularly in cases where the father chooses to be recalcitrant, is largely unfounded. It is estimated that over 5.8 million nonwelfare families in the United States have problems of nonsupport, in addition to the 2.9 million families on assistance. . . . Lack of effort on the part of states to enforce support is judged a major factor in welfare dependency in this study. The abused wife or former wife may also be subject to further abuse if she attempts to enforce support.

Ironically, the no-fault divorce statutes enacted in many states to make divorce more humane by replacing adversary proceedings with an irretrievable breakdown standard have contributed to the economic disadvantages of women. . . . The bargaining power which might formerly have been available to an abused woman in a divorce proceeding is lost when abuse is no longer grounds for divorce. Eisenberg and Micklow . . . have pointed out, however, that women did not gain much economically under fault proceedings either. Legally, it has never been easy for a woman to obtain any economic remedy for a spouse's abuse: married, she cannot institute a civil suit against him; and in a divorce action, she is likely to gain little more than the dissolution itself.

Downward social mobility as a consequence of marital separation is feared by some women as much as or more than poverty itself. In this regard, the motivational significance of loss, as opposed to absolute level of income, is evident. Finally, the prospect of poverty interacts with fear of social stigmatization. Stigma accrues not only to poverty in our society, but to the individual judged to be illegitimately dependent on others for support. The image of the female divorcee who leeches her former husband for alimony is contradicted by real-life statistics. . . . Nevertheless, the image persists, along with the socially devalued stereotype of the "welfare freeloader" to serve as a powerful deterrent to some women who are reluctant to accept even the economic aid to which they are entitled.

4. Love versus loss of attachment— The trauma of losing love is usually cited as a major dimension of marital separation. Abused wives not infrequently report that they love their husbands and hope for a change in the abusive behavior. This claim of love has been interpreted as a major support for the masochism hypothesis. There is, of course, an important logical distinction between loving a spouse in spite of his abusive behavior and loving him because of it. Even so, the statement that abused wives love their husbands need not be taken at face value. It may represent merely a denial of ambivalence or even unmitigated hatred. It is also likely to be bound up with the wishes for identity and social approval typically associated with marriage itself. And it functions as a rationalization for remaining in an abusive situation.

Those spouses who do love their husbands in spite of abuse face the prospect of a formidable loss should they decide to leave. Not infrequently, the submissive wife has focused all her affection on her family, sacrificing ties to adults other than her husband. Under these circumstances, the loss of the husband may threaten to isolate the wife from any close interpersonal relationship.

The professed love of an abused spouse for her abuser may also, from a clinical standpoint, resemble addiction. To conclude that such love is masochistic is to beg the question; the concept of masochism explains no more about addictive love than it explains alcoholism. In this regard, it may be significant that a high proportion of the spouses interviewed by Eisenberg and Micklow . . . reported that assault was associated with heavy drinking. This observation suggests that the interaction between some assaultive and assaulted partners may reflect a pattern of mutual symbiosis between addicts, each of whom looks to the partnership as a kind of security blanket but one of whom, the husband, is able to externalize feelings of rage when the sense of security is threatened. In order for an abused woman to extricate herself from such a situation, she would have to overcome her own addiction and find more reliable sources of security. Here, again, she is often confronted with few positive options.‡

‡ Elizabeth Waites, "Female Masochism and Enforced Restriction of Choice," *Victimology: An International Journal*, Vol. 2, 1977–78, Feb. 1978.

Indecision about staying or leaving is heightened by the mixed messages the battered woman receives from those around her. Her family, friends, and religious counselor may urge patience and tolerance, while her doctor and lawyer condemn her for staying and accepting the abuse.

In addition to staying or leaving, Lenore Walker lists several other issues around which ambivalent feelings tend to cluster: love/hate, anger/passivity, rage/terror, depression/anxiety, omnipotence/impotence, and security/panic.

Another area of conflict is a woman's decision whether or not to prosecute her husband in criminal court. Frequently, the abused woman turns to the criminal-justice system not because she wants to put her husband in jail but because she wants to force him to stop his use of violence. The courts by and large are incapable of influencing the batterer's behavior, but there is nowhere else for her to turn. She is faced with the unpleasant choice of jailing her husband or remaining a victim of abuse indefinitely.

Embarrassment and Shame: Ms. Resnick points out that a woman may feel embarrassed and ashamed of remaining in the abusive relationship. She may not want to admit that she is a battered woman, particularly if she is middle-class, since battering is assumed to take place only in low-income neighborhoods. Researchers note that the woman's shame and resulting isolation insulate the battering husband from disgrace and criticism, thereby giving him a psychological advantage.

Lenore Walker says that sometimes the battered woman's need for others to view her as successful is more important and stronger than her need to escape from violence.

Fear of Insanity: Ball and Wyman point out that if the abuser's perceptions of his use of violence are significantly different from the victim's, she may believe that she is going insane.* And when the battered woman is ". . . socially isolated, she has no one to confirm her sanity."†

Physical Illness: Those working with abuse victims usually observe a variety of physical disturbances and ailments. Ms. Cooper feels that the battered woman's problems are largely the result of

* Ball and Wyman, op. cit.
† Resnick, op. cit.

inadequate feelings of personal strength. She is reinforced in this conclusion by Hilberman and Munson, whose clients made frequent clinic visits for headaches, choking sensations, hyperventilation, asthma, chest pain, gastrointestinal symptoms, pelvic pain, back pain, and allergic phenomena. Other common ailments are heart disease and epilepsy. Epilepsy is particularly common. Whether or not frequent head injuries suffered by battered women cause subsequent epilepsy is unclear.

Physically disabled battered women report feeling especially trapped within their marriages. One blind woman told us that her husband would regularly rearrange the furniture so that she would be unable to move about the house. If she did attempt to get around, she would often trip and fall, occasionally suffering injury as a result. In spite of this, she was convinced that her husband was the only source of help and support available to her at that time.

Hilberman and Munson describe an epileptic who required multiple hospitalizations for seizures. For this woman, refusal to use anticonvulsants was her only escape from a savagely brutal husband who kept her from leaving the house unless she needed medical attention.

Learned Helplessness: The theory of learned helplessness as a psychological rationale for why battered women stay with their abusers has been extensively explored.‡ Ms. Walker describes a series of experiments conducted on dogs, rats, and humans during the past several years. The experimenters found that when animals and humans were subjected to repeated imprisonment and/or varied and random, painful stimuli over which they had no control, they soon ceased any attempts to escape or avoid harm. Later, when avenues of escape were made available, they were ignored. "In fact, even when the door was left open and the dogs were shown the way out, they remained passive, refused to leave, and did not avoid the [electric] shock. . . . It took repeated draggings of the dogs to the exit to teach them how to voluntarily respond again."

‡ See Walker, Battered Women and Learned Helplessness," and Ball and Wyman, "Battered Wives and Powerlessness: What Can Counselors Do?" *Victimology*, Vol. 2, 1977–78, Feb. 1978.

The experiments demonstrated that this acquired sense of powerlessness can be transferred from one situation to another and that the expectation of powerlessness does not have to be accurate. That is, if a person does have control over the outcome but does not believe such control is possible, then he or she responds with the learned-helplessness behavior. If the person believes that he or she can control the outcome, then that person's behavior is not affected, even if the reality is that he or she does not have control. Whether one actually can or cannot control a situation is not as important as the *belief* that he or she can or can't. Ms. Walker notes, "This concept is important for understanding why battered women do not attempt to gain their freedom from a battering relationship. They do not believe that they can escape from the batterer's domination. Often their perceptions are accurate, but they need not be for this theory to work."*

Ball and Wyman theorize that socialization into the traditional feminine role as well as a history of family violence may account for later helpless behavior, but on the basis of these experiments, one could also argue that the passivity, almost paralysis, of many battered women is a form of learned helplessness acquired after repeated attempts to escape have been blocked by biased therapists, unsympathetic family members and friends, hostile police officers, an ineffective judicial process, degrading and humiliating welfare procedures, discriminatory employment practices, and having no place to go to escape the batterer.

The Victimization Process: Usually the abused woman has no knowledge prior to the marriage that her husband is going to be violent. It is not until after the wedding (or in the case of a boyfriend, until after they set up house) and she becomes "his" that the violence begins. Her first reaction is one of disbelief. She is shocked, hurt, and angry. But he promises never to do it again. Because she loves him, she believes him. But the violence continues, since battering rarely ends with one incident. It takes her a while to face the fact that not only is it continuing, it's getting worse. She feels she can change him, however, and that they will work it out somehow. When solutions fail to materialize, she

* Lenore E. Walker, "Battered Woman and Learned Helplessness," *Victimology: An International Journal,* Vol. 2, 1977–78.

seeks help, perhaps from a marriage counselor. But it does no good, because she can't figure out what it is that she does to provoke him. Her husband refuses to go. He sees it as a sign of weakness. By now, some time has gone by; perhaps several beatings have occurred. Although she may not realize it, the abuse has begun to take an emotional as well as a physical toll.

An analogy: Many social scientists are familiar with the effects that terrorism has on a community. Individuals become jumpy, fearful, insecure. They never know when the next attack will occur. It could be argued that wife abuse is terrorism on a personal basis. The battered woman finds herself living in fear, feeling powerless and without hope. Her self-confidence evaporates. Paranoia develops. She starts to think less and less of herself, because she is neither fighting back nor getting out. She takes to staying in the house, particularly when she's bruised and swollen, which is often. She isolates herself, withdraws, becomes the criminal instead of the victim. She thinks, "I must have asked for it. If only I hadn't said this or done that, maybe he wouldn't have exploded." She becomes paralyzed—emotionally as well as physically crippled. She reinforces the myth of her own masochism by her inability to take concrete action. Living in a state of chronic anxiety, she may no longer feel the pain. She makes up excuses to justify her continued acquiescence. "It's just his drinking that's a problem" or "I have to stay for the sake of the children." She no longer thinks about leaving. She accepts the abuse as part of her life, although she is in constant fear for her life She no longer calls the employment office; she no longer visits the therapist; she no longer cries to her mother. Her victimization is complete. She has given up.

COUNSELING APPROACH

There are some therapists whose counseling to the battered woman focuses upon how her behavior has contributed to the violence and how it might be changed to prevent future attacks. According to Natalie Shainess, "There are a number of questions a woman can ask herself, if she is willing to consider her own contribution to the problem, and would like the marriage to continue.

Among them are: At what point in my marriage did this assault take place? Is there some unusual circumstance in my husband's business (or other) life which has made him more volatile? What was my role in eliciting his anger? Was I or have I been unfair to him? Have I baited him, criticized him or been extremely demanding? Is hate a predominant affect (feeling-tone) in our marriage? Is there constant discord?"†

Although this approach might be seen as a means of assisting women in avoiding further assaults, implicitly it assumes several things that are part of the ideology that actually supports and rationalizes her assault. First, by counseling her, rather than the husband or both, the problem is tacitly assumed to be hers. Since it is her problem, the counseling focuses on her behavior and what she can do to avoid provoking her husband's violence. The search for provocation is the implicit acceptance of the idea that a man has the right to beat his wife if the circumstances warrant it. In effect, the counselor has said, "Your husband has the right to beat you as long as you engage in behavior he does not like."

This approach serves to reinforce the abuser rather than help the woman. Ms. Shainess advises the victim to comply with a husband's insatiable demand for sex if she wants the marriage to continue. She states that it "makes for a more tolerable marriage." One wonders for whom it becomes more tolerable, the abuser or the victim?

Ms. Shainess believes that battered women choose violent men in order to fulfill their neurotic, perhaps unconscious, need to be abused, and her counseling approach reflects that belief. We, of course, categorically reject such an approach. The vast majority of battered women have no inkling prior to their marriages that there is going to be violence. Problems, yes; violence, no. (Lately, we have learned some of the common characteristics of men who will tend toward violence, and we are now more capable of alerting women to the warning signs. See Chapter VI.)

Del Martin points out that wife beating is, without question, an example of power abuse. "The underlying factor that breeds and perpetuates hostility between the sexes is the male-supremacist patriarchal system, which depends upon the sexist structure of the

† Shainess, op. cit.

family unit and other social institutions. . . . Expecting the husband to be a benevolent despot is no guarantee that physical force will not be used."‡

Dr. Lion contends that it is important not to view the woman as the underdog, but we feel that this is precisely what is needed, since she *is* the underdog.*

Beverly Nichols says: "Because most family caseworkers are philosophically linked to the preservation of family life, some of their reticence in being true advocates for the abused wife is understandable, but is in need of examination."†

People in the helping professions must learn to reexamine old and trusted theory and develop new and different counseling techniques. Battered women are *victims,* and counseling must be approached with that understanding. Otherwise the problem will simply be perpetuated.

Although we take the position that the abuser's behavior is his problem, not the victim's, that doesn't mean that couple counseling and working with the batterer (both of which are discussed in Chapter VI) are the only acceptable therapeutic approaches. Working with the victim is extremely important so that she can develop the emotional and material wherewithal to remove herself as a victim. Even when couple therapy is indicated (when the woman wants it and the husband is willing to participate), it may be more appropriate to work with the individuals involved, at least in the beginning, than to deal with the relationship itself. As Lenore Walker points out, "There is less success in overcoming helplessness when women remain with their battering partners and try to change the relationship to a nonbattering one. . . . Before the specific couples therapy can begin one must sever the symbiotic dependency bonds that have developed between a couple engaged in battering behavior. It is necessary to treat the couple as two individuals, strengthening their independence and teaching new communications skills, in order to reverse the learned-helplessness process."‡ At the Victim Information Bureau in Suffolk County, New York, women are given their choice of counseling

‡ Martin, op. cit.
* Lion, op. cit.
† Nichols, op. cit.
‡ Walker, op. cit.

modalities. If the victim wants to remain with her husband, she is
encouraged to bring him in for counseling. If it is impossible to
involve him in the counseling process and she is unwilling to consider leaving him, then she is encouraged to join a group with
other women in the same situation.

For these women, the traditional mental-health approach of
strengthening and reinforcing the family unit should be aban-
doned. Instead, the counseling method must be one of developing
the victim's emotional independence to the point where she will
be able to leave her husband. There is no hope for the marriage if
the husband is not willing to work on changing his behavior. In
fact, violence that is not stopped will escalate. The battered
woman who chooses to remain with her husband must be made
aware of this fact. Ms. Walker stresses that in order to end her
victimization, the battered woman must leave and never return:
"At the present time . . . the most effective alternative for the
battered woman is to end her relationship with the batterer."*

This does not mean that she should be pressured to leave or
that she should be condemned for not doing so. Hilberman and
Munson comment: "The clinician can expect a series of stormy
trial separations and should not view this as treatment failure. The
battered woman is well aware of what she *should* or *ought* to do,
and if she feels that she has disappointed or failed the clinician,
she will be reluctant to return in the future."†

Geller and Walsh add that "Mental-health professionals with
their treatment based on a medical model of pathology further
victimize the abused wife. They do so by identifying her situation
as satisfying 'deep-seated masochistic needs' if she refuses to leave
her husband. Since mental-health practitioners work toward helping people improve their lives, leaving the husband often becomes
a 'condition of treatment.' The choice to stay or leave must be the
victim's. To castigate, chide, or reject her for not leaving is a further victimization. To help her develop tactics that are effective
for dealing with her life affords feelings of power and improved
self-image. If a woman who wants to remain in a status-quo situa-

* Lenore E. Walker, "Treatment Alternatives for Battered Women." In
Jane Roberts Chapman and Margaret Gates, eds., *The Victimization of
Women* (Beverly Hills, CA, Sage Publications, 1978).
† Hilberman and Munson, op. cit.

tion is prodded to leave, she will drop out of treatment and be lost forever to the therapeutic process."‡ Monica Friedman, program coordinator for the Montgomery County (Maryland) Abused Spouses Programs feels that the counselor must be aware that "both sets of options open to her—i.e., staying in the current situation or facing a situation where she will be alone with her children, probably in a strange place, and almost always managing at a very reduced standard of living—are bad."*

While we agree that battered women should not be "prodded," we cannot endorse a therapeutic approach that allows the woman to deceive herself into believing that what she does or doesn't do will influence the degree of her victimization. And while we agree that she needs to be provided with survival skills and information, she should also be made aware of the physical and psychological cost to her of staying.

Bonnie Carlson points out: "Victims who choose to stay in their situation and hope to improve it also need support. But if the assailant's environment, either external or internal, does not change in a meaningful way, the prognosis for improvement of the victim's situation is not favorable."†

One possible approach is employed by Margaret Elbow, who has found it helpful "to point out that she [the victim] has three alternatives: she can leave, she can choose to stay and continue to hope that her husband will change, or she can decide to stay and relinquish the hope that he will change." Abuse victims will initially "choose the second or third alternative, continue counseling to build their self-esteem, and later, sometimes after terminating, make and carry out plans to leave. They report that sorting out the alternatives early in the treatment process provided them with a basis for thinking through their situation and for making plans in their behalf."‡

When working with the woman who chooses to stay in the abu-

‡ Janet A. Geller and James C. Walsh, "A Treatment Model for the Abused Spouse," 1977. Unpublished monograpth.

* Monica Friedman, "Montgomery County Social Services Abused Spouse Program," March 1977. Unpublished paper.

† Bonnie E. Carlson, "Battered Women and Their Assailants," *Social Work*, Nov. 1977.

‡ Margaret Elbow, "Theoretical Considerations of Violent Marriages," *Social Casework*, Nov. 1977.

sive relationship, a number of approaches can be helpful in moving the victim from a passive to an active state, which is the appropriate therapeutic goal. Lenore Walker mentions that it is important to label the woman battered, particularly after an acute battering incident, when the incentive to change is high. This precludes the use of denial, a typical coping mechanism that prevents her from considering action.

Ball and Wyman state that "one of the major goals should be to increase the woman's feeling of being in control of her life. The counselor or therapist must realize that a battered woman will initially demonstrate a lack of motivation and show poor cognitive problem-solving skills. The therapy process must begin with a very directive approach. The counselor or therapist should communicate a feeling of confidence that the client's problems can be positively resolved. This attitude can be helpful in changing client expectations. . . . Despite assertiveness training, individual and group therapy, some battered women will choose to stay in the battering relationship. The counselors should help the client explore the rationale for this decision to determine if the reasons are realistic or mythical. Joining a consciousness-raising group could also provide support for women during and after this difficult decision-making period."*

Betsy Warrior, in her publication "Working on Wife Abuse" points out that in a support group, the history of the relationship can be reviewed to assess the possibility of a real change.†

In general, the counseling approach for battered women (those who stay or those who leave) must be one of improving their coping techniques while helping them to overcome feelings of powerlessness and helplessness. As Ms. Nichols points out, "The most innovative approaches to the problem of wife abuse . . . are being developed outside the province of the traditional family agency and are primarily the work of people interested and involved in the women's movement. In general, women's groups are

* Ball and Wyman, op. cit.
† Betsy Warrior, Lynn Lyell, and Melissa Woods, *Working on Wife Abuse* (Cambridge MA: 1978). A directory of services and publications for and about battered women. Covers all of the United States and some other countries. Information on shelter procedures, hotlines, and support groups. Can be ordered for $3.50 from Betsy Warrior, 46 Pleasant St. Cambridge, MA 02139.

bound by fewer stereotypes than professional counselors, so that they are freer to see and try options that do not maintain the status quo."‡

GROUP COUNSELING

The support group has emerged as a major contribution of the women's movement to the counseling of battered women. The usefulness of support groups' peer counseling approach (women helping women) has been well demonstrated by grass-roots organizations, with two outstanding examples being the consciousness-raising groups and support groups developed for women in marital transition. This development capitalized on what social group workers have always known, that groups provided "a means of individual development through increased socialization and cooperative living," and "that there is a universal need for group associations."* Feminists, aware that "Traditional values and traditional therapy have been more concerned with women's relationships with men than with their relationships with other women . . . , also stress the importance and benefit gained from women working out their problems in close caring relationships with other women."† A group of feminist therapists working together in Philadelphia, called the Feminist Therapy Referrals Committee, strongly endorses the group therapy model as a mutual support system for women. (See the Committee's "Working Definition," in this chapter.)

Peer counseling, support, and/or therapy groups seem especially valuable for battered women because they are even more isolated than other women. They rarely meet other battered women, and if they do, the odds are that they do not talk about their abuse. Shame, guilt, fear of reprisal, and the feeling that they alone have this problem contribute to the isolation. Those women who are not isolated tend to be surrounded by people who not only have no understanding of their plight or goals but who actually interfere with attempts to ameliorate or to get away from abu-

‡ Nichols, op. cit.
* Helen V. Phillips, *Essentials of Social Group Work Skills* (New York: Association Press, 1974).
† Marjorie H. Klein, "Feminist Concepts of Therapy Outcome" (to be published in *Psychotherapy: Theory, Research and Practice*).

sive situations. Our experience indicated that the group was the one stable force in the lives of these battered women that was consistently operating in their behalf. The usual "magic" of the group process—losing the feeling of being alone, giving support, ideas, and encouragement to each other, and receiving understanding from women who have had similar experiences and who really understand—is even more "magical" for the previously isolated battered woman.

The following information is based upon our experience at WRN in conducting emotional-support groups for battered women. As in individual counseling, the organization has a choice regarding the kind of group "leaders" they will use and the kind of therapy introduced, depending on their philosophical base. According to Esther Fibush and Martha Morgan:

> Women have a special stake in therapy because it has been one of the ways by which masculine domination has been reinforced in recent years. A number of women have started to raise some serious questions about psychotherapy, and the subject has been drawn into the battle for women's liberation.
>
> There are many different kinds of therapy, and it would be a tedious, perhaps impossible, task to list them. Each person's therapy is different from every other person's even with the same therapist, for the therapist responds in different ways to different people. There is one kind of therapy, however, that is especially in tune with the needs of women; it was originated by women and has been practiced predominantly by women. This is the therapy developed by the social work profession. It arose from a concern for people and the realities with which they have to contend. Practiced under a variety of names—social casework, . . . psychosocial therapy, and clinical social work—it remains humanitarian in conception and equalitarian in conviction. Its basic principles are those of democracy: the dignity of the human being, the right of self-determination, the acceptance of individual and group differences, the freedom to seek and to speak one's own truth. It is grounded in a profound respect for the wisdom of intuition as well as for the findings of research. It stands midway between science and art and draws on both.‡

‡ Esther Fibush and Martha Morgan, Introduction: "Forgive Me No Longer—The Liberation of Martha," *Family Service Association of America*, 1977.

Whatever the choice, whether to use professionally trained therapists or not, it is imperative that the facilitators operate from a feminist frame of reference, be willing to learn about the special aspects of the problems that battered women face, and have some knowledge of group process and dynamics. As in individual counseling, there are many group "treatment" modes and the choices may depend on the experience, style, and training of the facilitator and, even more important, on the group itself. In essence, the group members should determine what they want from the group experience and define goals for themselves. (Throughout, we use the term facilitator, rather than leader, because the function is an enabling one: to help women find and develop their own strengths and leadership abilities.)

The facilitator needs to be flexible in order to modify, change, or discard group techniques, depending on the composition and needs of the group. In other words, the models and techniques should fit the group members, rather than having the members fit the group model.

In our experience, with several group facilitators and with battered women, some of whom were living in shelters and others at home, we have drawn the following ideas.

In terms of the groups of women living at home, it is helpful to have an initial individual interview with each woman seeking help. The purpose of this interview is to learn about her situation, assets, liabilities, and goals and to provide an opportunity to determine together with her what type of help would be most useful to her at that point in time. It would be preferable for this "intake" interview to be done with the woman who will be the group facilitator, as it both provides for the chance to get some sense of each other and makes entering into the group easier for the participant. The intake interview could be done on the phone, though a face-to-face interview is preferable whenever possible since it provides visual as well as auditory connections and gives the applicant a chance to check out the setting, transportation lines, room, etc. The potential usefulness of a group experience and the woman's suitability and readiness for this experience need to be explored in the intake interview. Because support and/or therapy groups are not a panacea for all at all times, a certain amount of screening is necessary. Certain combinations of factors operating in the woman's life might very well preclude a group experience.

Women who are so depressed that they are having trouble functioning or are so preoccupied with their own problems that they would not be able to interact with peers; alcoholics; drug addicts; and women with psychotic disorders would most likely not benefit from a support group. For these women, other services should be considered and appropriate referrals made. If possible, a follow-up contact should be arranged, as a group might be suitable at a later time.

Having described the group as envisioned, and having ascertained the woman's interest, practical considerations as to whether or not she would be able to get to the meeting place with the regularity necessary to benefit from the experience should be reviewed. If child care is not provided by your organization, the questions to ask are the following: Can she arrange baby sitting? Is transportation possible? Is her situation sufficiently intact to allow her to make the time commitment? If the answers to the above are negative, then a group is not appropriate and another plan is in order. Incidentally, we have found that providing child care during sessions may seem like a valuable service to offer, but unless it can be set up without introducing distractions to the group, it tends to detract from the focus on the woman. For many battered women, coming to group may be their first experience with something that is just for them and where their needs are the primary consideration.

We now need to consider the form of the group we wish to develop. Should it be open-ended, allowing participants to enter and leave the group as their situation and needs change? Should it be limited to a specific number of original participants? How long should the sessions last? How frequently should the group meet? Should there be a specified number of sessions or an indeterminate number with the members setting the time of ending? What is optimal group size? Should there be one or more facilitators? As to content, should the group be structured, semistructured, or determined by what the women bring to each session? How about a combination? What group techniques will be used?

Some of the answers to these questions depend in part on the style and experience of the facilitator, what feels comfortable to her. Optimally, groups for battered women should be kept small, because of their isolation and of the multiplicity of problems, concrete and emotional, that battered women face. A group of five or six women meeting weekly for two to three hours with one facilitator would provide opportunity for maximum participation and in-depth consideration of issues. If two facilitators are to be used, the group population can be larger, but for the above reasons should not exceed eight or nine. The rationale for using two facilitators is that they can provide a model of shared responsibility for the participants, can balance each other by picking up on questions that the other missed, can be supportive of each other, and can offer a wide range of responses. Using two facilitators can also provide training opportunities for inexperienced personnel, by pairing them with the experienced staff.

The advantage of using one facilitator is that it allows more time for group participation and for the engagement of group members with each other instead of with the "leaders." Be it one or two facilitators, the issue of the participants interacting with and using each other is an important factor in group process and individual growth.

"Unique to working with groups is the stimulation and conscious use of group relations in interaction with the leader, toward the goal of the individual and social growth of the members. Attention should be given to each member and the group as a whole while entrusting part of the growth process to the engagement and interaction of the members with each other. . . . The leader should not be like a Maypole to which each ribbon (participant) is firmly and separately attached."*

Regarding open or closed groups, we have found that most people feel more comfortable with a group that does not admit new members once sessions have begun. They feel that it interferes with their own process by having to get to know new people and having to review old material. If the group is adequate in size, we would opt for not admitting new members after the first few sessions. If the group requires enlarging, new members can be ab-

* Helen Phillips, op. cit.

sorbed constructively by including the group in the decision and dealing with their questions, problems, and reservations. The same would apply to the person joining the group.

One common problem in forming an ongoing group is attrition. For a variety of reasons (reality problems, lack of motivation, personality clashes, class and race issues), some women seemingly eager to participate in a group do not continue beyond the first or second session. In general, a useful technique is to start each group with a testing-out period of three sessions to give the members a chance to learn not only what the group experience is like but whether or not they see it as beneficial to them. By the end of the third session each member should be in a position to make a more realistic decision about whether to continue as a participant. The reasons, questions, and problems involved in making the commitment should be explored. The group can then decide on a given number of sessions, at the end of which the members again recontract regarding the continuation, nature, goals, and timing of the group. Recontracting can also be used at any point in the group process if, in the opinion of the facilitator or a group member, the group is losing its effectiveness and value to its members.

If a group member does not attend the three trial sessions and has not shared with the facilitator the reasons for her break with the group, the facilitator should attempt to contact the woman to learn why she discontinued, and help her rejoin or seek other resources, whichever is appropriate. The issues regarding a woman's continuing should also be discussed with the remaining group members so that their feelings, questions, concerns, and sense of loss can be vented. This is important, for it is not uncommon for some group members to feel that they may have caused the discontinuation.

Group Composition

Theoretically, it would be good to have a group consist of members from various classes, races, and sexual orientations. Practically speaking, because we are geared to providing help when it is needed, we cannot wait for the right percentage breakdown and must work with whatever composition presents itself (exclusive of those identified earlier as not being adequately served by a group experience). The issues involved in working with women from a class, race, or sexual orientation different from the helper are addressed later in this chapter and apply to women in the groups as well. The facilitator, in addition to examining her own racial, class, and sexual orientation as they may create therapeutic blind spots, must be sensitive to biases conveyed implicitly or explicitly between group members. Sexism, racism, classism, and negative reactions to gay people run deep in our culture; and as it is not uncommon for these biases to find their way into participant interactions, they must be handled openly and thoughtfully. Dealing candidly with a conveyed prejudice may seem very difficult and potentially embarrassing, but our experience has been that most women who involve themselves in a group want to change and grow and thus may welcome becoming sensitized to the biases and prejudices that can interfere with their growth and development.

If battered women are to free themselves from abusive situations, to find internal strength, and gain control over their lives, they need to come to grips with their own prejudices toward others and with their own sexism. This is tantamount to recognizing the prejudices you have against yourself and the habit you have of seeing yourself as inferior and beholden to others.

Mindy, a young woman with whom we worked, came to understand that she was not responsible for her husband's addiction to heroin, nor was she responsible for his cure despite his insistence that he "could not detox without her . . . that it was her responsibility because she was his wife." She also became aware that her husband resented her going to the library or reading and prevented her doing these things whenever possible. However, after a period of separation, she was considering returning because he promised her: "I will let you go to the library. . . . I will let you continue with your women's group. . . . I will let you. . . ." It took five minutes of group interaction for Mindy to hear what she was saying, that nothing in the relationship had really changed— that her husband was still controlling and determining what Mindy could and could not do and, in essence, conveying his ownership of her. It is hard to shake sustained and protracted indoctrination. Another woman was pleased that her husband, who was living in her dream house, the house she had to leave to avoid abuse, had arranged for them to meet with his lawyer to arrange for the disposition of the house. That she needed to look out for herself and have her own lawyer to represent her was discussed and accepted as a valuable suggestion. She needed to shake the old notion that her husband would take care of her. As she put it, "My world was this man, there was no other side to me."

Though support groups for battered women are not consciousness-raising groups per se, there is need to sensitize the participants to the sexist issues that play a critical part in their lives and grip them in abusive situations. This can be done by addressing the issues around problems that the women bring into discussion as in the above examples and by making occasional didactic presentations from a feminist point of view growing out of common issues identified by the group. In other words, conditioned responses and prejudices, whatever the "ism," play a large part in the problems these women face, and the facilitator has the responsibility to hear and to respond constructively to the attitudes that interfere with a member's growth and coping capacity.

Group Modalities

The use of the group experience as a medium for helping people work through problems and/or in serving as personal growth experiences is currently enjoying wide popularity, and the literature is rife with methods and ideologies: sensitivity training, encounter or T groups, transactional analysis, assertiveness training, etc. Facilitators, therefore, have many options available to them, and what they choose will depend on their experience, training, ideology, and what each group teaches them. Since all methods work for some and no one method works for all, we again emphasize the need for a peer approach that is responsive to the needs of the group. We also again emphasize that whatever therapeutic model is used (humanistic, functional, behaviorist, gestalt, etc.,) the facilitator must operate from a feminist or a nonsexist point of view. This should include an understanding that human conflicts and problems do not develop in a vacuum but are related to the social, cultural, and economic systems under which we live.

We have already learned that battered women are not sick women needing a cure for their "masochistic tendencies." They are, basically, well women who have problems in living that, to a high degree, are created and maintained by a sexist society. In the group process it is important to pitch to the inherent strengths in these women, that they may realize their potential as strong, independent, capable individuals who can survive, cope, grow, and succeed in their self-determined goals. Because many battered women face problems rooted in economic dependence on their men and in their responsibilities as mothers, it is important for the facilitator to be knowledgeable about the health, welfare, and legal resources available in the community. If not personally knowledgeable, the facilitator should familiarize herself with where the information can be found in order to make appropriate referrals.

Getting adequate legal help, finding a job, applying for welfare, arranging child care, continuing one's education, securing job training, or finding an apartment (particularly if there are young children involved) are among the myriad of problems with which battered women need help. This help takes two major forms: One is practical or informational, regarding available resources— where they are, how to get them, and how to consider options. The other form of help is an enabling one. It involves getting help with whatever confusion or difficulties interfere with goal achievement: lack of assertion, fear of authority figures, fear of failure, and ambivalence, for example. Group members can help each other by sharing experiences and giving leads and suggestions that serve to avoid common pitfalls, as well as by offering encouragement. If several women have the same problem, an expert in the given area should be invited to a group session to share her know-how with the members.

Actually working on and through these kinds of problems constitutes the heart of therapeutic intervention. Dealing with how to cope with problems will yield much information about the psychic economy of the person involved—the strengths that can be enhanced and the weaknesses that need modification. Many of the common difficulties women have, such as low self-esteem, lack of assertiveness, putting others' needs before their own, and poor problem-solving techniques, will emerge in the discussion of life's problems and can be dealt with in context, rather than in a vacuum. For example, if a woman is having trouble securing financial assistance because the welfare worker is tying her up in red tape, she needs first of all to know her rights and that one of the most effective ways of cutting red tape is to suggest to the worker that she discuss the matter with her supervisor. If the worker finds this suggestion unacceptable, the woman should contact the supervisor herself, and the supervisor's supervisor, right up to the department head if necessary. If the group member likes the idea but can't execute it because she has difficulty standing up for herself, the facilitator has a perfect entry to discuss the issues in assertive behavior and to institute some assertiveness-training exercise. Self-awareness, personal-growth, and emotional-support groups seem to work better with a population not having to deal with the harsh reality problems with which most battered women have to deal. However, using these approaches in relative isolation from real-life problems may account for some of the failures organizations report in their attempts to provide group services. In other words, getting emotional support is great, but this needs to be accompanied by concrete help geared to problem solving and increased independent functioning. Getting help with finding a job that enables one to leave an abusive situation can be very growth-producing and is inherently emotionally supportive.

If your organization cannot provide small-group service with the combined concrete and emotional assistance just described, it is also useful to develop emotional support or rap groups for larger numbers of women, as long as there is a structured tie-in with a resource giving practical or concrete help. For example, the Marital Abuse Project in Delaware County, Pennsylvania, successfully conducts large support groups with their hotline providing the practical and emergency-service backup.

Should your group have members who are not plagued with such problems as the lack of job skills or economic dependence but are staying in abusive homes out of fear, psychological dependence, a sense of failure, and other more "internalized" problems, they will usually require more intense therapy over a longer period of time. It is possible to provide this within a group if the group is small enough and the facilitator feels comfortable with intensive long-term counseling. If this is not the case, then the group experience should be augmented with individual counseling or therapy. Actually, we have found that the combination of group and individual counseling has been very effective with many of the women with whom we have worked. The main concern with this kind of concurrent help is that there be communality of goal and philosophical stance to ensure that the therapies are complementary and not conflicting. Collaboration between the individual counselor and the group facilitator, in which the "client" is included, can be of value in coordinating effort and in speeding up movement and change.†

Group Methods and Structure

Again the key word is flexibility. The usual model of groups meeting once a week for an hour and a half with a planned agenda does not work well for women who are living in abusive situations or have been out on their own for a short period of time. These women are in crisis and are facing new difficult matters daily requiring timely intervention. Attempting to hold to a fixed, restricted time schedule is highly unrealistic, as important problems can't wait until next week with women who might not be able to leave their homes next week. We originally started one group on the hour-and-a-half schedule and found ourselves deeply involved four hours later. About three to three and a half hours became the pattern for that group, which had five members and one facilitator. This gave each member a chance to work through, as much as possible, her concerns at the time. It also allowed for some socializing, which filled a critical need for these women, who were otherwise very much alone.

In addition to time flexibility, the facilitator indicated her availability by phone during the week for emergency purposes. We found that this was not misused and it provided added support. In general, knowing that something is available if needed provides assurance and adds to people's ability to cope. The members themselves exchanged addresses and phone numbers, thereby

† See, in this chapter, *Why She Stays* for amplification of the issues involved for these women.

developing a support system of their own. This over-all communication network provided a major breakthrough from previous isolation.

We are emphasizing the time-and-energy investment required in order to be realistic about the demands of running a group so that provision can be made to allocate sufficient time to fulfill the commitment. In this connection, having two facilitators instead of one has the advantage of sharing the demands and of ensuring that one person is accessible when the other is not.

As to the actual structuring of the sessions themselves, many possibilities are open to us. One format we have found useful is that of having one member at a time interact with the facilitator about an area of concern, much as though she were in individual counseling. The other group members are focused on this interaction and are encouraged to raise questions and share insights and ideas out of their own experience, knowledge, and sensitivity. This could be considered cofacilitating, as it were, requiring a kind of disciplined attention to the needs of another. For the contributors it is an experience in leadership and increased self-esteem, particularly when one is rewarded with "That is a great idea" or "You hit the nail on the head." If this scheme is used, it is important to determine at the beginning of each session what each member's concerns are, so that priorities about who goes first and approximately how much time each person will have as the focus of the group can be established by consensus. With this method, each member is assured that she will have her turn, which, among other things, is of immeasurable help in concentrating on the problems of another. Setting priorities and a disciplined use of time are also good lessons in problem solving within the natural context of the group.

The format can be enhanced by interweaving exercises and brief didactic presentations about the general issues involved in problems that the members share. This essentially nonstructured model requires the utmost in flexibility on the part of the facilitator, a playing it by ear and drawing on one's repertoire of skills, knowledge, and techniques as they seem appropriate and geared to what is going on in the group at the time.

Semistructured sessions have also proved effective. Therein, the facilitator determines with the members pertinent topics to be reviewed during upcoming sessions. This gives the members a chance to think about the subjects. It also gives the facilitator the opportunity to prepare in advance the exercises to be used and to consider the important points to be addressed. Of course, ample time should be allowed for group discussion of problems and concerns.

The group itself will bring forth topics of specific and current interest and should be encouraged to do so. Also there are many issues of general and critical concern to women, that should be addressed in group sessions. Among these issues are assertiveness, anger, self-esteem, self-validation, self-image, life planning and options, alternative life-styles, sex roles, autonomy and interdependence, self-definition, and problem solving. When considering such issues, it is important to deal with them in the context of societal indoctrination. For example:

> Self-esteem is a core criterion for health; improved self-esteem is almost a universal condition for a favorable outcome. Unfortunately, most concepts and measures of self-esteem are biased against women . . . traditional ideals for women . . . contain fewer desirable traits than those for men . . . and are heavily influenced by sexist stereotypes as a matter of course, and often find them, rather than the self-image, to be the focus for major therapeutic change. A successful feminist outcome, in short, would be more likely to involve redefinition of the ideal. . . .
>
> Apart from the content of self-esteem, the source of self-esteem is also an important issue. Women traditionally have been taught and expected to anchor their self-definition and esteem externally. . . . The pitfalls of this "other-directedness" are obvious. . . . Measures developed to overcome this problem must appraise the source of the respondent's self-esteem . . . a shift [is needed] from external to internal anchorage—e.g., the difference between woman's self-concept, woman's own ideal, and woman's concept of man's ideal. . . .‡

Group discussion of these ideas plus such exercises as go-rounds on "things I like about myself" and fantasy trips on "what

‡ Marjorie H. Klein, "Feminist Concepts of Therapy Outcome" (unpublished paper to be published in *Psychotherapy: Theory, Research and Practice*).

I would be and what I would like to be if I had my wishes" are useful devices in identifying and modifying attitudes and behavior. Incidentally, the facilitator should include herself in whatever exercises are used, as it adds to the perspective, helps to demystify the power relationship inherent in any therapeutic situation, and lends credence to the fact that as women we have common problems and struggles. Also according to Klein:

> Choice and decision making are important steps to personal growth. . . . Women traditionally have been viewed as deficient in decision making: unable to make up their minds, changing their minds often, not knowing what they want, seeking others' advice and guidance. One of the most important gains that a woman may make in treatment is learning to trust her own decision-making and problem-solving skills and to give up accepting others' decisions.
>
> . . . the most prevalent model for problem solving and decision making in our society is a rational, logical one [that is] stereotypically masculine [and] highly valued. [However,] when we speak of growth, self-actualization, personal integration, etc., intuitive, aesthetic (feminine) processes come into play.*

Again, didactic amplification and group discussion of the concepts involved can be used in conjunction with exercises. One effective exercise in developing problem-solving skills is the force-field analysis, which, in essence, calls for a member's using paper and pencil to identify a goal and list the assets and liabilities involved in reaching the goal. Capitalizing on the positives and conquering the negatives are then discussed, and a plan of action is further broken down into short-term and long-term goals and approximate timing. The other group members, of course, can contribute ideas. Putting something down on paper is frequently a clarifying experience. We have also found that many women tend to maximize the obstacles (probably rooted in the self-esteem issue) and minimize the positives if they see them at all. Here the facilitator and other members can be helpful in reversing this by pointing out assets that they know exist in the participant and/or in her experience.

Other popular and effective exercises are role playing, dyads,

* Ibid.

relaxation techniques, anger ventilation, and psychodrama. The possibilities are limitless, and for those readers who are particularly interested, there are many books detailing exercises and techniques available in most libraries. Talking with women who have had experience in this area and taking advantage of training workshops given by feminist organizations can also be enriching.

As is true with models and methods, any given exercise is not effective or meaningful to all, therefore variety should be sought, and the groups' response should help you with the choice. Also, exercises should be tied in meaningfully with the issues and problems the members face and not be offered in a vacuum.

The group models and methodologies covered in this section can be used independently or in a variety of combinations. They are not the final word, as each group experience adds knowledge and a new dimension. The best teachers are the group members themselves; we should listen and incorporate their ideas into our work. The best device available to ensure this input is to build in feedback and evaluation as an integral part of the group process.

Groups Within Shelters

Working with a group of women living in a shelter is different in a number of ways from working with a group of women living in their homes. The differences call for a different model or models from those already presented, while the techniques, composition, exercises, etc., remain fairly applicable. The differences are primarily qualitative. Starting with the obvious, the women in a shelter are a captive audience, as it were. The variable of choice in deciding to join a group and the dynamics and desire for change implicit in the motivation shown by the "home" women are missing. Women usually get to shelters out of a desperate need for safety, and rightly that is where their attention is focused, not on getting help to change an intolerable situation and starting a new life. Once the healing takes place and they feel safe, then the factor of having to come to grips with planning their future emerges. If a group is part of the shelter's service, a decision must be made as to whether group participation is mandatory or optional. If there is free choice and a resident joins the group, it may indicate motivation to get added help in dealing with problems, or it may mean conforming to what she thinks the staff expects of her. So, why she joined the group needs to be understood and handled. If there is no choice and group attendance is required, then the rationale for this requirement must be offered by the staff. The facilitator must also deal with this issue and its aftermath: the anger and reluctance to participate, which can be conveyed implicitly or explicitly. If the facilitator genuinely understands these feelings to be valid responses, the group-member residents will in turn probably accept her saying that although they had no choice about joining, they do have a choice about whether the group has any pertinence or value for them. As with the "home" group, the shelter group defines the goals and provides feedback regarding the effectiveness of the group.

The structure for the group could be a weekly meeting at a specified place for a specified period of time. If so, it is important to include the residents in these decisions to insure their availability. It is also very important to arrange for child care during the sessions, making the sessions a time just for the women, enabling them to think about their own needs and goals and to learn ways of fulfilling both.

Another option is the more informal, Pizzey model wherein a staff person is available for designated periods of time to talk with residents. Residents come and go depending on their need in this "open house" arrangement.†

A third option is to use part of house-meeting time to work on group issues.

Whatever option or combination of options is used, we will have, in essence, an open-ended group, with constant population change as women enter and leave the shelter, in contrast to the kind of closed group possible for the "home women." In view of this, an unstructured or a semistructured group (as already described) seems to be a more appropriate model.

In contrast to the home group, the shelter group appears to have a larger number of women who have sunk low in the victimization process. Many have never earned a living and have be-

† E. Pizzey, *Scream Quietly or the Neighbours Will Hear* (London: Penguin Books, 1974).

come economically dependent on their men. In addition, the women may have few or no survival skills, having received no training from their parents before moving in with men who handle and control all the money, including their welfare checks. We were startled to learn, when working with our first shelter group, that some of the women could not cook. It is, therefore, critical that shelter groups concentrate on teaching survival techniques as a priority. House meetings can be useful in this area. An even better approach would be to incorporate the teaching around the residents' participation in running the shelter. Cooking, shopping, handling money, etc., are part of the fabric of living in a shelter, and these skills can be taught experientially very much in the manner of those of us who were privileged to learn them from our families. The same vehicle for teaching applies to using banks, to learning about public transportation, etc. Such teaching can be augmented during group meetings by handling the embarrassment of not having skills as well as confronting the fear of trying new things.

It should go without saying that the shelter group needs more intensive help in all the areas described above than their home-group counterpart, in which the women are much higher on the victimization scale and tend to have more resources at their disposal.

If possible, it is important to provide a sustained follow-up group for women who have left the shelter. This services allows for a continuation of the shelter's support system in order to provide help for further development and growth inherent in what is now a home group.

Both home and shelter groups could make use of the guidelines for support groups included in Betsy Warrior's manual.

GUIDELINES ON
SUPPORT GROUPS FOR BATTERED WOMEN

For battered women only. No observers.
This is a *support* group. People should not criticize or be disapproving of how a woman has handled her situation, but offer support and suggestions for alternatives that will be more constructive and helpful in the long run.

Keep the atmosphere as informal and spontaneous as possible.

Give everyone a chance to speak if they want to without going around the room in a formal way. Be aware of who hasn't spoken yet, so that when they do start to speak they'll get a chance to discuss their situation or finish what they want to say.

Allow women in immediate crisis situations the most chance to talk—if they want to.

Define the problem. Don't get bogged down in individual details too long without relating it back to other woman in a social context —how all women are socialized and battered (or discriminated against in different ways), how we can deal with this more effectively or change the situation. Each woman must know that she individually is not to blame for her battering, but instead understand the circumstances that are making it hard for her to struggle against it.

Keep to the subject of what we are at the support group for.

Don't single out shy women to speak. Wait until they are ready and then encourage them and try to make them feel comfortable. If they look like they'd like to say something, ask them how their week was, instead of saying something like, "Do you want to talk now?" or "Tell us something about yourself." This way they can offer as little or as much information as they want without feeling pressured. Sometimes a shy woman will speak up at first only when everyone else is talking at once, because then all the attention isn't focused on her. At this time try to allow her some space to be heard and finish what she's saying. Otherwise:

Try to keep everyone from speaking at once and separate conversations from going on at the same time so everyone will have a chance to know what's going on.

Try to keep people from interrupting or monopolizing all the time. Keep the group small so people can get to know and trust each other and have plenty of time to talk (about six people).

Support-group participants must remember that what is discussed within the group is confidential. When relationships between participants in the group develop outside the group, these confidences should never be abused.

If a woman in the group shows a lot of hostility, aggression, or manipulativeness towards the other women, or is disruptive, consistently unsupportive, or doesn't seem to understand what the group is for, she should be asked to leave.

The support group isn't equipped to handle women with heavy alcohol, drug, or emotional problems. They should be referred to other sources for help.

Support-group facilitators should be contacted through the shelter hotline or the Women's Center and should not give out their phone numbers.

The group can't lend money or provide transportation.‡

Lenore Walker reminds us that there is often a risk factor for women who facilitate support groups for battered women. Some abusers have unleashed their rage on the facilitator. One group in Seattle was held at knife point for several hours before being released. Another group had a car driven through its front door. Take precautions.

The prevalence of emotional-support groups for battered women reflects the development of an alternative to the traditional therapeutic approach which has come to be known as "feminist therapy." In general, this approach is by far the most appropriate when working with battered women (or all women, for that matter).

Patricia Ball and Elizabeth Wyman provide the following description of the feminist approach:

"Feminist therapy is a therapeutic approach for the resolution of individual psychological problems which encourages the development of healthy, fully functioning individuals who are not limited, confined, or defined, by sex-role stereotypes. Mander and Rush . . . refer to feminist therapy as "the missing link therapy" because it is a synthesis of modified traditional therapies and of the creative developments of the women's movement. Feminist therapy is not a new technique but rather a new orientation and philosophy that determines the nature of the therapeutic relationship.

In feminist therapy the client is viewed as being the expert on her experiences, feelings, and needs. Lerman . . . states that the assumption of client competence goes hand in hand with the assumption of personal power. She defines the role of the therapist as one that helps the client validate her own self and experiences. Feminist therapy also holds the assumption that "the personal is political." Women have been taught to internalize anger and aggression and they must learn to differentiate between those difficulties for which the individual may be responsible and those problems which are due to sex-role stereotyping. For example, it is not uncommon for the

‡ Betsy Warrior, Lynn Lyell, and Melissa Woods. op. cit.

battered wife to feel "guilty" for being abused or to blame herself for causing the beating. Feminist therapy would help the client examine her situation from both a personal and environmental perspective, and enable her to redirect her anger away from self and into constructive channels of her choice. This ability to separate the internal and external gives the woman a greater sense of personal power. It also helps her learn that she is not "crazy." The feelings of self-doubt and low self-esteem characteristic of most women have their roots in the ambivalence generated by the socialization process. Living in a battering relationship can only serve to magnify these feelings of powerlessness and worthlessness.

One goal of feminist therapy is teaching women to become self-nurturing and self-loving. Critical to the battered women's survival is her initiation of self-nurturing acts including: talking to a neighbor, seeking professional help and eventually canceling the "hitting license" of her spouse. Rawlings and Carter . . . say that any relationship where the power is unequal is pathological. A relationship in which one spouse feels that physical violence against the other spouse is an acceptable way to communicate one's feelings is pathological. Feminist therapy does not support the notion that the nuclear family unit must be maintained at all costs. However, in counseling battered women, the therapist must take precautions against encouraging women to leave their spouses before they are self-sufficient."*

From the Feminist Therapy Referrals Committee, in Philadelphia, comes a working definition of feminist therapy:

1. The basis for feminist therapy is a recognition of the harmful effects of the sexist society in which we live. Real oppression of women based on gender as well as class or race is the basis for the conflicts, low self-esteem, and powerlessness reported by many women who seek psychotherapy.

2. Feminist therapy explores with clients the inner contradictions in the prescribed social roles for women. It rejects the medical model of psychiatry which locates the source of human conflicts within individuals, that is, in a vacuum, with no relation to the social and economic system under which we live. Instead, it emphasizes a sociocultural and systems approach to psychological growth and change.

* Ball and Wyman, op. cit.

3. Feminist therapists support women in an exploration of their inner resources and recognize their capacity for nurturance and self-healing. They encourage the process of individual goal setting and support those client goals that transcend traditional sex-role stereotyping. They encourage the exploration of various lifestyles and sexual orientations and support the acquisition of skills for self-directed and interdependent living.

4. Feminist therapy distinguishes itself from traditional therapies by the nonsexist frame of reference. Feminist therapists utilize appropriate existing therapeutic modalities as well as develop new techniques compatible with the underlying philosophy of feminist therapy.

5. Feminist therapists work on demystifying the power relationship inherent in any therapeutic situation. This process requires that a feminist therapist work toward being open about her own values and attitudes.

6. Feminist therapy affirms that matching women clients with women therapists is often most therapeutic for women. Feminist therapists use both individual and group approaches to therapy. They affirm, in particular, the value of an all-women's group therapy model. The group model enables women to: a) validate each other's strengths, b) develop mutual support systems, c) break down their isolation, and d) help each other perceive a variety of possibilities for growth.

7. Feminist therapy requires that a therapist: a) conduct an ongoing evaluation of her practice; b) make provision in her practice for low-income clients; c) examine her lifestyle and values as they relate to her therapeutic approach; d) identify with the goals and philosophy of feminism; and e) examine her race, class, and sexual orientation as they may lead to therapeutic blind spots with clients, especially those of a different race, class, or sexual orientation.

8. Feminist therapists acknowledge that psychotherapy per se is not a cure-all, and they encourage women to consider other avenues for growth and support instead of or in addition to a therapeutic experience.†

While short-term counseling goals for the battered woman may focus on reducing or stopping the violence, the long-term goal

† Feminist Therapy Referrals Committee: Muriel Fondi, Jean Hay, Marylou Butler Kincaid, and Kate O'Connell, *Feminist Therapy: A Working Definition* Philadelphia, PA, Feb. 1977.

must be one of empowerment. The real and perceived powerlessness of the battered woman is what stands between her and
self-determination. Providing her with the support that she needs
to retake control of her life is the primary function of the counselor or therapist.

Whether or not male therapists can adequately fulfill this function is questionable. Of course, any therapist, male or female, who
uses the traditional approach may do more harm than good. But it
is our feeling that the male therapist, no matter how sensitive or
sympathetic, will most likely be perceived as an authority figure
by the majority of battered women. Trained to look to men for
guidance, approval, and their own sense of self-worth, most battered women will find it impossible not to transfer their dependency needs to a male therapist. While this happens with female
therapists too, it is not as likely to occur, and it is easier to handle.

In order for male therapists to be of service to abused women,
it will be necessary for them to come to grips with the power positions that they occupy. This can be difficult, because nobody
wants to admit that he or she is in an oppressive or privileged position. But this is a necesssary step for male therapists who must
deal with battered women outside of the traditional dynamics of
the male-therapist/female-client relationship.

Accomplishing this involves a personal struggle. It means
dealing with the threat that feminism poses on a personal level.
Wrestling with personal power and privilege is difficult, because
feelings such as defensiveness and guilt will surface. It is important that the therapist avoid shifting his struggle onto the client.

Male therapists should make every effort to augment their therapy with a support group for battered women or a consciousness-
raising group. If there is no organization in the area that works
specifically on the battered-woman issue, the local chapter of
NOW or the local women's center, if there is one, should be helpful. Female therapists who are familiar with the feminist therapy
model should be consulted regularly.

Safety is another issue that should not be overlooked during the
counseling process. Ms. Elbow discusses the need to underscore
the gravity of marital violence. "It is not uncommon to find that

professionals such as social workers, attorneys, clergymen, and doctors do not acknowledge the threat of homicide as a real possibility. Not only is the safety of the victim of concern, but that of agency staff, the victim's family, friends and co-workers as well. All too often, the victim herself is not aware of the danger to her life. Recently I had a difficult time convincing a woman threatened with death to take precautions, and in another situation, which led to the death of a woman, discovered that the victim had not discussed the violence and the threats on her life with those who might have been able to protect her."‡

For the safety of the counselor, Ms. Resnick recommends that she should not visit the client at her home, nor should she meet with the assailant unless, of course, couple therapy is the agreed-upon counseling modality.

Yet, setting time and energy boundaries is important not only to prevent overwork and possible "burn-out" for the counselor, but also to ensure that the woman does not become overly dependent on the counselor or therapist.

Earlier in the chapter, we discussed the wide range of emotions experienced by battered women. From suggestions developed primarily by Resnick in *Counselor Training Manual #2* and Ball and Wyman in "Battered Wives and Powerlessness," we offer what may be some useful recommendations when encountering some difficulties:

Anger

The victim should be encouraged to express anger and direct this energy into constructive action on her behalf. She may need support to avoid feeling overwhelmed by her anger.

Guilt

As previously discussed, battered women often feel guilty because they have internalized society's tendency to blame them for their own victimization. It is important for the counselor to explore prevailing biases and misconceptions about battered women with the client and to let her know that she doesn't think

‡ Margaret Elbow, "Theortical Considerations of Violent Marriages," *Social Casework*, Nov., 1977.

that they are true. Providing the woman with feminist reading material related to domestic violence may be helpful.

Emotional Dependency

The battered woman must be encouraged and helped to make important decisions and may need active positive reinforcement. This cannot be stressed too strongly. Learning to make decisions is an important first step for the battered woman to regain control of her existence.

Fear

Practical suggestions may be helpful, such as changing locks on doors and windows, etc. Helping the client to realistically assess the amount of danger she is in and developing workable contingency plans such as the survival techniques discussed in Chapter I are important.

Embarrassment

Abused women who feel shame or embarrassment will probably welcome the opportunity to vent their feelings in a supportive atmosphere. The victim should be reminded that there is no reason to be ashamed of mistakes (such as returning to an abusive spouse) as long as she learns from them.

Fear of Insanity

It is important that the counselor be comfortable with and accepting of all expressions of emotion. As in all counseling, it is important never to discount the client's feelings.

COUNSELING SKILLS AND TECHNIQUES

Hilberman and Munson believe that the focus of psychotherapeutic work should be "the woman's markedly impaired self-esteem, emotional isolation, and mistrust."

With the more direct focus on the affective impact of the violence, the woman may share information, for the first time, about other aggressive acts against her, so that the clinician must be prepared to deal with an earlier rape, incestuous relaionship, or abuse as a child. One may also hear about aggression directed toward her children and her confusion about mothering. Basic work on the differences between limit-setting, discipline, and battering is necessary, and this may include the involvement of child protective services and/or direct work with the children.

Understandably, this has been a crisis point for some women, who may require hospitalization or intensive outpatient work to support their controls. This is also a time when one sees dissolution of the passivity in favor of a more active position, with embryonic plans for work, job training, school, and termination of the marital relationship. Because of the real possibilities of escalating violence as a result of changes in her behavior, it is stressed that the woman should not be pushed to move beyond what she feels are safe boundaries in terms of her acknowledgment of anger or actions to confront her husband. The clinician must assume that her assessment of her own controls, the extent of the danger to herself and children, and her husband's potential for violence are accurate.*

Lenore Walker points out that "It becomes important to find ways of motivating battered women to attempt new behaviors so that they can experience success. Each new success helps to return some individual power to them. Self-esteem rises as these women take back control of their lives. Most helpers agree that once battered women leave the relationship and learn new skills to reverse helplessness . . . they do not choose to relate to another batterer as the popular myth has it.†

Psychotherapy modalities that strengthen the battered woman's successful coping strategies while helping her overcome her powerlessness have proved effective. Supportive psychotherapy during the separation and divorce period has proved successful . . . Although the kind of psychotherapy modalities vary in technique and scope, the goals remain constant. Current behavior is the focus, although exploring the past is sometimes helpful in interpreting present problems. It is important to clarify the ambivalent feelings of the bat-

---

* Hilberman and Munson, op. cit.
† Lenore Walker, "Battered Women and Learned Helplessness." Appearing in *Victimology: An Internatinal Journal,* Vol. 2, 1977–78, Feb. 1978.

tered woman . . . A combination of behavioral, insight-oriented, feminist therapy has proved the most effective therapeutic approach.‡

Ms. Elbow also mentions ambivalence: "The abused wife is frequently protective of the abuser, a characteristic also found in abused children. Consequently, it is important that the helping person not berate the abuser either directly or by innuendo, but instead identify the victim's ambivalence: 'It must be difficult for you to know how you feel about him; at times you describe him as thoughtless and cruel, and at other times, you describe him as comforting and sensitive to your needs.' If the victim senses that the counselor sees her husband as one without any positive qualities, she may become defensive of him. Furthermore, if there has been a history of her leaving and returning, it is helpful to point out the pattern and acknowledge the difficulty of giving up her hope for change. Without the recognition of her ambivalence, she feels alienated, not only from her husband, friends and family, but also from her counselor."*

Ball and Wyman refer to several basic areas in which women can begin to assert ownership and control over their lives. "Success in these basic areas can develop the confidence necessary to begin tackling major issues such as financial independence and severing relationships."

These basic areas include money, space, time and talent. Does the wife know how money is budgeted in the family—for housing, transportation, insurance, repairs, utilities, entertainment, clothing, food, and medical bills? Can she arrange to have money of her own that she does not have to account for—money that she alone controls?

Is there a space in the house that is hers alone? In this space she can do what she wants, she can arrange it in a way most pleasing to her. It may be a place to work or relax. Somehow it should reflect some aspect of her identity.

‡ Lenore Walker, "Treatment Alternatives for Battered Women." In Jane Roberts Chapman and Margaret Gates, eds. *The Victimization of Women,* Vol. 3, (Beverly Hills, CA: Sage Publications, 1978).
* Margaret Elbow, "Theoretical Considerations of Violent Marriages," *Social Casework,* Nov. 1977.

Can she set aside some time during the day when she can do anything she wants? Preferably it should be a time to do something for herself. She can learn that she is capable of giving pleasure and meeting her own needs.

What talents does she have that she would like to develop? There should be some regularly scheduled activity that is engaged in for her own self-improvement. It is not necessary that the talent be career or job oriented. The important point is that the woman learn she is still able to learn, grow, and develop as an individual.

These are some suggested activities that could be encouraged in a directive manner. Ideally the client would be part of a small group, of six to eight women, who have experienced battering. The above-mentioned activities could be given as homework assignments during one of the initial group meetings.†

In addition, assertiveness training is a counseling modality recommended for abused women:

Assertiveness training is one of the therapeutic techniques for counseling battered women. Baracek . . . describes assertiveness training as one of the few therapeutic techniques designed to teach the client how to exercise more power. Women in general benefit from assertiveness training because the socialization process encourages women to be passive and self-denying. Ball . . . found that increased assertiveness increases self-concept in women. Mueller and Leidig . . . describe increased verbal assertiveness as a strategy for dealing with physical expressions of anger. Assertiveness training is a combination of cognitive restructuring and behavioral techniques such as modeling, behavior rehearsal, role playing, coaching, homework, and feedback. These techniques are designed to teach the individual to express her/his thoughts without attacking the other person or denying her/his own feelings. Alberti and Emmons . . . provide the following definition:

Assertive behavior is behavior which enables a person to act in her own best interest, to stand up for herself without undue anxiety, to express her honest feelings comfortably, or to exercise her own rights without denying the rights of others.

In assertiveness training for battered women, the counselor would want the client to clarify her rights and develop a personal belief system. These rights may include:

† Ball and Wyman, op. cit.

she has the right not to be abused.

she has a right to anger over past beatings.

she has a right to choose to change the situation.

she has a right to freedom from fear of abuse.

she has a right to request and expect assistance from police or social agencies.

she has a right to share her feelings and not be isolated from others.

she has a right to want a better role model of communication for her children.

she has a right to be treated like an adult.

she has a right to leave the battering environment.

she has a right to privacy.

she has a right to express her own thoughts and feelings.

she has a right to develop her individual talents and abilities.

she has a right to legally prosecute the abusing spouse.

she has a right not to be perfect.

In a group setting, the counselor could ask group members to generate "rights" from their individual perspectives. In addition to this type of cognitive restructuring, assertiveness training with battered women would also include teaching the nonverbal and verbal components of assertiveness through role playing and behavior reversal. Each participant would construct a hierarchy of assertive situations from least difficult to most difficult scenes. By increasing her verbal assertiveness, the wife is communicating a new message to her spouse. The new message is that she will no longer tolerate physical displays of aggression and violence. Straus (1977) states that our societal values must change so that the marriage license no longer becomes a hitting license. This assertive message may increase the hostility of the battering spouse. The counselor should explore the realistic consequences of increased assertiveness with the client before she begins a new style of communication.‡

Ms. Walker discusses interdependence as a possible counseling goal when working with battered women:

In designing treatment alternatives for battered women, stopping the battering is the immediate concern, but the long-term expected outcome is economic and psychological interdependence. To be interdependent means to be capable of either independent or dependent behavior within a relationship as appropriate. Each person in the

‡ Ibid.

relationship can provide strength (independence) which the other can lean upon (dependence); while, at the same time, the person who is independent can depend upon the other for certain needs.*

Individual Counseling

Although we feel that the support-group model is the most effective for promoting the emotional independence of the battered woman, we recognize that many battered women will seek a one-to-one counseling modality. We stress the importance of the feminist approach described earlier in the chapter. Ms. Walker offers the following observations regarding individual counseling:

> The battered woman who comes to the therapist . . . is usually trying to cope with her feelings of guilt, anxiety, and anger. The therapist can help her express her guilt by having her recount the details of battering incidents in which she could not stop her own battering . . . Control of anxiety may be accomplished through relaxation training, hypnosis, or recommending that the battered woman join a health club to focus on positive body feelings. It also is important to help the battered woman recognize and control her anger. She should be encouraged to anger each time it occurs, rather than suppressing it and releasing it all at once, perhaps triggering an acute battering incident.
>
> The realities of present alternatives and future goal planning are explored in individual therapy. The battered woman needs to recognize concrete steps she can take to improve her situation. . . . The therapy is more action-oriented than analytic, as unstructured psychoanalysis is too risky.†

Whenever possible, individual therapy should be augmented with a support-group experience.

In working with battered women, crisis intervention may at times be helpful and productive. Ms. Walker notes:

> Crisis intervention techniques are often very appropriate for intensive therapy after an acute battering incident. Battered women or the batterer individually are concerned enough about their lack of control to want to understand and change their behavior. Crisis ther-

---

* Lenore Walker, "Treatment Alternatives for Battered Women." In Jane Roberts Chapman and Margaret Gates, eds. *The Victimization of Women,* Vol. 3, (Beverly Hills, CA: Sage Publications, 1978).
† Ibid.

apy usually focuses on a specific critical incident. The goal is to teach the client how to resolve possible future crisis by applying conflict resolution techniques to the present one while motivation is very high.‡

Ball and Wyman make a similar point:

The counselor or psychotherapist working with a battered wife may employ a combination of strategies. First, consideration must be given to the crisis aspect of her immediate situation. If she has contacted a competent counselor or therapist, she has taken the initial step necessary to break out of her isolation.

She will need continued support to combat the secrecy and isolation which have become part of her life. She may need to be reminded that neither her husband's reputation nor hers is worth her physical and psychological pain. The second crisis consideration entails anticipating the worst and preparing for it. A place of refuge must be found. A list of possibilities should be available for the client if she has no local resources. It is helpful to find a refuge which will also accept children.*

When a battered woman is part of a minority group, her problems are more complex and difficult. The added burdens of racism and perhaps poverty make the process of achieving an independent existence doubly difficult (in Chapter VIII, we discuss the special problems and concerns of minority women who are battered). In what follows, we address some of the cultural and social factors that influence minority women. Counselors who come from racial and/or cultural backgrounds that differ from those of the women with whom they are working must have a heightened awareness of and sensitivity to these factors.

Carol Angell, of the Battered Women's Project, in San Diego, California, has provided us with some valuable insight regarding several different groups of minority women:

NATIVE AMERICAN WOMEN— Native American women living on a federal reservation have problems all their own. Historically, battering, like alcohol, was not part of the Native American culture.

‡ Ibid.
* Ball and Wyman, op. cit.

Both were imported and had a profound impact on life on the reservation.

In addition, the influence of Catholicism should not be overlooked. A great many Native Americans, particularly in the Southwest, were converted by the early missionaries. The church reinforces subservient female roles within the family and teaches that men are the authority figures in the community and church. In the church's eyes, marriage is a sacred, life-long commitment.

In contrast, the women's movement has begun to have an impact on some reservations. Women are being offered courses to develop their skills and have started to leave the reservation during the day for jobs in the wider community. They have begun to be more economically independent. This, coupled with the high male unemployment, produces strains in families where the man is traditionally the breadwinner. The Native American woman is exposed to conflicting values on and off the reservation.

MILITARY WOMEN— The military establishment is built on the premise that it is appropriate to use force as a means of control and to get what you want. Military training reinforces the male socialization that says that feelings are not acceptable and aggression is. Servicemen are given little or no opportunity to vent their frustration within the authoritarian superstructure. The high level of stress related to work is often compounded by tensions within the family. The young man who joins the service finds that suddenly he has a high degree of responsibility that his age does not equip him to deal with. The military family is relocated frequently, making it difficult for family members to develop close friendships or community support systems. Thus, the wife tends to be extremely isolated and lonely. There tend to be long separations when the man is at sea or on assignment. New pressures surface when he comes home. In his absence, the woman has often found new independence and the ability to make decisions and care for herself. He tends to reenter the home and want to take over and be the authority figure.

CHICANAS— A great many Mexican women living in the U.S., both citizens and non-citizens, are isolated from the dominant culture by language, customs and socialization. They are kept ignorant of their legal or economic rights and have difficulty finding adequate bilingual and/or bicultural social services.

Many Chicanas have learned to play passive roles in relationship to men. Their socialization and the Catholic Church have encouraged them to expect future rewards "in heaven" but little in their day-to-day lives. Men are expected to play a "super macho" authority role and put their needs and the needs of the children before the needs of the women. The church stresses the marriage vows and encourages women to endure bad family situations by condemning divorce and separations. The ban on birth control leads to large families, more work for the women, and more children to help the women to feel trapped. Societal oppression and racial discrimination have accentuated the economic and emotional stresses that may lead to alcohol abuse and/or battering in the Chicano family.

ASIAN WOMEN— When working with Asian women, it is vital that non-Asian counselors not lump them into a cultural stereotype. There are a wide variety of Asian cultural groups in the U.S.A. For example, in San Diego there are eleven distinct Asian groups. Their cultures differ as do their languages. Some groups have had substantial historical conflicts between them that have not dissolved upon entry into the U.S.

With that in mind, many Asian families do share certain problems and characteristics that should be handled with sensitivity by counselors. The women's needs are subjugated to the needs of the family and particularly the husband. She is expected to be humble and meek, while the man is expected to be the authority figure. There is strict morality within the family, and divorce and separation are considered to be shameful. Resisting the power of the man may be seen as rebelling against the entire community—therefore, it may be hard for her to get the support she needs.†

Mary Peterson, of the Solano Shelter for Battered Women, in Fairfield, California, points out that American servicemen often marry Asian women for their submissiveness and dependency. When she arrives in this country, however, the Asian woman becomes more assertive after exposure to American ideas of female independence. Her husband may react with violence. He attempts to keep her isolated from the larger community to maintain her dependency on him and to prevent her from finding any support for becoming more assertive.

Ms. Nichols makes the following comments regarding minority women:

Marital abuse crosses all economic and social lines, but certain minorities, whether ethnic or religious, present special problems.

Experts in the menace of racism advise us that respect and sup-

† Carol Angell, "Battered Women: Special Problems and Needs" Battered Women's Project, San Diego, CA, 1978 (unpublished).

port for the cultural differences of a given client population are necessary responsibilities of caseworkers. Again, these are patriarchal
societies, so that the problems that beset a family suffering from cultural shock are defined in terms of how the men have fared. The
male's role as head of the family and his prestige as protector and
wage earner, are considered crucial to the family's well-being, while
at the same time they are related to its misery. Wife abuse is an act
of male violence. It is especially difficult for a social worker to find a
point of intervention that does not, in some way, threaten or violate
the cultural norm.

In groups with strong ethnic ties and as established cultural identity, what matters is the fact that this identity is separate from the
mainstream of a community's thrust. The incidence of wife abuse, in
these groups, is also high and may be treated as a "fact of life."

Social work has often been criticized for maintaining the status
quo in relation to issues of power and economic structure. Similarly,
professionals may be criticized for maintaining, by adherence to tradition, power systems that favor one group of human beings
(males) over another (females), especially when physical abuse has
occurred.

It would be helpful if professional social workers from minority
groups would write more specifically about how to deal with the serious problems that ethnicity creates for minority women. Most social workers are aware of the effects of urbanization on the man
who moves his family into a predominantly white, middle-class community. But the stress on women, though less recognized, is equally
great. Because women in subordinate or complementary roles are
often the recipients of male frustration and anger, interventions that
help them gain a sense of self-worth, even independent of their
families, are valid.

In short, one may know and understand a culture and still see
how parts of it restrict or inhibit individuals. . . . there is a rich potential for contribution to a helping relationship in full understanding of different cultural orientation.‡

Although it is clear that wife abuse cuts across all lines of class
and race, we have found that there are significant differences between the experiences of battered women from low-income communities and abused women from middle-class suburban areas.

‡ Beverly B. Nichols, "The Abused Wife Problem," *Social Casework,* Jan.
1976.

One difference is the tendency for low-income women to fight back on a physical level. Many low-income women have had to know how to fight to survive, and it is not uncommon or unusual for them to defend themselves vigorously, often to the point of causing physical injury to the batterer.

The availability and utilization of resources is another area of difference. Although middle-class women have more resources, they tend to use them less. They are controlled by shame and embarrassment. They are more likely to protect their husbands, due to their anxiety about harming his career, which represents their means of support and survival. Middle-class women are less likely to be believed when and if they attempt to let others know what is going on or to seek help. This is especially true if the husband is well known in the community, which is often the case. People find it difficult to believe that the charming, ingratiating person with whom they are familiar is actually a brute behind closed doors. If the middle-income woman has a history of emotional breakdown or psychiatric hospitalization, she is even less likely to be believed and could be labeled a "hysterical female."

As mentioned in Chapter I, middle-income women face particular difficulty in utilizing social services. This is due to the fact that many programs will base eligibility for service on the husband's income, even though the woman herself may be penniless.

Often, middle-income women are more frightened of the prospect of leaving the husband, particularly if they have never lived independently. Usually, they have no knowledge of the family finances and no access to any property, stocks, bonds, etc.

If the husband is a professional with influence in the community, the wife may find herself unable to obtain a good lawyer, a decent job, or sympathetic medical care. The woman who fears that her husband will be able to wreak havoc upon any attempts toward independence on her part is not paranoid. Her fears are justified.

The low-income woman may be more accustomed to struggling for survival. Although she has fewer resources, she will use them more. She is more likely to have some knowledge of the welfare system or other social services. Due to fostered independence, she is more likely to take concrete action in her own behalf. Although the low-income woman may act more aggressively in removing herself as a victim, she faces massive resistance from those agencies and institutions that are supposedly designed to meet her needs. Hostile and racist attitudes on the part of welfare workers and other bureaucrats often make it difficult for her to collect what is due her.

The low-income woman has more difficulty than others in relying on family members for assistance, since however sympathetic and supportive they may be, they are less likely to have the financial resources to help her.

The counselor or therapist who works with battered women faces a wide array of problems and stumbling blocks. Although rewarding, such work is difficult and emotionally draining. In "Sixty Battered Women," Hilberman and Munson state that working with abused women is "slow, frustrating, and intensely anxiety-provoking, with the knowledge that the client's self-assertion could prove fatal . . . the client's progress may seem small or inconsequential, for example, a wife asserts her right to attend church. For the middle-aged woman who has been battered and isolated for twenty years, however, this may be a monumental step forward.*

Some additional thoughts are offered by Ball and Wyman:

The need to protect their men and themselves may be partially responsible for the tendency of battered women to retreat from the assistance of helpers even when they themselves have initiated requests for such help. Helpers report becoming exasperated and angry with battered women. The helpers try to bring whatever legal and social assistance is possible under a limited system. This often occurs at considerable effort to the helper. Just when some assistance is found (restraining order, a police call, hospitalization, foster home, psychological help, etc.), the battered woman often turns it down. Understandably, helpers become exasperated when she returns to the dangerous relationship, denying that any harm can come to her. She assures herself and others that she can handle her man and returns to him, leaving others speechless at her behavior. They question her intelligence and sanity. It is probable that battered women do not accept the helper's assistance because they do

---

* Hilberman and Munson, op. cit.

not believe it will be effective . . . They see the batterer as all-powerful. Thus, there is no safety for them.†

One common problem that counselors face is the tendency of battered women to perceive them as "rescuers." Occasionally, counselors see themselves in the same way. Margaret Elbow writes:

A final appeal is made to avoid trying to rescue the victim of marital violence. All too often those who are concerned about the well-being of a battered woman prematurely plan for her escape from a destructive situation, which only leads to additional frustration and perhaps, on the husband's part, a feeling of resentment toward a woman already alienated and alone, as well as a possibility of homicide. Professionals respect the right of self-determination for other adult clients; they need to examine why they cannot give the battered woman the same measure of respect.‡

Ball and Wyman address the same issue:

The counselor or therapist must not allow the client to simply shift her dependence from her husband onto them. Wyckoff . . . refers to this process as playing "rescue." The "rescue" game consists of attempting to save someone who views herself as helpless and powerless. "To rescue someone is oppressive and presumptuous, since it colludes with a person's apathy and sense of impotence. Rather than demanding that a person take power and ask for what she wants, it reinforces her passivity." . . . There is a fine line, in counseling battered wives, between the need to be initially directive and the danger of playing "rescue."*

Ms. Cooper, in *Counselor Training Manual #2,* provided the following helpful information to counselors:

"Problem solving is sometimes described as a highly complex and structured set of activities. It need not be complicated or difficult. What it is is an objective and orderly way of looking at the problem,

† Ball and Wyman, op. cit.
‡ Margaret Elbow, op. cit.
* Ball and Wyman, op. cit.

the resources potentially available to resolve the problem, and the selection of a way to use those resources to resolve the problem. In providing services to assaulted women, good common sense can go a long way toward problem solving. Establishing realistic goals for yourself and your client, making use of and expanding the limited resources available directly from the project and making referrals where appropriate will provide your client with some of the help she needs. . . .

As a volunteer-peer or professional counselor, it is important to set realistic expectations for yourself. A common hazard of crisis intervention work is a tendency for counselors to expect too much of themselves. Client problems can be overwhelming to the client, but they should NEVER be overwhelming to the counselor. The client's problems may be of many years' standing, involving many other persons. They may be part of a life situation which is inadequate to meet basic physical and emotional needs. Faced with a crisis, the client frequently communicates a sense of panic, fear, and urgency. Clients may tell themselves that they must immediately solve all their problems, bringing an end to problems that have gone on too long. They often tell themselves and the counselor that they need an immediate and effective solution to their problems, and it is needed now. This is unrealistic, but clients are often so frightened and overwhelmed that they are willing to give up responsibility for themselves and their problems.

The message from a client is often, "Rescue me, take care of me." These clients, however, need more than temporary rescue. What they do need is a supportive listener who believes in the client's own ability to cope with the problem. A listener should convey the belief that the client has inner strength to draw on. A listener/counselor can communicate firmly and supportively that the client's problems *can* be solved, that the client *can* get help in solving those problems, but that a final solution may not be reached immediately. The counselor should offer alternative solutions, and access to resources; however, it is always the client's responsibility to make decisions concerning her life.

It is sometimes difficult for counselors to maintain their belief in a client's strengths and ability to cope with the problem. As helping persons concerned with the well-being of their clients, counselors may accept responsibility for their clients. Counselors may expect immediate improvements in their clients' behavior. Often a counselor becomes disappointed after investing time, energy, and faith in a client, only to realize that the client has slipped back into old patterns and behaviors. It is important to realize that no one is capable of performing miracles with another person's life. If a counselor expects the client to respond immediately with initiative and motivation to the counselor's assessment of her situation, and to the counselor's proposed solutions, she may soon become discouraged.

If and when a client refuses to cooperate with a counselor's suggested solutions, the counselor may naturally get angry at either herself or the client. It is important for a counselor to acknowledge and express that anger to a supervisor or fellow counselor. This anger should not be internalized, nor should it be overtly directed at the client (although a counselor may directly express her disappointment and feelings of frustration to the client). . . . A client in a crisis stating extreme intolerance for her situation and making desperate resolutions about change should not be expected to follow through on any or all statements. Alternatively, a client who appears unable to make any plans, or is paralyzed by fear or ambivalence, should not be expected to respond immediately to a counselor's efforts to help her, to organize information and select alternatives.

On-call counselors are expected only to assess immediate needs, and to help the client list available alternatives and solutions. This includes helping the client recognize her inherent abilities and strengths. The client may or may not be willing to recognize these or accept the help her counselor has to offer, but *the choice is up to the client.* Counselors must protect themselves and their clients by clarifying expectations of the counselor and the limitations of the Project. Remember, even an assault victim is responsible for herself —all the counselor can do is to help her define the problem, and explore ways of responding to the problem.†

On the subject of care for the counselor, the following is important:

Crisis work is difficult to do. It requires a cool head. It usually requires a counselor to expend a lot of emotional energy in a short space of time. A little attention to yourself can go a long way to assure you have the resources you need to make working with your clients rewarding. . . .

To prepare yourself for crisis intervention with assaulted women,

† Cooper, op. cit.

take a few minutes to recall situations from your own life in which you felt either in a crisis or dead-end, trapped situation. Did it take you some time to decide the situation was intolerable and to resolve to take action? Did you slip back several times into known unsatisfactory solutions, even after resolving to make positive changes? If you are female, have you ever been frightened at the prospect of terminating emotional and/or financial dependence on men in your life? What happened to your self-esteem?

If you have had these experiences, recall your attempts at problem-solving. Perhaps you will remember temporary paralysis, or high states of anxiety. Were there other obstacles to problem solving which you experienced? Think about how you handle crisis now—perhaps you turn to trusted friends, withdraw for a while, or resort temporarily to some less-than-mature behaviors. A friend who accepts your anxiety, and your need to talk, and who does not respond to your panic, but maintains a firm belief in you and your ability to cope is a valuable ally.

In your work with wife-assault victims, learn to expect and accept fear concerning major changes in clients' lives. Expect grief reactions if the client has chosen to leave her husband or boyfriend and begin a new life. These moves represent significant losses, and frightening independence. And learn to expect a victim's fear of being judged by you. If clients are judging themselves harshly, they will assume the same reactions from you.‡

Counselors who work with battered women would do well to perceive each other as sources of support and encouragement. In a program geared specifically to spouse abuse, regular staff meetings should be scheduled for skill sharing, information exchange, and feedback.

Counseling battered women is a relatively new field and those working on the problem are pioneering in the development of effective counseling approaches and techniques. It is important that these be shared as much as possible.

For those practitioners in traditional agencies, it is a good idea to establish contact with whatever battered-women's groups are in the area to reduce any feelings of isolation and for increased confidence and competence in working with battered women.

‡ Ibid.

The Women's Resource Network is currently designing and conducting training workshops to provide mental-health practitioners and medical and social-service-agency personnel with the skills, techniques, awareness, and resources necessary for effective counseling of battered women and the proper handling of intrafamily violence cases. Via the media of role playing, film, sample cases, discussion, didactic lectures, and experiential exercises, the following areas are developed:

> Understanding the problem
> Psychology of the victim
> Profile of the abuser
> Counselor roles
> Counselor bias

Counseling skills and techniques include initial interviewing, crisis intervention, long-term therapy, and survival-skills training:

> Couple counseling
> Group counseling for battered women
> Group counseling for abusive men
> Options for battered women
> Community resources and information

Our format emphasizes experiential skill learning with some didactic process. Evaluative procedures include verbal and written feedback from participants.

A sample workshop would be as follows:

A. Agenda review
B. Didactic overview of the problem
C. Involving the participants in role playing which portrays typical problems presented by battered women and typical counselor management of the problems. Correct and incorrect interventions are enacted, followed by a critique by the participants, into which the facilitators weave the psychology of the victim, why she stays, conselor bias, and effective therapeutic management.
D. Go-rounds on participants' feelings about working on cases involving domestic violence; their feelings about violence in

general and their basic feelings about victims and abusers in particular.

E. Discussion of actual cases counselors are currently carrying, geared to assisting with the dynamics involved and effective case management. Included are the unique aspects of couple counseling.

F. Showing the documentary film *Battered Women: Violence Behind Closed Doors,* which features interviews with both male perpetrators and female victims, examines the cultural aspects of the problem, and considers alternatives for the victims. This is followed by a guided group discussion of the issues involved.

G. Presentation re: setting up and conducting a therapeutic support group for battered women, followed by a question-and-answer period.

H. Presentation re: developing and managing group counseling for abusers, followed by a question-and-answer period.

I. Review of available options for victims and abusers and the distribution of printed materials listing community resources, information, and bibliography for continued in-depth study of the problem.

J. Verbal and written feedback and evaluation of the workshop.

Resource development is another critical counselor function: Hilberman and Munson discuss its importance:

The clinician also has an important role in supporting those actions which enhance the woman's sense of control over what happens to herself, her body, her children, and her destiny. There must be reinforcement of the idea that she is a person who is important, deserving, and capable of making decisions. In order to make choices, she needs to know what her options are. Thus, there is a need for concrete information and assistance from a variety of resources and community agencies with whom both the clinician and the woman may have contact.

They list the following resources that may have to be mobilized:
1) Women's groups for information, support and shelter
2) medical institutions

3) social service agencies
4) legal aid
5) vocational rehabilitation agencies.

As pointed out in the article, the counselor should be aware of the fact that the information she gives to a judge, social worker or lawyer may influence the degree of help, assistance and advocacy she obtains when utilizing community resources.*

Ball and Wyman suggest that another of these survival strategies consists of enrolling in a self-defense class or a martial-arts training program. It can be a critical factor in combating the victim's feelings of docility and resignation. Lessons in self-defense build strength as well as the self-confidence and self-respect necessary to stand up for one's rights. . . .

"However, educating battered wives in self-defense is made more difficult because their learned helplessness inhibits assertive behavior."†

From Ms. Resnick's *Counselor Training Manual #1,* we share the following specific skills and techniques:

Listening and Summarizing

The most fundamental aspect of good counseling is the ability to listen. Good listening demands intense concentration. Effective listening demands also not only that the interviewer hear and understand what is being said but that she/he also hear and understand what is being communicated through silence. Frequently the impact behind what was not said suggests clues about sources of difficulty. Again, a client should never feel pressured into discussing anything she doesn't want to talk about. The counselor should be aware of topics that are emotionally stressful for the client. After trust and rapport have had time to build up, the counselor may want to gently pursue these areas. Body language (the way a client sits, whether she looks the counselor straight in the eyes, whether she rocks, wrings her hands, etc.) should be carefully observed, as it offers important data to the counselor. Discrepancies between verbal and nonverbal communication should be noted by the counselor and if the atmosphere is appropriate, the discrepancies should be pointed out to the client.

* Hilberman and Munson, op. cit.
† Ball and Wyman, op. cit.

For example, a woman discussing how terribly angry she is at her husband, but is smiling as she speaks. This could be purely a nervous reaction or it could be an indication that she has difficulty in expressing her anger or dissatisfaction. This is all too common a problem and we must remember that if anger is not focused at its source, it is often turned inward, which leads to feelings of depression and guilt.

It is important to remember that there is a great difference between listening and hearing. It is often a very helpful technique to summarize the salient aspects of what you have understood from a client's verbal and nonverbal communication. Such a summary should never be put forth as a statement of fact. In other words, it is not appropriate to say, "I can see that you are very angry," but rather to say something like, "It sounds to me like you are feeling very angry." We must never assume that we understood or that a message came through clearly without first verifying it.

Summarizing can be very important for three reasons:

1) It gives the client a chance to point out things that she feels were misunderstood or that she needs to clarify.

2) It gives the client assurance that the counselor is really listening and trying to understand her.

3) By the summary, the client may well be helped to better clarify and conceptualize what she had previously thought a complex maze of data.

Ascertain whether the client has listened attentively and understood what you have said by asking her to summarize your communication to her.

Sorting Aspects

A victim may feel so enmeshed in her problems that there seems to be no logical way to begin fighting her way out. It is important to help the client dissect her problematic life—to segmentalize different aspects of the problem—to label each aspect of her problematic situation. A problem usually will not appear as overwhelming and unwieldy if its components can be identified and labeled.

Especially if the client is planning to make dramatic changes in her life, such as leaving a man whom she has been with for a long time, there are many decisions to be made and changes to plan. Labeling and dissecting each category of change can often help to reduce anxiety. A client in this type of situation may need help in prioritizing. Her options should be fully explored and discussed.

Labeling a Client's Feelings

The range of feelings that a victim often experiences has been previously mentioned. As an outsider, the counselor will be able to hear her feelings more clearly than she can recognize them and help her label her emotions. Very often, simply getting her feelings named will help her greatly. It will bring some order to the chaos she is experiencing. A client may be feeling a good deal of ambivalence. She may feel that she both loves and hates her assailant. In such a situation it can be useful to ask a client to enumerate or list the positive aspects of her husband, or boyfriend, and the negative ones. Writing the positive and negative traits of the man on different sides of the same piece of paper can be helpful in gaining a better grasp of her feelings.

Ventilation

With good listening and labeling skills, the counselor can provide the client with a supportive atmosphere in which to ventilate her problems, anxieties, fears, etc. She may need the counselor to function primarily in this role for the first few sessions. After a reasonable period of time, the client must be offered direction and encouragement to take positive steps to solve her problems. Ventilation is important but is usually not enough. It won't do the client any good to center her happiness around her counseling session, if no other steps are being taken to make her life a better one. Warmth, kindness and sympathy are important, but unless the client is also encouraged to take charge of her life and improve her situation, we are handing out bandages when we are prepared to assist with surgery.

Appraisal of Strengths and Weaknesses

Many of the clients we see feel weak, defeated and helpless. It is important to help them get in touch with and believe in their strengths and assets. It is often therapeutic to ask a client to list her assets and strong points as a person. This may sound like an easy question to answer: experience will show it to be quite the contrary. Most of us would probably have difficulty ourselves, answering such a question. The client will probably need a lot of encouragement and patience to get started. It is quite possible that she will be unable to say even one positive thing about herself. In such a case, it would be a good idea for the counselor to give an honest and realistic appraisal of what some of her strengths and assets appear to be. If she sees that the counselor believes in her, it may well be a first step to her believing in herself. The very fact that she came for help shows that she has not given up, and has the strength, the will and resolve to work for own happiness.

The counselor should also emphasize the client's external strengths, such as family and friends.

Realistic Goals and Sub-goals, Defining These Behaviorally

At all points in the counseling experience both the client and the counselor should be clear on the goals toward which the client is working. Since domestic violence is a multidimensional problem, she may be working with several, long-range goals. The client sets her own goals with the counselor's assistance, in objectifying and offering support and assistance in meeting them.

Objectifying a goal means putting it in behaviorally specific terms. For example, a nonbehaviorally specific goal would be "I want to start a new life." A behaviorally specific goal would necessitate defining "new life," such as "I want to get public assistance until I find a job," "I want to move to Ohio to live with my sister," etc.

Especially with behavioral goals, it is tremendously important to help the client set up short-term sub-goals so as to prevent a sense of discouragement. Behavioral and life-style changes take a long time and the process can prove frustrating if one keeps measuring their progress in relation to the meeting of such a long-range goal. The setting up of realistic short-range goals gives more direction and allows for more immediate gratification. For example, if the client sets up the goal of obtaining a job, some sub-goals may be

1) Investigating day care facilities.

2) Choosing and enrolling her children in such a facility so that she can begin job hunting.

3) Going to Employment Security Commission and employment agencies, etc.

Even if the long-range goal is, by its nature, behaviorally objective, such as obtaining a divorce, sub-goals, such as obtaining an attorney, filing, etc., must be stressed so that the client can see and internalize progress on a more immediate basis.

Plan of Action

Once goals and sub-goals have been set up by the client, plans of action to achieve these goals must be decided upon. Again, all options should be presented to the client. Caution: our values should never color the emphasis we place on the presentation of an option. Some of us may be pro- or anti-religion, abortion, welfare, etc. We must be in touch with these feelings, but we must always remember that they are our personal beliefs and not universal truths.

Once plans of action are decided upon, the client may be particularly apprehensive about certain contacts or conversations that she will be having in the future. Role playing can be a very helpful technique to allow the client an opportunity for behavioral reversal. Also, if it seems appropriate, the counselor can play the client's part, perhaps giving some suggestions, by modeling, as to how to get the information that she wants across.

Counselor's Roles

Practical Helper and Educator: Many victims may be uninformed as to where and how to go about seeking the kind of help they need. Counselors can provide them with the information they need to take action on their own behalf, especially in the legal, medical and social service areas, and can help them to arrange the necessary appointments with appropriate personnel. In some cases, there may be several options in agencies or persons that provide the same or similar services. Those who are being counseled should be informed as to all of their options.

Advocate: The victim may well be uncomfortable with medical, legal and social service agencies and authorities. Often in proceedings (particularly legal) she will become lost in the action and her needs may well not be fully met. As her advocate, the counselor should keep in contact with medical, legal and social service authorities in order to keep her informed about what is happening, and in order to insure that the appropriate personnel are taking as much action as possible in her case. Advocacy should be done tactfully but with resolve and persistence if necessary. Counselors will not just be functioning as a personal or peer advocate, but also as a representative and advocate from their parent organization.

Remember that, as an advocate, it is very often advantageous to ask to speak with supervisory personnel if the client is not getting the needed services and satisfaction. Again, this should always be done with tact and diplomacy.

Counselor-Supporter: The role here is to provide the victim with emotional support, to encourage her to talk about her experiences, and to help her to identify and understand her feelings. The presence of a concerned person will help her to realize the importance of her feelings. Support can be a tremendous help to her at all times.

Initial Interview/Intake

Victim Anxiety: In the first contact with a new client, it is important to remember that there is most often a great deal of anxiety involved in initial help-seeking efforts. The following are some of the possible reasons for this anxiety. The client may mention her concerns. If she does not, the counselor might explore these following sources of anxiety with her, because she might feel reticent about initiating such a discussion.

Worries About How to Communicate with Counselor:

The victim may see her life as so chaotic that, in anticipating her meeting with the counselor, she may worry about where to begin talking, what to say and how to say it.

The client should be assured that there is no rush for her to tell all that is on her mind. She should, further, be reassured that she need not feel compelled to tell anything that she doesn't feel comfortable confiding.

Fears That Counselor Will Be Judgmental: Especially if the beatings have been going on for an appreciable period of time, the client may be worried that her counselor will be critical or judgmental in attitude.

The client must be assured that the counselor will not be critical or judgmental and understand that motivations for any action or lack of action are complex. It is very important when counseling to be aware of personal feelings about the client. In order to be an effective counselor, feelings must not be allowed to color his/her work. Not all of the victims encountered will be likable, nor may the counselor agree with their way of thinking. A counselor must face these negative feelings about the victim or her case honestly. If they are ignored and counseling continues as if they didn't exist, these feelings will most likely be poorly hidden and the negative attitudes will leak out in nonverbal communications with the victim.

Some of us may have more difficulty than others in accepting the fact that some clients that we see may not want to leave the man who physically abuses them, let alone press criminal charges against him. This is the client's decision to make. She should be advised of her options, made aware of the support that she can expect from you, from your organization, from legal authorities, etc., and she should be encouraged to follow through on legal proceedings if she is so inclined. She might not want to do so at present but may change her mind in the future. If she does decide to stay with a physically abusive man, the counselor can help her clarify why she has made the decision.

Embarrassment in Labeling Self as a "Battered Wife": Because of society's attitude towards the victims of wife assault (They must like it—they are getting what they deserve—if they were better wives, their husbands wouldn't have to beat them, etc.), the client may feel embarrassed to identify herself as a "battered woman." It is important to assure the client that she need not feel embarrassed at being a victim, that it is not a reflection on her character or her worth as a human being.

Confidentiality: The victim may be concerned about her assailant finding out about her visit to you and, thus, be worried about physical retaliation.

The client should be assured that everything that she says and the very fact that she is seeking help are to be held strictly confidential. She is to be assured that the counselor will release no information to anyone without her consent. Further, if her assailant should find out or if she is worried about physical abuse for any reason, if she has no place to go for refuge, she should be assured that temporary safe housing is available to her, if such need is the case.

Commitment: The victim may be worried about what kind of commitment to action she is making by seeing the counselor. She may be worried that, against her inclination she will be pressured into filing for divorce or pressing criminal charges.

The client must be assured that her needs will be met as *SHE* defines them, that the counselor has no intention of pressuring her to do anything. Encouragement to follow through on her intentions, yes—pressure, never!

Some or all of the above mentioned fears may be so overwhelming that the client may not show up for a scheduled appointment. Having a client not show up for an appointment is always a frustrating experience for a counselor. A telephone call in which the counselor helps to identify and alleviate the concerns that kept her from coming can often open or reopen the channels of communication. Above all else, it is important to stress that anxiety when seeking help is normal, and that as rapport builds, her anxiety level concerning your meetings should decrease. Also, there may well be reasons other than those mentioned that caused her to miss her appointment. Some real detective work may have to be done to ferret them out and it is quite possible that the client herself cannot label the concerns that prevented her from coming to the appointment. Caution: The obvious should not be overlooked, such as: Was transportation or child care a problem? Did the husband or boyfriend prevent the client from coming?‡

Telephone Counseling

Telephone counseling is crisis counseling, done on the telephone. Therefore, we recommend that you read carefully the crisis-counseling guide developed by Barbara Cooper, of the NOW Domestic Violence and Spouse Assault Fund, Inc. The key elements to remember when doing telephone counseling are

1. to stay calm;
2. to take down vital, identifying information;
3. to assess the immediate situation of the caller;
4. to help the *victim* choose what her course of action should be;
5. to have at hand appropriate resource directories that can help you arm the caller with necessary numbers and information.

‡ Resnick, op. cit.

The Legal System

Chapter III

THE LEGAL SYSTEM

".. . and the next thing you know the female who's been beaten up starts on you, right, leave him alone, why are you picking on him, we didn't call for you, the neighbors called, right, so after a while you just have no feelings. You go in, you do your job. That's it."

"Why do you think she does that?"

"Because it's her man. I had an old-timer tell me this. I had a call and this guy was beating his wife up. My partner took me outside and said, 'Look, son. I'm going to tell you something. I've been married probably longer than how old you are.' He said, 'My wife feels as though I don't love her any more, so at least once a month, I start an argument, I slap her around a little bit, and we have a perfect marriage. I've been married thirty-five years.' "*

"So we get him to court. Now, what do we do with the courts? The general procedure has been to negotiate a settlement between the two parties and the usual outcome of that is a signed agreement whereby the husband promises to leave her alone. Well, of course, it can be easily documented that those agreements are generally violated left and right so, what are some alternatives at the court level? is one of the questions."†

* Interview with a policeman.
† Interview with Philadelphia judge.

"It is my view that police and later prosecutors and courts contribute to domestic violence by their laissez-faire attitudes toward what they view as essentially a personal problem. . . . This view is held because they are socialized to regard females in general as subordinate."‡

Unfortunately, the battered woman frequently gets little real help from the legal system. Often when she calls the police, she is met with disregard and lack of concern for her safety. Dispatchers who learn that the victim is married to her assailant may advise her to go to court in the morning and file for a civil order restraining her husband from beating her in the future. They may then classify the call in such a way that no police will come to her aid.

Police who arrive at the scene of a beating may not notice the woman's medical needs unless serious injuries are apparent. They may attempt some on-the-spot "mediation," with the object of encouraging the parties to settle their differences without disturbing the neighborhood. They may again advise the woman to seek a civil restraining order; they probably will not arrest unless there are serious visible injuries or the use of a weapon is involved. They may also tell the victim she can file a "private" criminal complaint, without explaining the relationship between these alternatives.

If the battered woman goes to court seeking either a civil order or a criminal charge, she must expect to spend a large part of several days during the next weeks and months waiting in rooms crowded with other battered women equally desperate and confused. In either civil or criminal court, the battered woman will feel substantial pressure from everybody from intake interviewers to judges to settle the "domestic" problem by means of a voluntary (and therefore unenforceable) agreement.

If the violence in the home is renewed, the same procedures will produce even greater frustration. There will probably be no report

‡ James Bannon, Executive Deputy Chief of Police, Detroit Police Department, "Law Enforcement Problems with Intra-Family Violence," presented to the American Bar Association Convention, August 12, 1974, unpublished.

of the earlier incident and no record of its result. If the woman has succeeded in getting a civil restraining order, police may refuse to "interfere" the second time because it has become a "civil" matter. In many cases, the cycle of violence and frustration continues for several years, or finally ends when one spouse kills the other.

Until now, the legal system has offered little help to battered women—not because there were no laws or procedures that applied but because of the many profound ways that sexism was institutionalized in the legal system. Common sense can find no reason to refuse to apply the law of assault and battery, for example, to cases in which a husband beats a wife with his fists, brass knuckles, or a belt. The same degree of force used upon a stranger would result in an arrest. The fact that some (few) states have recently enacted laws specifically prohibiting wife beating (California's "felony Wife Beating" statute—Cal. Penal Code Section 273d, for example) demonstrates that the law has treated and regarded this form of violent behavior as quite different from the less common violence between strangers.

The legal system has for centuries paid respect to an ancient legal doctrine giving husbands a "right of chastisement." Along with the wife's duty to obey her husband went his right to punish her disobedience or other improper behavior. Under the doctrine of "coverture" (according to which marriage makes of two persons one—that one being the husband), married women lost all separate legal identity. It was, therefore, legally impossible for them to sue their husbands or testify against them. It also meant that the husband became legally responsible for all of his wife's acts, just as for his cow's. Therefore, as William Blackstone (whose writing provided a major source of common law for American judges and lawyers throughout the nineteenth century) "reasoned":

> For as he is to answer for her misbehavior, the law thought it reasonable to intrust him with this power of restraining her, by domestic chastisement. . . .*

* Blackstone, *Commentaries*, 445.

Until very recently, little had changed since William Heale admitted, in 1609, that "In the strictness of the law, for a husband to beat a wife is lawful. . . ." In 1824 the Supreme Court of Mississippi upheld the right of a man to "chastise" his wife, specifically declaring that he should be free to do so "without subjecting himself to vexatious prosecutions for assault and battery."†

Laws have changed in the past 150 years, perhaps more than attitudes. Although there are now a sometimes bewildering number of legal avenues open to a woman who has been beaten, few of them work to make her life more secure or painless. One of the primary reasons for this is that the (mostly) men who are charged with enforcing and applying the law still agree with the North Carolina judge who, in 1864, felt it was better not to "go behind the curtain" of the marriage, "leaving the parties to themselves, as the best mode of inducing them to make the matter up and live together as man and wife should."‡

Very recently, the courage of battered women who speak out against the pain and humiliation inflicted upon them by men has begun to make a difference. Wife beating is changing from a private joke among men and a private nightmare for women to a public outrage. As a result, public officials in the law-enforcement, prosecutorial and judicial professions are beginning to respond to pressure and criticism of their long-standing failure to develop policies that treat battered women like other victims of personal violence.

WIFE BEATING: A COMMON PRACTICE

Law-enforcement officials estimate that there are 28 million *victims*.

Wife Abuse is the most underreported crime. Research indicates that *at least one sixth* of all married couples experience one "violent episode" every year.

† (Bradley v. State, 2 Miss. [Walker], 156, 158) (cited by Sue E. Eisenberg and Patricia L. Micklow in "The Assaulted Wife: Catch-22 Revisited," 3 Women's Rights Law Reporter 138–61 at 138. See also Stedman, "Right of a Husband to Chastise Wife," 3 Va. L. Reg. [n.5] 241, 1917).

‡ State v. Black, 60 N.C. 162, 163, 86 Am. Dec. 436, cited by Eisenberg and Micklow at 139.

Studies indicate that *up to 60 per cent* of all married women are subjected to physical violence by their husbands at some time during the marriage.

One study showed that 20 per cent of the husbands beat their wives "regularly"—from daily to six times a year.

Another indicated that 10 per cent of the men interviewed in a random sample *admitted to "regularly" engaging in "extreme physical abuse"* of their wives.*

SPOUSE MURDER

1 According to the International Association of Chiefs of Police ("Training Key ⚡246, Investigation of Wifebeating"), 25 per cent of all murders involved close family members; in over half of these, one spouse killed the other, with wives being the victim in 52 per cent of the cases and the "criminal" in 48 per cent.

2 Husbands and wives kill each other with equal frequency, but wives are seven times more likely than husbands to have killed in self-defense. (National Commission on the Causes and Prevention of Violence, 1969.)

3 A recent study indicated that 40 per cent of the 132 women detained on homicide charges in Cook County Jail (Chicago) had been repeatedly beaten by the men they killed.† Most had remained in abusive homes for five years or longer, because they feared being unable to provide a good home for their children.

4 A study of homicides in the city of Chicago revealed that in homicides involving minority persons, 69.7 per cent of the women were killed by people they knew well and/or lived with; 78.9 per cent of the white women were murdered by people close to them (including husbands, estranged husbands, boyfriends).‡

* "Wife Abuse and Police Response," *FBI Law Enforcement Bulletin*, May 1978, 4–5. The study referred to was conducted for the National Institute of Mental Health by Richard Gelles, Murray Straus, and Suzanne Steinmetz, reporting on separate research and interviews conducted by the authors.

† See "Study of Female Killers Finds 40% Were Abused," in "Around the Nation," New York *Times*, December 20, 1977, p. 20, col. 8.

‡ Harwin L. Voss and John R. Hepburn, "Patterns in Criminal Homicide in Chicago," *Journal of Criminal Law, Criminology and Police Science* 59 (4) (1968).

SPIRALS OF VIOLENCE: THE RESPONSIBILITY OF THE LEGAL SYSTEM

To date, police intervention has failed to interrupt the spiral of violence. A Kansas City study of "domestic assaults and homicides" reveals that prior to the last serious or fatal attack, police had responded to previous calls for help in 85.4 per cent of the cases. In over half of these, they had already been summoned *five or more times!**

A Detroit study revealed that police had attempted to intervene in previous domestic disturbances in *90 per cent* of the cases that eventually became spouse murder cases.

Ineffective responses from police and the rest of the legal system force many battered women to remain in abusive homes, becoming almost certain targets of escalating violence.†

A Reminder

This chapter describes the major forms of help and protection currently offered by the legal system, along with suggestions for how to make the best use of available programs and services and how to work toward establishing better ones. People who use this chapter should remember three principles when applying what it says to their own local situations:

Specific statutes (written laws), official policies, and specific programs may vary widely from state to state, city to city, and one rural location to another.

Official policy—written and unwritten—also varies from place to place, and may vary considerably from or even contradict the official local law.

Unofficial policy, made by on-the-spot decision makers, often has the most significant impact on battered women seeking help from the legal system.

* Keeny Jeanne Meyer, "Police Intervention Data and Domestic Violence, Exploration and Validation of Prediction Models," Kansas City, MO, Dec. 1977.
† Richard Gelles, "Abused Wives; Why Do They Stay?" *Journal of Marriage and the Family,* 1976.

Throughout this chapter it is necessary to use a number of legal terms. Important ones will be explained in the text and used later with no further explanation.

CIVIL OR CRIMINAL: WHAT IS THE DIFFERENCE?

The distinction between civil and criminal processes is one of the fundamental distinctions in the American legal system. Generally, the civil side of the law is used to resolve *private* conflicts (e.g., contracts, sex discrimination, divorce, child support), while the criminal side is supposed to vindicate the *public,* or state's, interest in the general welfare and public peace (e.g., prohibiting and punishing loan-sharking, fraud, and assault). The criminal law is said to be punitive and the civil law remedial. The purpose of civil law is to compensate (often by means of money but sometimes by means of an order requiring or prohibiting specific noncriminal acts) a person whose legal interests have been interfered with. The purpose of criminal law is to restore public order, vindicate the state's authority, and punish the offender.

The usually clear distinction between civil and criminal law grows hazy when a battered woman looks to the legal system for help. Often, she is referred to "family" or "domestic" court—a subdivision of the civil court system. Often, the same beating would have resulted in arrest and criminal prosecution if the attacker and victim had been strangers. The same assault is more likely to be treated as a criminal offense if the parties were never married or are separated or divorced than if they are married at the time of the attack.

"What does marriage have to do with the usual rules defining civil and criminal cases?" you wonder. The answer is, "Nothing." Marriage makes no difference in the physical pain involved; a wedding ring does not make a blow to the head less lethal or a prolonged beating less disruptive of public order and security.

When police and prosecutors refer battered women to the civil court *instead* of to the criminal system, they may be doing so to avoid becoming involved in "family disputes" or filling up the court calendar with cases they do not consider important. This is not to say that criminal prosecutions are any solution to the prob-

NAME OF LEGAL ACTION	TIME BETWEEN COMPLAINT AND REMEDY	LEGAL ASSISTANCE REQUIRED?	ENFORCEMENT MECHANISM
PEACE BOND	Relatively short (within 1-2 weeks)	No	Order to refrain from abuse pending a full hearing; may be extended after hearing. Cash bond may be ordered deposited with the court until order expires. Order may contain a warning that violation will result in arrest and/ or forfeiture of cash. Relatively informal hearing process. (May be civil or criminal process.)
TRO (Temporary Restraining Order) or INJUNCTION	Very short for TRO— within 3-5 days. May be extended indefinitely after a hearing, when it becomes an injunction.	Probably	Order to cease abuse; does not require notice to defendant or full hearing. Often limited to cases where serious injury or the likelihood that it will be carried out exists.
ORDER OF PROTECTION A. Family court	May be long delays—2 weeks to several months.	No	Approximately same as peace bond. Sometimes less effective. Often, these are little more than voluntary agreements not to abuse or threaten.
B. Under new legislation	May provide for emergency hearings almost immediately, usually within ten days.	Recommended	May evict abusive spouse for specific period of time (a month to a year) where there is evidence of serious injury or danger, or of child abuse. Does not otherwise affect abuser's property rights. May determine custody and visitation during eviction period.
SEPARATE MAINTENANCE or DIVORCE AMET (rare)	Several months or more	Yes	May order abusive spouse to support wife in separate residence, may enjoin harassment, may permit wife to live with children in jointly owned or leased home. Similar to rights under new "Protection from Abuse" laws, but permanent rather than temporary. Not available or exceedingly difficult to obtain in some states. May be called "Divorce AMET." May or may not resolve property ownership, alimony, custody or child support.

REMEDIES AVAILABLE	PENALTIES FOR VIOLATION	RELATION TO CRIMINAL AND OTHER CIVIL PROCEDURES
Often none. Maybe civil contempt. Enforcement by prosecutors more effective than enforcement by police. Enforcement proceedings must usually be initiated by victim; usual method is to contact judge or other issuing authority. In some jurisdictions, no record is kept of bonds issued, and victims are required to procure new bond for new violence.	Often none. May require forfeiture of cash bond (to court, not victim). In some jurisdictions, violation may result in arrest and contempt proceeding with possible jail sentence. (Rare.)	Frequently viewed as preferred and exclusive alternative to criminal process. It is not necessary to use this process at all, or to seek enforcement of the peace bond rather than initiate a criminal action. A history of ineffecitve peace bonds may strengthen claims for other kinds of relief.
Expires in ten days if not extended after hearing. Civil contempt is legally appropriate enforcement mechanism but is usually not invoked. Police may refuse to enforce or act because the matter is being treated in civil courts. Party obtaining TRO or injunction should inform her attorney or issuing authority of violation.	Fine or jail for civil contempt possible. Arrest for violation rare unless there are specific directives from local judges, prosecutors, or police officials requiring this. Victim may have to swear out warrant and/or locate violator for police.	This is preferred alternative set up to keep these cases from "clogging" criminal courts. Local practice may make filing criminal charges virtually impossible.
Approximately the same as peace bond. In some places, woman must begin process all over again for new abuse.	In theory, arrest is authorized in many jurisdictions. Local police practice may make this impossible. No criminal penalties; may result in violation hearing and warning.	Check local legislation. Need not be exclusive.
Check local statute; civil contempt common.	Legislation may specify arrest and/or prosecution.	Need not be exclusive, but a woman with a TRO or injunction is likely to be referred to civil courts to remedy violation. She still has the right to have criminal proceedings begun if a crime has been committed. Must be obtained as part of divorce in some jurisdictions.
Poor. Wife must institute proceedings for nonpayment of support or other violation. Violation of order to cease harassment may result in contempt proceedings if initiated by wife. Not likely to result in more than warning, although fine or imprisonment theoretically possible.	New proceedings to attach or garnishee wages for nonpayment of support possible in many jurisdictions. Procedure for collecting overdue payments varies widely but must always be initiated by party obtaining the order.	No relation to criminal process. Is usually an alternative to divorce which continues husband's obligation to support wife and prevents both parties from remarrying. As a practical matter, it may make obtaining all kinds of relief from civil and criminal courts easier.

NAME OF LEGAL ACTION	TIME BETWEEN COMPLAINT AND REMEDY	LEGAL ASSISTANCE REQUIRED?	ENFORCEMENT MECHANISM
DIVORCE AVM (common kind) or DISSOLUTION (no fault)	Varies widely from several months to a year or more.	Usually	Ends the marriage and man's legal right to physical access to wife. May also end or reduce duty to support wife. In some jurisdictions, it does not resolve property ownership, joint debts, child custody, or support. Restraining orders may be issued in connection with divorces sought on grounds of physical cruelty.
TORT ACTIONS (noncriminal actions seeking compensation for assault, battery)	Lengthy—months or years	Yes	May reimburse expenses incurred as a result of the violence, especially if parties are not married at the time of the attack.
TRESPASS/EVICTION	Varies—probably several months	Yes	Orders party with no legal interest in property to move.

1. NOTE: Not all these remedies are available in every jurisdiction.

2. "Legal assistance" includes private attorneys, free legal services, lawyers, and counseling from legal workers or advocates with experience in the area.

3. Local do-your-own-divorce manuals or classes may enable a woman to file for her own divorce without a lawyer if there is no contest about children, property, support, or the divorce itself.

lems of battered women, but to point out that advice to forget about the criminal process and seek relief in civil courts instead may be rooted in the belief that the violence is not really "serious" or that marriage is a "sacred" institution, which should be preserved by counseling obtained through the civil court.

In most jurisdictions, there are a number of procedures that may help battered women in limited ways. Some are criminal and some are civil. Usually, these two types of remedy are not exclusive (e.g., a criminal prosecution for battery and a civil action for divorce and child support), although in some jurisdictions choosing one action may prevent a woman from asking for another. The rules and names of these legal actions vary from locality to

REMEDIES AVAILABLE	PENALTIES FOR VIOLATION	RELATION TO CRIMINAL AND OTHER CIVIL PROCEDURES
Tends to be automatic, although violation of restraining order and support requires separate civil action.	None.	No-fault divorce or divorce obtained by husband may make it more difficult for woman to obtain other forms of relief. Divorce obtained by woman may make it easier to initiate criminal action but is not a prerequisite. Divorce may be a prerequisite to a tort action.
Money damages to compensate for expenses, including medical costs, cost of replacing broken objects, or moving, changing locks, or lost income during period of recovery.	Does not apply.	May be precluded if victim received victim's compensation after criminal trial. May be unavailable to victim married to attacker. Is not an exclusive alternative to the criminal process.
Separate enforcement proceeding must be initiated by legal occupant.	Arrest for criminal trespass.	Trespass is both a crime and a tort. Violator who enters property after warning not to, may be arrested for criminal trespass. As a practical matter, eviction proceeding may be necessary prerequisite for arrest on criminal trespass and may make it easier to press charges for assault.

locality, as does the relation among them. The best way to decide which court to go to and what to ask for is to consult with local lawyers and legal workers who have represented battered wives. Court personnel are very knowledgeable about the procedures used for specific kinds of legal action but tend to know only what happens in the system they are part of. Legal workers, lawyers, and others working on wife abuse are more likely to understand the full range of possibilities and be able to counsel a woman about which one or ones are most likely to accomplish the result she needs.

The legal action chart does not represent all the forms of action available in any particular jurisdiction but is a guide to those most frequently available. It is meant to provide some guidelines as to the advantages and disadvantages of various kinds of legal actions and the relation among them.

PEACE BONDS: THE DETROIT EXPERIENCE

The details of procuring, administering, and enforcing peace bonds, like those of other legal remedies, varies somewhat from one place to the next. The Detroit experience is interesting, because it illustrates a relatively successful one as well as an ineffective one. In Detroit, the difference depended on whether the prosecutor's office saw to the enforcement, or whether it was delegated to the police. The commander of Detroit's Police Department explains the history and use of peace bonds in that city. He introduces the peace bond by calling it one of "the novel ways police departments seek to avoid becoming involved." He describes the process:

> This non-document was issued to the perpetrator by an assistant prosecutor and admonished him to cease and desist beating his wife on pain of being prosecuted if he should repeat the offense during the time limits on the face of the instrument. Surprisingly, this was a fairly effective device. It was effective because the prosecutor would follow through on his commitment when the assault was later repeated. . . .
>
> Later the prosecutor withdrew from this role and the police took over issuing the peace bond. However, it has lost whatever effectiveness it once had because the prosecutor has no commitment to follow through if the offender repeats."‡

PRIVATE CRIMINAL COMPLAINTS V. ORDERS UNDER THE
NEW "PROTECTION FROM ABUSE" LAW:
THE VIEW FROM PHILADELPHIA

The Philadelphia District Attorney's Office classifies approximately 35–40 per cent of the cases processed as private criminal complaints as "marital abuse" cases. There is no record of how many times the parties have previously appeared in this process or how many times the police have been called to aid the victim. Most of the men appearing as defendants in this system are

‡ James Bannon, op. cit.

charged with simple "harassment." Harassment is technically not a crime but a summary offense, with a maximum penalty of ninety days and/or a fine. It includes incidents in which one person "strikes, kicks or otherwise subjects" another to "physical contact or attempts or threatens to do the same," as well as acts "which alarm or seriously annoy" another. 18 P.S. 2709. In theory, "simple assault" (classified as a second-degree misdemeanor with a maximum penalty of up to two years) may be charged whenever there is actual injury or intent to injure (18 P.S. 2701), but police may not arrest for many offenses or misdemeanors that they did not witness, unless they have an arrest warrant.

Within the past year, significant improvement in the prosecution process has taken place in the Philadelphia District Attorney's Office. In the past, however, the process was not unlike the current practices of hundreds of urban, suburban, and rural communities. Simple assault is charged only where there is physical evidence of an injury *at the time the complaint is made* or the victim has evidence of having received medical treatment for an injury. The regular criminal procedures are invoked only where the victim was admitted to a hospital as the result of an attack.

The ultimate purpose of the private complaint procedure is to get the victim and assailant to enter into an agreement and avoid prosecution. If both parties agree, there is no prosecution. Substantial pressures are exerted by court personnel and the magistrate presiding over the proceedings to resolve these cases by means of such agreements. The magistrate often recommends counseling or marriage therapy, and may order a psychiatric evaluation by a city psychiatrist. Stern lectures may be impartially delivered to both parties, who are generally admonished to go home and stay out of trouble. The entire process must be begun all over if there is a new assault, unless the woman is injured so badly she must be hospitalized. Occasionally, a few women will be adamant about refusing to "settle" their cases in this way and insist on proceeding with a criminal trial. There is a substantial attrition rate between the private complaint process and the actual criminal trial, but those cases that do survive often result in convictions.

As of this writing, under Pennsylvania's "Protection from Abuse Act," effective since the end of 1976, 471 petitions in Philadelphia alone have resulted in enforceable agreements or "consent decrees" in approximately 35 per cent of the cases. In the other 65 per cent of the cases, the court issued orders (enforceable by contempt proceedings). In about two thirds of these cases, the man was ordered to cease the abuse; in 41 cases the husband was ordered out of the house for periods ranging from one year (28 cases) to six months (11 cases). One assailant was sentenced to six months in prison and three were referred for counseling. Of the 471 petitions filed, only 28 were withdrawn before the hearing, which is scheduled within ten days of the attack.

Unfortunately, police practice has not been modified to take fullest advantage of the new law. Felony assaults are still referred to this civil process, and until recently, police could not arrest for a violation of an order to cease the abuse or stay away from the home unless it occurred in their presence. New amendments to the legislation now permit an immediate arrest for any violation of a protection or eviction order, but such authority has long existed in other jurisdictions without any noticeable effect on the traditional disinclination of the police to arrest when women are the victims of domestic violence.

In some states, battered wives may seek temporary restraining orders or civil injunctions ordering their husbands to cease the abuse, move out of the house, and/or seek counseling. If the husband is ordered to leave the home, custody and visitation may also be established in the judicial decree for a specific period of time. Violation of these orders may be punishable by contempt proceedings and possible jail sentences. In some jurisdictions, violators are allowed to continue working so as not to disrupt the income of the wife and children and are jailed only at night or on weekends. A civil-contempt jailing does not leave a criminal record. One defect of this remedy is that it may require that the victim be legally married to her assailant before she is eligible for this form of relief.

Marjory Fields urges that with an amendment that would make nonmarried women eligible, this may provide the most appropriate form of relief in almost every case except those in which the victim is convinced that her assailant's physical freedom represents a serious and continuing threat to her safety. Ms. Fields has also pointed out that to be truly effective, civil injunction statutes must be enforced (by contempt proceedings and jail, if necessary), they must be available in emergency situations in the evening and weekend hours, when most attacks occur, and they should provide victims with legal counsel (free if necessary).*

ABSOLUTE DIVORCE AND DISSOLUTION

Divorce is the legal system's favorite and, until recently, only remedy for wife beating. For many centuries, the battered woman did not even qualify for this relief, since marriage could be dissolved only in favor of a party whose spouse had committed a grievous breach of the marriage contract. That contract guaranteed the husband's right to use corporal punishment to "correct" his wife. Eventually, "physical cruelty," "extreme cruelty," or "cruel and barbarous treatment" became recognized grounds for divorce in favor of either spouse.

But as recently as 1975, a New York court refused to grant a divorce to a woman who had been beaten twice, at four-year intervals. The judge found that she had "provoked" her husband's behavior by denying him sex, refusing to prepare breakfast, and neglecting other wifely duties. He ruled that "As a matter of law, . . . if a husband beats his wife two times and there is a hiatus four years between each beating, that is not sufficient ground for a judgment of divorce." (Quoted in Brief of Plaintiff-Appellant to New York Court of Appeals; this decision is reported as Echevarria v. Echevarria, 40 N.Y. 2d 262 [1976]). The case was ultimately overturned on appeal, establishing that a single act of cruelty that constituted part of a course of cruel conduct was sufficient to grant a divorce.

Although the attitudes reflected in this case are not so unusual, most women will not find it difficult to assert legal grounds for a divorce by reciting the facts of their beatings. Having the proper legal grounds is, however, only one factor in using this form of legal action to get relief from a husband's abuse. The cost of ob-

* Marjory D. Fields, "Wife-Beating: Government Intervention Policies and Practices." In *Battered Women: Issues of Public Policy*. U.S. Commission on Civil Rights Wash., DC, 1979.

taining a divorce is another. Women who do not qualify for free legal services may want to consider filing for their own divorces if there will be no legal contest and there are no unresolved questions about property division, alimony, child support, custody, or visitation. This is particularly easy in states that have enacted "no-fault" or "dissolution" laws, but battered women may not qualify for this procedure, due to requirements that the parties attend a conciliation meeting or have lived apart under a formal separation agreement for a specific period.

Another important factor for women to consider who are looking at divorce as a possible remedy for spouse abuse is the effect a divorce will have on a husband's obligation to support them. In some states, divorce ends that obligation entirely. Because child-support payments are notoriously inadequate and difficult to enforce, the lack of alimony will, in reality, reduce the amount of money available to a woman with custody of children who depend on the father for help with their financial support. Even in states that recognize a husband's duty to support a divorced wife, a number of factors may operate to substantially reduce his support of the family once a divorce has become final. Among those factors may be the court's interpretation of the reason for the divorce and the relative "fault" of the wife. For example, a woman who left the marital home after physical abuse may still be judged somewhat "guilty" by a judge considering whether the husband should pay alimony. Of course, the wife's remaining in the marital home after a divorce and her relative earning capacity may also reduce the amount of alimony ordered.

The relationship between divorce proceedings and other civil and criminal remedies varies greatly from one jurisdiction to another. In some, a wife can obtain a civil restraining order against her husband's violence only by filing for a divorce and asking for an order pending the granting of a divorce. (See, e.g., Cal. Civ. Code Section 4359; Ann. L. of Mass. C. 208; Mich. GCR 723.3) The amount of paperwork involved, the necessity for having a lawyer, and the expense of divorce proceedings all make this a cumbersome procedure, which tends to be less effective than those procedures which permit women to file for civil restraining orders without having to file for a divorce. In many if not most jurisdictions, filing for any form of civil restraining order will make it almost impossible to have a husband who violates it arrested on criminal charges, and judges will probably be less willing to find men in civil contempt and jail them for violations of restraining orders issued in connection with a divorce than those obtained independently.

In jurisdictions that do not require civil restraining orders to be filed in connection with divorce proceedings, divorce itself should not be looked upon as a remedy that offers any immediate protection or security. It is a rather slow process which has not deterred many estranged husbands from continuing to assault their former wives, especially if they have contact at times of child visitation.

Divorce does have an unquestionable symbolic value for the battered wife. It is an official rejection of her legal subservience to her husband. Often, wife beaters have constructed elaborate fantasies and ruses by which they persuade themselves that their wives really love them and/or could not get along without them. If the abused woman obtains a divorce, there is symbolic proof positive that this is not the case. It is part of the syndrome of abuse that such a symbolic gesture will (at least temporarily) pierce some of those delusions. It should, therefore, be regarded not as an immediate solution to a crisis but as a final, symbolic resolution and termination of the legal relationship between the parties. As a practical matter, a divorce decree will probably make it easier to obtain help from the legal system if the ex-husband does not accept the fact that the relationship is over and he has lost his right of access and his authority over his wife.

SEPARATE MAINTENANCE OR DIVORCE AMET

Another civil remedy battered women may want to investigate is called separate maintenance (informally known as legal separation in some jurisdictions) or "divorce AMET." Originally, it was impossible for women to obtain absolute divorces; they were eligible for a special, limited form of divorce, *a mensa et thoro* ("from bed and board") in circumstances including extreme cruelty. This form of divorce does not permit either party to remarry but does order married parties to live separately and continues the husband's obligation to support the wife in a separate residence.

Because divorce AMET has traditionally been available only to married women, some states have declared it an unconstitutional violation of equal rights on the theory that it discriminates against men. There is no reason why this form of divorce should not be available to men as well as women, where similar circumstances of economic dependence and cruelty exist. In other states, either spouse may be eligible for a decree of separate maintenance, which requires the parties to live separately and sets the amount of a support obligation for the separation period. Again, this is not a final divorce, and neither party is eligible to remarry. Conduct on the part of the plaintiff that might be grounds for a divorce may interfere with the separate-maintenance decree, especially in courts with a strong "fault" orientation to the law of divorce.

The advantage of separate-maintenance or divorce-AMET proceedings over formal separation agreements between the parties is their theoretical enforceability. Separation agreements are private contracts and a party who believes the agreement has been violated must sue to enforce. This usually requires hiring a lawyer and suing for breach of contract in a court of small claims or other civil court. In theory, the separate-maintenance or divorce-AMET decree can be enforced by returning to the family-court judge who issued the order and petitioning for enforcement. The battered woman has the threat of civil contempt available to use against a husband who violates the order by beating, harassing, or failing to support her or her children.

TORTS AND OTHER CIVIL ACTIONS AGAINST ABUSIVE PARTNERS

Assault and battery and trespass are the subjects of civil remedies as well. Civil laws that attempt to settle disputes between private parties emphasize restoring the status quo between the parties. These legal actions initiated by victims of noncriminal violations of the social order are known as "torts." Most torts are concerned with violations of individual rights that interfere with the peace of the community (e.g., nuisances, negligence) but do not amount to violations of the criminal law. In some cases, the criminal and the civil laws overlap, with the result that victims can choose one or the other, or both.

For many generations, husbands and wives were not able to sue each other for torts, due to the fiction that they were, in reality, the same person. The legal doctrine prohibiting spouses from suing each other in tort actions is known as the "interspousal immunity doctrine," and it remains valid in many states today.† In some areas, however, state legislatures have passed statutes exempting some or all forms of tort action from this doctrine, and it has been annulled by court decisions in others.‡

In theory, women who are not married to their attackers, and those who can sue in states that abolished the interspousal immunity doctrine, are eligible for money to compensate them for any actual expenses incurred as the result of an assault or battery, including compensation for damaged clothing, furniture, medical bills, loss of income, and moving expenses necessitated by the attack. In reality, the likelihood of women recovering any of this money is remote, with married women living with their attackers least likely to recover anything. Women who have obtained divorces—especially on the grounds of earlier cruelty—may have a better chance of success, as will women not living with their assailants.

The practical value of tort action available to a few women is the civil action of ejection for trespass. Women who are legally the sole owners of premises they have bought, are buying, or rent may take men who persist in entering those premises to court for trespass even if police will not arrest, prosecutors will not prosecute, or the conduct does not amount to criminal trespass.

There are several major drawbacks to having to sue in tort for

† See, for example, "Tort Liability Between Husband and Wife: The Interspousal Immunity Doctrine," 21 *U. Miami L. Rev.* 423 (1966); Davis, "Torts—Action by Wife Against Husband for Personal Injuries," 34 Miss. L.J. 348 (1963); 43 A.L.R.2d 632 (1955).

‡ For example, the interspousal immunity doctrine was overruled in Michigan in 1971, Hosko v. Hosko, 385 Mich. 39, 187 N.W.2d 236 (1971). See also R. Calvert, "Criminal and Civil Liability in Husband-Wife Assaults," in S. Steinmetz and M. Straus eds., *Violence in the Family* (New York: Dodd, Mead, 1974).

trespass. This remedy is limited to those few women who have a legal right to property separate from their spouses or boyfriends. It is a relatively long, fairly complex procedure that usually requires a lawyer and attorney's fees. The availability of the eject-ment or eviction remedy may make it attractive to women who have not suffered enough physical brutality to qualify for this re-lief under a civil protection-from-abuse statute or similar proceed-ings. It may be especially useful to women with rich and/or pow-erful husbands who would not relish the attendant publicity and are determined not to leave a property in which she lives, either because of children or for economic reasons. For most women, the parallel remedy of criminal trespass is a better alternative, if the prosecutor will cooperate. The result of most civil actions for trespass is a declaration that the woman is entitled to sole use of the property and an order to vacate directed to the man. If he re-fuses to obey the order, a separate enforcement proceeding must be brought, resulting in his eventual eviction, by force if neces-sary.

THE POLICE RESPONSE TO CALLS FOR HELP

"The officer should be aware that most family disputes are not violent."*

The Initial Response: Call Screening

At least one study has confirmed that the police receive more calls for help from victims of wife abuse than of any other serious crime. (Raymond, "The Police Response to the Domestic Disturb-ance," 1967 Wis. L. Rev. 914, n.2.) In many places, the failure to keep any record of the police response obscures the fact that many of these calls are screened out by police dispatchers, who decide—either on the basis of their own judgment or official directives—that the call represents a low priority for police ac-tion. As a result, the police often do not arrive in time to witness or to stop the assault. Of course, not witnessing the crime and not

* *LEAA Training Guide* (National Institute of Law Enforcement and Criminal Justice), 1975.

knowing the location of the accused are factors considered in every criminal incident, but they rarely determine a policy of inaction, as they usually do in wife-beating cases.

Obviously, the priority assigned to "domestic" calls by police dispatchers is determined by overall police policy toward the problem, which in turn reflects society's attitudes toward it. Explanations for call-screening policies shed some light on the standard police attitudes toward the needs of battered women. Call screening is a system designed to "screen out" those calls for help which are least important and to reserve the police response for those cases in which it is most necessary.

The result has been that in many cities it is difficult for women being attacked by men they know, live with, or are married to, to get emergency police help. As James Bannon of the Detroit Police Department explained, "Since call screening began, in 1965, chances are excellent that if there is no weapon, police will not be dispatched."† The Chicago Police Department policy requires that all incidents in which the assailant makes physical contact with the victim be classified by the dispatcher as "batteries," while all domestic violence is rated as a "disturbance." The significance of these categories is evident in the New York Police Department policies that rate "family disputes" as *fifth* in priority rank, while all other assaults are ranked second or third, depending upon the seriousness of the threat, injury, or the presence of weapons. Of course, lots of women have figured out the system and refuse to identify their attacker as their husband, or allege that weapons are involved when they are not, but victims should not have to resort to such measures to get police response.

All of these classification policies that minimize the seriousness of the danger to battered women contradict the experience and facts of which police, as well as battered women, have direct knowledge.

Commander Bannon suggests that "police response to social conflict, particularly domestic social conflict, is intertwined with notions of sanctity of the home and quite possibly with traditional conceptions of male-female roles. There appears wider acceptance

† James Bannon, "Social Conflict Assaults," Part II of Police Foundation Study.

of the idea that a little corporal punishment to the recalcitrant wife is not all that deviant."

Given a great deal of discretion to exercise their own judgment about the importance of calls from battered women, police departments have tended to minimize them. Therefore, special efforts should be made to see to it that these calls are not "screened out" of the police process from the very beginning. The following suggestions may help police departments to adopt appropriate classification and priority procedures for dispatchers:

1. Appropriate dispatch policies must be based on the rule that calls should not be classified as less urgent merely because of the relationship between the victim and the attacker. Assaults and threats should all be categorized on the basis of the danger to the victim, based upon objective factors including presence of weapons, injuries already inflicted, nature of threats, and previous history of assault by the attacker. If anything, the potential for escalating violence in wife-assault cases should suggest a higher, rather than a lower, priority for these calls.

2. Review copies of local guidelines for dispatchers to determine what types of calls from battered women fit into each category. A memorandum giving examples of various factual situations and discussing why a particular classification is appropriate could be drafted and submitted for inclusion in training materials for new dispatchers, and circulated among those presently operating in this capacity.

3. Does the police department have special units or personnel specially trained for wife-assault cases? If so, is the dispatcher's classification such that these personnel are the ones who receive the calls? Is this an appropriate across-the-board policy, or should calls involving a high level of danger be routed to those with the fastest response capability (i.e., those in the immediate neighborhood, regardless of "special" training?)

4. Do local dispatchers have quick access to police records of prior calls to the same address and whether there are outstanding orders of protection, peace bonds, or other civil orders that should be enforced by immediate arrest if the police find the man in violation? Police who answer battered women's calls should be armed with this information when they arrive. It's usually too late to arrest after the police go back to the station and learn that the man was in violation of an order.

Groups interested in correcting improper classification and call-screening procedures will have to find the best approach for their locale, depending on the interest of local personnel. In some instances, advocate groups may want to call for public hearings on police policy toward domestic disturbance.

Reasons for low priority given to domestic calls

Call screening and low-priority classification of violence occurring in the context of "consensual" relationships is merely a symptom of overall attitudes and policies of police toward wife beating. If call screening does not result in removing these cases entirely from the law-enforcement and criminal-justice system, these attitudes, reinforced by training, are likely to appear over and over again as the victim deals with the legal machinery designed to protect and help her.

The first line of defense against dealing with the issue is the popular myth (among police) that domestic calls are not violent. This directly contradicts actual police experience as well as the fact that such calls are extraordinarily dangerous to police.

In 1974, more than one fifth of the officers killed on duty and more than one quarter of all those assaulted were responding to "disturbance" calls.‡ The police chief's *Reference Notebook* shows that 21 per cent of the total number of police officers killed on duty died while handling "disturbance" calls (IACP Police Reference Notebook, Unit 4A5, "Disorderly Conduct and Domestic Complaints."). The 1975 Uniform Crime Reports show that between 1971 and 1975, 106 officers were killed responding to "disturbance" calls, 129 responding to robberies, and 130 responding to other calls requiring arrest. (U. S. Department of Justice, FBI, 1975 Uniform Crime Reports, 225–26.)

The remarkably high level of danger to police has led to a number of attempts to (a) avoid "domestic" cases altogether, (b) teach police how to "defuse" them through training in "conflict resolution," "mediation," and other arrest-avoidance approaches,

‡ G. Marie Wilt and James D. Bannon, "Conflict Motivated Homicides and Assaults in Detroit," Detroit Police Department Study (1974). See also Ronald K. Breedlove, John W. Kennish, et al., "Domestic Violence and the Police" (1975), a Kansas City Police Department study. Both are available from the Police Foundation, Washington, D.C.

(c) create special programs and units within police departments to handle these cases, and (d) in a growing number of areas, develop training materials and procedures appropriate to what is recognized as a serious police responsibility. Unfortunately, traditional attitudes prevail in most police departments, as the result of a long history of inadequate and inappropriate training. And we are not likely to see the necessary nationwide improvement in police services to battered women until police appreciate the substantial risk of violence to themselves.

The Content of Police Training

Those police departments which do address the problems of battered women often take an outdated approach by teaching their officers that "common factors in chronically disturbed families" include "sadomasochism" and "the guilt of the victim."*

In a widely used police training guide, *The Function of the Police in Crisis Intervention and Conflict Management,* police are advised to follow their own instincts about the underlying cause of the "incident." It portrays the "typical" situation in which a woman calls for help after an attack by her husband essentially as a non-violent situation, and often no advice on how to determine the seriousness of the injuries or whether an arrest should be made. Instead, it suggests that the officer act on his instinct that "she sounds like a demanding nag. If she always sounds this way it could be driving her husband crazy. Or maybe the husband has been giving her too little of something. . . ."†

The LEAA guide suggests four "typical situations" that the police imagine themselves dealing with as part of their training: (1) A nineteen-year-old unwed mother instructed to "portray a dominant female figure who has control over the father and sides with him against the son." (2) A "very domineering" wife of an alcoholic whose mother was also "domineering." She is to be portrayed as "one who takes delight in controlling her husband." Her

* "The Function of the Police in Crisis Intervention and Conflict Management, A Training Guide" (LEAA, National Institute of Law Enforcement and Criminal Justice), 1975.
† Morton Bard, *The Function of the Police in Crisis Intervention and Conflict Management.* U. S. Department of Justice. Law Enforcement Assistance Administration, Wash. DC, 1975.

insistence upon the removal of her intoxicated and abusive husband from the apartment is portrayed as unreasonable. (3) A twenty-three-year-old drug addict whose husband is a Vietnam War veteran "with four years' service." The woman is abjectly passive, with "little interest in her children or her role as wife and mother." The police goal in all of these situations is to restore things to their "proper order" by calming "hysterical" or otherwise unreasonable or abnormal women and reestablishing the supremacy of the husband. They are taught that "there is evidence that they are expected to regulate the conflict, not to enforce a law," and specifically counseled to try to "mediate" the "conflict," refer the "couple" to counseling or other social services—and avoid arrest at almost all cost. If arrest appears inevitable, the police are advised to "explain all that's involved, . . . having to testify in court, the loss of income, need for bail. . . ."

And all too often these programs and policies do little to meet the needs of the victim. The Lincoln, Nebraska, Police Department Crisis Intervention Training Class Study Guide (George Hansen, Lincoln, Nebraska, Chief of Police) lists the goals of a "crisis intervention class" as follows:

> Reduce the number of officers injured or assaulted while on domestic calls.
> Reduce the number of repeat calls for service through proper referral.
> Reduce the amount of time spent on domestic crisis calls.
> Improve officer ability . . . , judged by the officers at work on domestic crisis calls.
> Increase job satisfaction.‡

While all of these are worthy goals, the narrow focus on benefits to the police precludes the adoption of many policies to aid the battered woman.

> Currently, American society is saying to its law enforcement officers, "Go in there and shoot it out or administer therapy, whichever is required." Is this a reasonable order?*

‡ R. Langley and R. Levy, "Wife Abuse and the Police Response," *FBI Law Enforcement Bulletin*, May 1978.
* Ibid.

"CRISIS INTERVENTION" AND "CONFLICT MANAGEMENT"

"Crisis intervention" and "conflict management" are Siamese twins popular in the police-training world. As basic emergency techniques, they represent skills every police officer should have. They should, however, be revised, expanded, improved, and updated if they are to meet the needs of the victim.

In 1967, the New York City Police Department instituted a "Family Crisis Intervention Unit" in response to the large number of domestic disturbance calls. Under this program, the department trained a few selected officers to work in biracial teams. The "crisis intervention" teams were given psychological training and training in using community resources to make referrals. Members of the team performed regular patrol duties but were on call for dispatch to "domestic" calls.

In two years, these teams handled 1,400 calls to 962 families and rated the program a success because none of these resulted in homicides or police injury.[†] Arrest was to be avoided, and the battered woman was to be treated as half of a troubled dyad or a member of a family "in crisis." While this approach does have some validity, it often results in a failure to recognize married women as individuals with rights, interests, and needs separate from those of their husbands.

The New York Police Department crisis intervention experiment has been used as a model for training in many police departments. Morton Bard, who is credited with developing the crisis-intervention approach and was responsible for much of the training conducted by the New York Police Department, explained that the theory of his approach was that "training police officers in interpersonal skills could improve and facilitate the management of domestic disturbances."[‡] He believed that using the term "crisis" would suffice to convey the seriousness of wife assault in contrast to what he termed the traditional attitude that wife beating consti-

† Fields, op. cit.
‡ Morton Bard, "Family Crisis Intervention: From Concept to Implementation," In Maria Roy, ed., *Battered Women: A Psychosociological Study of Domestic Violence* (New York: Van Nostrand Reinhold, 1977.)

tuted "an alcohol-inspired 'nothing' about which little could be done."* Essentially he viewed wife beating not as part of a social, political, and economic system that discriminates against women but as an "obvious expression of some deeper difficulty in the family." In recent years, Bard's approach to family violence has come to reflect the growing concern with the needs of the victim, but since his Family Crisis Intervention program and theoretical writings have exerted such influence on police training and programs everywhere, they deserve careful analysis by all who are working to make police responsive to the needs of battered women. Violence directed at a wife by a husband should not be treated in the same manner as violence between strangers, Bard assumes, because intrafamily violence is merely a symptom of a troubled relationship. While there may be some truth in this observation, the exclusive emphasis on the importance of keeping the "family" unit intact through counseling, referral, and mediation results in a deprivation of fundamental rights of the abuse victim. Because he presumes the paramount importance of the family, Bard treats the victims of this crime as "people in conflict" who "want an objective, skillful and *benign authority* who can negotiate, mediate or arbitrate a constructive outcome."

The words "benign authority" betray what may well be an essential weakness in the "crisis intervention" model for police responses to wife beating. While the police are indeed viewed as "authority" figures—and tend to be trained to behave in "authoritarian" ways—many people working on wife abuse question whether any authority figure who is "benign" to the assaulter can also be perceived as benign to the victim.

Nor are most police officers terribly comfortable with the "benign" image, as Bard recognizes when he criticizes the traditional police avoidance of anything that might be characterized as "social work" out of a fear that "any helping function requiring the use of interpersonal skills diminishes the masculine authority image of the police."† The great advantage of the "crisis management" and "crisis intervention" technique, it is suggested, is that it avoids the "feminine" social-work connotations by substituting

* Ibid.
† Ibid., p. 185.

images from the world of business, government, and the military —images much more consistent with the authoritarian view and masculine self-image of the police.

It may well be that the reliance on the "authority" of the police system as the key to its ability (or potential) to help battered women is entirely misplaced. Many battered women may want and need something quite different from another assertion of "masculine authority." While it cannot be questioned that the police constitute the single most important source of emergency help for victims of wife assault, their value lies in their immediate response-ability, rather than in their ability to be more masculine than the assaulter. In fact, the implicit threat to the masculinity of an already insecure wife beater may have something to do with the number of police killed on domestic calls.

The obvious flaw in the "conflict management" and "crisis intervention" approaches is that they are shaped by concern for individual police officers and the police department, for "the family," "the marriage," and the husband. They remain fundamentally ignorant of the needs of the victim, the battered woman. As a result of this failure to concentrate upon her needs, police policies for handling a widespread and serious law-enforcement and citizen-protection problem are inconsistent and self-contradictory. Police behavior must change before battered women receive the protection they deserve from the only agency organized to perform this service.

When a woman calls the police emergency number for help, she is asking first that her physical safety be restored. The argument that police do not arrest and prosecutors fail to prosecute in wife-abuse cases because the victims don't really want their husbands to get caught up in the criminal-justice system is not supported by experience. One study, conducted in Detroit in October 1972, revealed that only 19.4 per cent of the 144 women who received police help in assault cases believed the assaults would not continue. Eighty-one had already reported assaults. Of those who thought the assaults would continue, 70 per cent also believed they would get more serious; 47.8 per cent had already received medical treatment as the result of a prior serious assault; and 84.7 per cent believed serious, even fatal consequences were possible. Although only 4.9 per cent of those interviewed believed that the only solution was to "send him to jail," 13.2 per cent had no idea what would help, and almost two thirds (65.8 per cent) of the victims indicated that the nonjail alternative remedies had to protect their right to live separate and apart from their husbands. Marriage counseling and individual and couple therapy were not seen as desirable alternatives.

POLICE TRAINING: A NEW APPROACH

The focus of new police training materials and programs should be the battered woman as an individual citizen whose rights must be protected by law-enforcement officials and the legal system. This is not to imply that all the other approaches and techniques are irrelevant. Shorn of sexist, racist or middle-class prejudices, many of the "intervention" techniques developed by Bard and others are important techniques, with life-saving potential. They provide an interpersonal skill that is a safer and better alternative to the use of force and weapons to reduce the potential for violence between disputing parties. But they must be used as supplements, and not as alternatives, to law enforcement and victim protection.

Another potentially very valuable technique is police referral to a wide variety of community agencies, including shelters and other groups assisting battered women. Programs that train police as mental-health referral agents appear quite promising.‡ The object of training police to use these techniques in wife-abuse cases would not be to refer people out of the legal system and into general "family counseling" agencies, but to identify violent men as people who are likely to have serious disorders that will be played out in increasingly serious violence unless they are the object of professional attention.

A number of advocate groups have begun to offer various forms of police training, ranging from one-day seminars to comprehensive training programs.

As mentioned in the Author's Note, the Women's Resource

‡ James Bannon, "Social Conflict Assaults," Police Foundation Study. Unpublished monograph.

Network has been funded to develop a demonstration model for improving police response to the problem.

Working with the Philadelphia and Detroit police departments, training will be conducted for both in-service and recruit officers, and both supervisory and lower-level personnel. We are developing an expandable transferable model that can serve as an add-on to existing crisis-intervention training. Based upon our experience in Detroit and Philadelphia, we have developed the following sets of goals and objectives which may serve as useful models for those working to improve the police response. Overall training goals: (1) to improve police attitudes, (2) provide crisis-intervention skills, (3) reduce police injuries, (4) initiate a successful connection between the victim and the helping agency, (5) stimulate significant data collection within police departments regarding the incidence and disposition of wife-assault cases.

Specific training objectives are

(1) improved procedures for reporting, handling the situation, making an arrest, conducting an investigation, and record keeping;

(2) procedures for making appropriate referrals to social-service agencies,

(3) crisis-intervention skills and techniques,

(4) the development of working relationships with social-service agencies,

(5) implementation of local wife-abuse legislation,

(6) knowledge of civil remedies,

(7) general understanding of wife-abuse problem.

A few things to remember when initiating and developing police training programs:

(1) Training line officers without training supervisory personnel (sergeants, etc.) can be a waste of time, since line officers tend to "follow the lead" of their supervisors.

(2) A low-key approach will probably be most effective.

(3) Officers who have received training related to rape will be the most open to developing new attitudes and approaches to wife assault.

(4) Training should be conducted for both in-service and recruit officers and both supervisory and lower-level personnel.

(5) Training approaches and materials currently in use should be reviewed for sexist, racist, or class-biased content and revised if necessary.

(6) Training materials must stress that the police officer's job is not to solve the problem that leads to the incident, nor to save the marriage, but to stop the violence, protect the victim, and enforce the law as he would in a similar case involving strangers.

One valuable police training resource is a referral manual that lists local social-service agencies and other groups offering services to battered women. In large urban areas, social workers or police with a thorough knowledge of the community and special training may be stationed during peak wife-beating hours (evening hours, especially on the weekends) to receive complaints and do referrals and provide crisis intervention. Generally, referrals are made, if at all, by the officers who answer a call. In either situation, a referral manual that lists relevant agencies, their addresses and telephone numbers, major services, and eligibility guidelines as well as fees could substantially increase the effectiveness of police aid to battered women. Ideally, such manuals should be arranged by service, so that referrals could be quickly made on the basis of what kind of help was needed. Advocate groups may find that preparing such a manual, if one is not already used by the local police department, is a good way to establish cooperative working relationships between your group and the police department. Some departments have officers who carry a great deal of this information in their heads, and their informal knowledge and referral abilities should be acknowledged and incorporated into a written reference for other officers. All recruit training should include community orientation, to make new officers aware of the agencies and services available.

Officers should also be supplied with small printed cards listing emergency phone numbers that they can discreetly distribute to assault victims.

Depending upon your resources, locality, and the responsiveness of your local law-enforcement officials, the specific training approach can take a variety of forms. In Detroit, the Social Conflict Task Force (a committee that is representative of the Police Department and several women's, family-service and men-

tal-health community organizations) decided to apply to their
state planning agency for a grant to conduct an in-depth training
program for the Detroit Police Department. They have selected
one precinct in which all assigned patrol and investigative officers
will be provided two eight-hour training segments. The training
will involve a classroom seminar format. Along with lecture material and discussion, officers will participate in role-playing situations
that simulate domestic conflicts. As part of their training, officers
will be provided with and instructed in the use of a referral list of
resources and services that are available to abused women. After
the most effective training methods have been determined, the
training program will be expanded to include the entire department.

In Philadelphia, local wife-abuse groups will cooperate with the
Police Department in the development of film cassettes for use in
training personnel in the Philadelphia Department. We will be
developing eight three-minute film cassettes that will be shown for
ten succeeding days at officer roll call. The cassettes will be shown
at regularly scheduled intervals so that officers will have the opportunity to view the complete series. Due to the large size of the
Philadelphia Department (eighty-five hundred officers) and the
consequent impossibility of establishing one-to-one contact with
every officer, the cassette is the most appropriate vehicle for delivery of this type of training for in-service officers.

In suburban or rural areas, with significantly smaller police
forces, a classroom format may be the most appropriate model for
training delivery.

Whatever the format, the following information should be conveyed in any police training program.

Introductory material should include:

    The social roots of woman-battering

    Statistics on the prevalence of domestic violence

    The nature and extent of the problem

    Psychology of the victim

        a. Why she stays

        b. Why she may refuse to cooperate with police

        c. Why she may not follow through on legal procedures

    The role of drugs and alcohol

Psychology of the abuser

Danger to officers and victims

Appropriate Response—Initial Procedures:

Arriving at the scene, gaining entry, establishing control, and protecting the victim: These procedures are described in the International Association of Chiefs of Police Training Key ※246. Available from IACP, 11 Firstfield Rd, Gaithersburg, MD 20760

Addition:

Officers should offer to transport victim to emergency room *without husband.*

Decision to Arrest:

a. Officers should determine if there is a protective order or any other civil order. If such an order is in effect, officers should follow appropriate enforcement procedures.

b. Arrest is appropriate when injury and assailant are present or when serious injury (apparent or nonapparent) has been confirmed by medical authorities, whether or not such injury results in hospitalization.

c. Officers should not substitute their judgment about the value of arrest for that of the victim when arrest is legally justified.

d. When officers are in doubt as to whether victim has actually suffered injury, victim should be transported to emergency room for documentation of injuries and treatment.

e. When an arrest is appropriate but the victim refuses to cooperate, police should respect her opposition in the majority of cases. Occasionally, in a severe case, a felony can be pursued if there exists strong evidence (circumstantial and physical). In a few cases, there may be eyewitnesses to the assault. Based upon the available evidence, the officer may be able to make a probable-cause arrest in a felony case regardless of the wife's cooperation.

f. Officers should avoid the use of physical force.

g. Officers should refrain from any action that might provoke violence from either spouse.

h. When making a decision regarding whether or not to arrest, the desires and needs of the victim should be taken into consideration.

i. Officers should make note of or gather evidence: statements of witnesses, injuries, broken furniture, weapons, bloody clothing, general disarray.

When Arrest Is Inappropriate

a. In misdemeanor cases that do not occur in the officer's presence, the victim should be informed that she will have to follow through with the legal process if she wants to prosecute.

b. The victim should be advised of available prosecution procedures.

c. She should be advised to gather names and addresses of witnesses to this and prior assaults to provide the prosecutor.

d. She should be advised as to whether she will have to pay a fee to file a complaint with the prosecutor.

e. She should be advised to seek medical treatment as documentation of her injuries.

f. She should be advised of available civil procedures.

g. Officers should offer to transfer victim to a place of safety and provide protection while she gathers up children, clothing, I.D., etc.

h. The victim should be advised of emergency services: medical, legal, advocates, or victim/witness unit of prosecutor's office.

i. Officers should encourage victim to avail herself of appropriate resources to counteract her feelings of helplessness and isolation.

j. Officers should make appropriate referrals, as discreetly as possible, in addition to and not in place of appropriate law-enforcement action, unless victim specifically indicates desire to use services referred to instead of criminal or civil action.

k. Officers should encourage victim to file a complaint when appropriate.

l. If assailant is on probation or parole, victim should be advised to contact assailant's probation officer immediately.

m. Officers should explain the limitations and responsibilities of police in providing police protection.

n. Officers should give referral cards and leaflets with appropriate information to victim.

In General, Police Officers Should

a. demonstrate a serious attitude;

b. demonstrate concern for the victim;

c. inform assailant of the seriousness of his crime;

d. *listen* to the victim;

e. Reassure victim that talking to officer does not automatically mean that her assailant will be arrested.

NOTE: This material should cover all domestic-violence situations, including families of police officers and any other city employees.

Conducting the Investigation:

Interviewing the victim, interviewing witnesses, interviewing the assailant, and gathering evidence: These procedures are described in IACP Training Key #246.

Civil Procedures:

a. An overview of any civil procedures available to victims of domestic violence.

b. Instructions on enforcement related to any existing civil remedies.

Criminal Prosecution Procedures:

An overview of procedures involved in filing a criminal complaint.

One simple way to evaluate the training program in addition to getting feedback from the officers involved would be to compare data collected by wife-abuse groups prior to the training program that indicate dissatisfaction by victims with police performance, with data collected after training has been completed.

Providing police with this type of training should produce several positive results:

(1) the establishment of a more effective police response;

(2) increased protection for battered spouses;

(3) increased options for battered spouses, including the opportunity to prosecute abusive spouses;

(4) the establishment of successful connections between victims and helping agencies;

(5) more effective and increased services for victims of abuse.

Police Should Discard These Myths

1. *Women usually "provoke" the beatings* by nagging, whining, or petty jealousy. The law does not consider whining a legal "provocation" for any battery. The underlying premise of this

myth is that husbands "have a right" to control the behavior of their wives, punishing them for "unacceptable" behavior.

2. *The husband was just expressing his frustrations* and should not be punished for it. Again, battery or assault is not a legal means of expressing *anything!* This rationalization for wife beating is part of the "culture of violence" theory, which teaches many policemen that working-class and minority people are "not able" to express their feelings, so they resort to physical violence. A second dimension to this attitude is the conclusion that since "this sort of thing goes on all the time in poor communities, we shouldn't interfere." Police must assume that if a battered woman calls for help, she does not accept this behavior as a cultural norm.

3. *Women who have been beaten before and keep on living with the batterer must be masochists.* Chief among the reasons why women stay is economic dependence. Another major factor is despair of finding help outside the home (see Chapter II). New legislation, which gives courts the power to order abusers out of the home for periods of up to a year, is intended to break the cycle of violence and despair by giving the woman and her children an affordable place to live (Chapter IV).

Facilitating Policy Change

Obtaining the necessary policy changes from your local police department is a necessary part of improving the police response. It will be impossible to establish police training programs until it is clear just what the police should and can do in responding to domestic disturbance calls.

In Chicago, the Legal Center for Battered Women met with the Chicago Police Department to discuss the failure of police to assist battered women. As a result of these meetings, the following agreement was reached:

1. The Chicago Police Department has issued a patrol division special order stating that an incident in which a woman has been beaten is not a domestic disturbance but a crime, which necessitates an investigation to determine if an arrest is proper. The order emphasizes arrest as an appropriate response in a situation in which the woman is injured and the man is present. If the man

isn't present, the woman is to be told of her right to obtain a warrant at a later date and where to do so. In addition, the woman is to be provided with information about legal assistance, counseling, and shelter.

2. The Chicago Police Department will investigate the Center's complaints and any others against police officers who do not abide by the order. The Center will be monitoring the Chicago Police Department's implementation of the order.

3. The Chicago Police Department has asked Center staff to work with their training division to develop a film and other materials related to battered women and the appropriate police response to their calls for assistance.

The Chicago experience represents a good model for those working to facilitate change within their police departments. Attorney Candace Wayne, of the Legal Center for Battered Women, reports that it is important for advocate groups to have a thorough knowledge and understanding of the police response. They should be able to document police ineffectiveness if they feel that it is preventing battered women from obtaining police assistance. She also points out that it is important for groups to monitor the police response, once agreements have been reached regarding any changes in police procedure and policy. She suggests further that groups take steps to insure that policy changes enacted at the top filter down to the patrol-officer level. One way to accomplish this may be to meet with the individual district commanders to make sure that they have received the information and are passing it along to their subordinates.

Once advocates are knowledgeable about the police response in their area, it is important to reach the policy makers within the department to begin negotiations for initiating change. Although it can certainly be helpful to communicate with line officers as a way of gaining information regarding the current response, when it comes to changes in policy it is usually necessary to work from the top. Although it can be frustrating to discover that the police response is substantially less than appropriate, it is in the best interests of battered women to maintain a low-key approach when communicating with representatives of the department. Remember that police attitudes, like the attitudes of the public at large, won't change overnight. Patience is a virtue.

The establishment of cooperative working relationships with the police is an essential step in gaining the type of law-enforcement intervention that victims of domestic violence need. Helping the police to set up a referral system, develop a resource manual, or establish joint crisis-intervention teams are some ways of establishing the necessary rapport.

Call Screening

Official policies of nonresponse to domestic-violence calls should be abolished. The Detroit Police Department has recently taken such a step: "Be it resolved by the Detroit Board of Police Commissioners that there shall be no 'call screening' in the Detroit Police Department." The resolution goes on to specify that "in the future all legal distinctions or references between being battered as a wife and spouse as opposed to being a stranger, be eliminated."

Data Collection

The Detroit Department recently amended its general orders to include a section on data collection related to domestic violence: "Officers dispatched to or encountering incidents of domestic violence shall complete a P.C.R. [author's note: fill out a report] if the elements of a crime are established. In addition to the usual assignment of such complaints, an additional copy shall be prepared and transmitted to the Special Projects Section: The Special Projects Section shall analyze such reports and make the data available to appropriate agencies concerned with this issue."*

"Until A Better System Exists. . . ." The Decision to Arrest
Avoid Arrest if Possible

A. Appeal to their vanity.
B. Explain the procedure of obtaining a warrant.
    1. Complainant must sign complaint.
    2. Must appear in court.

* Detroit Police Department "General Order Pertaining to Domestic Disturbance."

   3. Consider the loss of time.
   4. Cost of court.
C. State that your only interest is to prevent a breach of the peace.
D. Explain that attitudes usually change by court time.
E. Recommend a postponement.
   1. Court not in session.
   2. No judge available.
F. Don't be too harsh or critical.†

The decision to arrest is one of the most important to be made by police officers responding to a family-violence situation.

While it is a mistake to suggest that every man who hits or slaps his wife should be immediately carted off to jail, we do believe that the strong preference for "nonarrest" resolutions by police should be reevaluated and modified.

A recent International Association of Chiefs of Police training guide acknowledges the error of discouraging arrest on the assumption that it will prove a waste of time or that "better alternatives" exist:

> To minimize pressure on the prosecutor, courts and social service agencies will only delay the time when adequate remedies and programs are provided. Ignoring the problem is an improper action of the police. Even if each family processed through the legal and social service systems receives no help from them, initiating the process remains the proper action for the police until a better system exists.‡

A policy of arrest when the victim consents and all the elements of a criminal offense are present serves the interests of battered women and society at large far better than a policy of arrest avoidance. It may also serve the crime-prevention function of the criminal-justice system better than the currently favored alternative provided especially for victims of "family" violence: the private criminal complaint.

One purpose of the nonarrest and "private" criminal process is

† Outline used by Wayne County, Michigan, Sheriff's Academy.
‡ International Association of Chiefs of Police Training Key #245, "Wife Beating."

to keep violence between spouses out of the already overloaded criminal-justice system. But the creation of separate standards and processes that are clearly inadequate to combat a veritable epidemic of violent crime is counterproductive. It is one of the fundamental assumptions of criminal law that impartial and effective enforcement of the law serves as a general warning to others tempted to engage in similar behavior, thereby deterring them. If this assumption has any validity, the criminal-justice system should apply it to family-violence situations as well as to violence between strangers.

CRIMINAL PROCEDURES AND THE LAW OF ARREST: A BRIEF PRIMER

Technically, an "arrest" is made whenever police stop and detain a person, usually by taking him or her into custody. In order to avoid discriminatory or arbitrary use of this power, the law prefers that no arrest be made without a warrant obtained from a judge or magistrate, who has to be convinced that there is "probable cause" to believe that the person charged committed the crime of which she or he is suspected. However, the law recognizes that there are some circumstances under which it would be impractical to require police to go before a judge and get a warrant before arresting a suspect. These include cases in which the suspect is likely either to flee in order to avoid arrest or to complete a serious crime in progress.

When police answer calls for help from a battered woman, they do not arrive with arrest warrants. Their decision to arrest or not arrest the man depends primarily on their interpretation of the seriousness of the crime and the likelihood that it will continue if they do not arrest.

As a rule, crimes are classified into three major categories which indicate their seriousness and serve as a guide to the maximum penalties. The categories are "summary offenses," "misdemeanors," and "felonies," with summary offenses being the least serious and felonies those that are likely to entail substantial prison sentences. People charged with summary offenses are usually not arrested and are rarely jailed; their maximum prison term is under six months, with fines and warnings common instead. The definition of misdemeanor varies greatly from one jurisdiction to another, ranging from offenses punishable by a maximum term of six months to one year to those punishable up to five years. In many jurisdictions, any crime punishable by a year or more in prison may be classified as a felony, while in others that term is reserved for offenses with maximum terms of five years or more.

The authority of police to make an arrest is determined primarily by whether the crime for which they arrest a suspect is categorized as a summary offense, a misdemeanor, or a felony in that particular jurisdiction. The two most important rules for arrests without warrants are

(1) Any police officer may arrest without a warrant when the accused has committed a felony; and

(2) a police officer who witnesses a misdemeanor may arrest the person committing the misdemeanor without a warrant.

In most instances, police will not arrive while the beating is going on; they will probably decide that the assault was not serious enough to be classified as a felony and will therefore inform the victim that they cannot make an arrest until after she has sworn out a complaint and they have obtained an arrest warrant. Usually this requires a trip to the police station or courthouse on the following day.

Many police departments tend to classify all "domestic" disturbances as summary offenses, for which immediate arrest without a warrant is not appropriate, or as misdemeanors, for which they cannot arrest without a warrant unless they witness the violence. A better policy would require the police to determine whether the case was a summary offense, misdemeanor, or felony on the basis of a thorough on-the-spot investigation of the facts of each particular case. Relevant factors would include: the extent of the victim's injuries (including those that are not apparent, such as injuries resulting from kicks in the stomach, blows to the back of the neck, etc.), and the use of weapons.

Once these facts are known, police can make an intelligent decision about whether to arrest, based upon their estimate of the seriousness of the crime and the needs and expressed desires of the victim. Victims should never be placed in the position of having to decide whether the man should be arrested, but their opposition to arrest should be respected.

If the police find that the beating amounts to a misdemeanor committed outside their presence (the most likely result when no serious injury is evident and no deadly weapons were involved), they probably will not arrest.

In this instance, they should inform the victim that she can file a criminal complaint with the local prosecutor. The likelihood of an arrest warrant issuing from this procedure is not great in many jurisdictions, but if the battered woman believes that an arrest would be appropriate, she should visit the prosecutor and ask that the accused be arrested. She should point out that her safety will be endangered if the defendant is allowed to remain in the home with her immediately after he learns of the charge. If no arrest is made, the defendant will receive a notice of the charge and a "summons," telling him to come to court. See Chapter I for more information on utilizing the criminal-justice system.

Toward an Appropriate Policy of Arrest in Wife-beating Cases

Many battered wives who tolerate the situation undoubtedly do so because they feel they are alone in coping with the problem. The officer who starts legal action may give the wife the courage she needs to realistically face and correct her situation.*

An appropriate policy of arrest in wife-beating cases must be based upon an appreciation of the unusual dangers to which the victim is exposed. At the very least, police should be no less willing to arrest in "domestic" cases than in incidents with an equivalent level of violence between strangers.

In addition, the likelihood of further and increasingly serious violence should be a factor in every decision to arrest or not to arrest. The fact that many victims make repeated calls to the police over a period of years suggests that effective arrest and prosecu-

* Ibid.

tion policies applied to early incidents may substantially improve the victim's safety and reduce the police caseload. A reasonable approach is suggested by Frank J. Vandall's *Police Training for Tough Calls* (1976, Center for Research in Social Change), which, among other things, advises police with probable cause to believe a felony has been committed to arrest and sign the criminal complaint themselves. The 1976 IACP training key on "Wife Beating" also advises that arrest must be made in these cases on the same basis as in any others—whenever there is evidence to support a finding that a crime has been committed, regardless of the relationship between the parties.

Citizen's Arrests: A Partial Solution?

In some jurisdictions, the refusal of police to arrest abusive husbands may be counteracted by victims or witnesses to the beatings who use their right to make citizen's arrests.† Some states have enacted laws describing when and how this may be done; in some there is merely a long-standing tradition of this form of arrest, while in others it is virtually unheard of or has been abolished. State and local law, policies, and practice should be thoroughly checked before attempting to use this procedure. The California law authorizing and regulating citizen's arrests is valuable as an illustration of how this procedure may be used in jurisdictions where it is still valid.

California Penal Code Section 834 specifies that an "arrest may be made by a peace officer or by a private person," and Section 837 describes the circumstances under which a citizen's arrest may be made. These are

(1) for a public offense committed in his presence;
(2) when the person arrested has committed a felony, although not in his presence;
(3) when a felony has in fact been committed and he has reasonable cause for believing the person arrested to have committed it.

† The relevance of the citizen's-arrest procedure was pointed out by Susan Jackson, and the information about the relevant California law comes from her unpublished monograph *"In Search of Equal Protection for Battered Wives"* (1975).

Obviously, the precise legal definition of "public offense," "felony," and "reasonable cause" are very important. Civil-rights lawyers and prosecutors, as well as independent researchers, must examine local cases and policies that interpret these words and phrases before citizen's-arrest procedures may be advocated. Citizens who misjudge the facts or legal standards may be found liable for false-arrest imprisonment and have to pay the falsely arrested person as the result of a civil suit.

The following description of circumstances under which it would be appropriate to make a citizen's arrest in a wife-beating case is meant to serve as a general guideline only. It should not be relied upon by any organization as the basis for policies promoting the use of this procedure without very careful checking to determine whether it conforms to local practice and law concerning the use of citizen's arrests for other kinds of offense.

GUIDELINE FOR THE USE OF CITIZEN'S ARREST IN BEHALF OF BATTERED WOMEN

A *VICTIM* who has been physically injured may make an arrest for assault and/or battery.

A *VICTIM* who has not been physically injured but who has been given reason to believe that threats to injure seriously or kill her will be carried out in the immediate future (e.g., if the man has possession of or immediate access to and inclination to use a deadly weapon) may arrest for assault or "menacing" (sometimes known as "terroristic behavior" or some other kind of "threat."

A *WITNESS* to an incident in which a woman has been physically injured may arrest for assault or battery.

A *WITNESS* to threats that would put an ordinary person in fear of immediate serious injury or death may arrest for assault or "menacing."

A PERSON WHO DID NOT WITNESS the events but has specific and reliable information about the kind of threats described above or very serious injuries (e.g., those inflicted with a deadly weapon or requiring hospitalization) and knows the identity and location of the attacker may make a citizen's arrest for assault, battery, or threats.

A CITIZEN'S ARREST MAY NOT BE MADE BY A PERSON WHO DID NOT WITNESS THE ATTACK UNLESS THE AT-

TACK CONSTITUTES A FELONY. This means that in most wife-assault cases, citizens other than witnesses may not arrest unless a recognized deadly weapon was used or brandished with threats to use it, or unless hospitalization (beyond emergency-room treatment) was required.‡

Procedures required to make an effective citizen's arrest vary from one place to another. In some jurisdictions, the citizen must take physical custody of the accused and bring him to a police station. Obviously, this may prevent battered women from using this procedure themselves and make it very difficult for witnesses to use it. In other jurisdictions, an arresting citizen need merely identify and locate the attacker, describe the facts of the crime, and state a desire to make a citizen's arrest to a police officer. The officer then has the duty to take the accused person into physical custody. This is a much more sensible procedure and could be used in many cases where police answer a battered woman's call for help but refuse to make an arrest.

Learning about citizen's-arrest procedure in your jurisdiction can have two effects. It may provide an alternative means of removing a dangerous man from the home long enough to help the woman escape. It may also encourage the police department to reevaluate its policies regarding arrest in these cases. In appropriate jurisdictions, groups working on wife abuse may want to advise advocates and clients to ask for police assistance in making citizen's arrests. They may want to work out guidelines and policies with local police officials. Police may be interested in cooperating with these procedures, because they relieve them of the responsibility for making legal judgments about whether to arrest, or it may serve as the initiative for developing appropriate arrest policies in behalf of battered women.

Sexism has, to a large extent, determined the way the legal system treats battered women. Likewise, a social and economic system based on the presumed superiority of some people to others has determined the way it treats working, poor, and minority peo-

‡ Other criminal charges, such as assault with intent to kill, aggravated assault, or illegal possession of dangerous weapons may be appropriate, depending on local law. Some form of assault, battery, or threat charges will almost always be appropriate.

ple, male and female. Constitutional amendments and historic Supreme Court cases have not prevented the arrest and jailing of poor and minority people in numbers dramatically out of proportion to their numbers in the entire population.

Groups working to change police policies and practices in wife-abuse cases should be ever aware of the dangers inherent in relying on authoritarian solutions and most especially of advocating more police intervention into the lives of poor and minority people. Susan Jackson has reminded us that:

> Because arrest has historically been used as an establishment tool for discrimination against minority and other unpopular groups, historically the struggle against discrimination has often taken the form of a struggle against arrest.*

PROSECUTION: WHAT BEST SERVES THE NEEDS OF BATTERED WOMEN?

One major source of differences between prosecutors and advocates for battered women is the prosecutor's understanding of and identification with the law-enforcement and criminal-justice system. Often, wife beating is not a high-priority crime for even the most conscientious among them. Many are truly confused about whether prosecution benefits battered women, but their main concern is making law enforcement and prosecution appear to work in highly publicized criminal cases and those with unanimous condemnation: crime against old people, public crimes of violence, random street crime. Prosecutors all know, for example, that no victim has the *right* to have her attacker prosecuted, while many victims and advocates assume there is such a moral, if not legal, right. The legal system could not function if every violation of the law had to be prosecuted and tried. Advocates for battered women who expect to work with the criminal-justice system should study the principles and mechanisms used by local prosecutors to determine what cases are formally prosecuted, and should research the alternatives to formal prosecution—both those available locally and those used elsewhere. Advocates' ob-

* Jackson, op. cit., p. 16.

jectives must be carefully chosen with the goal of enhancing the ability of battered women to use the power available to prosecutors to escape from or stop the abuse.

The cardinal rule of the criminal-justice system is that it exists to punish criminals who threaten the peace and order of the state. It is concerned with redressing *public,* rather than *private,* wrongs and is, because of this focus, inevitably more concerned with the offender than the victim. Once the victim has performed her essential service as the primary witness in the state's case against the accused, she is no longer an object of any interest to the criminal-justice system. It is the job of advocates to create more sensitivity and concern for the victim.

The accused, however, becomes the focus of intense debate and study, and considerable public expense. Should he be severely punished in the hope that his fate will serve as an example and deter others from similar conduct? Or should he be "studied" in order to learn his real problems so that he can be "rehabilitated" and commit no further crimes? The American criminal-justice system has no definitive answers to these questions, nor to the questions about what behavior is worthy of punishment and whether the responsibility for "crime" is entirely individual or is largely social and/or economic. As a result of confusion about these fundamental questions, the ability of the system to deliver what a broad spectrum of people consider "justice" is severely limited. As a result, battered women and their advocates must organize their demands in such a way that they can become the subject of positive negotiation and program building. The deep confusion about the role of the legal system in providing justice for individuals and groups in conflict should also be given careful attention by advocates seeking to make it work for them.

Initially, battered women must recognize that they play a somewhat secondary role in a prosecutor's scheme of things. Technically victims are merely "complaining witnesses" in the state's case against the abuser. Of course, if there are no other witnesses and the state's complaining witness decides not to testify, there is not much evidence and not much of a case. If police were trained to investigate wife abuse properly, and potential victims were educated in the importance of prompt complaints and preserving evidence, the victim would often play a much more decisive role in the prosecution.

Because police procedure and pretrial prosecutorial preparation are often very poor in these cases, battered women are often left with the full responsibility for providing the prosecution's case and, therefore, the ultimate decision to prosecute. Given any understanding of the criminal-justice system, the decision to prosecute is often a difficult one for individuals to make, even when the accused is a stranger. The fear of reprisals and genuine concern for the accused forces many women to reconsider the wisdom of prosecuting even seriously abusive spouses. In many cases, their economic dependence compounds the quandary. Perhaps one of the most important services advocates can provide is to help the victim sort out her own goals and alternatives in order to decide whether criminal prosecution will benefit her.

Advocates will find that it is worth investing time and energy in attempting to sensitize prosecutorial personnel and in pushing for the adoption of policies and guidelines reflecting a serious commitment to prosecute wife-abuse cases—not because the result in any one case will be gratifying but because the threat of effective prosecution is probably the most effective weapon the criminal-justice system can create to delegitimize the popular pastime of wife beating.

"Prosecutorial Discretion" and the Decision Not to Prosecute

The decision to charge someone formally with a crime can be made only by a prosecutor. Although police or victims may sign a complaint accusing someone of violating a law, only the prosecutor can force the accused to answer the charge. Criminal laws describe the prohibited conduct (and the penalty for violation); they do not require that every person accused of a prohibited act be charged with or tried for a crime. Prosecutors have a great deal of latitude in deciding which accusations will become the subject of a formal charge and which will not. There is virtually no review of this decision and virtually no guidelines, so prosecutors tend to exercise this power of "prosecutorial discretion" on the basis of their own values, their perception of society's view of the crime charged, and the likelihood of success in getting a conviction. Their calculation of these factors and their decision to prosecute or not is final.†

The aforementioned study by James Bannon illustrates what most victims and advocates of battered women know; prosecutors frequently exercise this discretion to deflect the cases of battered women from the official criminal process. In Bannon's study, 92 per cent of the cases were not prosecuted. Often, battered women's cases are "resolved" by referring them to other mechanisms in the legal system established to protect them. For example, in Detroit, most of the cases that were not prosecuted were referred to civil courts for peace bonds. In many places, women are referred to civil courts without being told that civil remedies are not exclusive: they do not all rule out prosecution.

In some areas, prosecutors refuse to go ahead with a prosecution on behalf of a battered wife unless she has already begun a divorce action. They reason that the divorce action is a good test of her sincere desire to use the legal system to resolve her problems regardless of its consequences for the marriage. This kind of policy tends to overlook the often staggering cost of obtaining a divorce as well as other factors that may determine the success of a prosecution: court personnel who advise her not to follow through, the time and expense involved in coming to court for repeated continuances obtained by the husband, or the lack of child-care facilities in the courthouse.

Prosecutorial discretion means that prosecutors may decide who must formally answer criminal charges, and what those charges will be. A defendant may challenge a specific decision to charge him or her with a particular crime, alleging that decision was made on the basis of some irrelevant factor and amounts to discriminatory use of the prosecutor's power. However, the decision *not* to charge or the decision to charge for a lesser offense cannot be challenged by an individual victim. In some cases, a large group of victims who believe nonenforcement of specific laws amounts to discrimination against them may challenge a prosecutor, but the *individual* whose attacker is not prosecuted has no recourse. For this reason, it is important for advocates of battered women to take a systematic approach to working with

† See Comment, "Prosecutorial Discretion in the Initiation of Criminal Complaints," 42 So. Cal. L. Rev. 59 (1969).

prosecutors and/or counseling women about using the criminal process.

Usually, the decision about whether to prosecute is made on a case-by-case basis, after considering four or five basic issues: the extent of the injuries and their seriousness, the defendant's apparent intent, the victim's desire to prosecute, the defendant's history of similar or other violent conduct—especially whether he has a criminal record—and the prosecutor's own estimate (based, among other things, on the existence of tangible evidence and other witnesses) of the likelihood of success at trial.

Advocate groups working closely with district attorneys and the police may make a large difference in a prosecutor's estimate of these factors. They may, for example, have convinced the police to preserve evidence and/or investigate these incidents in such a way as to substantially increase the likelihood of obtaining a conviction. Later in this chapter, we discuss a number of other things that advocate groups may do to improve the likelihood that prosecutors will pursue these cases. Advocates should take care to concentrate their efforts on the most serious cases of abuse, which, if unprosecuted, are most likely to result in even more serious harm to the battered woman. Insisting on prosecution of every single case is unrealistic and not in the best interest of many victims.

In reality, many criminal laws describing the conduct of men who abuse their wives are virtually useless to battered women. In some places, this is because of a specific law or informal understanding that such matters belong in family, rather than criminal, court. In others, it is merely the result of prosecutors' use of their discretion not to prosecute particular cases. In still others, prosecutors have created internal alternatives to the regular criminal process, so that a woman who takes her complaint to the district attorney's office will be automatically referred to a "family bureau" or "domestic" division of the district attorney's office, where their cases are eventually settled by way of informal hearing, referral, or conciliation. This illustrates one of the ways in which the criminal-justice system has attempted, in recent years, to substitute a less formal alternative procedure for a prosecutor's decision to ignore entirely those cases he does not want to prosecute.

Advocates should learn whether civil (family) courts have "exclusive" or "concurrent" jurisdiction over wife-abuse cases. When there is "concurrent jurisdiction," the victim may have a choice about whether her assailant will be prosecuted in a criminal court or sent through a "civil" system, which is more likely to provide mandatory conciliation or counseling and will probably not result in imprisonment or any criminal record. When jurisdiction is "concurrent," victims have the option of using the coercion of the civil-court process to let their husbands know they intend to stop the abuse and, perhaps, to get help for the accused. If this does not work, they have not sacrificed the threat of a criminal prosecution, which threat is often more effective than the prosecution itself (although generally only as effective as the prosecutor's reputation for serious prosecution). "Exclusive" civil-court jurisdiction is the worst alternative, from the point of view of battered women, because it immunizes their assailants from the threat of criminal prosecution. Exclusive criminal jurisdiction may render the threat of prosecution meaningless, it puts the battered woman in an all-or-nothing position the first time she seeks help from the legal system. Advocates should press for concurrent jurisdiction.

THE MOST COMMON CRIMINAL CHARGES IN WIFE-BEATING CASES

1. A woman who has been hit, slapped, punched, kicked, or assaulted in any other way has the right to expect police protection and arrest of the assaulter. The most likely criminal charge appropriate to any case in which the attacker made *contact* with the victim is assault and battery. "Disorderly conduct" and "disturbing the peace" are not appropriate charges.
2. If serious injury resulted, the assailant should be charged with some form of aggravated assault or other felony.
3. A woman with reason to fear that her assailant's threats to inflict serious bodily injury will be carried out may have the person making the threats arrested for assault (in some jurisdictions), for "menacing" (making serious, believable threats), or for "reckless endangerment," where a weapon such as a gun is used to back up the threat. A previous history of violence between the parties is reason to fear the threats may be carried out, as is a history of violence with others on the part of the assailant.

4. Severe beatings and/or attacks with deadly weapons should be treated as felonies, such as aggravated assault, assault with intent to kill, or assault with a deadly weapon. In some cases, attempted murder is the proper charge, depending on the assailant's apparent intent and statements.

5. A man who enters property owned or rented separately by his wife and who has been notified of her desire that he not enter the premises may be charged with criminal trespass if he enters without her consent. The woman should have a copy of the lease, deed, or order of ejectment to show police. Otherwise they may not arrest on trespass charges. If physical force has been used to gain entry, the man may be charged with breaking and entering.

DIVERSION

The word "diversion" has many meanings, all of them related to the process whereby an accusation of crime is channeled out of the regular criminal process. These cases are literally "diverted," or turned away, from the usual process that leads to trial and a finding of guilt or innocence, with some penalty imposed for guilt.

Many communities now have some form of diversion in their criminal-justice system. Generally, these programs seek to screen out of the regular criminal process all the less serious cases, which might be more quickly and appropriately resolved in a setting other than a courtroom, in a process offering a wider range of alternatives than fine or sentence. The director of the American Bar Association's Special Committee on Resolution of Minor Disputes describes the impetus for many such programs:

> A visit to a small-crime court is all that is necessary to prove the point [that courts are not the best places to resolve these conflicts]. A harried and overworked judge presides over structured chaos in the misdemeanor courtroom. Every conceivable wrong-doing, dutifully codified into a criminal act, is before him: squabbling neighbors, fighting spouses, owners of indiscreet animals, revengeful complainants and belligerent defendants.‡

‡ Fred Dellapa, "Mediation and Community Dispute Center." In Maria Roy, ed. *Battered Women: A Psychosociological Study in Domestic Violence* (New York: Van Nostrand Reinhold, 1977).

Clearly, diversion is a boon to "harried and overworked" judges and to prosecutors attempting to mete out justice in the structured chaos of the misdemeanor courtroom. Unfortunately, we are not told much about how the squabbling neighbors, fighting spouses, and owners of indiscreet animals feel about being structured into the chaos (or out of it), and we are left to wonder whether the cases of battered wives should be resolved along with those of neighbors squabbling over loud stereos or owners of indiscreet dogs—either within or outside of the formal criminal court. The juxtaposition of all these cases certainly tends to minimize the extent of harm done to battered women.

Advocates for battered women may be able to use the diversion process to improve the treatment of victims, inside the process as well as outside. Unlike many of the people who champion diversion for wife-abuse cases, we are not suggesting that it is a good idea because the victims want nothing more than to save the marriage and/or help for their attackers but because the criminal-justice system itself is unlikely to provide any help beyond confining a few of the most violent men.

Cases may be diverted at any point in the criminal process prior to conviction, and may be channeled into a wide variety of programs. Most often, diversion comes prior to prosecution, in order to save the largest amount of time, money, and energy possible. And it generally results in the parties' "resolving" their conflicts by way of some more or less formal agreement reached after an informal fact-finding process conducted by a person who is not a judge. The system that allows victims to file "private" criminal complaints after a prosecutor decides not to initiate prosecution may be seen as a primitive form of diversion. Usually the parties are pressured to drop the action and/or resolve their differences by way of an agreement. Extreme persistence by the complainant and/or a failure to reach an agreement may result in formal prosecution. This technique was developed to save prosecutors from having to try minor cases and is the way in which most wife-abuse cases are processed by the criminal-justice system in many places.

Since this early form of diversion, many more programs have been created, some of which remove prosecutors almost entirely from the process and some of which offer the promise of responding more directly to the needs of battered women. Most still treat battered women as individuals with interpersonal or intrapersonal problems that result in social conflicts (these cases are not treated as those with common legal, social, and economic causes differing from those involving loud stereos and indiscreet dogs). A description of several "community dispute settlement" programs to which many battered women are referred by prosecutors in several cities will illustrate the advantages and disadvantages of this approach to diversion.

The Minneapolis Citizen's Dispute Settlement Project handles primarily neighborhood disputes and spouse abuse. A local official cites "tremendous" "emotional and oftentimes financial pressures" upon battered women as one of the reasons for attempting to divert these cases. Many battered women are subjected to such pressures, which are hardly considered sufficient reason to excuse a witness from testifying at an ordinary trial, much less to support a system-wide policy of diverting cases out of the criminal system. However, the test of the program's value is not its inspiration but whether it offers the victim a better solution than criminal trial. Because the "settlement" reached through the dispute project is likely to specify actions to be taken by both parties, clarify issues that may have been the subject of specific disputes, and prohibit specific action, it may in fact be more valuable to the battered woman than a criminal trial, which results in a stern warning, a suspended sentence, a fine, or a brief term in jail. The fact that the Minneapolis project works closely with local women's support groups and offers referrals from a resource book compiled with the cooperation of a battered women's consortium and with a community health-and-welfare survey on the problems of battered women in the area, increases its potential for helping victims and certainly gives it an advantage over current practices in the ordinary criminal process.

Follow-up is an essential but often neglected component of diversion programs. In Minneapolis, the agreements are signed, filed with the dispute center, and monitored by way of a telephone call after two weeks, three months, and six months. The follow-up may be cursory however, and many of the agreements may not be specific enough to settle an underlying dispute or may not be enforceable.

The entire "dispute settlement" process assumes, of course, that there are specific disagreements, perhaps even legitimate differences of opinion between the parties, and that a rational discussion and agreement about specific behavior is all that is necessary to stop the violence. Often, this is far from the case, especially where the beatings are frequent.

An annual evaluation of the Minneapolis program revealed that it had the effect of reducing the number of domestic cases in which police became involved, and that parties who had a history of violence were more likely to present their cases at the dispute center than they were to call the police. The annual report suggests that this is because victims knew that police would not arrest, knowing that prosecutors would not prosecute. The results of the annual evaluation do not prove that a dispute-settlement approach is superior to treatment of wife abuse in the criminal system. But, obviously, dispute settlement is preferred over a policy of "benign" neglect. Whether it is adequate to meet the needs of most battered women remains to be seen.

COMMUNITY MEDIATION

Mediation Center, Coram, New York
Another model of mediation/diversion has been established in a suburban/rural area and appears to function quite differently from the Dispute Settlement Center in Minneapolis. The differences are not merely those one would assume from the differences in character of the locations The Coram center relies largely on trained volunteer community members and sees its goal as allowing "parties to self-resolve their disputes":

> Arrest records with their stigma, court delays, and attorney's fees are all avoided. Impersonal bureaucracies do not impose arbitrary rules. Disputing parties come to the realization they can reassert control over their own problem and their own lives.

This approach follows in part from a conviction that a breakdown in community functions is responsible for the overload in the criminal-justice system, and tries to revitalize that community by substituting its judgment for the official machinery of the criminal system. This philosophy suggests a return to the institution of the community "moot," in which conflicts in the community were settled before the whole community, relying on mediators to help get out all the facts and reflect the community consensus about the best resolution. In this model, clients come both from official referrals from justice and mental-health agencies and by word of mouth. Their services and referrals are free, but many private arbitration or mediation services charge fees based on the time and number of parties involved.

Other Mediation/Referral Diversion Models

The Rainbow Family Crisis and Counseling Program, Phoenix, Arizona (3251 W. Thomas Road, Phoenix, AZ 85009) is the "only diversion program to deal uniquely with spouse abuse." This program provides immediate crisis intervention in domestic-violence situations, as well as ongoing counseling. Its ability to provide immediate intervention distinguishes it from most services, in which there is a lag of several days to weeks between the violence and any attempt at mediation. "Crisis-intervention experts" believe that immediacy is a key to success and use this belief to argue for police training in crisis intervention. If outside agencies can provide the same kind of 24-hour-a-day, 365-day-a-year response availability and have personnel trained in crisis intervention, there is hope that police intervention will not be the only solution to emergency help for battered women. In the later, counseling phase, the Rainbow project concentrates on helping clients to develop "new skills of communication, higher levels of self-esteem and self-acceptance, and new coping skills." A violent husband cannot be diverted into this program without consent of the victim, and the injuries received must not have been serious enough to require admission to a hospital. Counseling groups meet for six months on a weekly basis, and the program makes further referrals to other community agencies.

Washington, D.C.'s Citizen Complaint Center, on the other hand, conducts crisis intervention sessions by police referral only and operates on a work-week-only schedule (8:30 A.M. to 5 P.M. Monday to Friday). Its services are not available during the times most domestic assaults occur. At the Center, a trained social worker conducts intake interviews to determine whether a specific case should be prosecuted or referred for counseling. The victim is consulted about this decision. The decision to prosecute is usually made after an informal hearing at which an attempt is made to define the areas of conflict. The major drawbacks to this kind of program appear to be its conventional hours, its lack of immediacy (hearings are held several weeks after the assault and may be postponed for defendant's failure to appear), and its failure to concentrate on the specific problems of battered women. The advantages appear to be the individual decision to prosecute or refer to other agencies, the attempt to mediate prior to prosecution, and an effort to consult the victim about the decision to prosecute or not. In addition, personnel at the Complaint Center are able to counsel victims on the availability of noncriminal alternatives such as civil protective orders.

Finally, a Battered Women's Project of the Citizen-Victim Complaint Unit worked with local women's groups in behalf of battered women in Milwaukee, Wisconsin, but is no longer funded. This project counseled victims and made referrals to women's groups (which taught women how to file for their own divorces) and other groups providing services needed by battered women. Defendants were ordered to appear at the prosecutor's office for a conference and were usually placed on a form of "informal probation," which would result in a formal charge if the conditions of the probation were violated.

Charles B. Schudson, a Milwaukee County assistant district attorney who helped with this project, commented that only the "first offender" can really benefit from the threat of prosecution as motivation to become involved in counseling or other programs to which he might be referred. The same might be said about any informal or diversion process.* Women whose husbands are impressed by or afraid of the law or who cannot risk the publicity or criminal record that might be attached to a criminal trial will benefit most from diversion programs.

---

* This is true for all the diversion programs that are simply "deferred prosecution," without counseling or referral. This is probably the most common form of diversion; it does nothing but warn the accused that a repeat performance will result in formal prosecution.

Victim/Witness Units

Almost every major American city and many smaller towns now have official victim/witness advocates or victim/witness units as part of the local prosecutor's office. The purpose of these units is to encourage people who have witnessed criminal activity to participate in trials for the prosecution as witnesses. Generally, they do not provide counseling or referral and focus primarily on the mechanics of getting a witness to cooperate with police and come to court to testify against a defendant.

Some victim/witness units do provide crisis-intervention and social-service referrals. The Pima County (Tucson, Arizona) Victim-Witness Unit is particularly sensitive to the relation between police and battered women, noting that "In almost every one of the marital discord police calls, law-enforcement officials would prefer to divert the spouses to community social-service and/or mental-health agencies . . ." than arrest and refer them to the criminal-justice system. The Pima County unit is an exception in that it recognizes that battered women have special needs and interests in common. For example, it has concluded that the fear of following through on criminal prosecutions suggests the possibility of economic coercion, which could be eliminated through job-training programs with placement capabilities.

The victim/witness approach to battered women's problems will probably never serve more than a few women whose cases do survive all the diversion mechanisms. In those cases, battered women should use all the services available and advocates should push for the creation of well-staffed free day-care facilities and help with transportation and witness fees for each court session. Local prosecutors should consider hiring a battered women's advocate to provide counseling and referrals and liaison with police and other relevant parts of the legal system.

ADVOCATES AND THE CRIMINAL-JUSTICE SYSTEM: WORKING WITH PROSECUTORS

Battered women need legal counseling and practical help throughout their interaction with the criminal-justice system. They need to know how the system works generally, how special exceptions have been made for their situations, and how to challenge those which may not be legitimate. Ideally, advocate groups should have their own legal counsel, with whom they could consult about general policies and local practices as well as specific cases. Short of that, they should seek friendly lawyers with extensive experience in the criminal-justice system (defense attorneys as well as prosecutors and judges) to conduct training on applicable laws and procedures.

Some groups working on wife abuse, such as Women Against Abuse, in Philadelphia, have established formal liaison with local prosecutors and are now conducting intake interviews for prosecutors in their own, nearby offices. There are advantages to this arrangement for both advocates and prosecutors, but probably the greatest advantages are those experienced by the battered women who are automatically referred by the prosecutors to their advocates. In one meeting with a trained advocate, the battered woman can get advice about whether to file a civil or criminal petition, about whether she should consider filing for a divorce, how to get support for her children, and, in some cases, how to get into a temporary shelter or find a group to provide moral support and practical help until she gets relocated.

Advocate groups interested in this model should carefully consider some of its drawbacks, which include proximity to and identification with the prosecutor, daytime and generally downtown hours, and possible accessibility of their records to the prosecutor and police. Short of establishing formal liaison with the prosecutor's office, advocates can have considerable impact on how battered women's cases are treated. In addition to setting up their own counseling and referral system for battered women, they can have their own intake interviewing process, which seeks to document witnesses, counsels the victim on how to preserve evidence, and provides a written reminder of the events in the incident, should the victim later testify in court. They can establish a court-accompaniment program, which provides the victim with moral support and an advocate to speak in her behalf if necessary (see Chapter VIII). And, if resources permit, they can offer independent legal advice about all the available procedures, their likely outcomes, and their interrelation.

Finally, advocate groups should not ignore their ability to influence policies and practices of local prosecutors. In cities where these are elected, the treatment of battered women and other victims of violence against women may be made an election issue. In any town or city, advocate groups should meet with prosecutors to question them on their policies related to battered women. Some of the most important questions that will apply to almost any setting include:

1. Do prosecutors distinguish between assaults of strangers and of spouses? For what purposes? Do they distinguish between cases in which the parties are formally married and those in which they are just living together? If they do, why?

2. When a battered woman's case comes to the prosecutor's attention, is it automatically referred to some other division or department for screening and preliminary attention? If so, where is it referred to and for what purpose?

3. What are men who hit, slap, kick, or punch their wives charged with?

4. Are there any written guidelines for prosecutors to follow in deciding whether to prosecute a wife-beating case or what to charge?

5. Are these cases usually channeled into a diversion program? If so, what remedies can victims get there? Is there any record of how many defendants who go into the diversion program reappear in the criminal process? What effect does the diversion program have on a victim's ability to have her husband arrested for further violence?

6. Does the prosecutor keep a record of wife-abuse cases under that category, or under some other category that would enable her/him to give an accurate answer to the following questions:

    a. How many battered women seek help from your office each year?

    b. How are their cases usually disposed of?

    c. What services, if any, do you provide them? Victim/witness programs? Referral to shelters? To battered women's groups?

    d. Based on your records, do you believe the criminal-justice system is doing all it can to help battered women? How many come to your office to report more than one incident?

e. How many cases has your office processed in the past year in which the *defendant* was a battered woman? What was she charged with? What was the result?

f. Who is responsible for enforcing civil protection orders, peace bonds, or temporary restraining orders? Does the prosecutor advise police on whether to arrest or not for alleged violations of civil orders? Do prosecutors routinely check to see if men accused of criminal assaults or threats have been the subject of a civil order?

g. How long does a battered woman have to wait before getting an appointment with this office? What is the average length of time between the assault and a criminal trial if any?

h. Are there any informal or formal policies that attempt to discourage battered women from pressing criminal charges or filing a private complaint? If so, at what points are they advised against doing so and for what reasons?

i. How do you prepare the victim for a trial?

j. Could you refer a victim to a shelter, a battered women's group, or other community agency? Does your office often make this kind of referral? Do you have a handbook for referrals? Does your office follow up on referrals or evaluate agencies referred to?

Advocates are in a position to be very helpful to prosecutors who are interested in assisting battered women. They can do much of the thorough interviewing and documentation that police and intake officers at prosecutors' offices rarely do; they can help a victim track down witnesses and help both victim and witnesses prepare for trial. In offices with interested prosecutors, it may be possible for advocates to be trained as legal workers and hired to work on battered women's and similar cases, such as rape.

Groups should be careful, however, to assess their own goals and those of their clients before they invest a great deal of energy in doing work that the city should provide through the prosecutor's office. If there is no formal relationship between prosecutor and advocate group, advocates should concentrate on assisting in some of the most serious cases. Advocate groups may also want to act as consultants to a diversion program and take referrals from diversion, or train personnel in diversion programs in the special needs of and services available to battered women.

Communities that have established victim/witness programs and/or community mediation centers that attempt to meet the needs of battered women include:

1. Dade County, Florida, Victim-Advocate Program
   515 N.W. 7th St.
   Suite 112
   Miami, FL 33125
   (emergency shelter by police referral only; some counseling; LEAA-funded)
2. Rainbow Diversion Project
   3251 W. Thomas Rd., Bldg. B
   Phoenix, AZ 85009
   (part of Maricopa County Adult Diversion Program of the District Attorney's Office)
3. Community Mediation Center
   356 Middle Country Rd.
   Coram, NY 11727
   (specializes in "neighborhood dispute resolution" through use of community members trained as mediators)
4. Northwest Mediation Service
   1700 Westlake Ave., N., Suite 420
   Seattle, WA 98109
   (private, fees charged; relation to court system not clear)
5. Columbus Night Prosecutor Program
   Police Prosecutor's Office
   100 West Gay, Room 105
   Columbus, OH 43215
   (handles private criminal complaints; attempts to divert through mediation.)
6. Pima County Attorney Victim-Witness Unit
   900 Pima County Courts Bldg.
   111 W. Congress
   Tucson, AZ 85701

To find out about the many theoretical approaches and practical explanations for alternatives to formal court processes, including the community moot, a publication entitled *Readings on*

Community Mediation of Interpersonal Disputes—collected and printed by the Pennsylvania Pre-trial Justice Program of the American Friends Service Committee, 1300 Fifth Avenue, Pittsburgh, PA 15219—is useful. This program is very prodiversion and does not address the issue of battered women directly.

COURTS

Judging the Judge

Judges sit at the pinnacle of the legal system. They get an eagle's-eye view of the problems of battered women. Their perception of the issue is filtered by the great distance that separates the public from the judge; the issues and incidents they learn about are screened by police, prosecutors, and the socioeconomic system, which discourages battered women from taking their assailants to court. They are the ultimate arbiters in every spouse-abuse case that is not diverted from the criminal process by formal or informal means. They may also decide who is eligible for a divorce, how much money a father should pay to support his children, and whether a woman is entitled to compensation for the years of unpaid labor she contributed to the home and child raising.

In theory, the legal system is set up to insulate judges from all kinds of pressures that might color their judgment or influence their decision in a particular case. They are supposed to put aside all their personal sympathies and allegiances and impartially evaluate the facts before them on the basis of nothing but the evidence presented in the courtroom. Of course, this ideal is impossible to realize. No one can overcome sympathies and prejudices based on personal experiences and race, class, and sex identification by an act of will. Sometimes, the result is that battered women end up feeling more like the criminal than the victim.

This does not mean that battered women and their advocates should avoid dealing with judges. Most advocate programs have tended to concentrate their energies on working with and/or reforming policies and practices in police departments and prosecutors' offices, to the exclusion of judges and judicial officers. While putting the greatest resources into the areas that have the most immediate and widespread impact on the lives of the greatest number of battered women is wise, people working on wife abuse should not ignore the important role of judges and the courts in the lives of abuse victims.

Advocates should consider instituting some sort of court-monitoring program to learn what particular judges tend to do in wife-abuse cases. Volunteers can monitor judges on a regular basis and establish a profile of how cases that do survive all the screening mechanisms are resolved by the courts. This information can prove very useful in documenting the inadequacies of the legal system's treatment of battered women and helping police, prosecutors, and judges to revise their treatment of victims and offenders in these cases (see the "Sample Court Monitor Form" on the following pages).

SAMPLE COURT MONITOR FORM

Name of Observer
Date
Courtroom
Name of Judge

1. *General Court Calendar*

1. How many cases were scheduled for trial in this courtroom for this day?
2. How many were continued to a later date? How many dismissed? For what reasons?
3. How many miscellaneous matters were heard by this judge on this day (e.g., adoption petitions granted, argument on various motions, guilty pleas other than in spouse-abuse cases)?

2. *Cases Involving Battered Women*

NOTE: IF MORE THAN ONE CASE IS TRIED IN THIS COURTROOM IN ONE DAY, FILL OUT A SEPARATE FORM, BEGINNING WITH QUESTION 2, FOR EACH CASE, AND STAPLE FORMS TOGETHER.

Name of Victim   Name of Prosecutor
Name of Defendant   Name of Defense Lawyer

Charge.
Trial or guilty plea?

If guilty plea
To what charge did defendant plead guilty?
Was sentence imposed immediately or postponed?
If postponed, to what date and what courtroom?
If sentence imposed, what result?
Record any outstanding remarks during sentencing
(a) by defendant or his attorney,

(b) by prosecutor,

(c) by judge.

If trial
Jury or judge trial elected?
If postponed for jury trial, to what room and what date?

If judge

A. The prosecution's case:
   How long did prosecution case take?

   What evidence was presented?

   What arguments presented for conviction?

   What sentence requested? Reasons for the request.

B. The defense case:
   How long did the defense take?
   What evidence was presented for the defense?

   What witnesses?
   What arguments presented to avoid conviction? Sentence?

C. Cross-examination:
   Of prosecution witnesses (by defense):
   Did the defendant testify?
   If so, did the prosecution cross-examine him?
   For how long?
   What were the most important questions asked?

   What other defense witnesses were cross-examined by the prosecutor?

Of defense witnesses (by prosecution):
Did the victim testify?
If so, did the prosecution cross-examine her?
For how long?
What were the most important questions?

Do you believe the victim was adequately prepared
  (a) generally?
  (b) for the cross-examination?
Explain.

D. Judge's attitude
  Did the judge express any attitude toward the defendant, the victim, or either lawyer?
  If so, what was the attitude and how was it expressed?

If jury trial
Selection:
  How long was the jury-selection process?
  Did the judge or attorney question prospective jurors? Were there any questions that suggested a particular attitude about this case? About women in general?

  Any statements from the jurors that reflected an attitude? What were they?

  What did the jury look like? How many were: Male: White:
                                             Female: Minority:

  What were jurors' approximate ages?
  Did you learn their occupations?

Juror Reaction:
  Whom did jurors appear to pay most attention to? Judge? Other witnesses? (Which ones?) Prosecutor? Defense attorney? Each other?

  What significant juror reactions did you observe? (Snoring, snickering, whispering, expressions of sympathy, appearing to identify with victim or defendant?)

  Deliberation: Note the most significant instructions given the

jury just prior to deliberation; try to get a copy
from the prosecution and attach; otherwise record
as accurately as possible

How long did jury deliberate?
Did jurors ask for clarification of instructions at any point during
deliberation? Did they ask to review evidence or testimony? What
was their final verdict?

(Advocates should attempt to interview jurors to learn as much as
possible about the deliberation and what facts and evidence
seemed most important to them. CAUTION: In some cases,
judges may order that jurors not be interviewed. Unless such an
order is made, interviewing jurors *after the verdict has been announced* is perfectly legal, although jurors' wishes for anonymity
should be respected.)

Was sentencing scheduled? If so, for what time and place?
Did defense attorney announce s/he would appeal?
Was defendant freed on bail pending appeal or sentencing?
If bail continued, in what amount?

3. *General Observations*

Did you observe any comments or behavior that suggested that the
race or economic status of the victim and defendant influenced the
attitude or behavior of the judge, the prosecutor, the defense attorney, the other witnesses (e.g., police), or the jury? Describe in detail.

Did you observe anything that suggested that one or more of the
participants in the trial did not consider it a serious or important
matter? Describe in detail.

What do you think could have been done to improve the experience
for the victim or help her obtain a better result?

Did the judge make any remarks of a sexist or racist nature? Did he
express disbelief in or impatience with the victim? Describe in detail.

Did the defense lawyer make any remarks or otherwise use sexism
or racism to help the defendant? If so, describe in detail.

Monitor should attend later proceeding to follow up, or see that another monitor does, and attach results of that proceeding to this form.

Court monitoring can also be very effective in training advocates and for gathering information to prepare campaigns for strategic reforms in prosecutors' and court procedures. The court-monitoring sheets can provide important data to be used as part of a public-education campaign at election time or as part of a media campaign to raise consciousness about the treatment of battered women in the legal process. It may also help advocate groups raise funds for shelters, court watching or other programs designed to remedy the deficiencies documented by the questionnaires. Finally, court monitoring programs are the best possible source of information about how the legal system deals with serious cases of wife abuse in your locality. Without this information, it is difficult, if not impossible, to make intelligent decisions about how to use the limited resources of advocates to make the biggest possible improvement in the system on behalf of battered wives.

Short of an all-out court-monitoring program, advocates should attempt to meet with the presiding judge in the jurisdiction to discuss judicial attitudes and policies toward wife-abuse cases and their disposition.† Advocates should be prepared to explain why prosecution is valuable in some cases, and which ones. Among the things judges may need to be told are

Spouse abuse tends to escalate from relatively minor blows to more serious attacks of increasing frequency and severity.

The failure of the criminal-justice system to intervene in "domestic" problems may well be responsible for the number of women jailed for spouse murder.

The threat of successful criminal prosecution and serious penalties being imposed is an effective deterrent for many men but only if that threat is supported by consistent policies on the part of police, prosecutors, and judges.

† For a general survey report on how judges tend to deal with wife-abuse cases, see Parnas, "Judicial Response to Intra-Family Violence," 54 Minn. L. Rev. 585 (1970).

Battered women must be allowed to decide for themselves whether their economic dependence on an assailant makes prosecution worthwhile. Victims should be informed of alternative remedies but permitted to choose from among all those authorized by law.

Judges should also be questioned about their knowledge of and willingness to use a number of alternative sentencing procedures. In some areas, judges will impose supervised probation with the condition that a husband not attack his wife again or with more demanding conditions such as mandatory counseling. Other alternatives include ordering men to serve "work-release" time, which allows them to continue at their jobs to avoid depriving the victim and her children of his income. Advocates should study all the alternative-sentencing remedies available to other criminal defendants to determine if there are any more appropriate for wife beaters than those currently available.

Extreme examples of judicial prejudice and/or incompetence can be brought to the attention of the local presiding judge, the bar association, or the judicial conference. All these agencies have some responsibility for upholding the professional image of the law and the courtroom, especially as these are personified in the judge. Advocates should, however, be prepared to provide careful documentation of such grievances.

Judging the Legal System: Suing court administrators, prosecutors, muncipalities, and other official agencies for failing to protect battered women

As explained in the section on prosecutorial discretion, no victim has a *right* to have her assailant charged with a crime. Until very recently, it was assumed that this meant that battered women must simply rely on the remedies provided or forget about trying to obtain help or protection from the legal system. However, as battered women have become more outspoken, and more and more lawyers, legal workers, and advocates have become interested in their cause, a number of theories have been used to challenge official policies that ignore their needs and their rights.

Most of the ensuing legal actions are undertaken in behalf of a group of "named plaintiff" individuals on behalf of all other battered women who have been discouraged from using the legal system or given inadequate or inappropriate advice or remedies there. Defendants have included chiefs of police and the head of the New York City Probation Department, charged with enforcing civil orders of protection. Family-court officials have been sued as defendants, as have entire muncipalities.

The largest single hurdle faced by all these lawsuits is the issue of who—if anyone—has a legal and enforceable duty to protect battered women? The tendency toward separate and parallel "family court" systems further complicates the question with regard to married women.

Several of the legal theories that have been used in recent cases are discussed in some detail below. All have one central theme: battered women are legally entitled to the same protection from physical abuse as any other citizen. The state cannot maintain a "hands off" attitude toward violent crime merely because it takes place behind closed doors in the privacy of the parties' home or because the parties are married or involved in a particular economic, emotional, or sexual relationship.

Large-scale lawsuits involving numerous plaintiffs and/or defendants (usually referred to as class actions) can be very time-consuming and expensive ways to call attention to or remedy a problem. It is probably wise to view them as last resorts, when every other form of negotiation and cooperation has been refused or has failed to produce necessary improvement in the treatment of battered women. In addition to the mechanical problems involved in class actions, they require effective use of the press and the news media to maximize their impact on public officials, and require a commitment to organizing by many people in addition to the legal team filing the action.

Battered women's groups should carefully evaluate their resources and their goals before deciding to launch a class action against local officials. How would a lawsuit affect efforts to start a shelter or a counseling and referral service for battered women? Are there enough energy and other resources to do both well— and at the same time? Would the publicity about the issue help to raise support for services to battered women? Or would a suit at this stage create unnecessary friction and freeze prosecutors and police officials into positions of adamant noncooperation? Or are relationships between advocate groups and public officials already so bad (or nonexistent, despite persistent efforts by advocates) that a little adversary process can't do any more damage?

The decision to invest the resources of the community of women concerned with abuse should not be made without consultation with as many segments of that community as possible—also with other communities where such suits have been filed. If there is a great deal of local support for taking such legal action and a consensus that there is little or no danger of damaging productive relationships with any of the defendants, the groups interested in participating in the suit in various ways should discuss the political implications of taking the plight of battered women to courts that may already have demonstrated their lack of concern. What does this action say to victims of abuse? What does it imply about long-range strategies for battered women and other groups traditionally ignored or mistreated by the legal system? There should be broad consensus on these questions long before the legal papers are filed; otherwise the legal case may have a career and a constituency of its own without any accountability to the community it was intended to serve.

Three legal theories on which government officials might be sued are discussed below, by way of introduction to what has been done in some areas already. These are by no means the only possible theories; local institutions and policies may suggest others, more suitable to your particular area. Before discussing the various class actions that have been brought in major cities, some mention should be made of a suit brought on behalf of a single individual, to dramatize the fact that governmental neglect of battered women can be anything but benign.

Plaintiffs in Hartzler *v.* City of San Jose, (page 306 of the California Reporter, 1975), sued the municipality for failure to provide police protection to a battered woman who asked for protection after a death threat from her husband.

The plaintiffs charged that the woman called the police to report that her estranged husband was on his way to her apartment after having threatened, over the telephone, to kill her. The man had been arrested once before for wife assault; the victim had called police over twenty times in the previous year. In this case, the police refused to respond. Forty-five minutes later, the husband arrived and stabbed her to death. Her survivors sued the city of San Jose, alleging it was responsible for her "wrongful death." The suit apparently foundered on the legal doctrine that municipalities, like other "sovereign" entities, may be immune from suit for violation of some legal duties. Although the facts certainly suggest "wrongful death" as an appropriate legal theory, the suit may have fared better under a theory that the city neglected to protect battered women or administered its protective services so poorly that it could be held liable for "negligence," rather than "wrongful death." Attorneys considering suit against municipalities or other governmental entities that might fall under the sovereign-immunity doctrine should carefully research the status of that doctrine according to the most recent local rulings.

Scott v. *Hart* is a major suit that has been filed in federal court in the Northern District of California,‡ charging that police and various city agencies in Oakland use their official power and legal authority to violate the rights of battered women to due process of law as guaranteed by the Fifth Amendment The law under which this suit was filed was enacted soon after the Civil War and the passage of the Thirteenth Amendment (abolishing legal slavery), the Fourteenth Amendment (guaranteeing equal protection of the laws), and the Fifteenth Amendment (granting the right to vote to all male citizens) to the United States Constitution. These Amendments were passed, and special federal legislation was enacted, to secure the right of black people to use the federal courts to enforce their new legal rights, which state and local officials often conspired (and continue to conspire) to deny them. Today these laws may be used by any individual or group that has reason to believe that the local government has official policies or practices that have the purpose and effect of discriminating against them.

‡ For more information about the status of this suit, contact Eva Jefferson Patterson, Committee for Urban Affairs, 21st Floor, Mills Tower 220, San Francisco, CA 94104.

One interesting legal theory that does not appear to have been used as the basis of any well-publicized suits against local officials is particularly applicable to the decision to arrest and prosecute. The legal theory is known as "mandamus,"* and it is used when a government official fails or refuses to perform a duty imposed by law. Courts may issue what is known as a "writ of mandamus" to compel a public official to perform an act she or he is legally required to perform. A writ of mandamus may order an official to exercise authority, but usually does not specify how that authority is to be exercised. For example, a court could order a prosecutor's office to process the complaints of battered women but could not order a prosecutor to charge a particular man with a specific offense.

In cases in which a particular right has been clearly established by law, courts may also use the writ of mandamus to correct a decision that clearly constitutes an abuse of discretion. System-wide policies of nonintervention in battered women's cases may be corrected, but specific individual decisions may not. Like the doctrine of sovereign immunity, the questions of when courts will order a writ of mandamus and how explicit they can be in shaping future policy require careful research into recent local precedent.

Finally, we should consider the class action brought on behalf of battered wives in New York who had been unsuccessful in obtaining police protection (in the form of arrest) or criminal charges brought against their husbands.

In December 1976, twelve New York City women who had been beaten by their husbands filed suit against nineteen defendants, including the police commissioner, the chief clerk of the family court, and the director of probation for the City of New York. The women charged that the defendants all failed to do their duty to protect them from abusive husbands as required by existing New York State law. Police officers were charged with failing to arrest for assault and other serious crimes, and refusing

* The relevance of the mandamus procedure is pointed out by Susan Jackson and discussed at some length op. cit. She also discusses the use of civil-rights statutes (42 U.S.C. 1981 et seq.) to remedy discrimination against battered wives.

to arrest for violations of orders of protection.† The suit charges that both police and court personnel "either deny the existence of violence against married women or they treat it as a privilege of marital discipline in which the state should not interfere." One plaintiff's husband put it directly: "The fist is the truth." The 102-page complaint illustrates, among other practices, how police "refer" women to family court and the family court "refers" them back to the police. "Neither agency enforces the law," say the plaintiffs.

New York law permits police to arrest without a warrant any person an officer reasonably believes has committed a crime. Ordinarily, a victim's identification of her assailant offers enough reasonable belief to authorize arrest for assault, attempted assault, menacing, or reckless endangerment. However, the *Police Patrol Guide* recommends that an entirely different process be used when the accused has committed "an offense against a member of his family."

In 1962, the New York legislature decided that women whose husbands beat them need "practical help," rather than "criminal punishment" for their attackers (Family Court Act, Section 811). Family court was therefore given the power to issue orders of protection to wives whose husbands committed assault, attempted assault, menacing, reckless endangerment, or disorderly conduct against them. Women who were not legally married to their assailants were not eligible for orders of protection but could go to criminal court, where the defendant might face penalties of up to seven years. The maximum penalty (very rarely imposed) for violation of an order of protection was six months' imprisonment.

It became common practice under this system for police to refuse to arrest a man unless his wife had already gotten an order of protection, claiming the Family Court Act made his conduct noncriminal. Family-court personnel often made it virtually impossible to obtain an order of protection. One staffer candidly ex-

† The complaint in the suit *(Bruno, et al. v. Maguire, et al.)*, was filed by the Litigation Coalition for Battered Women, New York, NY. Copies of pleadings and the consent decree are available from National Clearinghouse for Legal Services, 500 North Michigan Ave., Suite 2220, Chicago, IL 60611.

plained, "An order of protection is just another way the police have of sending you down here and dragging it out so that they don't have to do anything." In the unlikely event that a woman did get an order, police refused to arrest for a violation in spite of a printed statement of their authority to do so, on the face of the order.

In response to the complaint filed in the New York suit, defendants argued that they had violated no law or duty and asked that the suit against them be dismissed. The Manhattan Supreme Court denied this motion, declaring that "the police owe a duty of protection to battered wives, in the same manner they owe it to any citizen injured by another's assault."

Soon after this declaration, the New York City Police Department entered into an agreement, dated June 26, 1978, obligating them to change dramatically their arrest and "referral" policies in cases involving battered wives. Under this agreement, they acknowledge that

> The Police Department and its employees have a duty to and shall respond to every request for assistance or protection from or on behalf of a woman based on an allegation that a violation or a crime, or violation of an order of protection . . . has been committed against her by a person alleged to be her husband (Bruno v. Maguire, N.Y. Supreme Court, County of New York, Index ⚹21946/76, "Consent Decree").

Police officials also agreed that henceforth

> When reasonable cause exists for a police officer to believe that a husband has committed a misdemeanor against his wife or has committed a violation against his wife in the officer's presence, the officer *shall not refrain from making an officer arrest of the husband* without justification (emphasis added).

Specifically ruled out as factors to be considered as "justification" are the fact that the parties are married, the fact that the woman has not previously sought an order of protection from family court, or the officer's belief that mediation and reconciliation are more appropriate. Police are given no discretion to refuse to arrest if there is reasonable cause to believe that the husband has committed a felony or if there is reasonable cause to believe that the husband has violated an order of protection.

Finally, police are also obligated, by the terms of the consent decree, to remain at the scene of an attack long enough to stop the violence and prevent any further violation of either criminal law or an order of protection, and to help the woman get medical assistance. The Police also agreed to help victims make civilian arrests where authorized by New York law and to use normal investigative procedures to locate and arrest husbands who have left the scene by the time police arrive. In addition, police supervisors are required to rescind all regulations, training materials, and other documents inconsistent with the new policies and to investigate every complaint of failure to follow these directives on the part of individual police officers or of the department.

One particularly positive result of the consent decree is the fact that other cities are developing guidelines and policies for their police departments modeled on provisions contained within the decree.

That part of the suit concerning the practices of family-court and probation-department officials was dismissed and is currently on appeal.

The legal system can be an important tool in winning basic civil rights for groups of people previously considered legal nonentities. We must remember, however, that the legal system is a two-edged sword and can sometimes be used against battered women and others struggling for equal rights. Litigation and other strategies must be planned with this possibility in mind. If you sue the prosecutor, is he going to subpoena the records of the local shelter for battered women in order to prepare his defense? If he does so, how do you respond?

Most programs serving battered women have policies guaranteeing the clients' rights to absolute privacy and confidentiality. Advocates should *always* refuse to disclose any information obtained from or about a client without her express consent.

Some states have enacted specific laws protecting all confidential communications between social workers, psychiatrists, and ministers, and their clients. Such communications between attorneys and clients are also protected in every state.

Counselors or staff at shelters or other services for battered women should never voluntarily turn over this information to police, prosecutors, or others. If records are subpoenaed, the person in charge of the records should seek legal help and file a "motion to quash" the subpoena. All clients whose records are involved should be notified and asked to indicate whether they wish to waive the privilege of confidentiality.

Groups working in prosecutors' offices should discuss carefully the question of access to their files by prosecutors and police.

Have other suits found ways to avoid problems of reverse discovery, expensive or time-consuming depositions, waiver of confidentiality between advocates or counselors and their clients, or other legal issues? In many large cities, litigation coalitions for battered women are being organized (under that title or similar ones); in other areas, groups working on establishing shelters or other programs for battered women will be familiar with local legal and other experts in the field.‡

NO EASY ANSWERS

For centuries, women have suffered physical abuse at the hands of men with whom they lived in legally and/or socially sanctioned relationships. For the most part, they have suffered in silence, because the physical abuse was a tacitly accepted part of the spousal relationship.

‡ Copies of pleadings in many of the major suits on behalf of battered women are available from the National Clearinghouse for Legal Services, 500 North Michigan Ave., Suite 2220, Chicago, IL 60611. Cases are arranged by number; a preliminary letter should request information about cases on battered women. (Pleadings in *Bruno v. [Codd and] Maguire* are available through the Clearinghouse as ⅙19951; pleadings in *Scott v. Hart* are available under ⅙19947.)

The New York Litigation Coalition for Battered Women is keeping a file of major litigation presently pending or about to be filed. People involved in or contemplating litigation in this field should contact the Coalition (Amy Herman MFY Legal Services 759 Tenth Avenue, New York, NY 10019). Those organizations responsible for bringing the New York class-action suit are MFY Legal Services, Inc., Center for Constitutional Rights, and Brooklyn Legal Services Corp. B., all of New York City.

Generations of struggle within and without the legal system have resulted in declarations that women are entitled to be treated as independent citizens with the same rights as men—in some areas. While women are now entitled to vote and married women can own property apart from their husbands, legislators in some states are still opposing a national declaration outlawing any discrimination on the basis of sex. The strength of the opposition to the Equal Rights Amendment is a measure of the commitment in the United States to male superiority. Until this commitment is renounced by millions and denounced as public policy, there is little hope for real improvement in the plight of battered women from within the legal system.

Ultimately, the legal system does not create and enforce a new social order but reflects and enforces community norms and values. While advocates must press for structural changes in the legal system to make it easier for women to process their complaints and prosecute their abusers, the success of these reforms depends upon their integration into a community-wide and nationwide campaign of public education about the extent and cost of violence against women. Wife abuse will cease being a major law-enforcement and criminal-justice problem when it is no longer a socially acceptable institution. And it will not become socially unacceptable until the entire society is committed to real equality for women, and sexism is universally understood to be the name of a dangerous social disease that poisons individual relationships as well as the quality of life in the community.

In the Meanwhile . . . Minimizing the Damage to Victims

Meanwhile, battered women, must use the legal system to assert their right to be free from physical interference and violence from husbands as well as strangers. The following suggestions represent goals for advocates working to change one or more of the major components of the criminal-justice system. Advocates should keep in mind that improvements made in one sector can be undone in another, and that when a strategic decision has been made to concentrate on one, careful coordination with other branches of the legal system is essential to any real gains for battered women. For example, convincing prosecutors to keep records of civil restraining orders and prosecute for violations can be virtually useless unless police are notified of the new policy and are instructed to make summary arrests whenever they have reason to believe a violation has occurred.

Goals for Improving Police Response to Battered Women

1. All recruits should receive crisis-intervention training as well as training in handling wife-abuse calls. Crisis-intervention training should be conducted by a person or team with expertise in that field; handling wife-abuse calls should be taught by a team including a police instructor, a prosecutor, and a member of an advocate's group. The course in handling wife abuse should review the law of arrest in criminal cases and the law of summary arrest for violation of civil orders. It should include instructions on the duty of police in cases in which a citizen wishes to make an arrest, as well as instructions on investigating wife-abuse cases and the importance of police testimony at trial. Women's advocates should train police in the origins of spouse abuse, its extent and serious nature, the reasons battered women remain in abusive homes (stressing lack of economic alternatives), and the importance of heeding the victim's choices regarding arrest and prosecution. Police should also be taught to use and make effective referral to community agencies, including shelters and groups for battered wives. Finally, they should be instructed in proper record-keeping procedures to facilitate recognition of incidents posing the most serious threats to victims.

2. In-service training should be conducted so that every member of the police force who is likely to respond to a wife-abuse call understands the new protocol with regard to wife abuse. New guidelines should be issued to each member of the force, and supervisors should monitor compliance for the first six to twelve months.

3. Police departments should recognize community-service achievement in the same ways it recognizes achievement of more traditional police goals—with public commendation, promotions, and other rewards. Nominations for community-service awards should come from the communities served.

4. Police policy and guidelines on wife abuse should be made available to the public.

5. Police departments should issue and circulate written guidelines on dispatch, priority assignment in various fact situations, the law of arrest and citizen's arrest, the proper procedure for making referrals to shelters and other services, the appropriate charges in various fact situations, and the proper procedure for issuing a criminal complaint in spouse-abuse cases.

6. Police record-keeping procedures should be modified so that police are required to report, for every spouse-abuse call, the following information: names and address(es) of parties, relation of parties; dispatch priority assigned, police response and responding officers; nature of injuries, use of weapons, names and addresses of witnesses, whether an arrest was made, whether a complaint was filed, charge (if any), what referrals were made, and what follow-up (if any). These records should be maintained for at least five years and filed together with copies of any civil restraining orders granted to the complainant for a similar period.

Goals for Improving Prosecutorial Response to Battered Women

1. Prosecutors should prosecute violent spouses in the same manner as they would if the assault occurred between strangers, unless prosecution is diverted by the consent of the victim.

2. Prosecutors should distribute written guidelines on appropriate charges in wife-abuse cases.

3. Pretrial diversion should be used for first offenses only; men with a history of wife beating should not be eligible. Diversion should be permitted only when both parties consent. "Deferred prosecution" should be used with diversion so that the accused will understand that failure to succeed in the diversion progam and futher abuse will result in prosecution for the initial offense as well as for the violation of the diversion agreement.

If prosecution staff makes referrals, staff must follow up by contacting the victim at two-week, six-week, and six-month intervals. The final contact should include a face-to-face evaluation of the diversion program with the diversion counselor and both parties. A period of "probation" should follow the conclusion of the diversion program, and the assailant should be warned that subsequent assaults will result in summary arrest and prosecution for initial as well as later assault.

4. Prosecution officials should take affirmative steps to inform the public about the new policies with regard to wife assault. Public-service announcements, talks to local organizations and community groups, and other means should be used to urge battered women to call local battered women's groups or prosecutors' offices for more information or help.

5. Diversion programs may consist of referrals to independent projects, staffed by or jointly run with women's groups, professional counselors, and advocates concerned with wife abuse and the legal rights of women. Job- and training-program counselors and welfare advocates as well as others who could provide concrete assistance to women seeking to escape from violent homes should be employed, as well as persons trained in mediation and community dispute resolution.

6. The goal of diversion programs should be to help both parties find the help and/or services they need. It should not be assumed that the parties want to continue living together. Diversion counselors should help each party evaluate her or his needs and make further referrals if necessary. The crisis that led to the call for help should be used as an opportunity to help the parties evaluate the relationship and their own goals.

7. During the counseling period, both parties should be interviewed separately as well as together to determine whether the problem is truly one of interpersonal conflict or whether wife abuse is symptomatic of serious psychological problems on the part of the husband.

8. If the parties indicate that both want the relationship to continue, mediation/conciliation techniques should be used to isolate major sources of conflict and help define specific actions to be taken by each party to resolve the conflict. These should be embodied in a contract that describes the mutual obligations in enough detail that an impartial third party could determine whether the obligations had been met or vio-

lated. Every contract should also describe a mechanism for its enforcement (e.g., return to the diversion counselor or referral to arbitrator or other counselor, with party found guilty of violation bound to pay for cost of extra sessions).

9. Prosecutors should be trained by advocates for battered women so that they become aware of the extent of wife abuse, its seriousness, and the importance of the threat of prosecution in preventing repeated attacks. The causes of wife beating and reasons for remaining in abusive homes should be thoroughly explored. The not-uncommon situation of women who kill their attackers in self-defense should be explored, with careful probing to determine a prosecutor's attitude toward self-defense in situations in which the victim is physically smaller, weaker, or ill prepared to defend herself with less-than-lethal means.

10. Prosecutorial programs to counteract wife abuse should be evaluated by outside evaluators at least yearly to determine the effect of diversion programs on the number of wife-abuse complaints received, the number of repeat cases, the number of prosecutions and convictions for assault, aggravated assault, and related cases, and the number of complaints withdrawn. An effort should be made to ascertain client satisfaction with diversion and prosecution programs.

Goals for Improving the Judicial Response to Battered Women

1. Court organization/jurisdiction: If parties do not consent or diversion fails, wife beating should be prosecuted in criminal courts in the same manner as assaults between strangers.

2. Judges should instruct juries to the effect that the fact of a relationship between attacker and victim should not affect their decision as to whether accused should be held liable for acts charged.

3. Sentencing: Judges should order presentence consultation and/or evaluation reports from psychologists or psychiatrists in all cases resulting in serious injury. Various forms of "supervised" probation should be used when recommended or indicated by presentence interviews. These should include partic-

ipation in therapy, alcohol or drug detoxification programs, or job-training or other programs. Jail or prison sentences should be imposed in ways that minimize the loss of income to the victim and children; work-release programs should be used as much as possible. Fines should be avoided, as these only deprive the family of income. Suspended sentences should be imposed with a warning that subsequent attack will result in summary arrest.

4. Court personnel should be instructed to inform battered women of all their legal rights and options, and refer them to appropriate legal-service attorneys if they qualify. Court personnel should be retrained to reflect new prosecution and judicial policy regarding wife abuse as a serious offense. Court personnel should not consider it their duty to discourage women who wish to prosecute their attackers or obtain civil protective orders but, rather, should consider it their job to facilitate the decision and help the victims file the proper papers.

5. Court personnel should be instructed to refer battered women to a local advocate group if there is one providing help to women during the legal proceedings, or to the local victim/witness unit. If there is a local shelter for abused women, court personnel should advise women how to contact it.

6. Free child care should be provided in the courthouse for the children of victims who must spend time in court to file complaints, testify, or appear for other appointments.

Battered Women and Homicide: The Responsibility of the Legal System

Explicitly or implicitly the criminal-justice system says to the citizen, "Look we can't solve your personal problems." It seems that police agencies are inept in their efforts to successfully intervene in social conflict situations—they are adept however at homicide investigations. If our present attitudes continue, we will become increasingly good at homicide resolution.*

* James Bannon, executive deputy chief of police, Detroit Police Department, "Law Enforcement Problems with Intra-Family Violence," presented to the American Bar Association Convention, August 12, 1974, 7.

A New York City study released in June 1978 shows that homicide among those with close personal relationships is increasing and that "of every five murder victims in 1977, . . . one was killed by a family member, a common-law spouse, or a boyfriend or girlfriend."† Just a year earlier, the figure was one of every seven. The New York study does not indicate how many of those killed were battered women murdered by their husbands or boyfriends. Nor does it indicate how many of those charged with homicide were battered women who, faced with a kill-or-be-killed choice, defended themselves.

A study conducted between 1974 and 1976 by the superintendent of the Women's Correctional Center, in Chicago, Illinois, revealed that in 40 per cent of the cases of "women who had killed their husbands, common-law husbands and/or boyfriends, the dominant reason these women gave for slaying their loved ones was continuous abuse."‡

This survey demonstrates that the self-defense homicides were the fruit of years of abuse and inadequate responses by the legal system. The married women had lived with their attackers an average of 6.3 years before the fatal incident, and those not legally married had lived with their assailants an average of 3.7 years. All of those jailed on murder or manslaughter charges had called police at least five or six times.

Only two of the women charged with homicide had any prior record: one for a traffic offense and another for battery—a charge made in retaliation against her when she attempted to prosecute her assailant. Forty-two of the fifty-three women had children, and thirty-six (over two thirds) said that the children were the main reason they had not packed up and left the violent home. Only fourteen of the fifty-three were employed outside the home. The others were either entirely dependent on their assailant's income or on welfare.

All of the jailed women had used either knives or guns to kill their attackers, each one stating that, despite many other attacks, she felt that the last one was different, that her attacker was deter-

† (New York *Times,* June 25, 1978, p. 1)
‡ Claudia Y. McCormick, "Battered Women—the Last Resort" (unpublished and undated).

mined to kill her or just would not stop short of killing her. In most of the cases, the woman has used a gun kept in the house by her assailant, and in many cases she killed her attacker with a gun used earlier in the attack to pistol-whip her.

The most important finding, in terms of the responsibility of the legal system, is that

> All of the women claimed the police were called on numerous occasions, and twenty-seven claimed that after continuously calling the police and having the men arrested, the beatings became more severe after each arrest. All of them stated that after the beatings became more severe, they stopped calling the police.

Many of the women whose husbands were arrested indicated that their husbands had been intoxicated at the time of the assault and were taken to jail to "sleep off" the alcohol and then allowed to return home with no charges being filed and no referral, counseling or follow-up. Fear of reprisals and guilt about being responsible for having their husbands or boyfriends jailed were the primary reasons mentioned for not attempting to follow through on prosecution, although it is likely that further efforts to have the assailants prosecuted might not have met with much success.

Eventually, seventeen of these fifty-three women were given sentences of two to nine years for defending their lives against a particularly violent attack.

The conviction and sentencing to prison of women who are denied protection by the law and end up killing in self-defense is one of the most cruel ironies of today's criminal-justice system. In theory, the law respects "self-defense" as a justification for taking another's life. In fact, the legal definition of self-defense is based on the assumption that the assailant and attacker are approximately equal—men.

Juries deliberating the fate of women such as those described in the Cook County survey are not ordinarily instructed to consider whether the relative size, physical strength, and training of the victim and the assailant justify the battered woman's use of a lethal weapon. Many judges will not allow the defense to present evidence of a long history of prior abuse, ruling that only incidents immediately preceding the final incident are relevant to the issue of whether the deceased "provoked" the defendant. These defendants are not arguing that they were "provoked," but that they had a reasonable belief that they had no other source of protection from deadly force.

While an ancient tradition justifies homicide on the part of a man "provoked" by finding his wife in bed with another, it does not recognize the physical, psychological, and social handicaps that may give a battered woman no choice other than to turn her attacker's knife or gun against him. Of twenty-five nationally publicized cases* involving battered women accused of homicide in the past two years, only seven were acquitted by reason of self-defense. Several were acquitted by reason of "insanity." The vast majority (approximately twenty of those tried by April 1978) were found guilty and given sentences ranging from five years (suspended) to life in prison.

Ironically, the seven acquittals of women who defended themselves or their children from violent attacks and/or sexual abuse created a wave of journalistic indignation. It has been suggested that the women's movement and the campaign to enact the Equal Rights Amendment is responsible for "an open season on men." (See, e.g., "The Right to Kill," *Newsweek,* September 1, 1975, p. 69; "A Killing Excuse," *Time,* November 28, 1977, p. 108.) As the Cook County interviews show, this is far from the truth. Defense attorneys for these battered women *are* using insights gained from the women's movement to argue that the standard notions of "self-defense" contain sex biases that make it impossible for juries to apply this fundamental human concept to situations in which victims save their lives by killing their attackers.

Attorneys who succeeded in having the conviction of Yvonne Wanrow overturned in a landmark decision explain:

* This information is taken from Elizabeth Schneider and Susan Jackson with Cristina Arguedas, "Representation of Women Who Defend Themselves in Response to Physical or Sexual Assault," *Women's Rights Law Reporter,* Spring 1978. Information about pending cases and consultation on representing women accused of homicide in response to abuse may be obtained from the Women's Self-Defense Law Project, 853 Broadway, New York, NY 10003, c/o Center for Constitutional Rights.

Our analysis assumes than an act of homicide by a woman is reasonable to the same extent that it is reasonable when committed by a man. We do not argue for a separate legal standard for women. However, sex-based stereotypical views of women, especially women who act violently, and a male orientation built into the law prevent an equal application of the law. . . .

The goal of this analysis is the presentation to the jury of the defendant's conduct as reasonable. The crucial point to be conveyed to a judge and jury is that, due to a variety of societally based factors, a woman may reasonably perceive imminent and lethal danger in a situation in which a man might not. (Schneider, Jackson and Arguedas, op. cit, p. 5.)

In the *Wanrow* case (State v. Wanrow, 88 Wash. 2d 221; 559 P. 2d 548 [1977]), the Supreme Court of Washington reversed the murder conviction of a woman after considering the impact of a "long and unfortunate history of sex discrimination" on the law of self-defense. The decision is a landmark because it represents the most explicit statement of the theory of self-defense for battered women to be adopted by an appellate court. The heart of the decision is its rejection of the standard self-defense instruction given to the jury. The jury that convicted Ms. Wanrow was instructed that a lethal weapon was not permitted in self-defense unless the party assaulted "believes and has reasonable grounds to believe that he is in imminent danger of death or great bodily harm."

Rejecting this instruction as ignoring the effect of sexism on the woman's perception of danger and lack of access to less drastic means of protection, the Washington Supreme Court ruled:

[This instruction] leaves the jury with the impression that the objective standard to be applied is that applicable to an altercation between two men. The impression created—that a 5'4" woman with a cast on her leg and using a crutch must, under the law, somehow repel an assault by a 6'2" intoxicated man without employing weapons in her defense—violates the respondent's right to equal protection of the law. The respondent was entitled to have the jury consider her actions in the light of her own perceptions of the situation, including those perceptions which were the product of our nation's long and unfortunate history of sex discrimination. Until such time as the effects of that history are eradicated, care must be taken to assure that our self-defense instructions afford women the right to have their conduct judged in the light of the individual handicaps which are the product of sex discrimination. To fail to do so is to deny the right of the individual woman involved to trial by the same rules which are applicable to male defendants. (*State v. Wanrow,* 559 P. 2d 559, citations omitted)

Until such recognition of the effects of sexism represents the norm, rather than the exception, both within the legal system and the society as a whole, battered women will have little hope for justice in the United States either as victims or as defendants. Unfortunately, the attitude reflected in the Washington Supreme Court decision is still far from the norm. Following the decision in that case, the Washington State prosecutor announced he planned to retry Ms. Wanrow.

The absurdity, futility, and injustice of jailing women who kill their attackers in self-defense was summed up by Claudia McCormick, superintendent of the Women's Correctional Center, in Chicago, when she wrote,

I question how one rehabilitates a person who is not a criminal but who, if services were available could be living productive lives, without guilt and remorse for taking a human life, to save their own. (Op. cit., p. 12)

CONCLUSION

For battered wives, advocates are often the most important, responsive, component in the legal system. They have a tremendous responsibility to press for specific, concrete changes that will eradicate the effects of sexism from specific laws, procedures, and practices that discriminate against battered women with tragic results. Discrimination in the legal system is directly responsible for the number of women killed by husbands and boyfriends and for the number of women jailed for killing a "loved one" who had a penchant for physical abuse.

Professionals in the legal system may be committed to instituting reforms in procedures and laws concerning battered women, but unless all involved ensure that these reforms are consistent with each other and with the overall needs of battered women, the violence is not likely to decrease. Concerned individuals, therefore, must remain constantly aware of a continuum of abuse that begins with petty forms of violence and ends in the jailing of battered women who kill their attackers in self-defense. The public, as well as legal professionals, must realize that today's battered woman is tomorrow's casualty or prisoner. In addition to providing direct services to battered women, we must constantly pose the question: "How long is our society willing to tolerate this preventable violence and tragic waste of life?"

Legislation

Chapter IV

LEGISLATION

During the past few years, advocates for battered women have turned to the legislative process as one avenue for the development of effective tools in working with wife-abuse victims. On the state level, a variety of legislative proposals have been considered and in some cases adopted. Proposed bills focus on providing shelters for abuse victims; streamlining criminal court procedures in assault and battery cases involving a spouse; establishing concurrent jurisdiction in criminal courts over family offenses; creating public education programs concerning family violence; developing improved data-collecting and reporting procedures; enforcement of restraining orders by police; repeal of intraspousal tort immunity (laws that prohibit spouses from suing each other); and a program of temporary residential, counseling, and supportive services for women in transition, along with authorization to use Title XX funds for the program. A number of states have modified their arrest procedures in misdemeanor cases to permit a police officer to make an arrest when he has probable cause to believe that one spouse has assaulted the other.

The Center for Women Policy Studies has published a valuable chart, reprinted below, that lists the major provisions of passed and pending state legislation related to domestic violence.

STATE LEGISLATION ON DOMESTIC VIOLENCE

The following is a chart of the major provisions of state legislation generated by the concern about battered women that has grown over the past several years. The statutory material was collected with the help of the contacts for each state, listed in the journal RESPONSE. These laws and pending legislation were assembled in January, 1978 and updated July, 1979. We have also included older, comprehensive laws of the District of Columbia, Hawaii, and New York that deal with domestic violence. Similar statutes of other states may have been omitted because the criminal and civil codes of each state were not researched. The chart was composed for CWPS by Barbara Harvis, a third-year law student at Georgetown University Law Center.

STATE	CIVIL REMEDIES— INJUNCTIVE RELIEF	SHELTER SERVICES	DATA COLLECTION	POLICE TRAINING	SPECIAL CRIMINAL STATUTES	CONCURRENT RESOLUTIONS
ALABAMA						
ALASKA		Laws of Alaska, Ch 72 (1977) • Shelter in Anchorage for one year • Appropriation: $216,000				
ARIZONA						
ARKANSAS						
CALIFORNIA	Laws of Calif., Ch 720 (1977) • Includes cohabitants • TRO for maximum of 30 days • Ex parte relief: "great or irreparable injury" • Relief is independent of Marriage Dissolution Proceeding • Copy of order to LEA if requested by π • Violation: Misdemeanor	Laws of Calif., Ch 892 (1977) • Statewide network of 4-6 pilot centers • Appropriation: $280,000 • Data collection • Confidentiality of Information	Laws of Calif., Ch 908 (1977) • Separates reporting of spouse abuse and child abuse		Laws of Calif., Ch 912 (1977) • Makes spouse abuse a felony • Includes cohabitants • Penalty: Imprisonment for not greater than 1 year.	

State			Abbreviations in chart
	HB 1633 (Failed) • Record-keeping requirements by police • Annual statistical compilation by general assembly		PO = PROTECTION ORDER RO = RESTRAINING ORDER VO = VACATE ORDER TRO = TEMPORARY RESTRAINING ORDER LEA = LAW ENFORCEMENT AGENCY Δ = DEFENDANT π = PLAINTIFF TOP = TEMPORARY ORDER OF PROTECTION Footnotes † Relief is without notice to the defendant • Provisions are substantially the same as those listed on the chart under the Pennsylvania "Protection from Abuse Act" of 1976. Additional provisions not found in the Pennsylvania law are listed. †† Relief is "in addition to" any other available civil or criminal remedies.
COLORADO	HB 1633 (Failed) "Domestic Violence Abuse and Protection Act" • See Penn. law* • Includes additional police enforcement and reporting provisions (temporary custody not to exceed 24 hours for violation of order and likelihood of assault) HB 1143 (Passed 1978) • RO to be issued by county courts		
CONNECTICUT	Pub Act No.77-336 (1977) • PO Hearing within 14 days of application. Relief includes RO and VO • Maximum duration 90 days unless action for marriage dissolution commenced • Copy of order to applicant upon request • Non-exclusive remedy†† • Ex parte† relief: "immediate and present physical danger"	Special Act No. 77-87 (1977) • Pilot program for shelter services • Appropriation: $75,000	
DELAWARE			
DISTRICT OF COLUMBIA	DC Code Title 16, Ch 10 (1977) • Includes cohabitants • PO: Relief includes RO, mandatory counseling • Maximum duration: 1 year • Ex parte† relief: "safety or welfare ... is immediately endangered" • Penalty: Contempt • No husband-wife privilege in proceedings		

STATE	CIVIL REMEDIES—INJUNCTIVE RELIEF	SHELTER SERVICES	DATA COLLECTION	POLICE TRAINING	SPECIAL CRIMINAL STATUTES	CONCURRENT RESOLUTIONS
FLORIDA		HB 74 (Passed) • Establishment and funding of diagnostic Intervention centers • Educational and informational programs • Spouses only • Confidentiality of information • Mandatory police referral			Subsection 901.15(6) (Chap 77-67), Fla. Statutes (1977) • Provides for warrantless arrest when abuse not in officer's presence	
GEORGIA						
HAWAII					Sec 709-906, Haw.I.Penal Code (1973): • Makes spouse abuse a misdemeanor • Warrantless arrest if abuse in officer's presence • 3-hour cooling-off period if abuse not in officer's presence • Violation: Arrest • Record-expungement provision	

IDAHO				HB 742 (Failed) • Provides for warrantless arrest when abuse not in officer's presence
ILLINOIS	Ch 69 Sect. 25. Laws of IL (1977) • Spouses only • Injunctions include RO, VO for maximum of 30 days, temporary custody counseling • Ex parte relief: "Immediate and present danger of abuse"			
INDIANA				PL 358 (1978) • Compensation for victims of violent crimes
IOWA	HF 2267 (Failed) "Protection from Domestic Abuse Act" • Includes cohabitants • PO or consent agreement: hearing within 10 days • Relief includes RO, VO, possession of residence or alternate housing for π, temporary custody or visitation • π has right to counsel • Defines PO violation ("mere presence on premises" = violation of eviction or alternate-housing order) • Max. duration of PO: 1 year	HF 2147 (Failed) • Includes cohabitants • Authorizes counties to provide emergency shelter and support services S 2057 (Pending) • Funding for four pilot shelter and support programs • Educational programs • Uniform method of data collection and evaluation • Appropriation: $500,000	S 2057 (Failed) • Mandatory data collection by hospitals, doctors, nurses, and police HF 2267 (Pending) • Mandatory collection of data by state and local LEAs • Information relayed to central registry for child abuse • Limits access to registry information • Confidentiality of records	

STATE	CIVIL REMEDIES— INJUNCTIVE RELIEF	SHELTER SERVICES	DATA COLLECTION	POLICE TRAINING	SPECIAL CRIMINAL STATUTES	CONCURRENT RESOLUTIONS
IOWA (continued)	• Ex parte† relief: "present danger of domestic abuse" • Emergency night and weekend relief • Non-exclusive remedy†† • Violation: Contempt (jail sentence may be on weekends)					
KANSAS	SB 579 (Failed) "Protection from Abuse Act" • See Penn. law* • Support payments; costs and attorneys fees • Provision for possession of personal property					
KENTUCKY	HB 501 (Passed 1978) • Provides protective services to abused adults that agree to prosecute • Provides that people report such cases to the Department of Human Resources KRS 403.270 (Amended 1978) "Child Custody Act" • Abandonment of house where abuse is threatened not relevant in custody cases	HB 750 (Failed 1978) "Prevention and Treatment of Domestic Violence Act" • Establishes Governor's Commission on Domestic Violence • Authorizes six shelter facilities • Education program • Standard system for collecting and analyzing data • Appropriation: $1,000,000	HB 750 (Failed 1978) • Mandatory data collection by social service agencies and LEAs • Annual reports to Governor			
LOUISIANA						SCR 21 (1977): • Requests La. Department of Health and Human Resources to study problem

	• Establishment of emergency shelters • Appropriation: $200,000				HJR 32 (Passed 1978) • Record-keeping by state police of incidents and resolutions
MARYLAND	Md Ann Code, art 88a, 101-105 (Supp. 1977) • Spouses only • Establishment of model shelter home	HJR 32 (Passed 1978) • Record-keeping by state police of incidents and resolutions			
MASSACHUSETTS	Chap 647 (1977) • Establishes temporary supportive residences H 1828 (Failed) • Victims of domestic violence included in assistance programs to persons deprived of living quarters				
MICHIGAN	HB 6127 (Pending) "Protection from Abuse Act" • See Penn. law* • More expansive relief (support orders, possession of residence) • Penalty for contempt, imprisonment for not greater than 6 months, fine not greater than $1,000, or both • does not have right to jury trial HB 5350 (Incorporated into HB 5349) • Violation of preliminary injunctive order = felony HB 5351 (Passed 1978) • Proof of service of preliminary injunctive order must be filed with LEA HB 5352 (Passed 1978) • Mandatory filing with LEA of RO in divorce actions by clerk	HB 5355 (Canceled; is now subHB 5306) • Establishment of temporary supportive residences • Includes cohabitants • Data collection • Appropriation: $500,000 HB 5306 (Passed 1978) • Establishment of pilot assistance center • Includes cohabitants • Data collection • Appropriation: $500,000 HB 5281 (Pending) • Establishment of shelter	HB 5353 (Passed 1978) • Uniform crime-reporting system by local and state police	HB 5354 (Pending) • Police training in investigation of domestic assault cases HB 5349 (Passed 1978) • Includes cohabitants • Warrantless arrest when abuse not in police officer's presence • Mandatory arrest if probable cause to believe violation of preliminary injunctive order or peace bond	HCR 108 (1977): • Creates special committee to study the problem

STATE	CIVIL REMEDIES—INJUNCTIVE RELIEF	SHELTER SERVICES	DATA COLLECTION	POLICE TRAINING	SPECIAL CRIMINAL STATUTES	CONCURRENT RESOLUTIONS
MICHIGAN (continued)					HB 5356 (Passed 1978) • Special probation provision for spouse with no previous convictions, may require mandatory counseling	
MINNESOTA		SF 1689 (Passed 1978) • Appropriation: $100,000 • Permits 4 shelters, research, and educational programs	Chap 428 (S.F. 124) (1977) • Mandatory reporting of data by hospitals, doctors, nurses, and LEAs		SF 318 (Passed 1978) • Arrest on probable cause without warrant if made within 4 hours of abuse • Allows 24-hour detention period	
MISSISSIPPI						
MISSOURI	HB 1023 (Failed) • See Penn. law* • Right to relief not affected by self-defense or by leaving residence to avoid abuse • No execution of bond by petitioner • Attorney fees paid by ▲ if ▲ loses • Relief is independent of marriage dissolution proceedings • Emergency night relief		HB 1023 (Failed) • LEA record-keeping requirements • Confidentiality of records • Immunity to record-keepers	HB 1023 (Failed) • Establishment of domestic-crisis teams		

MONTANA	• Temporary custody (20 hrs.) for abuse and violation of court order				HJR 103 (Failed) • Requests study of battered-spouse needs
NEBRASKA	LB 623 (1978) "Protection from Domestic Abuse Act" • Includes cohabitants • Relief includes TRO and TVO • Ex parté relief: "irreparable harm, loss, or damage" • Applicant gets two free copies of order		LB 623 and LB 623a (1978) • Establishes comprehensive support services to victims, families, and abusers. • Compilation of statistical data • Confidentiality of information • Appropriation: $176,000 for three pilot shelters	LB 623 (1978) • Education and training program for LEA	LB 623 (1978) • Mandatory counseling as condition of probation for abuser
NEVADA					
NEW HAMPSHIRE					
NEW JERSEY	S 3156 (Pending) "Battered Persons Act" • See Penn law* A 844 (Pending) • In divorce proceedings, physical abuse is an affirmative defense to desertion claim A 874 (Pending) • TRO may be issued by municipal court		A3168 (Pending) • Establishes shelters and comprehensive services • Includes cohabitants	A 3170 (Pending) • Special police training	A 3171 (Pending) • Person accused of assault, assault and battery, or atrocious assault and battery may be kept away from marital residence for up to 72 hours.
NEW MEXICO					

STATE	CIVIL REMEDIES— INJUNCTIVE RELIEF	SHELTER SERVICES	DATA COLLECTION	POLICE TRAINING	SPECIAL CRIMINAL STATUTES	CONCURRENT RESOLUTIONS
NEW YORK	Family Court Act, Art. 8, NY Jud. Law (McKinney) amended by Chap. 449 (S 6617-A8842) (1977): Spouses only • Initial concurrent jurisdiction in family court and criminal court, but exclusive remedy • PO (restraining, vacate, visitation, custody), Maximum duration: 1 year • Ex parté relief • Notice of PO to LEA • Violation: Maximum of 6 months in jail • Conciliation procedures (pre-filing of petition); Probation services, written agreements (court may enter PO in accordance with agreement)	Chap 450 (A8843), Laws of NY (1977) • Permits Board of Social Welfare to approve establishment and operation of shelter homes	Chap 449 (S6617-A8842) laws of NY (1977) • Compilation of data by judiciary		Chap 449 (S6617-A8842) laws of NY (1977) • Gives criminal courts power to issue TOP as condition of pretrial release, and, upon conviction, to enter PO. • Copy of order to police	
NORTH CAROLINA						
NORTH DAKOTA						
OHIO	HB 835 (Pending) • See Penn. law*	HB 1080 (Pending) • Loan and grant program for purchase or renovation of buildings to be used as shelter; max. loan for 1 building: $75,000 HB 987 (Pending) • Establishes program of family protective services • Includes cohabitants • Record-keeping provision • Appropriation: $5,000,000			HB 957 (Pending) • Makes second or subsequent criminal assault against spouse a felony of 4th degree • Includes cohabitants • PO during pendency of action, 24-hour/day court,	

OKLAHOMA	HB 1620 (Failed) "Protection of Household Members from Abuse Act" • See Penn. law*		
OREGON	Chap 845 (HB 2438), Oregon laws (1977) "Abuse Prevention Act" • Includes cohabitants • Relief includes TRO, injunction or consent agreement, temporary custody or visitation • Maximum duration: 1 year • No undertaking required • Relief not affected by leaving household to avoid abuse • Nonexclusive remedy ‡‡ • Petitioner must deliver copy of order to LEA • Mandatory arrest for violation of retraining order. May be released on bail pending contempt hearing • Limits criminal and civil liability of arresting officer·	Chap 846 (SB 769), Oregon Laws (1977) • Grants for programs (including shelters) designed to prevent, identify and treat domestic violence.	copy of order to LEA • Probation provision (suspended sentence) if participation in psychological treatment programs

Chap 845, Ore. Laws (1977) • Provides for mandatory arrest (unless victim objects) if police officer has probable cause to believe assault or fear of assault on spouse • Includes cohabitants • Limits criminal and civil liability for arresting officer |

STATE	CIVIL REMEDIES—INJUNCTIVE RELIEF	SHELTER SERVICES	DATA COLLECTION	POLICE TRAINING	SPECIAL CRIMINAL STATUTES	CONCURRENT RESOLUTIONS
PENNSYLVANIA	Act 218, Laws of PA (1976) "Protection from Abuse Act" • Includes cohabitants • Right to relief not affected by leaving household to avoid abuse • PO or consent agreements: Hearing within 10 days of filing petition, proof by preponderance of evidence, ▲ has right to counsel. Relief includes: RO, VO, possession of residence, temporary custody and visitation, alternative housing. Maximum duration: 1 year • Ex parte† relief: "immediate and present danger of abuse" • Emergency weekend relief • Copy of order to ◄, π, and LEA • Nonexclusive remedy†† • Violation: Contempt →	SB 964 (Pending) Amends Act 218 • Clarifies when π may gain possession of household • Provides that relief may include support order • Emergency relief by Philadelphia Municipal Court Judge • Violation: Indirect criminal contempt, maximum penalty 6 months in prison, $1,000 fine, or both, no right to jury trial • Warrantless arrest for violation of order if probable cause (whether or not in presence of arresting officer) →		SB 964 (Passed -1978) with Amendment: • Must be taken before court that issued order. If possible must be arraigned before district justice or Phila. Municipal Court judge		
RHODE ISLAND	78-H-7868 sub A, Ch 15519 • RO may be granted if petition for divorce is filed • Court may prescribe counseling				77-S-1009, Chap 259, RI Public Law (1977) • Makes domestic assault a misdemeanor • Includes cohabitants	

State				
SOUTH CAROLINA			S 795 (Pending) • Includes cohabitants • Establishes pilot programs for shelter and support services • Community education program • Data collection and program evaluation	• Arrest must be made within 24 hours after commission of crime • No recognizance requirement
SOUTH DAKOTA			SB 335 (failed) • Provides for RO and VO • Ex partel relief	
TENNESSEE				Tenn. Code Ann Sect. 39-602 (1976) • Makes domestic assault a misdemeanor
TEXAS				
UTAH				
VERMONT				
VIRGINIA			Code of VA 16.1-279 (amended) 1978 • Court order for counseling or treatment for either spouse • ʌ may have to pay for shelter care	HB 683 (Pending) • Two-year pilot shelter program • Department of Welfare pays one half cost for shelter

STATE	CIVIL REMEDIES—INJUNCTIVE RELIEF	SHELTER SERVICES	DATA COLLECTION	POLICE TRAINING	SPECIAL CRIMINAL STATUTES	CONCURRENT RESOLUTIONS
WASHINGTON						
WEST VIRGINIA	HB 1082 (Failed) • Includes cohabitants • Right to relief not affected by leaving household to avoid abuse • PO or consent agreements: Include RO, possession of residence or VO, custody to party with possession • Maximum duration: 10 days (renewable for 10 days) • Ex parte† relief: only after notice to ∆ hearing within 72 hours, "immediate and present danger of abuse" • Non-exclusive remedy†† • Violation: Contempt • No husband/wife privilege under the act					
WISCONSIN						AJR 36 (Failed) • Directs legislative council to study the problem of abuse of spouses
WYOMING						

Legislation that has been enacted falls into three general categories: shelters for battered women, improved court procedures, and expanded authority for police officers to act in domestic disputes. We have researched one bill from each of these categories in order to provide you with the kind of background information that will be useful should you attempt to enact similar legislation in your state.

IMPROVED COURT PROCEDURES—PENNSYLVANIA

Enacted in January 1976, the Protection from Abuse Act provides that a woman who has been battered can petition the court asking for a protective order. The order may specify that the abuser is to vacate the home for a period of up to one year. If the abuse is short-term and mild, it may simply restrain the assailant from further harassment or abuse. The protective order can be issued immediately, but a hearing must be held within ten days of the filing of the petition. The order may grant custody and support as well as specify who will make mortgage or rent payments. Effective enforcement of the act has been aided by recently passed amendments. Once the order is violated, the police have the authority to make an arrest whether or not the abuse or harassment occurs in their presence. Under the new amendments, a spouse who violates a protective order can be fined up to one thousand dollars and/or incarcerated for up to six months. Previously, the maximum penalty for violation was fifteen days in jail.

It should be noted that when a protective order is issued, a copy is filed with the local police department. Thus, when a woman calls the police claiming violation of the order, they can immediately check and order the man off the premises by threatening him with arrest or by actually arresting him if they believe that violence has occurred.

Prior to the passage of the Protection from Abuse Act, battered women in Pennsylvania had very little response from the legal system. As in most other states, the police were relatively ineffective. The only legal remedy available was criminal prosecution, which was technically difficult. In addition, many women were loath to give their husbands a criminal record, because they feared retaliatory measures such as increased violence. For economically dependent women, incarceration meant the loss of income. Under the new legislation, the obtaining of a protective order is a civil action. Thus, the assailant receives no criminal record.

The legislation was the brainchild of young Community Legal Services attorney Larry Mass, who had become frustrated by the lack of remedies available to his clients, many of whom were battered women. He was able to gain the support of State Senator Louis Hill, then chair of the Senate Judiciary Committee, who held hearings. Senator Hill's staff helped with the redrafting of the bill as well as drumming up support and devising strategies for passage of the measure. His legislative assistant, Ken Neely, turned to the various women's groups throughout the state that were beginning to develop shelter and support services for battered women, for their help in getting the bill passed. In addition, the State Commission on the Status of Women was alerted. All these groups sent representatives to the hearings held by the Senate Judiciary Committee in the summer of 1976.

Neely proved to be an extremely effective force during the legislative process. He notified the women's groups when hearings were held, made suggestions concerning whom they should personally lobby, and made recommendations for how and when to initiate letter-writing and telephone campaigns. According to Neely, his intensive efforts on behalf of the bill almost cost him his job, but he persisted. The effectiveness of his work demonstrates the need for support for this type of legislation from within the legislative halls as well as from without.

Neely is also credited with another effective measure: bringing Marjory Fields, of the South Brooklyn Legal Services Corporation, to testify before the Pennsylvania Senate Judiciary Committee. She spoke about the effectiveness of similar legislation in New York State, impressing the legislators from both the senate and the house, and the bill gained a broad base of support.

According to Larry Mass, there had been some concern regarding evicting a man from his own home, but this was submerged in the deeper concern and awareness of the legislators regarding the pervasiveness of the domestic-violence problem. Their awareness stemmed from experiences that many of them had had in previous roles as prosecutors in their home counties and attendant frustration in finding suitable remedies to the problem. As a result, there was no need to present much testimony regarding the enormity of the problem. Rather, the focus was on the potential efficacy of the proposed legislation.

It is important to note that the legislators were already sensitive to problems of violence against women, as a successful effort to revise the state's rape laws had recently been concluded. Not only was the evidence of unreported violence against women clear and convincing, the various women's groups that lobbied the rape legislation had been extremely effective in educating the legislators. The legislators had become aware that these women's groups were wielding increasing political power; and very pragmatically, they approved the legislation.

Since the bill contained no allocation of funds, it was not opposed on fiscal grounds, as often happens to many pieces of legislation geared toward social change. There was serious consideration of how the bill would affect family and property law, but these concerns were not sufficient to prevent passage.

After enactment, gaps and loopholes quickly became apparent. Enforcement provisions turned out to be inadequate. By this time, the women's groups working on the issue had organized themselves into a state coalition (Pennsylvania Coalition Against Domestic Violence) and worked hard at getting the necessary amendments introduced and passed. Neely kept the amendments from getting bogged down procedurally.

Yet the bill did not pass without controversy or opposition. Some organizations within the black community were concerned that the bill would perpetuate the breakup of the black family, historically encouraged by the powers that be. Originally, the bill contained a provision that a social worker, welfare worker, or other third party could initiate a request for a protective order. Expressed opposition from the black community changed this provision, so that only a member of the household (except in the instance of child abuse) could initiate a petition.

According to Elaine Sanders, of the Marital Abuse Project of Delaware County, Pennsylvania, passage of the act has enabled a

sizable number of women who heretofore had no relief, to be protected from the violent acts of their husbands or male cohabitants.
However, Linda Quiring, a paralegal worker, has serious reservations regarding the bill's effectiveness—particularly about police
enforcement measures. Ultimately, the effectiveness of the bill
hinges on this factor.

Even assuming that the police can and will enforce the protective orders, Ms. Quiring points out that many women may hesitate
to utilize the act due to the potential loss of financial support from
their husbands. And even though the order may specify that the
assailant is obligated to provide support, enforcement is difficult.
These problems point up the importance of shelter and supportive
services in addition to legislative remedies for battered women.
No one tool will suffice, but a combined set of legal mechanisms
and social services could constitute an effective support system.
As of this writing, advocates are working for the passage of additional legislation that would appropriate funds for shelter and
support services.

EXPANDED POLICE AUTHORITY—OREGON

The state of Oregon has recently enacted a law that provides
for mandatory arrest of an abusive spouse or cohabitant not only
when there is evidence of an actual assault but when the police
officer has probable cause to believe that there was an assault or
fear of assault.

Prior to passage of this legislation, the only statutes relevant to
domestic violence specified that pushing and shoving was a class
A misdemeanor, subject to a citation from the officer—much like
a parking ticket. Police automatically assumed that the majority
of domestic violence incidents were trivial.

Restraining orders were available as a civil remedy only when
the wife filed for divorce. The new bill makes the restraining
order available whether the woman is presently married, was formerly married, or is just living with her assailant. Once a restraining order has been issued and filed with the police, violation
will result in arrest. Violation can consist of harassment and
threats as well as actual assault.

According to Rose Gangle, of Bradley/Angle House, a shelter in Portland, the legislation was enacted as a result of the efforts of the Oregon Coalition Against Domestic Violence. The Coalition came into being after a conference on battered women was held in Portland and attended by various women's groups from throughout the state. The Coalition established a legislative task force, which drafted the bill and asked State Representative Gretchen Kafoury to introduce it. An all-out effort was then made to get passage of the legislation; a variety of women's groups across the state contributed funds to hire a lobbyist, who worked full time for six months on getting the bill passed.

The Coalition also decided to publish a newsletter on a regular basis. The newsletter readership generated an impressive network of women actively interested in seeing the legislation through. In addition to using the newsletter as an effective tool in gaining passage, the Coalition made a major effort to gather large numbers of women for the hearings. They also arranged for battered wives to be present to testify. Passage of the bill was aided by the fact that there were many in Oregon's legislature who were sympathetic to the special problems of women, since the legislature had recently enacted an employment discrimination act and changes in the rape laws.

Contrary to the Pennsylvania experience, minority women were significantly involved in drafting and working for passage of the legislation. Black, Native American, and Polynesian women testified as battered wives at the hearings.

As in Pennsylvania, enforcement proves to be a problem. Police are reluctant to arrest, but the Coalition is reporting instances of nonenforcement and applying pressure for improved response from the law-enforcement community. The badge numbers of nonenforcing officers are reported to the police liaison officer of each police department throughout the state. In addition, public forums are being conducted in each city on spouse abuse and the new law. The forums are sponsored by the National Organization for Women, the Women's Political Caucus, and the Governor's Commission on the Status of Women. These measures have created widespread awareness of the problem.

Marilyn Miller, executive director of the Governor's Commission, has made enforcement of the new law a priority concern. She has developed questionnaires that are filled out by police officials during meetings in cities and towns throughout the state. In many small towns, police officials were unaware of the new law prior to these meetings.

According to Ms. Gangle, the District Attorney's Office in Eugene, Oregon, failed to enforce the law and instead initiated a seven-day cooling-off period for the couple involved. In response, the local NOW chapter applied pressure and the cooling-off period was eliminated.

Another enforcement problem occurs when the assailant violates the order in a county other than the one in which the order was issued. This can occur if the battered woman lives in one county but works in another. In addition, if the woman has previously cohabited with her assailant but is no longer living with him, she is ineligible to obtain a restraining order.

Clearly, amendments are needed and will probably be introduced. The need for legislative action regarding shelters and other services is also seen as a must. These issues are currently under legislative consideration.

Ms. Gangle notes that the Alaska Coalition Against Domestic Violence utilized the experience of the Oregon group in gaining enactment of similar legislation in their state.

SHELTERS FOR BATTERED WOMEN—CALIFORNIA

California has enacted legislation that provides funding for four to six shelters for battered women. The appropriation amounts to $280,000 for a two-year period and has been allocated to groups that are already in operation as shelters or crisis centers. The crisis centers are utilizing the funds to open shelters and provide other supportive services.

Once again, we find that the state coalition (California Coalition Against Domestic Violence) was instrumental in the enactment of the legislation. The Coalition has sixty members, fifty of whom represent crisis centers and shelters. There is significant minority involvement.

The group as a whole drafted the legislation, and State Senator

Robert Presky introduced it into the legislature. State legislator George Moscone (later mayor of San Francisco) held hearings in the Bay Area, and the Coalition mobilized women to attend and testify.

There was no paid lobbyist to see the bill through. Instead, the Coalition applied continuous pressure to legislators and their aides while educating them on the extent and nature of the problem. National and statewide publicity regarding the issue was helpful. So was a local case in which a San Jose judge declared a state law that made it a felony for a man to beat his wife unconstitutional. Public reaction was strongly against the decision, and with pressure from the Coalition the decision was reversed, making spouse abuse a felony and extending the statute to apply to cohabitants as well as married couples. Giving added momentum to passage was the enactment of a civil remedy that enables a battered spouse to obtain a restraining order against her assailant.

According to Linda Berland, of Sacramento, police enforcement of the restraining orders varies from community to community. In localities with organized wife-abuse groups, enforcement tends to occur more readily. Otherwise, enforcement is sporadic or nonexistent.

The passage of Proposition 13 has made many people uneasy about the continuation of shelter funding. Several communities have already withdrawn their financial support. CETA money, which is an important source of funds for shelters (see Chapter VIII), has been cut. The two-year allocation was designated for a "pilot program," which means that refunding is by no means automatic, unless the shelters are to be written into the ongoing budget of the Department of Health, which administers the program. At this point, the Coalition is looking to the federal government as a source of future funds. Unless such funds are forthcoming, the California people believe that their programs are in jeopardy. Since, as of this writing, Proposition 13 seems to be the wave of the future, advocacy groups should keep the California experience in mind.

Based on information from our contact people in each of the three states and material from a kit on battered women developed by the Department of Labor, we offer the following thoughts and suggestions regarding the enactment of state spouse-abuse legislation. From the Department of Labor: ". . . Women's groups desiring to develop a legislative component for a comprehensive program dealing with battered spouses can obtain information and assistance from legislators and commissions on the status of women in their states.* After studying the laws and enforcement policies in their state, some groups may find that existing laws are adequate but that enforcement is lax. In other states, gaps in the legislative authority may be identified. Also, after the need for new legislation has been determined, it is recommended that the state bar association, judges, and legislators be included in the planning process at the earliest possible moment; it may be difficult to enact legislation without their support. In fact, they may be very helpful in your initial study of the legal situation in your state.

In states where the laws are adequate but enforcement is lax, it may be necessary to bring a court action to compel public officials to discharge their responsibilities. As a practical matter, the situation should be discussed with public officials before resorting to legal action. On the other hand, a lawsuit pending in the background often facilitates speedy negotiations. Class actions have been brought in New York City; Cleveland, Ohio; and Oakland, California, against police and other public officials, to secure better enforcement and protection for women in domestic-violence cases."† (Author's note: see Chapter III.)

Some additional suggestions:

1. Raise the public consciousness regarding the issue. Publicize the problem and gather statistics.

2. Get legal input during the drafting process.

3. Find someone in the legislature that will take responsibility for introducing the measure and guiding it through the legislature.

4. Lobbying and legislative liaison are important. A legislative aide could fulfill this function. So could a committed volunteer or a

---

* The Center for Women Policy Studies has published a list of state contact people. The list was compiled by Ernest Caposela, of the Council of State Governments.

† Kit on Battered Women, Women's Bureau, Department of Labor, Washington, D.C. 20210.

person funded specifically for this purpose by constituency-based organizations. You may be able to afford a lobbyist by banding together organizationally.

5. Check out various legislative procedures and make sure that you don't get enmeshed in them.

6. The presence of numbers of concerned citizens and battered women at hearings is essential.

7. Letter writing to both the legislators and the press is important.

8. Court friendly people in the legislature.

9. Adapt successful techniques employed by others.

10. If your group is a coalition, make sure that it is as broadly based as possible.

11. Consider special problems of minority groups. Anything that may threaten family solidarity may be viewed suspiciously by minorities and perceived as an attempt to break down racial or ethnic cohesiveness. According to Susan Flint, of Cambridge, Massachusetts, the concerns of Third World women resulted in an important change in a bill under consideration in the Massachusetts legislature. In an article appearing in the National Communication Network, she writes: "The most significant change is the deletion of a provision that would have allowed probable-cause arrest in cases of misdemeanor assaults not witnessed by a police officer when the people involved are married, were married, or live together. Currently, in Massachusetts, when the assault is not witnessed by the police, arrest is permitted only for felonious assault and battery in cases in which a deadly weapon is used or there is intent to murder.

The Battered Women Action Committee decided that in extending the power of arrest to misdemeanor assaults, the potential for harm was greater than the advantages to be gained. Our feeling was that the arrest provision would certainly be enforced more stringently against poor and Third World men than against white, middle-class men. It would also open the door for fewer restrictions on arrest, which could increase police abuse. Thirdly, we saw no guarantee that this provision would not be used against women."‡

‡ Excerpted from *NCN* (National Communications Network Newsletter), now merged with *FAAR* (Feminist Alliance Against Rape) to become *Aegis: A Magazine on Ending Violence Against Women*. This bimonthly publication is available from Aegis, P. O. Box 21033, Washington, DC 20009, for $8.75/year/individuals, $20.00/year/institutions, and $25.00/year/sustaining subscription. Two-year subscription and bulk discounts are available. Checks should be made out to FAAR. This is an invaluable resource, containing reviews, articles, and news items for all those working on any aspect of violence against women in an active or research capacity.

12. Don't let your efforts flag after the legislation is passed. Bird-dog to see if it is being applied and enforced.

13. Be prepared to offer amendments to close up loopholes, and be prepared to see them through.

14. In the case of funding appropriations, make an effort to build yourselves into a decision-making role regarding distribution of funds. Immediately after the passage of the legislation in California, the California Coalition Against Domestic Violence came forward and offered their expertise on the issue to the Department of Health and Welfare (the administrating agency). As a result, the Department, which had no expertise of its own regarding domestic violence, selected two representatives of the Coalition to work with them on the distribution and allocation of funds.

One controversial aspect of the bills that provide for eviction of the abusive spouse is the question of the constitutionality of evicting a homeowner from his property. There are some who believe that such provisions are unconstitutional. Others argue that property rights are not fixed things; they consist of personal rights to the property. In the instance of an eviction of an abusive spouse, his property is not being taken away; rather, his use of it is being restricted. There have been precedents set for these types of restrictions in zoning-law and nuisance proceedings. Historically, the courts have exercised authority regarding the use of property; for example, in disputes over water rights, etc. Since they have regulated the use and value of property for economic reasons, eviction provisions merely extend this practice to the civil as well as economic area. In addition, in the instance of joint ownership, the law specifies that owners shall each have access to the property. If one owner is being abusive, then his eviction may be the only means by which the other spouse can achieve access to the property.

FEDERAL LEGISLATION

Several bills concerned with spouse abuse have been introduced into the U. S. Congress. In June 1977, Lindy Boggs (Louisiana) and Newton Steers (Maryland), of the House of Representatives, introduced the Domestic Violence Prevention and Treatment Act of 1977. That same day, an identical bill was introduced in the Senate by Wendell Anderson (New Mexico) and Edward Kennedy (Massachusetts). In September 1977, Barbara Mikulski (Maryland) introduced the Family Violence Prevention and Treatment Act in the House of Representatives. In the spring of 1978, two more bills were introduced. The Domestic Violence Prevention and Services Act, introduced in the Senate on March 16, 1978, was sponsored by Alan Cranston (California) and fourteen others. This bill would commit the federal government to funding domestic-violence programs for a five-year period beginning in fiscal year 1979. The bill provided that a minimum of 19 per cent of the allocated funds ($30 million a year) be granted to nonprofit private organizations working on the problem. The bill specified state participation in matching-grant programs and established a National Center on Domestic Violence to be administered by the Department of Health, Education, and Welfare. On the House side, the "Domestic Violence Assistance Act of 1978" was sponsored by George Miller (California) and co-sponsored by Barbara Mikulski (Maryland), Lindy Boggs (Louisiana), and Newton Steers (Maryland). Funds appropriated under this bill would be administered by a newly created council established within the Department of Health, Education, and Welfare. This bill provided for $15 million in fiscal year 1979, $20 million in fiscal year 1980, and $30 million in fiscal years 1981, 1982, and 1983. Public agencies and nonprofit organizations providing services to victims of domestic violence would apply for funds. State and local governments would not be required to participate.

Although the Senate version of these bills was passed, the House bill was defeated there on May 23, 1978, by a vote of 205 to 202. Because it was raised under a suspension of the rules, it needed a two-thirds majority for passage. Suspension of the rules allowed only forty minutes for floor debate; amendments from the floor were not permitted. Failure to secure even a simple majority demonstrated a lack of support among House members.

Objections to the bill included criticism of government intrusion into family matters, the designation of the Department of Health, Education, and Welfare as the administering agency, and the allocation of any more money for social-service programs.

Due primarily to these criticisms, there is some doubt (as of this writing) as to the passage of similar federal legislation which was introduced during the 1979 session. Writing to congresspeople, visiting representatives, and obtaining media coverage of the nature and extent of the wife-beating problem will all be helpful measures for getting legislation introduced and enacted. For information on how you can help, contact Kathy Fotjik, contact person for the Legislative Task Force of the National Coalition Against Violence, 1917 Washtenaw Ave., Ann Arbor, MI 48104.

The overwhelming concern regarding federal legislation within the battered women's movement is that the largest possible share of appropriated funds is channeled to direct services for victims of domestic violence.

University of California sociologist Mildred Pagelow expressed the feelings of those within the shelter community in a letter to Senator Cranston published in a recent issue of the FAAR and NCN newsletter, *Aegis:* ". . . we do know that the best method we currently have of preventing (more) violence is by the establishment of shelters and the variety of support systems that assist victims and their children. The shelters themselves serve as a preventative measure. Shelter staffs have developed the understanding of the problem and the skills to train others, including many in the criminal-justice system, in innovative and workable crisis-intervention techniques. Outreach and advocacy is performed by shelters' staff volunteers, and ex-victims. Since traditional public agencies have historically been insensitive to the problems of victims of domestic violence, there is little reason to believe that the way to sensitize them is to give them more money. Let us put the money where the work of prevention and service has been performed—with the grass-roots nonprofit service organizations and shelters—and let them continue to lead the way in prevention of domestic violence and in assistance to victims."*

On the opposite side are those who argue that funneling money into traditional agencies will establish within those agencies mechanisms structured not only to address the needs of abuse victims but to remain in existence long after federal funding runs out.

* Ibid.

Whether or not this is true, it is clear that any federal legislation should provide for substantial funds for those already working on the problem. Funds allocated for research should be minimal and should be earmarked primarily for applied or evaluative research programs that will make concrete contributions to the reality-based efforts of battered-women advocates.

In addition to working for the passage of federal legislation, it is important that groups working on the issue stay on top of what is happening at the federal level. If and when legislation is passed, funds may very well end up being distributed on a first-come, first-served basis. Often this leaves grass-roots groups at a disadvantage, because they are not as informed about what is happening on a national level as larger, more traditional agencies and institutions. So if you are part of a group that provides assistance to battered women, it is in your best interests to learn about the proposed legislation, work for its passage, and develop plans if and when it becomes law. Keeping informed and involved may enable you to sit on advisory boards and panels that make decisions about the allocation of funds, etc. In taking part in some of the decision making related to implementation of the legislation, you may contribute to making sure that as much of the money as possible is channeled toward groups already working on the issue.

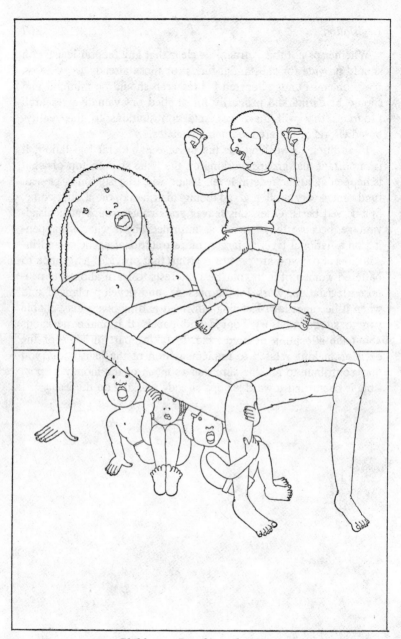

Children—Breaking the Cycle

Chapter V

CHILDREN—BREAKING THE CYCLE

JO-ANNE

"I saw it affecting the kids finally. They had no respect for anyone, really. The way they talk to people. The way they act. It was all because of him, the way he talks to me and the way he acts with me. My kids before—when they were younger they were never like that. But seeing the abuse constantly has influenced them."

LITTLE GIRL SPEAKINGS

Ain't nobody better's my Daddy,
   you keep yo' quauter
   I ain't yo' daughter,
Ain't nobody better's my Daddy.

Ain't nothing prettier'n my dollie
   heard what I said,
   don't pat her head,
Ain't nothing prettier'n my dollie.

No lady cookinger than my Mommy
   smell that pie,
   see I don't lie
No lady cookinger than my Mommy.

—Maya Angelou

The direct ancestor of our present nuclear family is the Roman patriarchal structure from which its name derives. The Latin word *familia* referred to the sum total of a man's goods and property, including his wife, children, and servants, over whom he had total control, including the power to inflict death. Even today, men in some Arab countries have the legal right to kill their wives if they commit adultery.

Although English common law, from which our current marriage laws are derived, took a more humane attitude toward a man's human property, the expression "rule of thumb" can be traced to the right of the husband to chastise his wife with a stick no thicker than his thumb; and the notion that a wife is the property of her husband is still entrenched in many areas of law affecting the rights of married women. The concept that woman and child are the property of husband/father serves as the basis for the rationalization of the use of violence against them. Obviously, a man should have the right to control his "property" by any means necessary.

Although "women and children first" may be a gentleman's rallying cry for protection of his most prized possessions, it also identifies the primary victims of domestic violence. This, then, is our heritage: the man is undisputed ruler of his family.

Although men no longer have the legal right to use unlimited violence to reinforce their supremacy in the family, cultural reinforcements for such violence remain relatively intact. Frequently, it is the *degree* of violence that is challenged, not the assumption that one person has the right to harm another physically. Prevailing attitudes reflect the belief that parental violence is appropriate as long as it's not excessive, and that wife beating is an acceptable prerogative of the husband. This attitude is illustrated by an experiment that was conducted by a group of psychologists who set up simulated assaults on various people in public places. The results were striking: bystanders would intervene when they saw what they believed to be assaults by men upon men, women upon women, and women upon men; no one interfered with a man assaulting a woman.*

* G. L. Borofsky, G. E. Stollak, and L. A. Messe, "Sex Differences in Bystander Reactions to Physical Assault," *Experimental Psychology*, May 1971.

Until recently, it was assumed that men in general tended to be "benevolent dictators" and used physical force only in amounts sufficient to maintain their control. This assumption was severely challenged when child abuse and wife abuse were "discovered" as far-reaching and devastating social problems.

There was great resistance to acknowledging the severity of the child-abuse problem, as it created a strong challenge to society's belief in the sanctity of the family. The idea that some children might actually need protection was so abhorrent that society long resisted the attempts of some reformers to set up protective mechanisms. In the earlier days of attempted child-abuse reform, doctors and hospitals were often reluctant to become involved in reporting incidents; children with highly suspect injuries were frequently treated briefly in hospital emergency rooms and released. Some of these children were to return again and again, others only when brought in "dead on arrival."

Why the widespread prevalence of child abuse came as such a surprise is rather mysterious. It should be common knowledge that abuse is an inevitable result of unfair power relationships whether it be men over women, women over children, or whites over blacks. Perhaps the tendency to romanticize the nuclear family, an institution that operates on a basic pecking order (men, women, children), is one way to assure its perpetuation.

The horrifying case of Mary Ellen, in 1905, was a landmark in the history of social-welfare reform. Mary Ellen, a young child, was found in her New York home bound and subjected to constant extreme forms of abuse and neglect, but there were no laws to liberate her from her life of inhumane torture and suffering. In desperation, welfare workers finally argued that human beings are categorically considered a form of animal life and thus were able to remove the child under laws set up by the Society for the Prevention of Cruelty to Animals. Shortly after this, the first society for the protection of children from cruelty was founded.

The difficulty in gaining public recognition of the problem of wife abuse parallels that experienced in the area of child abuse, and is further compounded by the mixture of fear, scorn, and devaluation with which women have historically been viewed.

Lately, however, through pressure exerted by women's groups

that have "discovered" the problem, society is beginning to address the issue. In so doing, the connections between wife abuse and child abuse are being explored. While there is little information available, some things are clear:

1. Men who abuse their wives tend toward child abuse.

J. J. Gaylord, in his study "Wifebattering: a Preliminary Survey of 100 Cases,"† found that 54 per cent of the husbands in the study beat both their children and their wives. It is hardly surprising that men who vent their rage through wife beating often abuse their children as well.

Parents Anonymous, a national organization that assists in the development of local self-help groups for parents who abuse their children, reports that in almost every one of its over 750 chapters there are mothers who are victims of wife abuse.

The child-protection program in Milwaukee County, Wisconsin, estimates that there is a battered woman in one of every three referrals of a battered child.

The director of the National Center on Child Abuse and Neglect, Douglas J. Besharov, reports that of the officially validated cases of child abuse and neglect, the spouse was also assaulted in almost 20 per cent of the cases.

Sociologist Richard Gelles found that pregnant women are frequently the targets of spousal assault. He sees this as a possible conscious or subconscious form of child abuse, or resentment toward an unwanted child being expressed even before its birth.

> Oh, yeah, he hit me when I was pregnant. It was weird. Usually he hit me in the face with his fist, but when I was pregnant he used to hit me in the belly. It was weird.‡

2. Women who are abused may vent their rage and frustration on their children.

According to Besharov, data also indicated that in 30 per cent of the officially reported cases, the mother who is a victim of

---

† J. J. Gaylord, "Wifebattering: a Preliminary Survey of 100 Cases," *British Medical Journal,* Jan. 25, 1975.
‡ Richard J. Gelles, "Violence and Pregnancy: A Note on the Extent of the Problem and Needed Services," *The Family Coordinator,* Jan. 1975, pp. 81–86.

assault abuses the children. Gaylord found that 37 per cent of the women he studied used violence against their children.

3. Children frequently become "accidental" victims of spouse assault.

A project funded under the child-abuse program in San Diego found that there was a significant incidence of "accidental" injury to children when the spouse was the target of the assault.

Often children are injured when they attempt to stop a fight or protect their mother.

Parents Anonymous also found that children often receive abuse that was intended for the spouse.

Frequently, women who stay in abusive situations become more motivated to seek help at the point when the violence is extended to their children.

4. Just as children who are abused tend to grow up to be child abusers, children who witness wife assault tend to grow up to be wife beaters and beaten wives.

The San Diego project discovered that the abuser and the assault victim had experienced childhood violence either as a victim or as a witness.

Suzanne Steinmetz, a researcher at the University of Delaware, found that "violence as a problem-solving method is learned in a family setting which reflects the general societal attitude toward the use of physical force, and this permissiveness in the use of physical force in intimate interaction acts as a training ground for potential abuse."*

In her article "Battered Women and Their Assailants," Bonnie E. Carlson discusses the modeling effects of aggressive and violent behavior on children:

It is known, for example, that one does not have to be rewarded directly for aggressive behavior to learn aggression as problem-solving strategy. Simply observing aggressive behavior occur without punishment is sufficient for learning such behavior. This clearly suggest that children growing up in violent homes, especially boys, are far more likely to learn such patterns of behavior and to use them

---

* Suzanne K. Steinmetz, "The Use of Force in Resolving Family Conflict: The Training Ground for Abuse," *The Family Coordinator*, June 1977.

when frustrated than are children who do not observe domestic violence in their homes.

The following personal anecdote illustrates the link between observing and performing acts of aggression and violence. The author worked with a client who had been badly beaten by her husband. The victim's 14-year-old son (who, incidentally, was beaten so badly by his father that he was covered with bruises) immediately began to defend his mother by attacking his father with a hockey stick. The parents subsequently separated and the home situation improved. But, about a year later, whenever the mother disciplined the boy verbally, he would respond by attacking her physically—and this was the same son who had defended her against physical attacks by her husband.†

Of the victims who contacted the Ann Arbor NOW Domestic Violence Project, 33.3 per cent had witnessed violence between their parents. Of the assailants, 49.1 per cent had witnessed such violence.

In her article "One of These Days—Pow Right in the Kisser," Judith Gringold quotes a mother who grimly admitted that her six-year-old tried to overrule her attempts to put him to bed by threatening to "call Daddy to hit you."‡

A study discussed by Maria Roy points to the long-range effects that domestic violence can have on future generations:

Thirteen of the 30 mothers (43%) indicated that violence may have affected their children's attitude toward marriage. These same women reported that their daughters expressed fear of marriage or general distrust of men and intimate relationships. One woman reports, "Although young at the time of the divorce, my daughter recalls that 'Daddy used to hit you.' This was never talked about in front of her after we separated. Her remarks are based on memory." Another woman said, "At ten my daughter vehemently stated she never wants to marry or have children."

Children are normally expected to be affected by the quality of their relationship with their parents, and women's reports suggest

† Bonnie E. Carlson, "Battered Women and Their Assailants," *Social Work*, Nov. 1977.
‡ Judith Gringold, "One of These Days—Pow Right in the Kisser," *Ms.* magazine, July 1976.

that children form attitudes about marriage and sex roles by observing their parents. The reports of these women also suggest that children begin to develop behaviors or typical responses to marital violence which could form the basis of their response to disputes later in their own marriages.

There may be some concern over what children learn from their parents' physical violence. Both sexes may learn that violence is one way of settling disagreements. Children themselves may tacitly come to expect that the use of physical force in marriage is a legitimate expression of authority. More specifically, boys and girls can learn that physical abuse is a form of control exercised by men over women, and unfortunately for their own marriages later on, they may receive the impression that violence is a way to "win" a disagreement. If these impressions are carried over into adulthood, they could be detrimental to marital problem-solving ability. Not only can children learn about the use of violence through their parents, but more important, in terms of developing children's skills to deal with conflict, the tendency for children to withdraw may preclude their ever viewing rational argument as an alternative way of ending disputes. When women and men possess good communication skills, unmet expectations can be clarified, behavior can change, and compromises can emerge. Children, by withdrawing, may fail to develop an understanding of the positive role of communication. Differences in childhood socialization of boys and girls, particularly in the areas of aggression and verbal skills, may tend to reinforce what children learn about the appropriateness of violence and communication in male and female sex roles. If mothers are tolerant (and the object, as well) of their sons' physical aggression, and if mothers are more likely to talk with their daughters, men and women may enter adulthood with different expectations about the use of physical force and different expectations concerning the importance of communication in conflict.*

It seems clear that violence as a means of solving problems is a learned form of behavior. A child learns how to "be" from the models available, and when parents act as if they have no internal means of control, they are demonstrating sanctioned behavior to

* Suzanne Prescott and Carolyn Letko, "Battered Women: A Social Psychological Perspective." In Maria Ray, ed., *Battered Women: a Psychosociological Study* (New York: Van Nostrand Reinhold, 1977).

their kids. Del Martin points to the horrifying potential for escalation of the problem as battered children grow up with violence as a way of life to become the next generation of batterers.†

Surely, there can be nothing more terrifying for a small child than listening to a mother's screams in the night while powerless to do anything. Yet the same child will eventually come to see violence as a way of life and may very well serve as the vehicle for perpetuating family violence in the next generation.

IDENTIFYING PROBLEMS IN CHILDREN EXPOSED
TO DOMESTIC VIOLENCE

Children growing up in an atmosphere of extreme violence are bound to have strong emotional reactions to the stress and trauma as well as to the inadequacy of their emotional, and perhaps physical, nurturance. This may take an easily recognizable form, such as high degree of aggression, but may be manifested in other ways. Kids may become irritable, moody, have low frustration tolerance, or, on the other hand, be extremely passive, actually too "well behaved." This last may be particularly common among girls.

Hilberman and Munson's article revealed that emotional neglect and abuse as well as insecurity were common due to frequent parental separations. Evidence of physical and emotional disturbance was found in over one third of the children and was suspected in many more. The children were terrified of physical examinations and had high anxiety levels about dying. Young children exhibited intense fear of and resistance to going to bed at night. Older male children were aggressive, easily frustrated and engaged in disruptive behavior (fighting with siblings and schoolmates). Female children were likely to become "withdrawn, passive, clinging and anxious." The article concludes, "Finally, there are reports of married daughters who are battered and of grown sons who are alcoholic and violent. The cycle is then complete."‡

† Del Martin, *Battered Wives* (San Francisco: New Glide Publications, 1976).
‡ Elaine Hilberman, and Kit Munson, op. cit.

While social withdrawal, physical illness, hyperactivity, and wanton destructiveness characterize the child of violence, those working in domestic-violence programs are building effective mechanisms for helping these children to develop more positive behavior patterns.

In 1976, England's Chiswick Women's Aid purchased a separate house for adolescent boys whose mothers were living in the women's shelter. They found that the boys' degree of disturbance and violent behavior was too great to deal with in the shelter, far greater than that of girls, who were able to remain with their mothers. They felt that the violence must be confronted, rather than avoided, and the boys were engaged in learning various work skills within a one-to-one therapeutic atmosphere. Although all the boys had police records for violent attacks against others before coming to the house, a year after the house had opened not one of them had physically attacked anyone again.

Some shelters seek to provide a structured, meaningful experience for the children as well as the mothers who stay there. Mary Jo Gintz, of Cleveland's Women Together, describes that group's children's program, which is financed by a special private grant. The program, which runs from 9:30 A.M. to 7:30 P.M. provides child care as well as an organized approach to dealing with the children's problems. In addition to play therapy and art therapy, they have special counseling and evaluation services for the children during their stay, and make follow-up contacts with child-guidance agencies for future therapy if needed. Counseling is also provided for women and children together. Another facet of the program is a focus on teaching parenting skills. Gintz definitely sees a cycle of violence and abuse. The little girls tend to be passive, easily giving up their toys and generally displaying victim mentalities, while the boys often have horrible tempers and throw violent tantrums. She also notes that the children have stopped listening to their mothers, or to any female staff, because their fathers have devalued all women in the eyes of the children.

La Casa de las Madres Children's Program (Northern California) consists of child care, counseling, and other supportive services for the child residents of La Casa.

La Casa's overall objective . . . is to break the intergenerational cycle of violence breeding violence which results in children growing up in domestically violent homes to become child abusers, battered women, or battering men.

The more specific objectives are:

1. To provide therapeutic, supportive child-care services to the child victims of domestic violence who reside at La Casa.
2. To provide respite care for battered wives to enable them to
   (a) recover both physically and emotionally
   (b) carry out the tasks necessary to reestablish their lives
   (c) continue working at their jobs, if employed
3. To teach parenting skills to the mothers, who often have either very little control over their children, or else frequently resort to violence themselves when they deal with their children.
4. To teach assertiveness skills to mothers.
5. To teach assertiveness skills to children.
6. To screen and refer to the appropriate agency for service or intervention:
   (a) children who have need of more intensive therapeutic services
   (b) mother-child situations in which child abuse is occurring
7. To intervene with and facilitate the resolution of conflicts and other problems engendered by the collective living situation at La Casa.
8. To do interagency liaison for
   (a) children's medical problems
   (b) school placement
   (c) legal problems of particular concern for the children.
9. To conduct ongoing follow-up after families leave La Casa to determine if further help is needed and to document progress and outcome.

Methodology

The philosophy of the Children's Program is to facilitate the comfort and safety of the children, to provide nurturance as well as aid in working through intrapersonal, family, and group living problems. The Children's Program sees its task as making La Casa a supportive home for the children while they are living there.

Infants have their own safe space where they can crawl around, be diapered and fed, be watched by mothers, but be separate. Older children are encouraged to help take care of them.

An integral part of the Program is to take the children on field trips whenever possible, since the crowded group living conditions can become oppressive. Trips to the zoo, beach, Exploratorium, movies, puppet shows, parks, etc., are made frequently within the constraints of age groupings, numbers of children, and health.

The interactions at La Casa are a macrocosm of what goes on in each family; there are often covert as well as overt expressions of violence, anger, frustration. Frequently the children are scapegoated, and blamed for problems in the house or "used" by the mothers to express anger at one another. Much staff time and energy goes into facilitating the processes and communications among the women and children as they live collectively.

Morning meetings daily, held in conjunction with the Women's Advocates, are the primary vehicle for working through these problems, resolving conflicts, and helping the women to become assertive both in expressing their needs and anger, and in requesting child care.

The makeup of the child population changes almost daily and is very unpredictable. Consequently, it is imperative that each worker in the Children's Program be able to relate to all ages of children as well as to mothers and to mother-child problems. There is no specializing in the staff, with the exception of the follow-up worker; everyone else must by virtue of necessity be able to do everything. All workers in the Children's Program work in pairs, except the follow-up worker.

Parent Effectiveness Training is being experimentally modified for the residents, and will continue to be offered if successful.

Whenever possible, children are returned to their original school or placed in a neighborhood school through special arrangement with the local school administrator.

Community liaisons have been made with innumerable San Francisco and Bay Area institutions (this is only a very partial list):

Social Services: S.F. and San Mateo DSS; Family Service Agency; Center for Special Problems; Child Abuse Council; Coleman Youth and Children's Services; Protective Services; S.F. Unified School District; Bureau of Alcoholism; Harriet Street Center; SPARC; and countless psychologists, psychiatrists, and social workers in private practice.

An English study entitled "Yo Yo Children" examined domestic violence in twenty-three families. The researchers presented the following observations about the effects of wife abuse on children:

> The effect on children in these restless, rootless situations can vary. Some may be resilient enough to cope. However, the effect on others is much more serious. When one considers the known effects of separation from parents or parent substitutes, it is small wonder that in the cases studied, where the pattern of frequent moves was coupled with violent behavior between parents, the children were variously described as being extremely nervous and jumpy, frightened and withdrawn and, not unnaturally, their school work was suffering. To the casual observer other children may not seem much affected, but their sufferings are frequently hidden because they try to keep out of the limelight. . . .
>
> In 9 cases children were either physically hurt or threatened with violence, sometimes getting hurt in the cross fire of parental blows. The parents were so overwhelmed by their own needs that they were unable to fully appreciate the needs of their children. Indeed, were it not for the social worker's intervention it would be likely that such children could be irreparably damaged emotionally or physically, or both, and it would also be extremely likely that the pattern could repeat itself when these children become adults and had their own families. . . .
>
> When young children continually live in an environment reeking of family disruption, their fathers constantly physically attacking their mothers, their mothers perpetually screaming and weeping, they do not know where to go or to whom to turn. They are denied parental love and nurturing, important needs of young children. Parental interest, concern, and empathy give the young child his first feelings of his own familiar surroundings and confidence in the world at large. If these are not available to children when very young they are denied satisfaction of their basic emotional needs; they do not acquire the sense of trust in their surroundings that leads up gradually to the different senses of autonomy, initiative, accomplishment, identity, intimacy, generativity and integrity laid down by Erikson as fundamental steps to healthy personality development. These children, therefore, suffer from emotional neglect as well.*

* Suzanne Prescott and Carolyn Letko, op. cit.

The English researchers suggest that to treat children affected by wife abuse, a parent or parent substitute (such as a grandmother) who can provide a child with stability should be given a good deal of support so that person can continue carrying such an important responsibility. Where residential or foster-home placement is deemed necessary, care should be taken to insure that the placement be a stable, long-term one, as many children are already highly insecure and have been in "yo-yo" situations for far too long already. In working directly with the children, social workers must be "prepared to share and vent to children their deep feelings of anger, anxiety, and depression. Such sharing may make the worker experience acute discomfort as repressed feelings and fantasies from their own childhood, though long forgotten, are resurrected. Feelings of inadequacy may become overwhelming as the worker realizes that children of tender years may have to be helped to face up to situations of momentous proportions, but only if such sensitive and ongoing work is attempted directly with the child and real communication established can children caught in these problems be helped."

Given the fact that abused children tend to become abusers themselves, we need to address ourselves to every possible means of breaking this cycle. One member of a women's therapy group, in speaking of her difficulties with her sixteen-year-old daughter, said, "Well, no wonder she looks down on me. I don't blame her. She used to see my ex-husband knocking me around, so how could she possibly have any respect for me?" The other group members nodded their agreement, indicating that this was a perfectly reasonable attitude. However, when the therapist intervened, questioning why she should be the one to feel ashamed when it was her husband's behavior that was shameful, the group became involved in discussion, and soon all the members expressed appropriate, healthy anger and were indignant at the assumption that the burden of shame should rest on them.

Certainly one of the goals of the women's movement is to enable women to develop positive self-images as well as respect and caring for one another. Children who recognize that women feel confident of themselves and each other grow up with a very different set of attitudes and behaviors from those of kids who are exposed to a model that devalues women.

Writer Del Martin discusses the effect that police inaction has on children, many of whom will run to a neighbor's to call for help:

> If the police officers (usually male) identify with the husband and treat the incident lightly, they will be reinforcing the role models of violent imperious male and powerless female victim. But if police efficiently calm down the parents, and, whether or not an arrest is made, effectively communicate the attitude that violent behavior is not to be excused or tolerated, the children will receive healthier signals.

Ms. Martin stresses that we must focus on reaching society's children if we are to break the cycle of violence:

> . . . another influencing factor is the child's observation of adult behavior outside of the classroom. Children pick up far more from the ways in which adults act than from what they say. Boys can't help but observe that men have the power and that they, too, can have things their own way if they take the power their maleness commands in our society. Their observations, unfortunately, still reflect the reality. . . . Change will not come about by itself. To break through the cycle of violence that has our society in its grip is an enormous task, involving nothing less than a cultural revolution of attitudes and values. If we are to reduce aggression and violence in our society, we must begin with the children. They must be trained to relate to one another as individuals, as human beings rather than as stereotypes.†

† Del Martin, "Battered Women: Society's Problem." In Jane Roberts Chapman, and Margaret Gates, eds., *The Victimization of Women,* Vol. 3, (Beverly Hills, CA; Sage Publications, 1978).

Couple Counseling—Counseling the Abuser

Chapter VI

COUPLE COUNSELING—COUNSELING
THE ABUSER

> Your hostility swatted me dead
> today
> A flattened out fly
> no more buzzing
> flying
> walking on my legs.
> I'm dead now
> flat
> motionless.
> You seem to like me dead.

Sally Saunders
Philadelphia, 12/76

PAT

"And can you tell me what actually happened, was there an argument?"

"There was too much grease on his breakfast plate and he threw his breakfast plate at me."

". . . the boys went away, and I just locked the door and put the bolts in. I just turned and he was racing down the stairs at me.

. . . He punched me, he kicked me, he pulled me by the hair, my face hit a step. He had his bare feet, you know, with being in bed; he just jumped up and pulled on his trousers and he was kicking me, if he had his shoes on God knows what kind of face I would have had. As it was I had a cracked cheekbone, broken jawbone, two teeth knocked out, cracked ribs, broken nose, two beautiful black eyes, it wasn't even a black eye it was my whole cheek. It was just purple from one eye to the other. He had got me by the neck and now, he was trying, in fact, practically succeeded in strangling me. I was choking, I was actually at the blacking out stage, and I was trying to pull his fingers away. With me trying to pull his fingers away, I scratched myself, trying to get his fingers off."*

JUDY

Yes, he'd just start shouting and give me a swipe, you know. Well, he threw me about. He had me by the hair and he threw me and I landed on the table, across the table, and I was all sore across the front. I thought he was going to start me off since I was pregnant, and I was frightened and he was shouting and I was holding my stomach. He was shouting at me, "I hope you lose it, I hope you lose that baby" and things like that.

In this chapter, we hope to share available information about working with abusive men and about counseling couples who are trying to eliminate violence from their relationships.

Although the vast majority of abusive men refuse to enter counseling, some do, and a few programs have begun to develop counseling components to address this need. What follows is a description of those programs currently under development.

It should be stressed that these efforts represent only the barest beginnings. They are highly experimental, and to draw any conclusions from the available data would be foolish. Neither support groups for abusive men nor couple counseling should be seen as a panacea for the spouse-abuse problem. Any reduction in the amount of violence used by abusive men will occur only after serious commitment and hard work.

The cessation of violence against women, both in the home and on the street, will occur only when future generations have been

* R. E. Dobash et al., "Wife Beating: The Victims Speak," *Victimology: An International Journal*, February 1978).

raised without the crippling sex-role stereotyping and dominance/submission behavior patterns with which men and women are currently burdened.

PROFILE OF THE ABUSER

As is usually the case with stereotypes, the stereotype of the abusive man just doesn't fit. He doesn't beat his wife because he is mentally ill (although mentally ill men may beat their wives); he is not necessarily poor or one of the working class (although he may be). He could be anyone—lawyer or laborer, executive or ex-con, living on an independent income or on unemployment compensation. As with child abuse, wife abuse cuts across all class, racial, ethnic, and socioeconomic lines.

His stated reasons for his use of violence vary: he may say it's because of stress at work, because he was worried about money, because she taunted him, because she didn't have dinner ready on time, because he was drunk, because she was pregnant, because she bought the wrong kind of mustard. The one thing these excuses have in common is self-justification—it was not his fault.

Common sense tells you that people don't bully other people if they feel good about themselves. Abusers tend to feel weak and powerless, and must resort to violence to assure themselves that they are, in fact, strong and in control. Bullies are cowards inside. They need to find someone who is weaker, who is afraid of them, who will not threaten or challenge their shaky sense of "superiority." A strong person can acknowledge weakness; a confident person can acknowledge mistakes. One who really feels weak and inferior inside cannot do so.

Society equates strength with masculinity, weakness with femininity. The cult of machismo offers only one acceptable form of human feeling and behavior for men and forces them to repress or ignore all others. Thus many men tend to view weakness as a female trait and to deny any trace of weakness in themselves. Since abusive men secretly feel very weak, they work even harder at denying their feelings, projecting them onto available others, the most available being their wives. They can sidestep having to face their own inadequacies by translating their self-contempt into contempt for women. Since society itself views women with contempt, abusers find reinforcement for their views. Natalie Shainess notes that men have always been acutely aware of their superior physical strength and that legal codes have had the effect of strengthening men's sense of ownership over women. The Napoleonic Code, for instance, forbade women to inherit property, vote, sue their husbands, or sign contracts alone. English and American laws have also dictated the inferior status of women, and discriminatory legal policies continue to deprive women of their rights. Such codes encourage men to take advantage of women, by physical force or in other ways.†

A major means of justifying oppression has always been to devalue the victim. The very labels given to victims deprive them of their human status. When the law establishes women as inferior beings, why shouldn't their husbands do the same? Mary Metzger cites a case in which a husband, after years of severe, chronic wife abuse, was incredulous at being brought up on charges, crying, "Do you mean to tell me that *I can't beat my wife?*"‡

As we have seen, many abusers were themselves abused in childhood. This can produce a peculiar, dual identification. A man tends to identify with the aggressor, the parent who beat him, and learns that violence is the way one deals with conflicts and emotions. At the same time, he bears a victimized identity: as a child his needs were not met; he was frightened and powerless and learned that his behavior could in no way affect what happened to him. As an adult, he feels the same way. Since he was not allowed to develop a healthy ego, a strong sense of himself, he is in many ways infantile. Like an infant, he cannot tolerate frustration and has a low level of impulse control. Although he seeks to control by brute force, he still feels essentially powerless, because he has never really experienced being in control. Feeling powerless, he doesn't feel responsible, and his projections and scapegoating serve to shore up his feeling that he is justified in what he does.

† Natalie Shainess, "Psychological Aspects of Wifebeating." In Maria Roy, ed., *Battered Women: A Psychosociological Study of Domestic Violence* (New York: Van Nostrand Reinhold, 1977).
‡ Mary Metzer, "What Did You Do to Provoke Him?" *State of Mind,* Fall, 1977, p. 23.

Some men may feel regret later, but during a violent episode they are either convinced that what they are doing is right, or some outside force (liquor, drugs, wife's behavior) has caused them to lose control. Other men may not even feel regret afterward: "I never felt too sorry, because I felt that I had been hurt twice as bad as whatever I did to her. This was the way I felt every time."* Just as abusive parents see only their own hurt and rage, and cannot see the child as a separate being, abusive men tend to see women only in terms of the degree to which they have or have not met their needs.

This infantile level of development and sense of powerlessness make it evident that behavior that is often viewed as macho and controlling is really a manifestation of the extreme dependence of the abuser upon his wife. Monica Friedman sees this dependence as the basis of the great anger and violence some men use to try to get their wives to return to them.† They make such extreme efforts not because they love and want their wives so much as because they really can't function without them. Hilberman and Munson note that "when not aggressive, the men are described as childlike, dependent, and yearning for nurturance; this picture of fragility is confirmed by the occasional reports of the husband's suicidal or psychotic behavior when there is any threat to dissolve the relationship."‡

Abusive men are often extremely jealous, and this may be evident even during the early, courtship period. Unfortunately, many women are taught to feel that jealousy is flattering, and see it as evidence of how highly they are valued. In fact, excessive jealousy is usually a sign that the woman is not really being seen for herself at all, but for the degree to which she can make a man feel important. Someone with a damaged ego often needs another person to make him feel whole, and jealousy is an expression of this tremendous dependency need. It establishes a man's possession of "his" woman. One woman, whose husband severely beat her and pushed her down the stairs, was told, "I love you so much I'd like

---

* Stephanie Oliver, *What he felt beating his wife.* Bradley-Angle House brochure, Portland OR 1977.
† Monica Friedman, op. cit.
‡ Elaine Hilberman, and Kit Munson, op. cit.

to keep you in a cage so no one else can have you." Such possessive men often foster dependency and play on their wives' weaknesses. One husband of an extremely overweight woman would often bring her presents of chocolates after he beat her, while another, who knew his wife had a drinking problem, would bring her beer. This woman later spoke of her awareness of what he was doing: "He knows that if I had a few beers in me I wouldn't care what he did and wouldn't bother him about his gambling away the rent money, but at the time I told myself that he did it because he was trying to be nice."

Another characteristic of many batterers is a kind of Dr. Jekyll and Mr. Hyde syndrome. Imagine how frustrating it is for a woman to see the man who just gave her a black eye being charming to the neighbors or looked up to as a pillar of the community, while she is busy making up a story about how she walked into a door because she is too ashamed to say what really happened, or because she feels that no one would believe her. A woman who had been repeatedly and brutally attacked told of watching a television program on wife abuse with her husband; he expressed shock that men could do such terrible things. When she pointed out that he had done those things to her, he responded with genuine surprise, saying, "Oh, no, I may slap you a little once in a while when you need it, but I never hit you like that!"

Monica Friedman notes that ten out of thirteen husbands seen by the Abused Person Program of Montgomery County Social Services could be described as "Mr. Nice Guy" and wonders whether "these men took great pains to present themselves in as favorable a light as possible; or whether they usually repress normal hostility to an unusual degree, and use violence against the wife as a mechanism for a role reversal, sometimes facilitated by alcohol."*

Some abusive men use drugs or alcohol to an excessive degree, and this may be a form of self-medication, an attempt to control or deny the tremendous rage that they carry inside. However, the result is usually the opposite of what they intended, as the liquor or drugs destroy what little control mechanisms or inhibitions they might have and their irrational behavior is given free rein.

* Monica Friedman, op. cit.

Ms. Shainess also believes this loss of control is encouraged by certain societal changes, which allow for greater freedom of expression, less repression of previously unacceptable feelings, "letting it all hang out."†

The role of alcohol in domestic violence has traditionally been viewed as a paramount one. Del Martin, however, discusses the findings of Morton Bard and Joseph Zacker, specialists in police crisis intervention, which dispute this traditional view:

> These researchers found that alcohol was the primary cause in very few cases. When alcohol use *was* noted, it was by no means inevitably the cause of the dispute. The most that could be said was that alcohol use was one of a number of circumstances contributing to the dispute, most of which undoubtedly remained unknown to the police.
>
> Bard and Zacker's study points up the possibility that regular training of police—which almost never includes specific instruction on handling domestic disturbance—predisposes officers to simplistic perceptions and self-fulfilling prophecies. If they *expect* involved parties to be intoxicated they may easily perceive and report them to be intoxicated. In this light, police data is of very little use in determining the significance of alcohol use as a variable in wife beating.
>
> Gelles agrees that to view alcohol as a primary cause in interpersonal violence is to tread on very thin ice. He points out that alcohol is known to break down inhibitions, and often leads to "out-of-character" behavior. Therefore, a person who is potentially violent can drink with the sole purpose of providing himself with a "time out" in which he can lay the blame for his violent actions on the alcohol. "Thus, individuals who wish to carry out a violent act become intoxicated *in order to carry out the violent act*. Having become drunk and then violent, the individual either may deny what occurred ("I don't remember, I was drunk") or plead for forgiveness ("I didn't know what I was doing"). In both cases he can shift the blame for violence from himself to the effects of alcohol."

Thus, by pleading drunkenness, wife beaters and their families can deceive themselves as to what is really going on in their own homes. The aggressor, his victim, and other family members can admit that the violence occurred, but maintain also that the family

† Natalie Shainess, op. cit.

is "normal," and that alcohol was responsible for the temporary lapse in "normality." Violent actions often seem to be more acceptable—or at least more comprehensible—in our society when they are performed by a person who is intoxicated. There is even a legal precedent, through the "diminished-capacity doctrine," for reducing the degree of homicide to second-degree murder or voluntary manslaughter when the offender is proved to have been intoxicated. This legal qualification reflects the assumption that the intoxicated person is not fully responsible for his or her actions. Thus, even a battered wife can avoid seeing her husband as a wife beater, thinking of him instead as a heavy drinker or an alcoholic. Notes Gelles, families that do interpret their domestic problems in this way and actually seek help usually wind up focusing on the husband's drinking problem rather than his uncontrollable aggression.

Erin Pizzey, founder of Chiswick Women's Aid, is more direct in this regard. She says, "Some of the men who batter are alcoholics, but stopping them from drinking doesn't stop the violence. Anything can release the trigger of violence in a batterer. It can be alcohol, a child crying, a bad day on the horses. Alcohol is one of several factors that often contribute to the circumstances in which marital violence occurs. It may be used as an excuse for violence and it may trigger arguments that lead to violence. But, contrary to conventional beliefs, it is not necessarily a direct cause of violence and therefore does not help to explain the causes of wife beating.‡

Martin's analysis points up a very important concept: that of the distinction between "causes" and "triggers." Many violent men, and far too many therapists and researchers, have cited external factors, such as alcohol, job-related stresses, or the behavior of other family members, including the victim, as "causes" for wife abuse. This is not only a distortion but a dangerous one, as it tends to focus attention away from the source of violence, that is, the abuser.

As we have noted, some men have such great dependency needs and have developed such elaborate defense mechanisms, that they

‡ Del Martin, *Battered Wives* (San Francisco: New Glide Publications, 1976).

never need to confront their behavior as wrong or feel guilty about it. Del Martin cites the description of an abusive husband who was interviewed by Tracy Johnston:

Johnston describes Adam as a short, soft-spoken, delicate-looking man of thirty-one. He was a self-styled "genius," who made much of his IQ of 200. Although he came from a pleasant, happy family, Adam had developed an acid tongue at an early age to compensate for his size. Johnston saw in him a "combination of arrogance and helplessness."

Adam and his wife, Julia, met in college and married after a short courtship. From the beginning they had an unusual relationship. Adam saw himself as the genius in charge of the "long-range plans." Being a woman, Julia was to do the "immediate work" of earning the living, keeping house, and paying the bills. That Julia agreed to this arrangement says something about Adam's abilities. However, she failed to uphold her end of the bargain. Although she did support them during most of their marriage, she did not keep the house clean and she never managed to balance the budget. So Adam hit her. "I wanted her to take seriously the things I expected to be taken seriously," he explained. Adam also hit Julia when she said "something stupid." When he tried to control Julia's smoking and she defied him, he hit her because he was trying "to help her discipline herself." Her defiance put him into fits of rage and frustration.

Adam said he did not regret giving Julia one slap in a nonemotional way, but he did feel guilty about flying off in a rage. "I wanted to be more in control," he said. "One thing, though, in all four years of our marriage, I never really damaged her." But Adam did admit that he caused Julia pain; often she had to rearrange her hair or tie a scarf around her forehead to cover the bruises. Toward the end, Julia started fighting back; she broke dishes, hit Adam with a poker, and threw things at him. They both threatened each other —with "murder, stuff like that."

At one point, Adam did try to stop beating Julia. But she had developed an acid tongue like his and knew how to get to him. When things were at their worst, Adam hit Julia "maybe once a day." Finally Julia disappeared; she just walked out on him one day without a word. Adam has not seen her since. But even after five years, he does not altogether discount the possibility of their getting back together.

Adam is not at all the chest-beating bully we might expect him to be. His behavior is not beyond his control; he has reasons, however self-deluding, for his violence. Obviously, in talking to Johnston, Adam took the opportunity to justify his position one more time. Clearly, he did not see the beatings he gave Julia as reason enough for her leaving him. Were we to collect more data of this kind, we would undoubtedly begin to see patterns in the rationalizations that wife beaters offer for their violent behavior.*

Susan Edmiston discusses the theory that a man uses violence "to maintain the superior position society expects him to hold in the family. When a husband sees himself as inferior in education and job status to his neighbors and his wife, he may consider violence the only means of asserting his authority. . . . Often the wife has better verbal resources—either because of her better education or because women, in general, are socialized to be more skillful with words than men."†

Margaret Elbow points out that the abusive male tends to project blame for mental strife onto his wife, experiences her as an extension of his ego, relates to her as a symbol of his mother or some "significant other," and demands that she meet his rigid expectations of marriage. He is generally incapable of intimacy, although he can offer warmth, protection, and security to his wife. She goes on to differentiate four major personality types among abusers:

The Controller is a man used to getting his way, who sees people as objects to control. He tends to monitor his wife's activities, her money, friends, and interests, and expects her to jump at his wishes. He can become violent when he doesn't get his own way, and believes his abuse to be justified. He opposes her leaving, because then he couldn't control her, and will often threaten retribution. He sees her as the parent who controlled him and feels that if he doesn't control her she will control him. Women may be attracted to him because he seems so capable of handling things.

The Defender is also self-righteous but wants not so much to control as to protect his wife, in order to keep from facing his own need for protection. He encourages her to be dependent on him and likes

---

* Ibid.
† Susan Edmiston, "The Wife Beaters," *Woman's Day,* March 1976.

to see himself as the sole breadwinner, who can take care of his wife and family. He wants to give to her but not to receive, because that would be admitting that he needs her. The basic anxiety that triggers his violence differs from the controller's in that while the controller fears being controlled, the defender fears being harmed.

The Approval Seeker has inappropriately high expectations of himself and consequently gets little satisfaction from his achievements. He gets depressed, needs constant approval, and often goes out of his way to please others. He abuses when his self-esteem is especially low. He expects rejection from others because he sees himself as deserving it. His parents usually withdrew their love when he didn't measure up, and he sees his wife the same way— he may hope she is accepting, but he expects her to reject him. He may instigate fights in order to test her love. Feelings of sexual inadequacy interfere with his ability to achieve sexual or emotional intimacy. This man does feel guilty for abusing his wife but is afraid to seek counseling, because he is sure that the counselor will put him down confirming his sense of worthlessness.

The Incorporator is characteristically desperate to incorporate another's ego in order to make himself feel whole. He may use drugs or alcohol heavily, and he exhibits jealousy during courtship. He is insatiable in his need for support and comfort, fearful that his wife will be taken away from him. He is frequently also a child abuser, because he can't differentiate between himself and others and sees his kids as well as his wife as extensions of his ego.‡

Often the abuser witnessed his father assaulting his mother as a child, and the development of an identification with the aggressor is a causative agent in the tendency to assault in later years. Although by no means do all abusers come from violent family backgrounds, the use of violence as a problem-solving technique is present in many of the families of these men.

For quick reference, we have put together a list of common characteristics of the abuser:

Heavy drinking or drug use
Abuse during the courtship period
Extreme jealousy; a need to keep the woman totally controlled and isolated

‡ Margaret Elbow, "Theoretical Considerations of Violent Marriages," *Social Casework,* Nov. 1977.

A history of having been abused as a child, or of having witnessed abuse of his mother by his father

Inability to tolerate frustration

A violent temper, often sparked by little things

Cruelty to animals; great enjoyment of hunting for the sake of killing animals, or abuse and mistreatment of pets

Preoccupation with weapons

Mental illness

Poor self-image; insecurity about his own masculinity

A pattern of blaming others, particularly his wife, for his problems

Acceptance of violence as an appropriate problem-solving method

Unemployment or high levels of job dissatisfaction.

HELP FOR THE ABUSER

Most people agree that men who are batterers need help, although there are disagreements about what kind and who should provide it. One point of view is that assault is a criminal act and should be treated as such. Certainly the strengthening of laws for the protection of women and the restraining of violent men is a vital focus for attention. However, the fact remains that men who have been taught violence as a way of life may not know another way and therefore remain potential abusers. When a woman leaves an abusive husband, she may find safety and freedom—he may find another woman to abuse. A number of approaches have been developed for working with abusers, although a great deal more work needs to be done in this area.

Del Martin notes the difficulty of getting abusive men to seek help:

Because he believes not only that he has the right to beat his wife but that other husbands are doing it too, he considers his behavior to be "normal." Therefore, he believes he has no problem and no need for outside help. The only way to get him into therapy or counseling would be for a judge to order it as a condition of release. Lt. George Rosko of the San Francisco Police Department suggests that a first-time offender be remanded to a counseling center in the same way that traffic violators are sent to traffic school. The batterer would be warned explicitly that if he "ever lays a hand on his wife again" he will be sent to jail. If judges would take such a hard-nosed position and make it stick, Rosko believes, there would be a marked reduction in the incidence of wife abuse.

An assistant district attorney in Spokane proposes a quicker method of obtaining results: peer pressure to bear upon offenders and let them know in no uncertain terms that such behavior is not acceptable; if men would work with batterers in much the same way as women are working with victims, we might well be on our way to solving the problem.*

When an abuser does agree to get counseling, the counselor should be alert for possible manipulation:

Experienced shelter workers know that many times when a battering husband offers to get counseling, he's taking this step not to change his behavior but simply to get his wife back home. Once she's home, he frequently stops seeing the counselor and resumes his previous behavior. Counselors that are dealing with battering men should be aware that they are often being used as a ploy by the husband to blackmail his wife into going back. This manipulation usually takes the form of the husband stating or implying to his wife, "I'm doing something to save the marriage; now you do your part by coming home." These men sometimes give their wives a deadline to return by. When counselors aren't aware of this dynamic, they can contribute to a woman's feelings of guilt and make her an easy target for the husband's manipulation by tacitly supporting his demands. The counselor should address the batterer's unacceptable behavior, rather than focusing on "saving" the marriage. . . .†

Some judges will require that a convicted wife beater undergo counseling.

The merits of mandatory counseling are still debatable, and there has been very little work done in addressing this issue. It is quite possible that the practice of judges' imposing mandatory counseling as a condition of release would carry a lot of weight in combating the unwritten societal acceptance of wife abuse and in giving legitimacy to the seriousness of the problem. On the other hand, it has been generally found that people tend not to receive

* Del Martin, "Battered Women: Society's Problem." In *The Victimization of Women*, Vol. 3, Jane Roberts Chapman, and Margaret Gates, eds., (Beverly Hills, CA: Sage Publications, 1978).
† Betsy Warrior, op. cit.

much benefit from counseling unless they themselves recognize the need for it. Abusers who are ordered into a counseling situation may just feel resentful and therefore resist attempts at therapeutic intervention, although it may also be possible that a skilled therapist can help a client recognize and acknowledge that he does have problems.

Janet Geller describes a group model believed successful in working with abusive men. It was developed by the Victims Information Bureau of Suffolk, Inc., in Suffolk County, New York; its two main objectives were "to sensitize the men to their violence and to help them rechannel their aggression into more socially acceptable forms."‡ It was a short-term, goal-oriented group, because these men had such low frustration tolerance that it was felt they needed to see things concretely and to experience positive results quickly. Accepting the fact that the men have low opinions of women, the group was for men only and led by a male worker. Use of the word "therapy" was deliberately avoided, because it might be threatening. The group model itself was chosen to minimize the threat of feeling singled out in an individual therapy situation and to maximize the sense of support and safety offered by the group setting. Only one group member initiated contact for service; the rest were recruited either as husbands of women involved in women's groups or due to their having been in couple counseling. The group met for ten sessions, during which a number of important areas of group process and development were noted.

Only two of the original five men committed to attend showed up for the first session, which engaged in active outreach for those who did not attend. While seeking to establish a comfortable therapeutic atmosphere, the worker also spoke clearly and openly about the reasons for the group and its goals: "to discover why they hit their wives, and how to stop." During the second session, a developing group identification and cohesiveness was noted. Although all the members were able to discuss their love for their wives and their wish to have violent behavior cease, they were not ready to acknowledge any responsibility for their behavior. By the

‡ Janet A. Geller, "Reaching the Battering Husband" Victims Information Bureau of Suffolk, Inc., Suffolk County, NY. Unpublished paper, 1977.

third meeting, although members continued to use denial and to externalize blame for the violence onto their wives, they were beginning to display discomfort with their behavior. During this session, the worker explained that a hotline would be available in conjunction with the group, which they could call when they felt like using physical force against their wives.

> In this effort the worker began to help the men to find a way to rechannel their aggression, delay the impulse to hit, and help the men to be successful in their attempts to change. In addition, he fostered the notion of continuity of service and agency identification in that there are many people at the project to help and he will be informed should any group member call. Further, this illustrated to the men that the worker was taking their commitment to change seriously, as well as placing expectations on the members that they are to change.*

These first three sessions were seen as the beginning of the group.

The fourth session brought an interesting development in that, although the men continued to use the same mechanisms to keep from acknowledging responsibility, they were at the same time beginning to show sympathy for the position of their wives. They were also able to discuss how threatened they felt by the women's movement. As a further step in the process of development of a group identity, the members exchanged phone numbers so that they could contact each other for help.

During the fifth meeting, members were able to move from denial to real introspection and to acknowledge that they were indeed responsible for the violence. With these admissions came a developing motivation to change. The worker saw this time as an appropriate one to take a firm stand against violence, as the members were now ready to hear this, rather than react defensively and feel criticized. They were also now ready to consider the possibility that they could learn to deal with their wives in new ways, although they could not at this point see any real alternatives. This session was considered to be a turning point and led to increased gains during the middle phase.

An important breakthrough for one of the members was dis-

* Ibid.

cussed in the sixth meeting, when he told of using what he had learned in the group to curb his impulse to hit his wife. The sharing of this experience helped the other members to see that it was possible to use alternatives to violence.

The last four sessions were devoted to the termination phase. Members were angry and felt a good deal of anxiety about the group ending. They were encouraged to verbalize their feelings in order to be able to work through their separation anxiety. It was also noted that members exhibited regressive behavior as a natural reaction to separation. Plans were made to invite wives to the ninth session, and it was felt that the members were able to move into this planning because they had been successful in dealing with their feelings around termination. The session involving wives was "introductory and exploratory in nature and the discussion centered around the couples' relationships. The wives in particular interacted very well together, and were more verbal and articulate than their husbands. By the end of the session, all present felt the need to continue as a couples group, and a commitment was made to meet as such with new workers." The new workers were to consist of a male/female team in order to provide positive models, and the change in workers was seen as a way of symbolizing the beginning of a new group. Ms. Geller writes:

"It was felt that this was a very successful group. The goals were clearly stated and researched. A group identity and cohesiveness developed. The group members experienced growth and were able to change their attitudes and views. Members were able to use what they learned in the group in their lives. They internalized group values and the worker influenced them. These were hard-to-reach clients—both invisible to the project and prejudiced against therapy. It is believed that the initial success of the group lay in strategy—it was not called therapy, the men were reached in innovative ways, and they were minimally threatened. The environment was made as comfortable as possible for them by defining the group as short-term, and for men only, with a male worker. The offering of help was tailored to their needs. This author believes that often when treatment is unsuccessful the cause for failure is within the treatment model, not the clients. It behooves the helper to help, and how that happens is the responsibility of the helping agent. With this group, the major work was in understanding who our clients were and providing a structure that met their needs. The rest of the group's success can be attributed to the sensitive work of the group leader. A postscript is that all but one couple has continued in couple counseling. The couple that did not continue had separated, only later to reunite. By then, the group's membership was closed, although the couple did request group-couple therapy.

RECOMMENDATIONS

It is always difficult to offer service to hard-to-reach clients, because their resistance to treatment probably affects our sense of effectiveness. In working with battered spouses, there is no clinical literature in the field; this compounds the problem. In addition, violence is abhorrent to most of us. The knowledge that men have beaten their wives black and blue does not help to motivate a desire to tackle this clientele. Only since 1973 has attention been directed to the plight of battered spouses. The presence of violence might be the sole factor explaining why this problem had not been addressed sooner by society as a whole.

The attempt to offer help to husbands who inflict violence on their spouses provided a unique opportunity to learn about the dynamics of the spouse-abuse syndrome. It also afforded an opportunity to experiment with treatment techniques when working with battering husbands. Although the group met for ten sessions only, what was learned about the batterers was both illuminating and surprising. In all areas of functioning other than the marital relationships, these men appeared normal. All the men were steadily employed and some men had their own businesses. They were homeowners, good neighbors, and average citizens. They had the same concerns and desires as their wives and they possessed the gamut of human traits and emotions. In most instances the violence was exclusive to their wives.

For these husbands, psychotherapy was not part of their frame of reference. What brought these men to the attention of the project was the identification of a single presenting problem. They were able to become engaged in treatment because the focus was on problem solving centered around the violence, which was very specific. Working with them in a group was the treatment of choice, because meeting with other men in groups was familiar to them. It also allowed for a decrease in intensity, since the focus was not always on one person as in individual therapy. The fact that the group was short-term was an advantage to the clients and worker alike.

The men probably would not have tolerated the time and investment in reaching solutions in more traditional therapy. For the worker, based on the limits of time, short-term treatment fostered working toward solutions.

However, the use of the group alone would not have fully provided the service needed by these men. Another essential component for working effectively with battering husbands was the ability to provide immediate intervention. Because violence could occur at any time and could be life-threatening, it was not possible to wait until the clinic appointment to deal with the crisis. Further, if there was to be modification of this behavior and attempts to rechanneling the aggression, that must be demonstrated through intervention at the time of the incident, not afterward. Calling on the hotline instead of battering a spouse is in and of itself an attempt at an alternative solution to the violence.

This information has broad implications, as it points out that not all batterers are the same in personality and degree of pathology. While some men who beat their wives might be too severely disturbed to benefit from treatment, others are not, although they might be highly resistant, as were the members of this group. Pizzey's observations were similar. She speculated that some battering husbands might benefit from treatment. In some cases, violence may be a maladaptive response to particular situations that can be modified over a period of time. In the short period of time that this group met, there were marked modifications in the violence. There is reason to believe that with continued help the violent behavior could be further lessened.

If these group members are a typical sampling of certain types of batterers, then this information may shed additional light on why the women stay, which is the most frequent question raised. Research has supplied some of the answers to this question, but perhaps, based on the experience of this group, we can glean some answers from the men themselves. Since no wives were continuously beaten and batterings could be quite infrequent, the women may stay because their husbands are good husbands when not beating them. This is not to negate the seriousness of wife abuse, but it may aid in an understanding of the wives' reactions.

If violence in most cases is limited to the wives, one might question what there is in the marital relationship that fosters violence. The author rejects theories of the sadomasochistic relationship and believes that the salient issue is intimacy. One hypothesis is that batterers cannot tolerate the close contact and exposure that the intimacy of most marriages demands. An area for further exploration might be the relationship between spousal violence and fear of intimacy."†

Many women's groups have no interest in working with abusers. They feel that their energies and resources are limited and their goals are to help women, for they feel it is the role of concerned men to develop programs to help men. Some groups, however, do see working with men as an appropriate function for them, particularly since a number of women, even those who leave their husbands, wish to continue their marriages. At Rainbow Retreat, in Phoenix, individual, family, and group therapy are available, and 60 per cent of the men participate in one or other of these treatment modalities. In England, Chiswick House has established a residence, staffed by two men, where abusers who are upset or feeling extremely unhappy can live or come to attend support groups.

Any form of treatment, in order to be helpful, must be perceived as helpful. None of us likes to be put down, and a counselor who approaches a client with a condemnatory attitude is likely to see that client disappear. An effective treatment is not for the counselor or therapist to express his disapproval of the abuser's behavior, but for the abuser himself to be brought to recognize and admit his behavior as a problem and to acknowledge the need for change. Since abusers typically externalize their problems anyway, it is easy for them to find excuses to avoid treatment, so that a counselor who is heavily judgmental is falling into a trap. This is not to say that the opposite is true—that a counselor needs to approve of unacceptable behavior; it is only to say that if the

† Ibid.

abusing man sees treatment goals not as his own but as the counselor's, he will have no stake in attaining them.

The Rage Behavior Program, set up by the Clark County, Ohio, Mental Health Program was not developed specifically for men, but only men applied to it.‡ In this program too, the emphasis was on setting goals and reinforcing positive behavior and the program was based on a behavioral-therapy model. Insight-oriented, depth therapy, which looks at causative factors, does not seem to be a useful model for people who need instant gratification, who have little patience and short fuses. Behavioral therapy focuses on the here and now—how you got to be the way you are is not considered relevant or helpful; but, rather, identifying the behaviors that are unsatisfactory and finding ways to change them are the goals. This seems a particularly appropriate model for the abuser.

An initial step in the development of the Rage Behavior Program was to pull together the following list of common characteristics of people with severe temper problems:

a) Depression
b) Poor self-concept
c) Problems on job, either with the co-workers or boss or possibly even both
d) Marital difficulty
e) Withdrawal from people
f) Drinking behavior
g) Manipulative interpersonal relationships
h) Explosion on minor issues that would crop up
i) A definitive dislike for authority figures
j) No recreational pursuits
k) Inability to laugh*

(Note that many of these characteristics parallel those of the abuser.)

‡ Walter F. Foltys, "Summation of the Rage Behavior Program." Unpublished paper (1978, Clark County, OH)
* Ibid.

The treatment program was developed to incorporate several dimensions of behavioral therapy, including:

> goal setting and reinforcement for meeting these goals. This was primarily concerned around behaviors of the person taking care of himself. This included teaching some relaxation techniques as well as also teaching some social skills. It was felt that previous behavioral therapy had primarily focused on one of these areas. It was also felt that no adequate work had been done on the combining of treatment plans, which included all these different behavioral therapies.†

The first twelve-week program, begun in September 1977, was completed by four of the five initially referred men, as well as two who were accepted after the initial intake:

"The procedure for the group was as follows: the primary part of the group was set around behavior management. Goals were set for the clients in the first interview . . . in four significant life areas, a) symptomatology, b) family, c) social, and d) life plans."

Goals included learning to relax and not to act in an offensive manner. Goals along the social line concerned taking care of oneself by engaging in recreational pursuits and also getting out of the house and being able to engage in more positive activities with the family and perhaps spending more time with one's children and developing the relationship with them. Goals along the lifeplan lines were primarily centered on the ability to (a) find employment or (b) continue with some kind of schooling.

Each week, clients prepared written lists of behavioral steps to be used toward meeting their goals, to be reviewed at the following week's meeting. Relaxation techniques, involving muscle desensitization and creating fantasies were a part of each session, and clients were noted to be visibly sleepy after the exercises.

"An interesting point to note is that every one of the clients also became aware of some possible antecedents of rage behavior. Each of the clients admitted that they suspect that certain parts of their body would tense up before a rage episode. Clients were in-

† Ibid.

structed on how to become more aware of these particular muscle groups and to pay attention to them and take appropriate action at the time before they blow. Each client thereupon learned that perhaps his rage behavior was not a spontaneous emission, but could be predicted from perhaps his shoulders tensing up or his hands clenching into fists."‡

Foltys also notes that a fascinating aspect of group process was that clients started to see the group as a "men's group":

> Clients were stating to this therapist that they felt exceptionally comfortable about being there because (a) it was their night out away from the family and kids and they were able to express themselves with a bunch of other guys with perhaps their censors off and (b) they felt that they could learn how to talk to other guys even about football and other sports events without having four to six beers in them at the time.

It is difficult to assess fully the effectiveness of the model at this early stage, but it was noted that clients did seem to feel better about themselves and others after completing the program.

The October issue of the Center for Women Policy Studies newsletter, *Response,* describes two additional programs for abusive men. One is EMERGE, (P. O. Box 536, Somerville, MA 02143). The program emphasizes that "it is important for men to begin to talk about battering—why it starts, what leads to it, how it affects individuals and relationships, and what can be done to stop it."

To do that, EMERGE provides "a safe environment for men to explore the roots of their violence and to learn ways to change their behavior." According to the sixteen volunteer workers at EMERGE, "a person who has habits of violence is not sick or less than human." EMERGE volunteers wish to help each man "to understand the social conditions, cultural support, and personal history that encourage his behavior," while also allowing him to explore "constructive alternatives for dealing with frustrations, angers and fears that . . . men experience today."

Aside from the aid given directly to the men, the work of EMERGE includes a strong community education effort with

‡ Ibid.

classes, workshops, and in-service training provided jointly with women's organizations.

Another program concerned directly with the abuser is Therapy for Abusive Behavior (TAB), at P. O. Box 6420, Baltimore, MD 21230, run by three women volunteers with the assistance of the Southern Baltimore Police District commander and one of his community-relations officers.

The TAB team, of Patricia Erat, Carol Bailey, and Willida Hoffman, started the program to give abusers an "opportunity for self-help in the area of personal growth and development by actively participating in a program designed to identify and change violent behavior patterns." TAB teaches men more effective techniques for handling situations and relationships, while providing a supportive network for the men during and after the program.

TAB is unique in that it intervenes to help the abuser at the initial stages of his contacts with the courts. In a probationlike manner, TAB offers the judicial system a "therapeutic rather than punitive" option. Instead of allowing the litigation to continue, a judge may place the abuser in TAB under the condition that he attend the program regularly or else reenter the judicial system.

TAB also offers a "structured program which can be easily utilized by existing agencies." The program meets the needs of its clients through a community network of health, social, and other services. Furthermore, in an attempt to effectively address the problems of the abuser and his victim, TAB plans to begin a complementary program for the women who have been abused by the men involved in the program."

The Women's Resource Network is currently in the process of developing models for working with abusive males through group counseling, which explores their use of violence as a resource and develops nonviolent problem-solving techniques. This project is conducted in conjunction with the Probation Department and in collaboration with drug and alcohol programs, community organizations working with battered women, and other appropriate health and welfare resources.

We are conducting group therapy sessions for seven to ten men who meet weekly for twelve weeks. The two-hour sessions are semistructured, and various group process techniques and experiential exercises such as role playing, role reversal, anger ventilation, emotional catharsis, guided fantasies, and relaxation techniques are utilized. In addition, there are occasional didactic presentations by the group leader, dealing with the generic issues involved in some of the problems the men share as well as the societal conditioning that lends covert and overt support to the use of violence in general and the use of violence against women in particular.

Critical to working with abusive men is finding a basis for identification with them, their goals, aspirations, frustrations, and being empathic with their plight. In general, men are conditioned to believe that the need for counseling or therapy is a sign of weakness and inadequacy, so that it is vital to establish a basis for trust between the leader and the group members. To this end, an individual appointment with the group leader prior to joining the group is useful.

Many of the problems and issues discussed in the group come from the members themselves, as they have an active part in defining the goals and content of the group in order that it be meaningful to them. In addition, issues intrinsic to the problems these men are dealing with are addressed, such as:

—sex-role stereotypes,
—positives and negatives in developing and maintaining the macho image,
—use of violence as a learned behavior and the "bully syndrome,"
—finding one's wholeness (for men, their emotional, intuitive selves),
—power—constructive and destructive forms thereof,
—the influence of various socioeconomic backgrounds on current behavior,
—the subtle and not so subtle effects of the societal and cultural influences under which we live,
—the importance of the models we learned as children, with particular emphasis on breaking the cycle for those men who were beaten as children and/or witnessed spouse abuse,
—the contribution of drugs, alcohol, and reality problems such as unemployment.

The top priority in working with a group of abusive males is to develop with them ways of defusing anger. To make an impact in this area, the group engages in exercises in assertiveness training, learning to communicate verbally and openly, learning to handle frustration, and learning nonviolent problem-solving techniques.

Concurrent individual counseling is provided on an as-needed basis as well as in close collaboration with other agencies involved, such as the probation department, to insure uniformity of goal.

COUPLE COUNSELING

Many women feel that they want their marriages to remain intact, but without violence. Many of these women request couple counseling rather than individual therapy, and several couple-therapy programs are being developed in response to such requests.

As program development in this area increases, practitioners will need information regarding a couple profile as relates to marital violence. Not much information is available as yet, but we share with you what we have managed to find.

In their article, Suzanne Prescott and Carolyn Letko discuss the role that marital expectations and lack of communication play in the violent relationship:

Aspects of roles were of particular interest in the current study. Each partner possesses expectations concerning the use of physical force and how conflicts should be handled. . . . When traditional sex roles emphasize male authority, men may not only expect to influence important areas of family decision making, but may also expect that the final word in disagreements is theirs, and that physical force is justified in maintaining their authority. Should strain arise over lack of ability or desire to meet either explicit or implicit expectations, conflict may be settled through the arbitrary use of authority by the male head of household.

There is also the matter of changing roles of women and their effect upon marital stability:

The Women's Movement at its core represents expanding opportunities for women. For many women, this had meant rising expectations for marital satisfaction and personal growth. Often, however, men experience the Women's Movement as a threat to their own opportunities and sphere of influence. As couples enter marriage and go through their adult years, they encounter the often incompatible desires to more firmly rely on old values and early expectations in the face of changing social values and the lack of social consensus concerning current sex roles. At the same time, they may find that their marriage is a testing ground for trying out new behaviors, developing new expectations, and changing sex roles. The need for security of old traditions and the need for new growth may lead couples to face new frustrations and may lead to conflict in marriage.*

Extreme dependence of a reciprocal nature is another element in many relationships between batterers and their victims:

Most relationships that involve battered women are not interdependent on both emotional and economic levels. The woman becomes the victim because of her extreme dependence upon the batterer. She does not believe that she can be a totally independent person.

Interestingly enough, neither does the batterer believe he can stand alone. A bond seems to exist between the couple that says, "We may not make it together, but alone we'll surely perish." Both typically are traditionalists, who fear the religious, social, emotional and economic ramifications of divorce. Death is a more acceptable alternative. It is essential to understand this conviction when working with the troubled couple.†

The similarity between abusive marital relationships and parent-child relationships are pointed out in *For Better, For Worse*:‡

. . . the parent (husband) knows what is best for the child (wife), makes all the important decisions, takes care of the money because children (women) just "don't know how to handle these things,"

* Suzanne Prescott, and Carolyn Letko, op. cit.
† Lenore E. Walker, "Treatment Alternatives for Battered Women." In Jane Roberts Chapman and Margaret Gates, eds., *The Victimization of Women*, Vol. 3, (Beverly Hills, CA: Sage Publications, 1978).
‡ Jennifer Baker Fleming and Carolyn Kott Washburne, *For Better, For Worse* (New York: Charles Scribner's Sons, 1977), p. 321.

and, of course, is responsible for "discipline." We are considered inadequate parents if we don't properly discipline our children; perhaps many husbands feel inadequate if they don't properly "discipline" their wives. Husbands and parents can control through fear; by being bigger and more powerful they can intimidate their "lessers" into desired behavior.*

Monica Friedman, staff person of the Abused Persons Program, Montgomery County, Maryland, provides us with the following information:

Many of these couples are in a multistress situation, with severe financial management problems, and often additional health, mental health, employment, and children's problems. Poor self-concepts, sexual difficulties, unrealistic expectations, and extreme jealousy by the husband are also frequent. The stress seems to be both in the external situation, as when the husband is seasonally out of work because he is in construction, and in the family's inability to cope, such as in their incurring unmanageable debts, even with a higher than median family income. The violence typically occurs when there is an overload on the system, and does not seem to be used as an instrument of control.

Wives frequently report that they do not know what sets off a violent incident; and it appears that the violence is generally not "provoked." However, when we ask questions about a wider time frame than the point immediately preceding an incident, both spouses can sometimes pinpoint changes in the immediate or wider family systems which occurred at the same time as the beginning or increase of family violence. The fact that much violence to wives begins or increases when they are pregnant (and injuries are directed at their bellies at this time) is a case in point.

We have also found a number of other changes in a previously shaky family balance associated with an increase of violence. One such is a religious conversion by one of the spouses, especially to a very different or extremist sect. In one case, the abuser joined a charismatic sect; he then told the children his wife was Satan and he and the children were Christ crucified by her. In another family, the wife joined a fundamentalist sect. She then started worrying more about his sinful ways, leading to more arguments, culminating in vi-

* Ibid.

olence. Another wife said, "My husband became very religious in 1972. He was baptized and then our son died the next day. Now he goes to church every other week, and then comes home and fights."

Of course, the religious conversion cannot be seen as the *cause* of the violence, any more than can alcoholism, which is highly associated with family violence. Rather, it can be seen as part of the shifts in the nuclear family system, resulting from an increase in anxiety, sometimes located in either an extended-family system or in the work system.

A cycle theory of battering, put forth by Lenore Walker, deserves serious consideration by counselors working with partners in a violent relationship.

". . . Rather than constant or random occurrences of battering, there is a definite cycle that is repeated over a period of time. This cycle appears to have three distinct phases that vary in time and intensity both in the same couple and between different couples. The three phases are the tension-building phase, the battering incident, and the calm, loving respite."†

One therapeutic approach involves the therapist's attempt to "cancel the hitting license."

A beaten wife cannot wait for the norms of the society to change so as to redefine marriage as not including the unstated right to hit. Nor can she do it herself unaided. Assistance in bringing about this redefinition is one of the most important reasons for involving others. Having brought the issue into the open, and hopefully, with their support, she can make clear that the use of physical force by a husband (or wife) is never justified, and will not be tolerated.

Part of this is the need to keep clear the difference between a conflict and how one settles conflicts, and between being wrong about something and how one changes the behavior of the person who does something wrong. Even if the classic complaints of being a "nagging wife" or a "lousy housekeeper" are correct in a particular case, that no more justifies a beating than being a "griper" or a

† Lenore E. Walker, "Treatment Alternatives for Battered Women." In Jane Roberts Chapman and Margaret Gates, eds., *The Victimization of Women,* Vol. 3, (Beverly Hills, CA: Sage Yearbooks in Women's Policy Studies, 1978), p. 155.

"slacker" at work. In this connection, it is important to realize that friends, neighbors, relatives and therapists often start by trying to find out who or what is wrong. A beaten wife must reject that approach, even though these issues must ultimately be faced. Whatever else is wrong, all parties must acknowledge that hitting is wrong. So an essential first step is to make clear that irrespective of who is at fault, the use of violence is unacceptable.‡

Margaret Elbow discusses the sexual problems battered women face in the relationships:

> Battered women often describe their sexual relationships as distasteful because sex is imposed upon them, because they are criticized for their performance, or because their own satisfaction is of little or no consequence to their mate. Several women have reported having sexual intercourse imposed upon them upon returning home from the hospital after childbirth, or when they are ill. Others describe intercourse as nothing but a means of relieving his sexual urges, with no foreplay or allowance for her arousal or climax. Humiliation by comparison to other sexual partners is not uncommon.*

The Victims Information Bureau of Suffolk County, New York, which conducts one of the men's groups described earlier, has developed a couple-counseling program component as well. Janet Geller and James Walsh feel that without the involvement of both partners in counseling, violence will not stop.

In their program, a staff member will work with the woman toward getting her husband to become involved, but if she expresses fear of approaching him or feels that she would be in danger if he were to know of her involvement, this is accepted and she is steered to a different counseling component.

For couple therapy, the husband must make a commitment to wanting to end the violence. Couples are taught that anger and fighting are alright but should not involve violence and that

---

‡ Murray Straus, "A Sociological Perspective on the Prevention and Treatment of Wifebeating." In Maria Roy, ed., *Battered Women, a Psychosociological Study* (New York: Van Nostrand Reinhold, 1977).
* Margaret Elbow, "Theoretical Considerations of Violent Marriages," *Social Casework,* Nov. 1977.

fighting should instead be focused on the goal of resolving an issue or problem.

The Victims Information Bureau sees the basis of abusive behavior stemming from one or a combination of three major factors: 1) an organic problem, 2) an impulse disorder, 3) a poor self-image with feelings of impotence and inferiority. A pattern of repressing feelings or abuse of alcohol can be a compounding factor. They note that organic disorders can be uncovered by psychological and neurological work-ups.

The next two factors can be treated by a combination of behavioral and psychotherapeutic techniques. "Normally," feelings of anger are sublimated by aggressive fantasies or verbalizations in the form of ventilation. However, the person who acts out, rather than rechanneling those aggressive impulses, may have an impulse disorder. A man with an impulse disorder is asked by the counselor what he can do to rechannel the anger into more acceptable behavior. The method that usually works the best comes from the individual. The husband is also asked to call the hotline when he is angry, rather than lashing out at his wife. The hotline operates twenty-four hours a day, seven days a week. The hotline workers are given a treatment plan developed by the couple's counselor. The plan for treatment helps the hotline worker to offer appropriate alternatives to modify the caller's behavior.

In addition, an environment that allows for dissent between husband and wife has not been created. Creating such an environment in the therapy sessions can enable the couple to change the environment at home.

Both partners are taught new ways of "fighting" that do not lead to violence. Fight and anger in a marriage are viewed as normal. The couple is taught to accept anger as part of the range of human emotions. The goal of fighting now becomes the resolution of problems through the expression of anger without violence. Both husband and wife are encouraged to be understanding of the expression of feeling between one another. The emphasis, therefore, is on restructuring relationships through modeling and teaching changes in behavior, rather than on analysis of intrapsychic dynamics.

A husband's drinking problem is not the focus of therapy unless it inhibits the change process. In which case, he is referred to an alcohol treatment program. While he is in treatment for his drinking he and his wife are offered supportive counseling until the drinking is under control and the therapy can resume. In cases that do not require a referral for specialized treatment of alcohol abuse, the focus remains on the relationship, with the drinking seen as a symptom of the problem.

Spouse abuse is the presenting problem of 96 per cent of our clients. The techniques described have proven effective. Clients who have not been seen in couple therapy have learned new methods to cope with the abuse. They report feeling less isolated and having a better sense of self since being involved with VIBS. For every couple involved in couple therapy for a minimum of three weeks, the violence has stopped in every case. More than two thirds of the couples in therapy have remained with the program.

The results obtained from this model appear hopeful, but measurement of sustained changes and reasons for leaving therapy are just being analyzed. However, this model is based on general family therapy models with techniques that have been tried and proved effective, and indications are that these techniques are the treatment of choice when working with battered spouses.†

Urging couple counselors to focus on interpersonal connections, rather than on intrapersonal pathology, Murray Straus examines the possible contributions that increasingly popular marriage counseling can make to the battering problem.

Just as wifebeating was ignored by academic researchers in psychology and sociology until quite recently, there has been a similar gap in clinical practice. Actually, it is worse than a gap, because under the influence of Freudian theory, psychiatrists, clinical psychologists, and social workers have tended to focus attention on such things as presumed aggressive "drives," acting-out of impulsive "needs," and female masochism. In short, to the minor extent that wifebeating has been dealt with clinically, it has been through attempting to diagnose and treat sick persons rather than sick relationships. As previously noted, recent developments have moved the field of marriage counseling to just such a focus on relationships. Nevertheless, as of this writing, little has been published on the specific marriage-counseling methods to be used for husband-wife violence. But a start has been made. Several family service agency

† Janet A. Geller and James C. Walsh, op. cit.

conferences were held in 1976 (for example, by the Jewish Family Service of New York) and there has been one paper which details specifics.

Marriage counseling is undergoing a tremendous growth. It may be the fastest-growing type of clinical service in this country. Considering the large clientele in the immediate future—most of whom will have been involved in at least some violent incidents, the scope for a meaningful contribution to the elimination of wifebeating is evident. However, this potential contribution is not likely to take place unless therapists come to see wifebeating as primarily a problem of social relationships (especially power), rather than of mental illness. Marital therapy, to deal with wifebeating, must focus on treating the relationship. Of course, psychological problems, such as damage to a wife's self-esteem and sense of adequacy, do often accompany wifebeating, and the counselor can provide valuable assistance to these women.‡

The importance of therapy focused on reorganizing the pattern of husband-wife relationships is stressed because, as previously noted, marriage counseling still seems to be dominated by psychoanalytic and other "insight"-type therapies focused on the presumed deep psychological problems of partners. At best, such treatments are likely to be ineffective. Usually, they divert attention from the here and now issues which must be resolved. At worst, traditional therapy tends to reinforce the society's penchant for blaming the victim —the wife—rather than the husband or the relationship. This is most apparent in the use of such concepts as "female masochism," and in a subtle and usually unintended (but nonetheless powerful) encouragement of women to follow traditional passive-accepting female roles. Perhaps the direction in which therapy in wife abuse cases needs to go can be best illustrated by comparison with the treatment of the closely related (but far less common) problem of child abuse.

The still predominant method of treating child abuse consists of insight-type psychotherapy, and if this fails or is not available, removing the child and punishing the parents by fine or jail. This approach is slowly being replaced by programs which, instead of trying to reorganize the personality of the abusing father or mother, teach parents how to "parent" and thus to avoid the kind of situation which leads to child abuse. The same shift in emphasis is called for

‡ Daniel G. Saunders, "Marital Violence: Dimensions of the Problem and Modes of Intervention," *Journal of Marriage and Family Counseling*, 1976.

in relation to wife abuse and the larger pattern of less extreme husband-wife and wife-husband violence of which wifebeating is the most dramatic manifestation. That is, the treatment steps must continue to include the wife removing herself, as well as prison for intransigent assaultive husbands—just as these remain the ultimate mode of coping with the child-abusing parent. . . .*

The potential for treating couples within groups is shown by the following case illustration, which supports this as a useful modality in some instances:

In a couples group, one wife's disclosure of receiving severe beatings exposed the husband's great fear of loss of control and brought it into focus. By staying with the symptom of abuse, many facets of the couple's interaction were exposed. The members of the group were able to help the husband see that his frustration over a poor work situation was displaced onto his wife. He was encouraged to find appropriate outlets for his anger. The wife was urged to consider terminating the relationship unless it improved. This couple was young, motivated, and eager to work on their problems. Gradually, the abuse was curtailed.

Opening a discussion of the abuse issue was helpful to other members of the group. Two more wives revealed that they also were victims of abuse, which took the specific form of being spanked. These couples were severely disturbed; the abuse was more chronic and deliberate. The abusive behavior was not, however, encouraged by the wife solely because of her masochistic needs. Rather, it was an interaction in which control was the crucial issue and physical strength was the axis on which the outcome depended.†

Ms. Nichols considers that it is within the women's movement that the most innovative treatment approaches are being developed, rather than within traditional family agencies, which have neglected the issue. She points to the need for work geared to reaching both abuser and abused, to overcome the traditional theories, which place responsibility on the woman. Finally, she

---

* Straus, op. cit.
† Beverly B. Nichols, "The Abused Wife Problem," *Social Casework*, Jan. 1976, p. 31.

suggests, "Family caseworkers, the majority of whom are women, should be more assertive in designing these interventions."

The best treatment alternative with potential long-range usefulness "is to get out of the battering relationship. To end her victimization, she must leave and never return. Most helpers agree that once battered women leave the relationship and learn new skills to reverse helplessness, they usually also overcome the emotional and motivational deficits. These do not choose to relate to another batterer as the popular myth has it. However, there is less success in overcoming helplessness when women remain with their battering partners and try to change the relationship to a nonbattering one."‡ Walker challenges the assumption that if the abusing husband can be gotten into therapy his violent behavior will necessarily stop. She and Mort Flax have developed some new approaches to couple therapy, which they have found successful in limiting the severity of the abuse but not altogether eliminating it.

No game playing concerning the reasons the couple is in therapy is allowed. The man is labeled a batterer; the woman, a battered woman. Male and female cotherapists work with the batterer and battered woman, respectively. Initially the men and women work separately, and the couple lives apart. After a short period, they are allowed to move back together, and they begin joint therapy sessions. The issues discussed deal with strengthening each individual so the relationship becomes free of all coercion. The couple learns how to ask for what they want from one another without being limited by often erroneous assumptions. They are taught to recognize their own behavior patterns in their unique battering cycle so they can become aware of the danger points.
Contingency reinforcement management procedures are employed, as are individual reinforcers for battering-free time periods. Natural reinforcers are strengthened. Therapy time is spent strengthening the positives and dissecting the negatives to prevent explosions in the future. Behavior rehearsals and role playing on videotapes often are used.

Although problems exist with this type of therapy, couples benefit.

‡ Walker, op. cit.

They attend regularly, and life is better for them. The women do not work as rapidly toward independence as they do in individual or group therapy, but they lose the pervasive terror that immobilized them, and they learn to express anger more constructively. The men learn to be more assertive too, asking directly for what they want without having to threaten a woman if they are not satisfied. As difficult as it is, couples therapy is a workable treatment alternative for battered women and their partners.*

Ms. Walker feels that instead of teaching couples how to fight better, nonfighting techniques need to be stressed. She points out: "Most couples in a battering relationship have extremely poor communication skills. Their relationship has unusually strong dependency bonds that need to be broken. It is therefore more important to work with the two individuals in the relationship, rather than deal with the relationship itself. Ultimately, the goal is interdependence."

Monica Friedman, of the Abuse Person Program, supplies us with the following list of practice guidelines that were developed during the first nine months of their couple-counseling program:

Avoid lengthy discussions of present and past abuse.

Avoid the "yes but" gambit by recognizing with some clients that perhaps they're not ready to separate.

At intake, supply a list of legal resources; help client reach other appropriate services, such as public assistance, Judicare, employment, training, etc.

If wife agrees, contact husband as soon as possible.

Offer family counseling with a different worker; where appropriate, involve a male volunteer to work with the husband.

Make explicit the assumption of counseling that there be no further violence.

See all children at least once.

Recognize the difficult situation of wives who are separating, by providing family advocates, groups, and counseling.

Write up "summaries of observations" (instead of "case histories") so they can be shared with the clients."†

* Walker, op. cit.
† Ibid.

It has been noted that many abusive men refuse to acknowledge that they have a problem. Walker notes that men are not very likely to seek help while their wives stay with them. "It seems that the most successful motivation for a batterer to seek help is for the woman to leave him. He thinks therapy will help him get her back."‡ Even when they do enter therapy, some men feel too threatened by the closeness and intensity involved in therapy, whether couple, group, or individual. In such cases it is obviously best to help the women leave the abusive situation. However, many women really can't leave; they may be too frightened, and for good reason. They may have no resources to help them survive alone. They may feel too dependent on the relationship. Continued support and exploration of options may help a woman get to a point of readiness, but until or unless she reaches that point, she still needs help, support, and understanding.

The problems in providing help to those caught in abusive situations are clearly great; the causes, and solutions, lie not only in personal and interpersonal dynamics but in the tremendous historical and societal forces that have led to the development of violence as an important aspect of life. Bonnie E. Carlson, in her article "Battered Women and Their Assailants," says it well:

> As long as men believe that responding to stress and frustration with aggression or physical violence is acceptable behavior, the problem of the battered woman will continue to exist. Thus in addition to improving the ability of men and women to support themselves and their families, efforts should be made to eradicate the beliefs that (1) men's status must and should be higher than women's, (2) men who are not dominant and are not physically more powerful than women are in some way not masculine and adequate, and (3) physical power and coercion are valid means of solving disputes in the family or in any other interpersonal relationships. Until these fundamental changes in attitude have become widely accepted, helping professionals must try to reach out to a victimized population too long ignored. They must recognize that battered women are not women who are mentally ill, but rather are troubled women in need of emotional support as well as tangible assistance.*

‡ Ibid.
* Bonnie E. Carlson, "Battered Women and Their Assailants," *Social Work*, Nov., 1977.

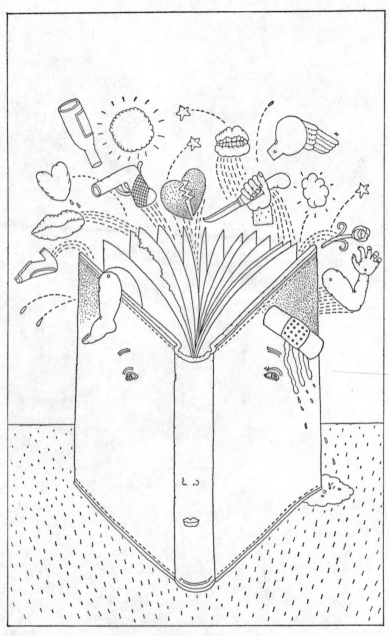

Research

Chapter VII

RESEARCH

When one examines the role that research has historically played in our society, it becomes clear that all too often the social sciences have reflected the biases of society at large. Social scientists, like the police and the courts, have sometimes contributed to attitudes that work against battered women and serve to perpetuate the problems they face. As a result, many people have come to mistrust such sources of wisdom as they seek to develop new ways of helping women who are victims of violence.

While it is important to challenge negative systems and attitudes, care should be taken not to cut off any potentially helpful avenue, no matter how tainted by misuse it may be. Research is an area often ignored by people providing services, because they don't trust it, don't understand it, or don't see it as having any value. Keep in mind that research is a tool, and tools can be used to destroy or to build. Because much research has been and continues to be biased and works against feminist values and goals, feminists and other concerned citizens should claim and use research as a tool to identify needs, develop programs, and conduct ongoing program evaluation. No less important is the use of good research to demonstrate clearly and irrefutably to potential funding sources the truths about domestic violence, and to counter myths and misinformation.

As is discussed in Chapter VIII, research in the form of a needs-assessment survey is important when planning and developing shelters and other services for women. Equally important and useful are research efforts to evaluate the effectiveness of such services to find out whether the program's original goals are being met, to determine what works and what doesn't, and to ascertain what factors make the difference in whether or not a woman seeks help.

Long-range follow-up studies on women leaving shelters should be done so that we begin to accumulate knowledge about what happens to them—how many return home or come back to the shelter, how many are able to lead freer, more satisfying lives—and what happens to their children. We also need to determine how well couple counseling or counseling for the abusive male affects long-term changes. Research may be geared to crisis intervention and long-range support and help, as well as to prevention. It can also provide a vital contribution to the woefully inadequate literature currently available.

In order to find out these things, we need to rely on more than instinct, and in order to transmit our knowledge, we need a structure and a method that "proves" that we know what we are talking about. One skilled and knowledgeable researcher, Norman Polansky, put it this way:

> Kurt Lewin, the great social psychologist, set down a famous prescription for rational social management. Intelligent intervention, he said, requires three phrases, repeated over and over: planning, execution, and fact finding on feedback. . . .
>
> Social workers have learned the hard way that, in professions where people are heavily burdened and mean well, they are apt to skip the phase of fact finding. Definite arrangements are needed to guarantee the feedback. Otherwise, an inept course of social treatment will continue uncorrected. So one way in which tested knowledge makes an important contribution to practice is feedback; sometimes this is organized into evaluative research.*

* Norman A. Polansky, ed., *Social Work Research,* rev. ed. (Chicago: University of Chicago Press, 1975), p. 2.

The trouble is that research isn't easy. It is a complex, exacting, and time-consuming process that requires considerable study to be done well—which is one of the reasons there is so much poor research around. Reading a published article describing a research project can be misleading, because the report is necessarily simplified and gives little indication of the intricacies that went into the final product or of the problems encountered along the way. One research text describes the following as the model generally used in writing a research report:

1. A statement of purpose is made in the form of formulating the problem;
2. A description of the study design is given;
3. The methods of data collection are specified;
4. The results are presented;
5. Frequently, there follows a section on conclusions and interpretations.†

All of this is not to scare you away from research but to make the point that it is not something to be ignored or taken lightly. There are certainly various levels of technical complexity, and not everyone has to become a professional researcher in order to do a good job. Compiling statistics on the women served and carefully logging the time spent in various activities can provide a lot of useful information and have practical value for day-to-day application. It might be a good idea to identify one staff member within an organization who has the time and interest to do further reading or perhaps take some courses in order to develop research knowledge and skills that can be shared with others.

Of course, many organizations don't have the time, staff, or money to spare for developing research studies. They may instead want to investigate the possibility of linking up with people within the academic community who are interested in studying domestic violence and need access to places where work is being done. College students, both graduate and undergraduate, frequently need to find a place to develop and carry out research projects in conjunc-

† Claire Selltiz, Marie Jahoda, Morton Deutsch, and Stuart W. Cook, eds., *Research Methods in Social Relations,* rev. one-vol. ed. (New York: Holt, Rinehart & Winston, 1959), p. 9.

tion with their course work. A college or university with a women's studies program would be an ideal place to recruit students for such a project, but departments of sociology or psychology or schools of social work, medicine, nursing, or law may also be good places to recruit women who are interested in exploring alternatives to traditional theory and practice.

BATTERED-HUSBAND DATA

Since research is a tool, it can serve many functions. Besides the pursuit of knowledge for its own sake (pure research) and knowledge pursued for a practical application (applied research), research can and often does serve a distinctly political purpose. A recent study of the so-called "battered-husband syndrome" by Suzanne Steinmetz, of the University of Delaware, is serving as an effective tool for those who would prefer to believe that spouse abuse is simply a result of breakdown in communication between husband and wife, rather than a direct and brutal consequence of the subjugation of women. Ms. Steinmetz seeks to establish that husband beating is a common phenomenon with deep historical roots. She cites post-Renaissance customs of shaming men who were beaten by their wives to bolster her hypothesis. This study has been seriously challenged from within the battered women's movement, and with good reason.

While it may be true that men were ridiculed if they were victims of violence perpetrated by women, such customs indicate nothing whatever about the frequency of husband beating. They do say a great deal about the prevailing attitudes that condoned wife beating but saw the use of physical force by women against men as an embarrassment to masculine supremacy.

Among many common expressions of this differential value system is the tendency to view preadolescent girls who pursue "masculine" activities with some amusement, as going through an appropriate, "tomboy" stage, which will be outgrown, while boys who express "feminine" interests are labeled "sissies" and customarily shamed and degraded. To be beaten by a woman brought forth public shame because it devalued men to be so treated by such greatly devalued people as women. This would not seem to indicate any great prevalence of husband beating; on the contrary, any group of people as oppressed as women have been would hardly be in a position to commonly use physical force against those with power over them.

Ms. Steinmetz also uses comic strips as evidence of the long-standing existence of husband beating on a wider scale than generally accepted. She considers that the typical theme of the nagging wife wielding her rolling pins against her long-suffering husband, as exemplified by Maggie and Jiggs, is an accurate reflection of cultural reality. There is no evidence whatsoever for such a conclusion, which is an example of what researchers call spurious reasoning. Comic strips are indeed powerful conveyers of culture, and serve to reinforce established values and beliefs. But to say that because Maggie hits Jiggs many women beat their husbands would be to ignore the mysogyny that has prompted so many degrading stereotypes of women. During the Second World War, comics portrayed the Japanese as shifty, cunning "yellow devils" with gigantic teeth and murderous hearts, which helped to solidify the chauvinistic attitudes considered necessary to patriotic feeling. It would be difficult to imagine someone conducting a serious survey of cartoons portraying black people and concluding that blacks indeed must roll their eyes, shuffle, and be lazy, childlike fools because that's what the cartoons showed. Yet this is exactly the line of reasoning that Ms. Steinmetz follows.

Ms. Steinmetz fails to understand that violence per se, and the particular social, cultural, and historical factors that produce the particular phenomenon of wife abuse, while related, are not analogous or interchangeable. She exhibits this same lack of understanding in her statement that "child abusers are more likely to be women, and women throughout history have been the prime perpetrators of infanticide."‡ Most responsible research has demonstrated that, in fact, women are *not* more likely than men to abuse children. The reported incidence of child abuse is about evenly divided between men and women. Allowing for the fact that

‡Suzanne K. Steinmetz, "The Battered Husband Syndrome," *Victimology: An International Journal*, Vol. 2, 1977–78, Feb. 1978.

women are far more involved in the care of children than men, it seems evident that men, not women, are the most frequent child abusers. As for infanticide, almost any good anthropology textbook can provide numerous instances of societally sanctioned killing of female children specifically because of the preference for males. Female children, throughout many cultures and many historical periods, have been considered inferior and less valuable in the same way as physically handicapped children, who were also considered worthless and were frequently killed at birth. Even when women, acting alone, were responsible for the death of their babies, this cannot be considered outside of the cultural context in which women bearing illegitimate children had no redress, no way of seeking support or even acknowledgment from the fathers, and were subject to the most punitive treatment that the dominant (male) culture could perpetrate. This is not an argument about whether or not women are capable of committing violent acts, as Steinmetz seems to think. Of course they are. But to fail to perceive the connections between sexism, child abuse, and infanticide is to display a rather dazzling ability to distort reality. Many of Ms. Steinmetz's inaccuracies and illogical conclusions are challenged and refuted by Pleck, Pleck, Grossman, and Bart:

Perhaps most serious is the misleading summary of the data presented in the paper. The concluding paragraph of the second section states: "The data suggest that . . . the percentage of wives having used physical violence often exceeds that of the husbands." In fact, in *none* of the five studies included in Table 1 do wives exceed the husbands in the total percentage having used violence ("use of any violence"). In four studies husbands are higher. In one study husbands and wives are equal. Inspection of the twenty-six components (filled) cells in the table further reveals that wives exceed husbands in only eight cells (about thirty percent of the cases), wives equal husbands in five, and wives show less violence than husbands in thirteen. Thus, a summary statement that the percentage of wives having used physical violence "often exceeds" that of husbands is incorrect and even irresponsible.*

* Elizabeth Pleck, Joseph H. Pleck, Marlyn Grossman, and Pauline B. Bart. "The Battered Data Syndrome: A comment on Steinmetz' Article," *Victimology: An International Journal*, Vol. 2, 1977–78, Feb. 1978.

Marjory Fields and Rioghan Kirschner offer data to support the conclusion that "serious violence by husbands against wives is more prevalent than serious violence by wives against husbands":

> In the period July through December 1977, Crisis Centers located in New York City public hospitals, staffed by both men and women, counseled 1,000 patients who received medical treatment. Of these, 490 were battered wives and 2 were battered husbands. An examination of the 503 divorce cases closed by Brooklyn Legal Services Corporation B in the eight months ending January 31, 1978, shows 442 women and 61 men divorce clients. Of the 442 women, 53% (233) claimed at least two acts of serious physical cruelty as the reason for seeking the divorce. Only 3% (2) of the men claimed physical cruelty. . . . From the data collected by New York City Crisis Center and Brooklyn Legal Services it is clear that women seek medical and legal help against serious violence by their husbands about 225 times more frequently than men."†

Unfortunately, the poor quality of Ms. Steinmetz's scholarship is more than a matter of academic concern. Fields and Kirschner point out that funding for a shelter in Chicago was turned down and justified in part by Ms. Steinmetz's work. Many people, including legislators, are only too glad to find support for ignoring the problems of abused women, and Ms. Steinmetz may be contributing to a backlash reaction that has serious implications for the future of service for victims of domestic violence.

FACTS AND FIGURES

Currently, the information available on domestic violence is limited and inadequate. Criminal-justice, legal, medical, and social-service systems have so far failed to develop the means of reporting incidents of abuse and of compiling meaningful data. The problem is further compounded by the large number of attacks that go unreported. Still, there is some information available that can be useful in writing grant proposals and interesting fund-

---

† Marjory D. Fields and Rioghan M. Kirschner, "Battered Women Are Still in Need: A Reply to Steinmetz," *Victimology: An International Journal*, Vol. 2, 1977–78, Feb. 1978.

ing sources in supporting proposed programs. Many women's groups have had to wade through huge amounts of material seeking statistics with which to justify their proposals. For this reason we are presenting the following, partial list of available statistics, in the hope that the sharing of such information will make things easier for newly emerging groups to get started. From a fact sheet put together by the Center for Women Policy Studies:

A study in 1966 of 600 couples applying for divorce in Cleveland found that 37 percent of the women gave physical abuse as one of their complaints.

In Lincoln, NE, in 1973 the police handled 2,000 cases of wife abuse—an average of five a day.

In 1974, San Francisco police reported that 50 percent of their calls were for family disturbances.

An information line on wife abuse in Hartford, CT, reported that more than 100 women called for help during their first two weeks of operation.

From 1969–1974, 457 persons in Dade County, FL, were homicide victims as a result of domestic disturbances.

According to a Kansas City Police Department study (1971–72), 85 percent of cases of domestic homicide showed that the police had been called at least once prior to the killing. In 50 percent of the homicide cases, the police had been called five times or more.

In Atlanta, 60 percent of all calls received on the night shift are reported domestic disputes, indicating more trouble in this area than any other crime category.

At Boston City Hospital, approximately 70 percent of the assault victims received in the emergency room are women who have been attacked in the home. Where the assailant is specified in these cases, it's usually a husband or lover.

The Citizen's Dispute Settlement Center in Dade County, FL, received 721 complaints involving "assault or battery" by a male upon a female in seven months.

The St. Paul, MN, police department said that about 100 police reports dealing with wife beating are written each week; however, this figure does not include police responses to domestic incidents in which the woman decides not to press charges.

Montgomery County, MD, one of the most affluent areas in the country, reported 650 incidents of wife assault in one year.

One District of Columbia study of 7,500 wives who attempted to bring charges against their husbands found that fewer than 200 actually achieved their objective.

Some 40 percent of the women admitted to a Santa Ana, CA, shelter for battered women are considered middle class, which is less than population averages, but still a sizable proportion. This and other studies indicate spouse abuse transcends class lines.

Del Martin, author of *Battered Wives,* estimates that wife beating affects at least three times as many women as the rape issue. FBI statistics for New York State in 1973 appear to support her statement with 4,764 rape cases reported to the police and 14,000 wife-abuse cases taken to Family Court.

English studies indicate that in 50 percent of the families where spouse abuse occurred, the children were also involved in the violence. In 25 percent of cases where babies were battered, it was found the father also battered his wife.

FBI reports 23 percent of the 132 policemen killed in 1974 were slain trying to stop family fights and 28 percent of the 26,094 policemen assaulted were attempting to halt violence within families. A Michigan study on woman abuse reported that: (a) 25 percent of the men were unemployed, (b) 50 percent of the men were skilled laborers, and (c) 25 percent of the men were white-collar professionals.

Some additional statistics:

Of 100 battered wives studied in Britain in 1975, all had bruises, 44 had lacerations, caused in 17 cases by a sharp instrument, i.e., razor, knife, broken bottle. All had been hit by clenched fists, 59 were kicked repeatedly. In 42 cases weapons were used. Nineteen women had suffered strangulation attempts, 2 suffocation. Eleven were burned, 7 bitten. There were 24 cases of fractured noses, teeth or ribs, 8 other fractured bones, 4 shoulder or jaw dislocations. Nine women, found unconscious, were taken to the hospital. One had a penetrating skull injury and two had epilepsy "which they claimed was caused through head injuries." (J. J. Gayford, 'Wife Battering: A Preliminary Survey of 100 Cases," *British Medical Journal,* Jan. 25, 1975.)

A Norwalk, Conn., study indicated that approximately the same number of wife-abuse complaints were received by police as in a comparably sized Harlem police precinct, 4–5/week. (J. C. Barden, "Wife-Beaters: Few of Them Ever Appear Before a Court of Law," New York *Times,* Oct. 21, 1974)

A Chicago police survey reported that 45.1 percent of all major crimes except murder, committed against women during a six-month period, occurred in the home. (Del Martin, *Battered Wives*. [*San Francisco, Glide Publications, 1976], pp. 11–12)

The Citizen's Complaint Center in the District of Columbia receives between 7,500 and 10,000 complaints of marital violence each year.

In 1974, Boston police responded to 11,081 family disturbance calls, most of which involved physical violence.

In Detroit, 4,900 wife-assault complaints were filed in 1972.

Almost one-third of all female homicide victims in California in 1971 were murdered by their husbands.

Nationwide in 1973, according to the FBI, one-fourth of all murders occurred within the family and one-half of these were husband-wife killings.

During the twelve months ending June 1973, 15,818 wives filed petitions in family court in New York State for Orders of Protection against their husbands.‡

CURRENT STUDIES

There are several research studies that we thought it important to mention. One is being conducted by the Colorado Association for Aid to Battered Women. Under a grant from the Department of Health, Education, and Welfare, they surveyed programs for battered women across the country and selected eight model programs for in-depth study. In June of 1978, representatives from these eight programs along with other individuals from the wife-abuse field participated in a conference in Denver at which they shared information on various service-delivery models, direct service to victims of abuse, research, and evaluation.

As a result of their site visits, the Colorado Association will write a monograph designed to assist programs in the development of a service-delivery system.*

Another study of importance to those working on wife abuse is the Police Foundation survey of domestic violence and police response in Detroit and Kansas City. Their report was summarized

‡ Minority Leader Manfred Ohrenstein, "Battered Women," New York State Senate.
* For more information, contact Susan Back, Project Director, Colorado Women's College, Box 136, Denver, CO. 80220.

by the Center for Women Policy Studies in the October 1977 edition of their newsletter, *Response:*

The study found a "distinct relationship between domestic-related homicides and aggravated assaults and prior police interventions for disputes and disturbances." The Kansas City study showed that "in the two years preceding the domestic assault or homicide, the police had been at the address of the incident for disturbance calls at least once in about 85 percent of the cases, and at least five times in about 50 percent of the cases." This finding has implications in predicting situations which have a high potential for violence.

Counselors and crisis workers who work with situations of family violence will find some of the victim data from this study helpful. The Kansas City data revealed that violence was preceded by threats in 50 to 80 percent of the cases, and the Detroit study confirmed the importance of threats as a predictor of violence. The Detroit data revealed that "53 out of 90 homicides involving family members were preceded by threats. . . ."

The Detroit study looked at patterns of conflict and considered the role played by sex-role definitions and perceptions in family interactions. The project analyzed the way homicide participants interpreted their male or female roles, as reflected in their interaction patterns. "In 66 out of 90 family conflict homicides . . . one person was defining another as an object of personal property and acting on the basis of that definition." Men were reported to take this attitude toward their spouses more often than women did.

The study indicates that there may be early warning signs of violence between friends, relatives, or acquaintances that could be recognized not only by the police but also by the victims. The study recommends further examination of conflict and disturbance disposition, conflict-intervention training programs, and characteristics of disturbance participants. For a copy of *Domestic Violence and the Police: Studies in Detroit and Kansas City,* send $3.00 to: Police Foundation Communications Department, 1909 K Street, NW, Washington, DC 20006.

In addition to the early research which was funded by the National Institute of Mental Health and carried out primarily by Richard Gelles, of the University of Rhode Island, Murray Straus, of the University of New Hampshire, and Suzanne Steinmetz, there are a number of spouse-abuse studies being conducted by individual social scientists across the country.

OVERVIEW OF RESEARCH ON WOMAN BATTERING

We are deeply indebted to sociologist Mildred Daley Pagelow, of the University of California, Riverside, for the following report, which she prepared for this chapter. Consisting of an overview of past and current research related to woman battering, it represents an invaluable addition to available information and analysis. Ms. Pagelow is currently working on a critique of the husband-battering study by Suzanne Steinmetz discussed earlier in the chapter.

RESEARCH ON WOMAN BATTERING

MILDRED DALEY PAGELOW

Sociology Department
University of California, Riverside

Introduction

The purpose of this report is to try to give an overview of some research that deals directly or indirectly with woman battering. It begins with a review of the theoretical perspectives underlying the studies. This section is written for present or potential researchers, and necessarily involves providing references—without references it would be useless to them. The balance of this paper will be less technical and directed toward a broad spectrum of persons interested in and involved with the serious social problem of woman battering. In the next section, I attempt to show the lack of consensus in the field, the differences (and inconsistencies) of definitions, and the focus of various studies. The definitions, focus, and parameters from my own research effort are provided to illustrate the way I attempted to provide clarity and to avoid ambiguity. Finally, recommendations are provided for needed research, and suggestions are made on how research can be designed and conducted that can be of greatest value to all of us: concerned citizens, service providers, victims, policy makers, and even other researchers or scholars, newly entering the field, who want to avoid some of the many pitfalls encountered when investigating a relatively unexplored subject.

It is my hope that these words will provide some degree of guidance to nonacademics who want to better understand certain studies and to discover what information they *really* provide us. Many social and behavioral scientists write their reports in technical jargon that impresses their colleagues but is all but unintelligible to people outside their particular disciplines. If this brief summary helps any readers to be more critical evaluators of research reports and to be able to draw some of their own conclusions independently of the professional researchers who *tell* them what it all means, then this effort shall have been worthwhile.

If it stimulates any others into new research projects of their own in the many areas that still need investigation, then writing this will have been doubly worth the effort. We need *much more* and *much better* research!

Finally, if this gives concerned citizens and feminists encouragement and inspiration in their own struggle to know that there are some people within academia who are truly concerned about the plight of battered women and who are dedicated to use their professional skills for enlightenment, understanding, and eventual eradication of crimes of violence against women—then so much the better!

Overview of Theoretical Perspectives on Woman Battering

Although some theories advance provocative and plausible ideas, none adequately explain why some women are battered by men with whom they have or had relationships, nor do they explain fully why some of these destructive relationships continue over long periods of time. A variety of theories abound despite the lack of systematic studies or replication, and despite there being only one large-scale representative sample to date. Theories range from individual psychopathology . . . to a "violent-culture theory" or "social-structural theory of violence." . . . Even a handful of case histories has provided the basis for generalizations of psychopathology of the batterer but particularly of the victim. . . . The violent-culture theory, briefly summarized, identifies woman battering as one of many manifestations of violence learned in the family which is legitimated by a violent society. The point these theorists seem to overlook is somewhat akin to the point overlooked in the "subculture theory of violence." What is ignored is that not *all* men are physically violent toward spouses, and women are recipients of violence, not the perpetrators, to a far greater extent than men, despite socialization in the same violent culture. Why, then, are some men physically abusive toward women, while some are not? And why are women almost exclusively the victims, rather than men? . . . Few of us would argue that ours is not a violent culture; we are surrounded by glorification, or at least acceptance, of violence as a fact of life in American society.

However, upon closer inspection, we may note that it is a society largely dominated by men, with laws created and enforced by men, with wars declared and fought by men, and with contests of physical strength, particularly body-contact sports, almost exclusively by men. While it is a violent culture, only one half of the population is encouraged in violence, while the other half is encouraged to avoid and fear violence. The study reported by Stark and McEvoy showed a high rate of approval of slapping one's spouse; yet men were more likely to approve of this behavior than women (1970). It seems safe to assume that not all men use force and violence on women, and probably very few women see force and violence as acceptable behavior when it is directed at themselves. As some proponents of the subcultural theory of violence have tried to explain high crime rates in poverty areas as manifestation of approval of antisocial behavior, including rape, they fail to account for the victims' disapproval. I suggest that a theory that can only "explain" the violent behavior of one segment of the population but ignores the nonparticipation of other segments of the same population (nonviolent men and most women) is not an explanation at all. In sum, these paradigms have been too broad and all-inclusive to be tested, since they either merge spousal assault with a variety of other social problems or subsume it with other forms of intrafamily violence. Conversely, other paradigms are too narrow to be tested beyond the interacting-dyad level, since they single out spousal assault as a relatively rare manifestation of individual psychopathological behavior, with no attention directed toward the social institutions that encourage or support such behavior.

As an alternative to these paradigms, I have proposed a tripartite theoretical perspective based on social learning theory that contains suggestions about the causation (Model I), the initial response of the victims (Model II), and the continuance of some women in battering relationships (Model III). . . . According to social learning theory, learning is accomplished by both negative and positive reinforcement; within a broader social-structural framework, cultural values are transmitted at both a personal and an institutional level. Individuals learn what is gender-approved behavior for themselves and the other sex, first from within the home and later from both the home and the "outside world." Sex-typed "appropriate" models of behavior for women and men lead to different—almost opposite—types of role-behavior conditioning, beginning at birth. Role definitions are individually and culturally prescribed and intermittently reinforced throughout life for women and men, and most actors can be expected to perform largely within those standards, since intermittent reinforcement has been shown to be most effective for learning and most difficult to extinguish. Examining feminine role expectations and comparing them to masculine role expectations leads to assumptions that, in the case of conjugal violence, the female is socially conditioned into the victim role and the male into the aggressor role.

Current Research and Research Problems

There is no simple and concise way to describe current research, research problems, and needed research on woman battering; there are obvious difficulties and complexities in the subject under study and in the investigations themselves and a host of important but less obvious considerations. Research to date has been extremely limited and there are very few empirical studies that have done anything more than scratch the surface. We have almost no concrete statistics to offer, because this is a particularly private crime, committed behind closed doors. Most statistics quoted and requoted have emanated from a few sources, who have tried to *estimate* the extent and severity of the problem. Even those who have based estimates on police records have had to extrapolate instances of spouse abuse from other forms of domestic disturbance such as "man with gun," sibling assault, etc. In addition, even if records had clearly differentiated between woman battering and other forms of domestic violence, police records still would not provide us with any reliable measurement of the extent of the problem other than the number of cases that come to the attention of law-enforcement authorities. As we know from other crimes of violence against persons, the vast majority of such crimes never become part of the official record. For example, the FBI estimates that only one out of ten actual rapes is reported, and woman battering has been estimated to occur three times more frequently than rape.

The only large-scale sociological research survey to date involving a representative random sample of married and cohabiting couples has severe limitations. It has added to our pool of knowledge about the prevalence of violence in our society, but tells us very little about the extent and severity of spouse abuse and has left many more questions unanswered. As the study's principal investigator pointed out, there are a number of methodological problems inherent in the study itself, such as the sample-selection criteria of intact cohabiting couples only, restriction of focus to violence committed in the year prior to interview, and the use of retrospective self-report—all of which lead to underreporting and thus to underestimation. The principal investigator estimated that true incidence rates of violence were probably double the rates obtained by his study; thus, even a nationally representative random sample of 2,143 couples ultimately yielded *estimates* of true violence rates!

But there are other important factors we should consider when discussing research on woman battering. In the first place, the differences in the focus of research itself begins with the terminology used for the phenomenon itself. Concepts are often vaguely defined, and there is no definitional consensus among researchers. Even titles of the phenomena being studied have important and distinct variations: some researchers are investigating "domestic violence," "family violence," and "violence in the home/family," all of which may include other forms of violence than woman battering, such as the one referred to earlier. Studies under this rubric may include intergenerational violence (child abuse and abuse of parents by their children), sibling violence, and other kinship relationships. "Violence" may include verbal, psychological, or physical acts of aggression, as well as property destruction, etc. "Spouse abuse," "battered wives/women," or the sensationalized "battered husband" may also include verbal, psychological, or physical violence between cohabitating couples and has, in some instances, been investigated only in either intact families (husband, wife, two children) or intact cohabitating couples. Most studies to date have limited criteria of "violence" to physical acts because of the ease of quantitatively measuring physical acts compared to verbal and/or psychological violence. An important exception is a new study by Lenore Walker, who will measure both psychological and physical violence against women.

Some researchers have failed to distinguish wife abuse from sadomasochistic practices engaged in by some couples for mutual sexual enjoyment. In addition, some have included in their studies *all* acts of physical aggression, not distinguishing between "mutual combat"—a rough form of aggression, sometimes very violent and potentially dangerous, engaged in by some couples well matched in ferocity—and battering, which is more of a one-way attack commonly described by battered women. Mild forms of "mutual combat'" may be the kick administered under the card table or the thrust of an elbow into the other's ribs, which are both nonverbal forms of communication for some couples, but for nondiscriminating researchers will be tabulated as violent acts.

Clearly missing from many studies is *intention,* which is a difficult variable to operationalize. Most of the studies do not investigate *victim precipitation,* which means that the victim is a direct, positive precipitator in the crime: the victim is the first to use physical force. The largest sociological study to date did not take into account victim precipitation in measuring husband-wife violent acts. But to do so involves another set of complications, including value judgments by the researcher/s. If a woman says, "I asked for it—I should have kept my mouth shut," is that victim precipitation? On the other hand, if a man comes home drunk, proceeds to beat his spouse, and she picks up the nearest heavy object and strikes him with it—is that victim precipitation? According to my value system, the former example is not victim precipitation and the second one is victim precipitation. Yet we cannot exclude verbal cues from victim precipitation, because some women frequently beaten by their spouses reacted to verbal threats by killing their spouses—and were found not guilty in courts of law on grounds of self-defense. On the other hand, some researchers report comments such as "I asked for it" as prima facie evidence of *provocation* or precipitation by victims.

Perhaps to resolve this dilemma we should measure the *intensity* of the acts or degree of *damage inflicted* on the victim. As I have pointed out in my papers, there is a vast difference between a well-aimed kick with a pointed-toe Western boot (or a steel-toed construction boot) and a kick in the shins with an open-toed sandal. Are both kicks the same? One can kill, another can hurt. A woman was kicked to death in Northern Ireland by her husband. Also, there are still some traditionally "feminine" women who resort to a Scarlett O'Hara type of open-handed slap on the face of a man who is making unwanted sexual advances or who makes a disapproved remark. Yet, for example, an open-handed slap on the face delivered by a marine sergeant with full force can bruise an entire half of a woman's face, dislocate her teeth, break her jaw, or snap her neck. Should both "slaps" be registered on a scale with equal weight? It seems unlikely, but it has been done.

Still, how can a researcher measure intensity or damage, particularly when it is being recorded in retrospect? From the viewpoint of the recipient? I have had respondents who said, "At first he only choked me, but later he began really beating me." Can *any* choking be *only*? Or should we investigate from the viewpoint of the aggressor to see if he *intended* to do the damage inflicted? Most men will deny intent or extent of the damage; e.g., "I only meant to bring her to her senses" (or to shut her up, etc.) or "I didn't really hit her that hard. She likes to exaggerate" (or she bruises easily, etc.).

The definition of battering used in my study attempts to settle some of these points just discussed. In the first place, the focus of this study is on *woman battering* (not *wife, spouse,* or *husband,* nor is it *abuse* or *beating*), because this phenomenon is placed in the context of violent crimes against women. For example, the following are my definitions of the problem I have been investigating, followed by the scope conditions or research parameters as they have been described in my manuscripts:

"Battered women" refers to adult women who have been intentionally physically abused in ways that caused pain or injury, or who were forced into involuntary action or restrained by force from voluntary action, by adult men with whom they have or had established relationships, usually involving sexual intimacy, whether or not within a legally married state. Battering is a willful assault on another to cause or attempt to cause harm, with or without provocation, i.e., one-sided aggressive acts that may or may not be defended against. (Sadomasochistic practices for mutual sexual enjoyment are excluded, as are forms of "mutual combat.") The term "battered" does not include nonphysical types of abuse such as intimidation, harassment, threats, or other forms of psychological coercion, unless they occur in conjunction with physical force or injury. Although these are undeniably damaging, painful, and injurious, the scope of the phenomenon addressed herein must be restricted to bodily injury. Physical abuse has been somewhat expanded to include force into involuntary or from voluntary action, so that being tied to a chair, locked in a room, closet, or house, or being locked out of one's home in the middle of the night, for example, which are clearly abusive actions, may be included. My sample of battered women has revealed accounts of each of these types of abuse. Excluded from this definition are short-term dating relationships, employer-employee relationships, social-acquaintance relationships, etc.

Scope conditions are expanded from conjugal relationships to also encompass: sexual relationships not involving cohabitation, marital relationships terminated by separation or divorce, and kinship relationships that include females residing in the same household with a father, brother, stepfather, stepbrother, or foster father. Although the vast majority of battered women appear to have been abused by men with whom they had intimate sexual relationships at the time of the assault/s, it is clear that many women are battered by men other than husbands or lovers. My sample of battered women reveals case histories of all the above situational relationships. Enlarging scope conditions to include nonmarital, nonsexual, or noncohabitational relationships places this perspective somewhere beyond the marital-familial setting advocated by some, and is too narrow for the more general interfamily violence in the home setting studied by others. Woman battering can be best explained when it is lifted out of the frame of reference that ties it so strongly to sexually intimate relationships, yet other types of familial violence, such as child abuse, are beyond these boundaries.

These statements have been included here not as an attempt to convince other researchers to adopt these same definitions and parameters but to support by example the necessity of clarity of concepts and conditions. If it is clearly outlined, we will all understand better what is actually being studied. We all need to take these matters into consideration when reading professional reports —to look critically for unambiguous definitions, how the research was conducted, what was being measured and how, and within what parameters—before we accept the researcher's conclusions.

With the foregoing, it becomes clear that there is no simple answer to research needs or the best forms of research designs to be employed. In addition, each researcher enters the arena equipped with her/his own set of life experiences, moral values, and ethics, as well as professional training and professional ideology. These factors enter into their projects whether they want them to or not —consciously or unconsciously. Social and behavioral scientists are human beings studying other human beings, not humans studying inanimate objects in a lab. Despite claims by many of "scientific, value-free neutrality," it is impossible to disassociate oneself from the personal framework from which life is viewed. Regardless of the best intentions and conscious efforts, none of us can throw aside the personal baggage of a lifetime when we conduct scientific research. To counteract this, some scholars have demanded that researchers make clear their own personal biases or ideology, their basic assumptions, i.e., to "tell where they are coming from." If they are willing to do this, the conclusions they draw from their studies can be evaluated by others in the light of this information. Unfortunately, very few do this: they usually maintain that they set aside personal biases and assumptions when they enter the lab or set out to do field research. In the social and behavioral sciences, the few who expose their basic assumptions are mostly to be found among feminist and minority scholars.

In my viewpoint, the best research on woman battering is and will be done by these people—the ones whose perspectives are clearly known in advance. Because I am a feminist, the reader would *expect* me to judge (and it is a value judgment) that the woman who talked instead of keeping quiet did *not* precipitate her own beating, even though the victim (from her traditional viewpoint) accepts the idea that a man is the "boss" and, as such, has certain rights to control and dominate her. Feminists and minorities have certain characteristics in common: they know the power of other categories to control and dominate them, the influence this has had on their life experiences and opportunities, and the difficulties encountered in trying to establish full personhood in a society where ascribed characteristics of sex, race, or ethnicity assign them to second-class status. Feminists and minorities are the ones who challenge the hierarchal power structure affecting both same-sex and cross-sex relationships. Feminist scholars reject inequality between the sexes, and domination-subordination in male-female relationships particularly, and for that reason, I maintain, they are best qualified ideologically to study, measure, and evaluate male-female interaction, whether such interaction be nonviolent (marriage, employment, social, economic, education, etc.) or violent (battering, rape, incest, or other criminal activities). At each stage of research, the intellectual baggage a researcher brings along with her or him affects the theoretical foundations of the study, the hypotheses introduced, the design, the methodologies employed, the questions asked, the scales used, the analysis, and finally, the interpretation of the data. Whether acknowledged or not, personal ideologies permeate their work every step of the way and influence the conclusions researchers draw. If a researcher believes that men are "naturally ordained" to be "heads of household" and supports the hierarchal structure of the patriarchal family, s/he may disapprove of the *methods* used to control women but will not object to the actual "need" for control of women by men, and this value judgment will imperceptibly affect her or his interpretation of the data.

Another present danger is that many people are cashing in on the current interest in women battering (dubbed this year's "fad" by some astute political observers). As Representative Barbara Mikulski described it, many "grant junkies" are ready and waiting to write proposals to support their professional and personal success—regardless of what the subject of investigation may be. Universities are pleased when faculty receive grants—it benefits the university both financially and by increased prestige—and they give recognition of this to faculty research-grant recipients in the form of rewards in promotion, salary increases, and tenure. It matters not to them whether the object under investigation is tsetse flies or battered women.

Within each discipline, the research design reflects the literature, training, methodologies, and ideologies that are passed along from one generation of scholars to the next. Within many disciplines, particularly psychiatry, psychology, social psychology, and social work, the traditional tendency has been to look for the source of the problems within the psychic makeup of the individual. Regarding woman battering, it is tempting to study the psyche or personality traits of the individual woman or man (or both) who are involved in a violent relationship. It is relatively easy to use research instruments—scales, questionnaires, and personality inventories—that have been utilized in earlier studies previously "tested" for validity and reliability. The fact that there is an underlying sexist bias inherent in their construction is frequently overlooked, and these instruments have been administered to battered women in some cases without question by traditionalist investigators. Then they draw conclusions about victims that are generalized beyond the subject sample to the population of nonresearch subjects. "Facts" thus drawn can have damaging effects on women's attitudes toward themselves and other women, and men's attitudes toward women.

Recommendations

1. Greatest credibility should be given to research conducted by feminists from a feminist perspective when any study is initiated regarding male-female relationships, especially those involving violence against women. Any study concentrating on victims them-

selves should be critically examined for "victim-blaming," i.e., looking for the *cause* of the problem within the victim herself. Personality studies should be discounted if the investigator fails to strongly warn against generalizing postbattering "personality traits" to a "victim-prone personality." *All* reports should be critically evaluated as to definitions, criteria, measurements, and conditions employed in the studies as much as possible, in order to draw conclusions independently of the researchers. Americans have a tendency to give unquestioning credibility to research reports written by people who have a Ph.D., Ed.D., or M.D. after their names or whose research is funded by large government organizations such as the National Institute of Mental Health or the National Science Foundation. No one is infallible. Nonprofessionals cannot be expected to analyze the data, even if they had access to them, but should guard against accepting the researcher's carte blanche.

2. Studies should concentrate their focus on male-female violence in society if we want to understand and eliminate violence in privacy between intimates. That is, it is far more pertinent to try to understand attitudes and behavior of men and women toward each other than to include other issues such as child abuse and sibling rivalry. These other relationships may have important causal or associational variables not directly related or nonrelated to adult cross-sex violence and tend to dilute and obscure the real issue. There are many funding sources for research on child abuse, juvenile deliquency, and problems of the aged. We need to conserve our energy and resources to direct our full attention to male-female relationships and male violence against females.

3. As I stated in the March 6, 1978, White House meeting on family violence, and in my testimony before congressional subcommittees, research needs to leave the sterile lab and exotic computers of the university and get its feet wet. Sophisticated technologies like path and regression analysis are by-products of quantitative methodologies until anything and everything that is encountered in the human experience must be numerically coded and quantifiable. Numerical tabulation of slaps or kicks produces raw material for the computer to feed upon, but we miss out on more than we get. It may seem glamorous to have paid inter-

viewers go into the living rooms of thousands of American couples to count the number of times respondents remember and are willing to admit they slapped, hit, or kicked their spouses in the previous year. But what have we really learned about the interactional dynamics before and after those acts, the actual force of the acts, the damage sustained (or lack of it), and the cognitions attached to the acts by both the actor and the receiver? In actuality, very little. Quantitative methodologies are limited in the amount of valid data they produce, often leaving more questions unanswered than answered or giving skewed results because questions are only partially answered. A variety of methodologies must be employed—both qualitative and quantitative—in order to provide depth as well as breadth to our understanding. The researchers who interpret data and draw conclusions from them that may affect social policy *must* do more than employ interviewers to go out into the field for them—they need to leave their computers and books and do some of the work themselves! It is *not* unknown for paid interviewers to "pad" the responses they turn in at the end of a day in the field or at the end of time periods at the telephone. Much research has become big business, in which principal investigators sit in their offices like executives and eventually analyze, at second hand, data turned in to them by their employees. I am suggesting that they leave the comfort and security of their offices and labs and join the hired workers, lower in the hierarchy, to find out for themselves what is *really* going on in the *real* world.

4. As also suggested to government leaders, I recommend that more research be conducted through the facilities of community groups and service providers, rather than exclusively through external institutions such as universities and professional research centers. Shelters for battered women and their children, for example, have a client population that are experienced in spouse abuse and staff that encounter relative problems within the community that impinge on shelterees. Investigations that could and should be conducted (and appropriately funded) through shelter auspices are

   a. The victims' perceptions of the problem—they are the *real* experts.

b. Victims' experiences with community agencies and services, and their perceptions of agental response to their problems and to themselves.

c. Staff's interrelationships with community agencies and services, funding sources, community educational success/failures, staff training programs, etc.

d. Longitudinal studies of victims for follow-up and evaluation purposes. This would serve a secondary purpose of providing a support system that extends beyond residence at the shelter, and could point out specific social, economic, and personal problems encountered by the women after they depart, *as well as successes.*

e. Longitudinal studies of the children-victims who accompany their mothers to shelters and beyond. We need to know what effect parental violence has on them (both short- and long-term), their reactions to communal living at shelters and effects of displacement from their accustomed environment by shelter residence, and eventually, their adult attitudes and behavior toward same and opposite sex.

f. Other studies on issues defined by shelter staff or shelterees —e.g., collective decision making, development of leadership roles, group responsibilities, advantages and disadvantages of programs available, receptivity and response of existing community agencies to shelters/shelterees, communal parenting, single parenting, employment, employment training, housing, economics, legal problems both within and beyond shelter residence, etc.

g. How to set up and operate shelters in ways that provide the greatest amount of service to the most women; how to evaluate the effectiveness of existing shelters. Many groups discuss this, but some of them forget to include in their discussion the shelterees, who are in the best position, from their own experience, to point out the positive and negative aspects.

5. Field investigations in law-enforcement, judicial, medical, and social agencies are badly needed. We should have investigators listen to and observe police dispatchers, accompany police on "domestic disturbance" calls, check police record keeping, tabulate and document the numbers of homicides that are preceded by

domestic disturbance calls, observe handling of prosecution, and monitor the judicial process concerning restraints against batterers, prosecution of batterers, child custody, property and financial settlements, and divorce. The same techniques of observation, participant observation, interview, and record analysis should be done within the medical profession with individuals, and in hospitals and clinics, as well as within social and other "helping" agencies.

6. Representative random samples should also be taken of the general population, but they should not be restricted to intact couples and they should use a variety of methodological techniques to provide depth. They should be designed and conducted carefully to reduce bias and misleading conclusions. These studies should be conducted in a wide variety of geographically and demographically distinct locations so that we can identify commonalities and differences within and between categorically different social groups. We will then be able to identify those features of woman battering which are generalizable and those which are not, unlike research conducted to date.

7. Most research so far has been permeated with a white, middle-class bias; racial and ethnic minorities have been either excluded altogether or included without considerations for subcultural variations. Racial and ethnic minorities should be included in sample populations, but I strongly urge that the strongest influence or control should be maintained by persons who are members of the same minority groups. For too long, women have been studied by men, who have then told us what we are like, how we feel, and why we behave as we do. *All* women have been victimized in various ways by men's sexist interpretations of us; we are only now beginning to study ourselves. As stated earlier, each researcher carries along her or his own basic assumptions, which inevitably permeate the work and the conclusions drawn. As much as possible, research utilizing minority categories should be designed, conducted, and analyzed by member/s of the same category. In addition, special care should be exercised in the construction or adoption of research instruments for use with minority populations, particularly where English is a second language or where the scales are translated into another language. Most existing

scales have an inherent ethnocentrism reflecting the white, male, middle-class biases of their designers. Intelligence tests are the best example of this, and most of us know the damage they have caused. (College entrance examinations are another example.) When we are studying such a social problem as woman battering, which obviously affects the lives, health, and welfare of so many women and children, researchers must exert special caution that the work we do does not become one more tool in the hands of those who oppress the powerless to further exploit and victimize our sisters.

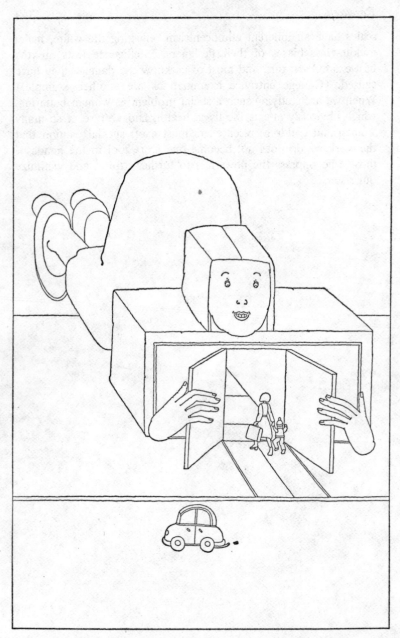

Establishing Shelter and Support Services

Chapter VIII

ESTABLISHING SHELTER AND SUPPORT SERVICES

ALONE

Lying, thinking
Last night
How to find my soul a home
Where water is not thirsty
And bread loaf is not stone
I came up with one thing
And I don't believe I'm wrong
That nobody,
But nobody
Can make it out here alone.

Alone, all alone
Nobody, but nobody
Can make it out here alone.

There are some millionaires
With money they can't use
Their wives run round like banshees
Their children sing the blues
They've got expensive doctors
To cure their hearts of stone.

But nobody
No nobody
Can make it out here alone.

Alone, all alone
Nobody, but nobody
Can make it out here alone.

Now if you listen closely
I'll tell you what I know
Storm clouds are gathering
The wind is gonna blow
The race of man is suffering
And I can hear the moan,
Cause nobody,
But nobody
Can make it out here alone.

Alone, all alone
Nobody, but nobody
Can make it out here alone.

Maya Angelou

CRYSTAL

"No. We usually are full to overflowing . . . but the thing here is
for some reason a whole week it's quiet. I mean simple quiet and all
of a sudden at the end of that week Friday nights, Saturday nights. I
mean it's total madness and it stays like that for about a good two to
three weeks. And all of a sudden you get another week of peace."

MARIA

"Yeah, and I'm still part of that house (I should say shelter),
and they had a number of Hispanic women there who had no one to
turn to, and I always said that I would like to someday—this was
about eleven years ago when this happened to me—and I always
said someday I'd like to see the shelter that didn't look like an institution, that had a home look to it and a number of my friends. . . .

We used to have it in our kitchens and talking and coming up with a creative idea of how to get it going. And three years we really sat and we planned it and planned it and that's what we are today."

MINNIE LEE

"Well, what we do with the women here is rev them up to show them what they're going to face out there and be damned if they're going to be turned away. . . . So what we do is rev them up and let them get out there and fight for what they need."

In many communities, shelters and hotlines for battered women have come into existence over the past few years. Although it is not clear just how many shelters and service programs currently exist in the United States, estimates put the figure at over three hundred. The most recent effort to determine the extent of services for battered women was conducted by the Center for Women Policy Studies, in Washington, DC. They have ascertained that as of this writing, there are 185 shelters and 138 other service providers currently in existence. Since 1976, Betsy Warrior, one of the early pioneers of the battered women's movement, has been producing a publication that lists almost every known group and many individuals working on the issue. The listing is updated frequently and is available by writing to her at 46 Pleasant St., Cambridge, MA 02139.

The vast majority of these services were spearheaded by feminists who were already providing assistance to women in need. As they staffed women's centers, antirape programs, and women-in-transition groups, they found that more and more of their calls were coming from women who were victims of violence within their homes. Stunned by the lack of options available (see Chapter I), these volunteers began to provide emergency housing and counseling.

These initial efforts in behalf of battered women did not come easily. With severely limited resources, no funds, and often little sympathy from the surrounding community, volunteers took abused women into their homes, and accompanied them to court, to the police station, to the hospital, and to the welfare department. They helped to find permanent housing, provided sympathetic and effective counseling, and worked to develop much-needed educational and employment opportunities.

Although many individuals and groups working in behalf of battered women are still in the early stages of growth, others have evolved into organized shelter and hotline programs. Lately, traditional agencies and institutions have begun to develop their own projects. The media are now paying attention, and some funds, although limited, are becoming available to support existing and emerging programs.

Although progress has been made, much remains to be done. Should you be part of a group or agency that is anxious to start a shelter or hotline, the way will not be easy. Although the problem has now become "legitimate," money is difficult to get. Operating such a program can be draining and difficult. Developing adequate resources is often frustrating and time-consuming. Despite the frustrations, however, the rewards are great. We offer you our unqualified support and encouragement.

STARTING A SHELTER

The first known refuge for battered women was founded by Erin Pizzey in England in 1971. Soon filled to overflowing, Chiswick Women's Aid rapidly expanded, and shelters began opening throughout England, the rest of Europe, and eventually the United States.

Women's Advocates, one of the first refuges in this country, says that "Refuges are the vitally necessary first step in eliminating domestic violence and oppression, because they serve to make the problem visible and to meet the immediate need for protection."*

A shelter is a sanctuary where a woman who has suffered a loss of self-esteem and self-confidence can find people who are committed to rebuilding the positive self-image necessary for her to

* *A Shelter for Abused Women and Their Children,* Women's Advocates, St. Paul, Minnesota, brochure.

regain control of her life. A shelter can be a place where a woman who has lived in fear and isolation can find security and safety as well as the love and support of other women who are struggling to rebuild lives shattered by domestic violence. A shelter can and should serve as a protective community to which residents and former residents can turn for confidential support, encouragement, and assistance.

The Beginning

The first step in establishing shelter and services for battered women consists of organizing a series of meetings with people who have encountered the problems of battered women in their work and wish to begin developing resources and support services. From these initial meetings, a core group of committed individuals who are willing to work on the problem will most likely emerge. Later, representatives from a variety of medical, mental-health, and criminal-justice institutions may get involved.

Next, we suggest you conduct a needs assessment and survey the existing services in your community. This is important both in terms of designing your program and in providing documentation of the need for such a program to potential funding sources.

There are many possibilities for gathering data. Letters or questionnaires can be sent to social-service agencies, hospitals, health departments, emergency rooms, police departments, courts, legal organizations such as Legal Aid, mental-health departments and agencies, churches, women's centers, hotlines—all organizations and institutions that may in some way be related to the problems of abused women. The Pennsylvania Coalition Against Domestic Violence suggests the following as examples of the kinds of questions you might want to ask:

1. In the past year, how many clients did you see that you could identify as abuse victims?
2. How many clients needed emergency housing?
3. Were you able to meet these needs. If so, how?
4. What services do you provide for abuse victims?
5. To what other agencies do you refer these clients?
6. (Police) How many domestic calls did you receive in the past year?

7. How many of these involved husband-wife conflicts?

8. What kind of service to victims of abuse would you see as best meeting the need?†

Depending upon the size and political orientation (conservative or liberal) of your community, you may want to do a more in-depth survey than that described here. If so, we suggest you read the phamphlet *How to Organize a Wife Assault Task Force,* written by Kathy Fotjik, director of Safe House, a program of the Domestic Violence Project, in Ann Arbor, Michigan.

The Pennsylvania Coalition Against Domestic Violence (PCADV) gives some additional information that may be helpful during the early organizational efforts of your group:

"Broad-based community support is vital to the successful launching of your program. If the project has evolved out of a felt need among the service providers in the community, the support is already there. If however, you are starting at the grass-roots level, it is imperative that you make contacts with important people and organizations in your area to solicit their support. Part of this work is accomplished by your needs-assessment survey. This serves as a consciousness-raising device and will attract those who see the need for the program.

The larger the number of supporters you can attract, the easier job you will have implementing your plans. It might prove helpful to personally visit those people whom you feel reasonably sure will be willing to assist you. . . . If you are seeking funding, it is important to be able to document your support in the community. Toward this end, it is advisable to request letters of support from those whose opinions impact on the community.‡

In addition to contacting those who you think may be helpful, it might prove worthwhile for members of your group to make a list of *personal* contacts who could aid in the development of your organization either through their influence in the community or through direct involvement.

A useful set of important resources needed to effectively de-

† Rie Gentzler, *The Abused: Advocacy Programs for Abuse Victims* (Lancaster, PA: Pennsylvania Coalition Against Domestic Violence, 1977).
‡ Ibid.

velop wife-abuse programs has been put together by Catherine Lynch, of the Dade County Victims Advocate Program, and Thomas Norris, of the Dade County Criminal Justice Planning Unit, Dade County, Florida.

PHILOSOPHY AND POLICIES

Having gathered as many data as time and energy permit, you are in a position to outline the structure of your program and to seek funds to implement it. At this stage, it is important to clarify and agree upon your philosophy, for it is out of this philosophy that goals and objectives are developed. You will need to decide whom you wish to serve, what kinds of services to provide, and how you plan to provide them. There are several important questions that you will need to address:

Decision Making: Who will make decisions regarding the operation of the shelter and its policies is an important consideration. At some shelters, only the board of directors has the authority to make such decisions. At others, the staff make the major policy decisions, sometimes in conjunction with residents of the shelter. This is the practice at Transition House, in Cambridge, Massachusetts. Many shelters consider it a priority to involve the residents in the decision-making process, particularly since they are the people who are most affected by whatever decisions are made. In any case, flexibility should be built in. Operating shelters for battered women is a relatively new undertaking. Much experimentation, change, and growth will be necessary. The Austin Center for Battered Women addresses this issue in "A Plea for Help: One Community's Response":

> The shelter program was developed following several basic assumptions: that woman battering is a social rather than an individual-family problem; that facilitating self-determination means actively involving the users of the program in the change process; that change is more effective if it is modeled as well as taught; and that an effective program listens to and learns from its users. These assumptions dictate that any program (if it is to be successful) must be flexible, responsive to the needs of its users, and help the users evaluate how and when to break the cycle of dependency and vic-

timization. The shelter program is predicated on a firm commitment to the belief that people learn more from behavior they see than from what they are told. Therefore, the shelter program must offer models that demonstrate the choices available to the residents. Concepts like individual worth, choice, self-determination, and interdependence are the foundations for staff-resident interaction. These concepts are modeled through the collective decision-making and administrative structures established for the shelter, as well as through the involvement of shelter residents and former residents in determining the goals, services, and procedures to be utilized in the shelter program.*

Counseling Models: Shelter clients are in need of many kinds of counseling services, but no matter what kind, all should be provided in a supportive, nonjudgmental framework geared to fostering independence and optimizing each woman's strength and abilities. In a traditionally run center, trained therapists may provide counseling to women, couples, and children. Nontraditional groups, on the other hand, seek to get away from the expertise model and focus instead on peer counseling, believing that women need to work with each other on an equal basis, sharing skills, strength, knowledge, and experience. According to Del Martin, experience shows the importance of women supporting women as *women,* rather than as professionals "helping" clients find solutions to their problems. She points out the reasoning behind this view as reflected by Sharon Vaughn, of Women's Advocates, who feels that the professional "treatment" model automatically serves to create a barrier that further dehumanizes and isolates the woman who has already been victimized not only by her violent husband or lover but by society itself. In addition, use of this model could lead to reinforcement of the concept of the battered woman as "sick," even though this may not be the intention of the practitioner.

The question of whether formerly abused women themselves are best suited to provide counseling to other women in similar situations is a continually debated one. Some argue that only those who have experienced such a situation are in a position to

* Deborah Novak and Deborah T. Meismer, "A Plea for Help-One Community's Response," *Victimology: An International Journal,* Vol. 2, 1977–78, Ns. 3–4, Feb. 1978.

understand the problems facing abused women, while others maintain that it is the counselor's skills and sensitivity that are important, rather than her background. We feel that since any woman is a potential victim of violence (rape, battering, etc.), it is helpful for counselors to perceive themselves as supportive allies, rather than as distant service providers in a separate category from those they counsel. From Casa Myrna Vasquez, Boston, Massachusetts:

> We don't pretend to offer ongoing, long-term therapy at Casa Myrna. Some of us are "trained" in different kinds of counseling work—advocacy, family work, rape counseling, crisis intervention, problem solving, etc., etc., etc. Others of us aren't "trained" as such but have good, strong instincts and insights. We can meet with a woman and begin to get a sense of what might be helpful to her. We can suggest she talk with a nun at Casa del Sol or with someone at the Health Center, and help that to happen. Or we can talk with her ourselves and help her through a hard time. If we are unsure ourselves, we can talk it over with another volunteer, with someone we trust to make a decision.†

A peer counselor with Project Outreach, in Hayward, California, Ann Leach, points to her source of expertise: "I have seventeen years of experience in a residential treatment facility—my home."

Nontraditional groups feel that it is important not to perceive the battered woman as "sick or seriously disturbed." For too many years, this type of assumption on the part of those in the helping professions has helped to lock the battered woman into a prison of shame and isolation. The staff at La Casa de las Madres, a shelter in San Francisco, share their views on this issue in their publication "La Casa de las Madres, an Overview," by Susan Jan Hornstein:

> "It has always been very important to us NOT to see the battered women who call or come to La Casa as "them" and the Casa staff as "us." The women who seek our help are not "sick" or crazy or dis-

† "Some Thoughts on Working a Shift at Casa Myrna," Casa Myrna Vasquez, Boston, MA, unpublished paper, 1977.

turbed. Rather, these women, as a result of circumstances, are more powerless than some of us. We see all women on a continuum of oppression and victimization: we are all victims, in various ways, of sexism in our culture—and we are all powerful, too. We see our job as helping these women to find and feel their power. We want to help residents to accomplish what they must, and to exercise their abilities to affect change. We don't have case conferences. Each resident's file (which is primarily an accumulation of information for statistical purposes) is open to her at all times.‡

Lisa Leghorn expands on the theme of self-help and its impact on women in abuse shelters:

> When a woman first comes in contact with a shelter group, the most refreshing and powerful aspect of her encounter is that her experience is *validated*. . . . Not only does she feel a tremendous sense of relief, but of empowerment. . . .
> Peer counseling, whereby the "helper" identifies with the "victim," constitutes a fundamental transformation in the way services are perceived and offered. No longer is a supposedly helpless, dependent, ignorant and masochistic client coming to seek salvation from a supposedly mature, wise and all-knowing counselor. . . .
> The self-help philosophy which is practiced by most shelter groups constitutes, in its content and process, an active support of each woman's empowerment. . . . Each step a woman takes in a support group, over the phone, or in a shelter, has been designed by her own hand. Although she has received validation, support and the information she needs to make a well-informed decision from external sources, she has assessed and evaluated her situation and defined her direction by herself. This explains why such a large number of women who have stayed in shelters go on to attend schools, job-training programs and make great changes in their lives that they never before had thought possible. . . .*

It is our feeling that the nontraditional approach offers the most flexibility and provides the most support for the battered woman.

‡ Susan Jan Hornstein, "La Casa de las Madres, an Overview," unpublished paper, San Francisco, CA, 1976.

* Lisa Leghorn, "Grass Roots Services for Battered Women: A Model for Long-term Change," *A Newsletter of the Feminist Alliance Against Rape and the National Communications Network*, July/Aug, 1978.

This is not to say, however, that those who have been traditionally trained have little to offer the woman who has been abused. On the contrary, a broad-based knowledge of counseling methods and techniques can be invaluable when combined with a supportive, pro-woman approach. In fact, these various counseling models are not necessarily mutually exclusive. Some shelters, such as the Women Against Abuse Emergency Shelter, in Philadelphia, incorporate both the traditional and peer concepts into their counseling components.

Weekly or nightly support groups, facilitated by staffers or volunteers, some of whom may be former battered women, are common. "The finest things happen at B.A. House when residents reach out to support other residents. We see the extent of our caring for each other at the Wednesday-night group therapy. On Wednesday night it is clear that we can each give what we all need: loving, comforting support as equals."†

At the other end of the spectrum, the Women's Transitional Living Center, in Orange County, California, feels that the traditional approach has value. "As controversial as it may be, counseling is mandatory for those residing at the center, and part of the counseling includes an initial interview with our consulting psychiatrist. Consultation with the psychiatrist enables other staff to better understand how to most effectively work with individual clients. . . . An argument that we've heard is that women are not sick but, rather, conditioned to respond as weak and nonassertive, and that we are contributing to the male-dominance syndrome from which women are struggling to escape. . . . The first part of the argument we agree with to a point. It is true that women have been conditioned to be nonassertive. At the same time, we have been taught to manipulate, seduce, and go along with our male counterparts, play a whole lot of games. Each woman is a unique individual, with her own set of coping and defense mechanisms, sometimes resulting in an imbalance."‡

† Staff of Bradley-Angle House, *Escape from Violence: The Women of Bradley-Angle House,* Bradley-Angle House, (Portland, OR, 1978).
‡ Sherry James and Susan Naples, *Establishing and Operating a Shelter for Battered Women . . . A "How To" Book,* Women's Transitional Living Center, Orange County, CA, 1977.

At the Domestic Violence Victims Assistance Program, in Dade County, Florida, nightly group counseling sessions are held for the women in the shelter. Each night, the group has a different focus. One night is devoted to emotional issues, one night to parent-effectiveness training, still another night to legal options or house rules.

An important part of the counseling process takes place when "older" residents provide help and support to newly arriving women. This occurs not only in a structured group setting but also on an informal basis during the day-to-day operation of the shelter. Often, this is quite beneficial to the "new" resident, since it reduces her feelings of isolation and provides her with an ongoing sense of support.

The style in which the shelter operates may also serve a counseling function for the residents. In some shelters, a great deal of responsibility is placed on the client from the time that she arrives. Strict house rules require her to prepare her own meals, care for her children, and organize her finances. She is encouraged to develop her survival skills and coping mechanisms as quickly as possible.

Other shelter environments are more communal in nature. Meals, child care, and other chores are shared tasks. In England, women in some shelters pool their money, and financial decisions are made collectively. Growth, independence, and a positive self-image are encouraged by the climate of warmth and support and sense of community generated within the shelter.

So counseling may be provided individually and in groups, on a mandatory or optional basis, by professionals or peers or both. In any case, it is important to keep in mind that many abused women have little or no experience in independent living and may need much encouragement and support to begin making their own decisions. A nonjudgmental approach as well as respect and acceptance for each individual are absolutely paramount.

We strongly urge you to read Chapter II, "Working with the Victim," before you finalize any decisions regarding your counseling components. Chapter II includes an overview of a variety of counseling techniques and methods as well as some insight as to their relative effectiveness.

Whom Does the Program Serve? Lately, there has been a lot of talk about battered husbands, although research findings don't support the increasingly common belief that husband beating is a widespread phenomenon. In fact, those working in the field find that women who physically attack their husbands are usually fighting back after enduring a prolonged period of abuse. Nevertheless, shelters are facing charges of reverse discrimination with increasing frequency. Many are reporting that funding sources want to know whether or not they will provide service to beaten men. Several of the shelters we have been in touch with would like to see concerned men begin to develop supportive services not only for battered husbands but for abusive men as well. They see their own priority, however, as providing service for women. La Casa: "We continue to uphold the decision to provide services only to women. Marriage counseling and therapy for men exist in abundance elsewhere. But there is little in the nature of support for women endeavoring to leave marriages."*

Should the *batterer* be served by shelter groups? Linda K. Boliger, chairwoman of the National Community Task Force on Women in Poverty, delineates her organization's position:

> As . . . a feminist long involved with the problems inherent in Family Violence, I am somewhat ambivalent about the inclusion of emergency shelter for the abusive spouse . . . especially since *he* does have a *nonthreatening* home situation in which to remain— Battered Women and their children do not. Further, the very last person Battered Women need to deal with in an emergency sanctuary is their, and/or anyone else's, abusive spouse. Asking Battered Women to deal constructively with male prototypes in the initial phase of trauma recovery is an unrealistic expectation, and one sure to incur the wrath of women's organizations that have worked to develop a supportive network of services for their abused sisters. . . .†

Some shelter groups, such as the Solano Shelter for Battered Women, in Fairfield, California, and Rainbow Retreat, in

* Hornstein, op. cit.
† Linda K. Boliger, "Sheltering the Batterer Too?" *A Newsletter of the Feminist Alliance Against Rape and the National Communications Network,* July/Aug, 1978.

Phoenix, Arizona, do provide services for men—both men who batter and the occasional men who are abused by their wives. In the event that your group is thinking about establishing such services, we suggest that you touch base with these and other groups providing this type of assistance. More information is available in Chapter VI.

In general, shelter clientele will depend on a number of factors such as location, accessibility, staff composition, etc. It is important to obtain as diverse a clientele as possible. Programs designed to provide services to women need to make sure that they meet the needs of all women, not simply those in the immediate neighborhood or those who already know how to utilize resources. Effective community work will help to insure diversity: a multicultural resident population.

Black women, Spanish-speaking women, Native American women, Asian women, military wives (both Asian and white), undocumented alien women, and rural women all face incredibly steep hurdles as they attempt to extricate themselves from the battering situation. They face all the dilemmas their many battered sisters in the majority culture face and, in addition, most contend with the discrimination that minority status carries.

Carol Angell, of the Battered Women's Project, in San Diego, California, has provided us with some valuable information regarding the special problems and needs of these women. She writes:

> All battered women's programs should include a well-grounded cultural and political perspective. Counselors need to expose themselves to many cultural groups and attempt to broaden their firsthand understanding. Shelters should make every attempt to hire bicultural and bilingual staff members. An attempt should be made to examine personal attitudes, bias and misconceptions in order to help prevent further oppression.
>
> Those of us working with abused women must look carefully at each of the women in context. We cannot know the appropriate responses or alternatives for her simply by hearing her story. The same events may have totally different meanings if looked at through different cultural, religious, economic, historical or political eyes. An option for one woman may be a barrier for another. Only

by understanding the context can we know what the events mean to her.

The military family, for example, poses some unique problems for those working on domestic violence. Often, the military couple is very young and far away from home. As a result there is an absence of any kind of family support system. Frequent relocation makes it difficult to develop any community ties. Many of the military wife's options and views of reality will be colored by her link to the military.

The Asian military wife and Asian women in general face special difficulties. Asian views of marriage prescribe a subservient, obedient role for the wife. Social services are at a minimum in many Asian communities. The Asian woman who has come to this country as a military wife finds herself in an alien environment where her culture and language are not understood. She is economically dependent on her husband, who may threaten to send her back. She has no marketable skills. Her only link with the new culture is through him. She often has no friends or family and is seldom aware of the services available in her community. She may not even know that it is illegal and unacceptable for her husband to beat, molest or imprison her, nor how to appeal for help. In addition, she may risk rejection from her family or particular Asian community if she tries to leave the marriage.‡

As you work to develop resources for this community of battered women, you will probably find that extra outreach will be necessary to increase awareness of available services. Resource development will be especially important. If possible, strong cooperative arrangements need to be built between your shelter and the appropriate military personnel.

Mary Peterson, director of the Solano Shelter for Battered Women, describes her program:

We are situated in the basin of two big military installations, Travis Air Force Base, which is the gateway to the Pacific, and Mare Island Naval Shipyard. Many of our clients are military dependents and many are Asian women. We have managed to develop a fantastic working relationship with these facilities, primarily

‡ Carol Angell, "Battered Women: Special Problems and Needs" (Battered Women's Project, San Diego, CA, 1978).

through the base chaplains and base commanders. Doctors from the base hospital participate in our in-service training programs. Other agencies, such as the Public Health Department, Mental Health Department and Red Cross, visit our shelter regularly to offer service and provide information as to what's available in the community. In fact, the director of the Public Health Department has made emergency house calls to the shelter.

Eventually, if we could raise the funds, we would like to develop a specialized immigration school which would teach English as a second language and would provide instruction in various trade skills.

We would like to include more Asian women on our staff, but this is difficult because of problems with citizenship, social security, and language. Often, military women don't qualify for our CETA-funded positions,* because their husbands' income is too high. So we have volunteers to do our interpreting for us.

Ms. Angell stresses that resources within the military and/or in the community at large should be well utilized. She provides the following information:

The military, at this point, has no uniform policies on how domestic violence should be handled. In some areas, such as Camp Pendleton, in California, the Human Affairs Officer is attempting to formulate such a policy. They are using past work on child abuse as a guide. Surgeon General William P. Arentzen, of the Navy and Marine Facility in Washington, D.C., has ordered that military facilities provide battered women with multidimensional services—more than just medical care. In many areas, the problem is referred to the base chaplain for counseling. This has some difficulties. According to a number of military personnel and wives who have been contacted, there is great reluctance to go to the chaplain, for two reasons. First of all, there is the fear that the man's position and therefore the family income will be in jeopardy. Second, there is a stigma involved in going to the chaplain and therefore much resistance.

If the woman does want assistance, either the counselor or the woman herself can call the Dependent's Assistance Board or the District Chaplain's Office to find out the appropriate chaplain for a particular demand.

The military does contain several other options. Many naval ships

* CETA stands for Comprehensive Employment and Training Act, a source of funds for many shelters. Funding is discussed later in this chapter.

have organized to support the wives. Most have an "ombudsman," a senior enlisted wife whose role is to assist other military wives. She can be located by calling the chaplain.

The battered woman can also go to the man's commanding officer to file a complaint. The C.O. is in the position to order the man to go for counseling or to move into the barracks—therefore leaving the woman in the home.

The different branches of the military also have drug and alcohol counseling programs that can be helpful in counseling the man or the couple. They also have some special relief programs, such as the Navy Relief Society, that can in certain situations provide shelter, and emergency funds. The Red Cross can also be contacted to help move military dependents back to where they come from across the country.

Confrontation with military agencies and programs should only be used after attempts to build creative linkage and trust have clearly failed. The military is growing in its awareness that family violence is a major problem and you may want to offer to do in-service education on family violence for chaplains, Human Relations Officers, and drug and alcohol counselors in order to help end many of the myths around battering.†

An outstanding example of the emerging recognition that military authorities are giving to the problem of abused women within the military takes place at Fort Campbell, Kentucky, where the Social Work Service Staff of the U. S. Army Hospital runs a shelter and offers counseling services for battered women. The project officer, First Lieutenant Nancy Raiha, reports that the women's community on the base, composed of both military wives and women working directly in the military, sought and won high-level official authorization and support for services for battered women. The shelter has been in operation since March 28, 1978, with an M.S.W. on call at all times. Presently, women's support groups and marital, family, and group counseling are available to battered women on the post. The staff plans to add legal services and more shelter space as soon as possible.

Education and outreach within the Asian community will be necessary to create a climate of concern for Asian battered women. Since wife beating is an accepted part of marriage within

† Angell, op. cit.

many Asian cultures, those social services that do exist within the Asian community may refuse to recognize wife beating as a problem. Mr. Zun Han, program director of the Korean Women Abuse Project, in Los Angeles, California, reveals that older and conservative Koreans have asked him, "What are you trying to do, spoil the Korean women?" when they have learned of his efforts to provide shelter and counseling for Korean women who are victims of domestic violence.

Native American women also suffer from additional problems and obstacles when they attempt to solve a battering dilemma. Ms. Angell addresses the issue:

Abused Native American women may be even more isolated and stranded than other women. The populations of most reservations are extremely small and they tend to function like an extended family. The majority of residents are related, either directly or indirectly. There is little privacy, so any action they take is public knowledge. According to several groups of women on the reservation, battery is frequently the norm—not the exception. Leaving the man would usually mean leaving the community—hardly an alternative for most women.

The majority culture and Native American cultures are different. Norms, perceptions of reality, humor and values vary—even from group to group. If it is hard for a majority woman to move to a new city for safety, it is doubly hard for the Native American woman. She would have to give up her community and go out into an often hostile environment. Her whole identity can seem to be in jeopardy. The residents of the reservation have many other major problems to contend with. Poverty is extreme, as is unemployment, particularly of the men. Suicide and alcoholism are rampant. These all contribute to domestic violence.

In addition, the women may have little access to outside resources. There are few phones and little transportation available. Medical care is inadequate, and police protection and jurisdiction on federal reservations is spotty or even nonexistent.‡

Ms. Genevieve La Pointe is a Native American woman from the Brulé-Sioux tribe, on the Rosebud reservation, in the south-

‡ Ibid.

central part of South Dakota. Her organization, the White Buffalo Calf Women's Society, is establishing a shelter for battered women on the reservation. She says, "A shelter would be one of the best things that could happen on a reservation. Often, you can find women and their children hiding in old battered cars or in dark alleys because there is nowhere for them to go when they are beaten. The police won't do anything and their families are afraid to take them in." Ms. La Pointe feels that couple counseling should become part of any effort to address battering within the Native American community. She points out that, historically, wife abuse has not been a problem for Native Americans and that poverty and discrimination contribute to a tense and stressful climate that leads to violence.

"Of course, our tribal laws don't help either. They view the female as the property of her husband. She is to bend to his will. If she wants a divorce, she will have to leave the reservation to get one, since tribal law doesn't recognize divorce."

Ms. La Pointe's group, which is composed primarily of Native American women, has managed to acquire an empty building that used to be part of a residential school. As of this writing, they are in the process of obtaining equipment and furnishings.

On some reservations, the feeling exists that establishing shelters for battered women could create problems as well as solve them. Ms. Angell points out that a confidential shelter location would be impossible. In addition, community support might not be readily forthcoming. "Many men would feel threatened by a shelter and might respond with increased violence,"* she writes. Ms. Angell feels that outreach is needed but that internal education and changing norms and values may have to slowly alter the situation.

One possible approach at this time is to stimulate the building of linkages among Native American women who are battered. Support groups might be a place to start. Here, feelings of fear, isolation, and self-blame can be addressed within the "safe" environment of the group. Eventually, these groups could lead to the development of an ongoing support community for battered women within the reservation.

* Ibid.

Ms. Angell's program is seeking funds for outreach workers to facilitate the development of such groups.

Those working with undocumented alien women describe their problems as "almost insurmountable." Ms. Angell writes: "The undocumented alien woman is caught in a situation of double jeopardy. She finds herself trapped between her fear of the man and her fear of the police and deportation. She may be lured to the U.S. by the promise of a new life, economic security and immigration as his wife only to find herself the virtual slave of the man who then refuses to marry her. She's extremely vulnerable and an easy victim of violence, abandonment and exposure."†

Unfortunately, we don't have many words of wisdom to share with you regarding the provision of services to these women. Those we've talked with who are working to alleviate the situation report that often there is little that can be done until the woman obtains the credentials that will allow her to work or qualify for welfare. Of course, ongoing emotional support and survival skills can be provided.

We spoke with Mr. Paul McKennon, deputy director of the Philadelphia office of the U. S. Immigration and Naturalization Service. He gave us some information regarding the immigration laws: It is illegal to harbor, conceal, or transport undocumented aliens. Whether or not providing shelter for abused undocumented women would constitute an illegal act is unclear. We suggest caution. It is not illegal to provide assistance to individuals who request it, and service providers are not obligated to turn anyone in. The right to confidentiality remains intact. (Recent court decisions have reaffirmed this.)

Depending on the circumstances of the case, the immigration authorities may be helpful in trying to straighten out the status of an undocumented alien woman, according to Mr. McKennon. "We will investigate the case, and if there is any way we can arrange for immigration, we will do so. If it is impossible for her to immigrate, we will give her time to arrange her return. We don't just scoop people up and put them on a plane or in jail." Again, we suggest caution.

† Ibid.

A movement is currently underway to change the immigration laws. One proposal calls for legal status for aliens who have been in the country since 1970. Federal legislation has been introduced and is being considered by Congress. Passage is pretty "iffy," says Mr. McKennon, due to heavy opposition.

Another group of battered women that face special difficulty is rural women. The Domestic Violence Project of the Nebraska Commission on the Status of Women has written a comprehensive report on the problems that abused women face in rural areas. The report points out that domestic-violence victims who live on a ranch, farm or in a rural town often need to travel five to fifty miles to get to their nearest neighbor or town, and therefore, to help of any kind.‡

The report goes on to discuss a variety of factors that compound the rural woman's difficulties: geographic and social isolation; lack of community resources such as legal aid, housing, shelters, crisis counseling, day care, job training; lack of anonymity; the ineffectiveness of rural law enforcement; traveling judges (which can mean a long wait for a court appearance); lack of shelter; lack of jobs; and nonexistent or ineffective hotline services. The wives of professional men are caught in a real bind, the report points out, because rural villages desperately need doctors, lawyers, etc., and these men are immune to social pressures if their reputations become tarnished by alcoholism, drug abuse, or child or spouse abuse. The report also describes the old-fashioned, conservative attitude in rural areas that perpetuate sex roles and the "no-win" situation experienced by victims of domestic violence.

The Domestic Violence Project has developed an effective model for establishing services in rural areas. Funded by CETA, the program focuses on developing community awareness of the problem as well as increasing the effectiveness of existing resources. The project itself acts as a resource and referral center. Four regional advisers in various parts of the state stimulate the formation of local task forces on domestic violence in as many communities as possible. The local task forces are, in turn, re-

‡ Domestic Violence Project, Nebraska Commission on the Status of Women, Lincoln NB, 1978.

sponsible for the actual delivery of services to victims. The task forces are made up of community volunteers, and the cost of services rendered to victims is usually underwritten by the volunteers. Services vary from hotlines to support groups to temporary shelter in YWCAs, YWHAs, or Salvation Army shelters.

One way of increasing the amount of services available to rural battered women is to sensitize as many agencies and county areas to the problem as possible. Then you might suggest that the agencies pool their resources so that a wider range of services can be offered.

The Pennsylvania Coalition Against Domestic Violence (PCADV) suggests that another way to reach outlying areas is to hire staff that would spend time in the field. Perhaps arrangements could be made to utilize the facilities of local churches for counseling and running support groups. In this way, women who lack transportation or who would be hesitant to travel could receive help.

In addition, if your program produces any publications (brochures, survival packets, etc.), you might arrange to leave them in grocery stores, post offices, doctors' offices, etc.

Hispanic women, both citizens and noncitizens, face difficulties similar to those of Asian women. They are isolated from the dominant culture by language, customs, and socialization. They are kept ignorant of their legal or economic rights and have difficulty finding adequate bilingual or bicultural services.

Carol Angell points out that the existence of the extended family in the Hispanic community can be both a blessing and a curse. On the one hand, fear of blackening the family name may lead to secrecy and avoidance. On the other hand, the family may be extremely helpful in providing support and protection. Counselors should make sure to investigate the family as a potential source of support.

For Hispanic women, moving out of the neighborhood (often a necessary step to escape an abusive husband) means leaving behind everyone and everything with which she is familiar. Every effort should be made to find a solution that does not require leaving the Hispanic community.

Some Hispanic communities, such as San Francisco, offer relatively comprehensive social services. Make sure you have adequately researched what's available in your community.

In general, minority women face all the same problems that majority women confront. In addition, they are burdened with lack of educational and employment opportunities, discrimination, and often poverty.

The necessity to rely on inadequate and biased delivery of community services significantly reduces the number of options available to them. Negative and insensitive attitudes on the part of social workers and welfare officials is frustrating and disheartening.

Racist attitudes and procedures on the part of law-enforcement officials, district attorneys, judges, and court personnel make a mockery of the criminal-justice system.

Low-income women in general find it difficult to rely on help from family members, since lack of financial resources usually means that not much help is available from home even when the family is sympathetic and wants to provide support and assistance.

When developing shelter and support services for minority women, sensitivity is the key. Every group or organization that proposes to address the problem of wife battering must have significant minority involvement if the program is to operate successfully. When a group wishes to establish services for minority women, it is essential to touch base with already existing groups and agencies within the community. An initial step may be to offer training on domestic abuse to those staffing community centers and organizations. If you already have a shelter or are providing service, the appropriate community agencies should be advised of the services you offer so that referrals can be made if needed. Sharing of resource information is another way of touching base and establishing cooperative relationships with already existing groups.

In some communities, there may be resistance to recognizing wife abuse as a serious problem as well as reluctance to work cooperatively with organized women's groups. If such is the case, community education will be necessary before services can be established.

Whatever the situation, it is important to remember that the need for services must be perceived by the community first if such services are to be successfully provided.

In Philadelphia, an effective working relationship was established between a group operating a hotline for battered women in a white working-class neighborhood (Hotline for Abused Women/Kensington) and community workers and counselors from an adjoining Hispanic community. In spite of long-term mistrust and hostility between the two communities, these groups held a series of meetings and rap sessions that eventually culminated in a joint undertaking to provide hotline services to battered women in both areas. Both groups of women have found the joint effort rewarding. Decisions to continue working together came after a spirit of trust and cooperation was engendered by the initial set of meetings. Although cultural differences dictate separate service components, the groups have agreed to conduct joint training and resource sharing. These women have managed to work together successfully to meet the needs of different groups of women with a common problem.

Within a shelter environment, various cultural groups with dissimilar value systems can sometimes meet head on. This can lead to difficulty in operating the shelter itself as well as related support services. These difficulties can take a variety of forms: specific groups keeping to themselves (at mealtimes, etc.) with no interaction with others, criticism of each other's child-care methods, placing blame for disorder and confusion on each other, refusal to actively participate in group meetings. Mary Peterson, director of the Solano Shelter for Battered Women, says: "Prejudice can be a problem. Recently, we had difficulty with a staff person who was still harboring resentment towards the Japanese from World War II. She was unable to work effectively with the Japanese women at our shelter."

Examples of how racism from the broader culture emerges among shelter residents are described by Renae Scott, of the Cambridge, Massachusetts, Transition House.

In our shelter, our biggest discussions have been around how different cultures view discipline. Some women would rather . . .

talk it out with their children. Other women feel spankings are the only way to discipline. Compound this problem with white and black women in a shelter on different sides of the issue—and you've got a Big Problem because they all have to live there in the house with the differences.

The next biggest issue has been around food. Who cooks with grease (shortening, lard, etc.)? Who doesn't and why? Do we have to have beans again? Or, that food looks, tastes funny—without ever eating or tasting it.

. . . Music—what radio station is listened to in the shelter? Is It soft rock, semi-classical? Is *Soul* Black Music—really that *loud?*

Do the Surroundings—pictures, books, magazines, etc., reflect other women's experiences? Do books reflect multiracial children—just as you would have them be nonsexist? . . .*

The best way to handle these problems is to deal with them directly. One approach used by Casa Myrna Vasquez, in Boston, is to schedule regular group meetings that address the question of racism. This usually gets hostilities out in the open, and with skilled facilitation, women from various cultural groups will begin to touch base with the things that unite them instead of continuing to focus on the things that divide them.

It is important, when dealing with these problems, that the staff members realize that they are setting an example. Often, the extent to which residents deal with differences is directly related to how successfully the staff accomplish the same thing.

As crucial as it is for shelter staff and volunteers to be aware of the distinctive cultures that battered minority women are part of, it is equally crucial that shelter workers remember that housing women is a *majority*-culture activity, variations of which are found in minority cultures. For battering is a societal crime, cutting across all classes, regions, ethnic groups, races, and religions. Arguments pointing to the alleged "culture of poverty" or "minority family structure" as sources of battering confuse cause with effect and reveal, at the same time, the race and class biases of the authors.

* Renae Scott, "Race and the Shelter Movement," *A Newsletter of the Feminist Alliance Against Rape and the National Communications Network,* July/Aug 1978, pp. 30–31.

Policy Making

No matter what your philosophic base, the development of certain guidelines is absolutely necessary to the effective provision of services. You will need to decide the nature and extent of your services, how many people you can realistically deal with at a time, where your referrals will come from, what kinds of priorities you will set when faced with more applicants than you can serve, and what kinds of limits you will need in order to be most effective.

Emotional Disturbance

Most shelters have found that severely emotionally disturbed women are not well suited to their programs, may cause too much disruption and upset to others, and are more appropriately served by a mental-health agency geared to handling their difficulties.

Drugs and Alcohol

Drug and alcohol addiction can also be extremely destructive forces within the shelter, and again, women with these problems need to be referred to other programs. Alcohol and nonprescription drugs are most often forbidden on the premises, and such a rule, made clear from the beginning, will help to avoid many serious difficulties.

Children

You will also have to address the question of children: who will be primarily responsible for their supervision, whether or not you wish to provide children's services, and whether or not you want to set age and/or sex limits. Be sure to see Chapter I's section "Your Children" and all of Chapter V.

In "Treatment Alternatives for Battered Women," Lenore Walker writes of the various difficulties that shelters face in dealing with children from violent homes—many of whom are emotionally disturbed from living through prolonged periods of stress and violence:

The withdrawn children are usually overlooked. Space is a problem for younger children, who need a place to run and play. Older children, especially the adolescents, engage in various acting-out behaviors that can make communal living in cramped quarters a horror. They often destroy the few meager furnishings. Much time, energy and money are spent trying to reverse the trends and prevent these children from perpetuating violence.†

Although there are many shelters that do not experience the extreme problems described by Ms. Walker, it is true that several groups have experienced difficulties with the inclusion of older boys in cramped living quarters with people in crisis situations. Some programs, such as La Casa de las Madres shelter, in California, however, do accept boys up to the age of eighteen and feel that separating families during the period of residence can be more disruptive than the problems engendered by their remaining together. La Casa has developed a children's program that deals with many of the problems described above, a description of which is included in Chapter V. If you feel that you can work more effectively without older or too many children, you will have to develop plans for helping mothers find alternative resources for them. This may be most appropriate for mothers who are having difficulty in coping with their children during their stay at the shelter.

The Solano Shelter for Battered Women has resolved this problem by establishing separate facilities for women with male children over thirteen years of age. Occasionally, instances of child abuse occur at the shelter. When this happens, there are several possible solutions. Since most shelters have rules that permit absolutely no violence, mothers who abuse their children can be ejected. Usually, however, this step is taken only when the abuse is severe and other deterrents have failed. Sometimes it is necessary to have the children removed and placed in a foster home. If it becomes necessary to institute this measure, we recommend that the woman remain in the shelter and receive additional counseling that will enable her to cope more effectively with her children as

† Lenore E. Walker, "Treatment Alternatives for Battered Women," In Jane Roberts Chapman and Margaret Gates, *Victimization of Women*, Vol. 3, Sage Publications, (Beverly Hills, CA. 1978).

well as her own victimization. Often, other residents will step in and try to demonstrate nonviolent parenting alternatives to the abusive mother. Quite possibly, the problem will be discussed during a house meeting. Sometimes this will result in more intensive counseling between the staff therapist and the mother.

Occasionally, a woman may want to place her children elsewhere during her stay at the shelter so that she can have the time and space to regroup and rebuild her life.

The question of how much child care the shelter will provide is an important one. Some shelters see child care as a priority and have instituted a variety of means to provide it. Frequently, volunteers provide this service. Some programs have obtained slots in local day-care programs.

The workers in some shelters feel that the mother should take primary responsibility for her child during her stay at the shelter. The "House Rules" of the Women's Transitional Living Center state: "Women are responsible for their children at all times. The Children's Activities Coordinator is at the Center daily Monday through Friday. She plans activities for the children. The only time she watches the children is when mothers are in group. She is not a babysitter and will not assume responsibility for the children."‡

Realistically, some child care will have to be provided if the women are to take care of their futures. They will need to visit the welfare office, legal aid, the housing authority, etc.

One of the things you may need to do is to make arrangements with the local school district to take the children temporarily until the family is resettled. If such arrangements are made, it is important that the school not release the address of the shelter and refrain from notifying the father of his children's enrollment at the school. (This has been known to happen.)

Many shelters have established parent-effectiveness training sessions on a regular basis for their residents to provide them with the tools that they need to counteract the negative effects that the abusive home has had upon the children. In addition, residents often learn effective parenting techniques from each other.

‡ Sherry James and Susan Naples, op. cit.

Length of Stay

Guidelines on length of stay may be quite flexible if necessary, but it is a good idea to have a general policy on this. Policies vary widely from no limit whatsoever to limitations of a few days. Of course, your policy will be partially determined by the size of your facility and the scope of your resources. Some shelters, however, place limits on the length of stay because they have found that some women are so relieved at the respite they find in the shelter that they have a hard time mobilizing themselves to make more-long-range plans, and it is helpful for them to know from the beginning that there is an expectation that they do so within a certain amount of time.

Policy on the number of times a woman may return to the shelter also needs to be set. Many shelters have no limit, recognizing that battered women need the time and space to break the cycle of violence as best they can. Del Martin puts it this way: "The reasons that kept her home in the first place beckon her back once she leaves: hope that her husband will change, fear of the unknown, lack of financial resources. Vacillation is inevitable."*

Transition House, a shelter in Cambridge, Massachusetts, sets the following limits: "The maximum stay at the House is six weeks for women with children and four weeks for women without children. Although women may return a second time for a shorter period of time, they may not return a third time. This guideline was made to prevent women from staying with violent husbands and using the House as a temporary shelter every time they are battered, while not resolving their situations."†

House Rules

House rules are a vital force in insuring the smooth operation of the shelter and avoiding the kinds of chaotic situations that cause only added stress to women already in highly stressful situations. You will need to address such issues as responsibility for

* Del Martin, *Battered Wives,* (San Francisco, CA: New Glide Publications, 1976).
† *Transition House,* by the Women of Transition House, 46 Pleasant St., Cambridge, MA, 02139, 1977.

house maintenance, for personal belongings, and for food preparation. These may be seen as individual or collective responsibilities, but either way it is important that everyone be clear about them. House meetings, both structured and impromptu, can be important in establishing, assessing, and modifying rules as needed. House meetings also serve to set up scheduling and address any problems that may be occurring in the shelter. They can also be used to orient "new" residents and as strategy sessions for women who are seeking employment, housing, etc.

As mentioned before, house rules almost always specify nonviolence. Usually they restrict visitors, and frequently there are strict rules against men on the premises. Dating may be prohibited, and sometimes curfews are in effect. One last consideration as you are drawing up your house rules: fees. Many shelters charge a small daily fee, usually no more than a couple of dollars. By paying their way, residents will not have to feel as if they are accepting charity, an important consideration for many women. If a woman is destitute, then of course she is not required to pay. Some shelters have a brief set of rules for children that address such issues as bedtimes and food preparation.

Intake

Intake procedures seem to be pretty much the same from shelter to shelter. Usually, the woman is received by a staff member and introduced to the other residents. If needed, medical care is provided immediately. She is given a copy of the rules and some linens and is made to feel at home as much as possible. Some shelters assign an "older" resident to serve as a "big sister" until the newly arrived client feels comfortable. Sometimes releases are signed and forms are filled out immediately. Often, women are given some time to relax and get acquainted first. Serious counseling and resource development usually don't begin until the second day.

Confidentiality

Since women arriving at the shelter are often escaping from life-threatening situations, the concept of a confidential location is no mere cloak-and-dagger one. Abusive men frequently seek out and severely punish women for leaving home. Therefore, the knowledge that the shelter's address is kept secret from all but those using the services can provide a very real sense of safety as well as psychological relief. Location may be kept secret by using a post-office box as a mailing address and by handling initial requests for service over the phone and making arrangements to meet women at a specified location and escorting them to the house. If the address is kept confidential, it is important to stress the seriousness of this to all staff, volunteers, residents, and other agencies.

Although the vast majority of shelter locations are secret, there are exceptions. Women's Advocates, of St. Paul, Minnesota, has a non-confidential address. This situation developed because in a city of 350,000 it became increasingly difficult to conceal the shelter's whereabouts. This may happen to many shelters over a period of time, especially if they serve a particular community within a larger city or are in a rural area. In the event that this does occur, it is important that good relations be maintained with the police so that they will arrive quickly in the event of trouble. It may be possible to get first priority on the police radio.

Loss of secrecy regarding your shelter location does not have to be a disaster. One positive aspect is that the community can witness the development of a family of independent women who at one time were virtually powerless and unable to exercise real control over their lives.

Staffing

Your philosophic base will be an important determinant of the kind of staff you have. Some groups feel that professional training and experience give staff members skills and expertise that enhance their ability to be helpful to abuse victims. Other groups may look with suspicion at professional credentials, believing that the record of professionals in dealing with battered women has been too dismal to give much credence to such credentials. Some even feel that professional training can stand in the way of sympathetic counseling and vigorous advocacy.

At the Bradley-Angle House, in Portland, Oregon, a staffer's credentials are not considered as important as her ability to relate well to the residents of the house. She must be able to identify with women of various backgrounds, she must have the ability to independently direct her own life, and she must have a willingness to share the personal strengths she has developed in a way that elicits strength from the women she works with. The position of program director lists the following qualifications:

1. Experience in program development for a related residential care facility or women's programs.
2. Experience and skill in relating to community-based organizations.
3. Experience in managing and raising funds.
4. Must have demonstrated administrative and group-process skills in past positions.‡

Whatever your stand on the appropriate qualifications for shelter staff, battered women need warm, sympathetic, committed counselors and advocates who are willing to make that extra effort in behalf of their clients.

Whether or not refuges should hire male staffers is currently under debate in the shelter community. Some organizations feel that men should not be present at all, since battered women have been recently victimized by men. Others feel that it is important that sensitive, caring men be present at the facility to demonstrate positive role models, particularly to the children. It is often as child-care providers that men are involved in shelter operations.

La Casa de las Madres cites several reasons for their decision to maintain an all-woman staff: "(a) The fact that we are all women—plumbers, electricians, child-care workers, organizers, speakers, architects, lawyers—is a powerful modeling tool for the women who stay at La Casa. Many of these women have never seen strong, independent women working together, accomplishing goals, being effective and supporting one another. (b) The presence of men on the staff would alter the dynamics and atmosphere of the support situation. (c) The house is a residence, a home where women are living together in intimate, crowded conditions, and we feel that the presence of men would make this situation more difficult and not as relaxed. (d) At this painful time in a woman's life, she is often thankful not to be in the company of

‡ *Women Sheltering Women from Violence,* Program Proposal for 1978, Bradley-Angle House, Portland, OR.

men, and prefers to come to La Casa because of this. (e) We live in a society in which men have power over women. Many battered women have been dependent and passive with regard to their husbands and/or lovers. All too often, in the mental-health and social-service system, we see that this dependency is duplicated in relationships between a dependent, passive female and a strong, authoritarian, "expert" male. We have no wish to duplicate this situation at La Casa. . . ."*

Although La Casa did consider hiring male child-care workers, they decided against it, because they did not want to indicate to women, many of whom have difficult and rebellious children, that men are needed in positions of authority over children and that women as single parents are not capable of exerting control over their children by themselves. It is important that single-parent women develop the skills to control their children, since they have to live with them. Men are involved at La Casa, however, in weekend outings and have volunteered to continue contact with children and mothers once they leave the shelter, if such contact is desired.

The Women's Transitional Living Center, Orange County, California, feel that males on the shelter staff can serve to enhance rather than detract from overall staff performance: "In some cases we would agree that having men work directly with battered women is inappropriate. The inappropriateness, however, centers on the personality of the man involved as well as on his position or function within the organization. It is our opinion that it is healthy for women and children to see that not all men are abusive and insensitive. Our psychiatrist is a person with a deep sense of compassion, aware of the problems women face, and one who does not do a one-up trip on women. He maintains a low, supportive profile, and in many cases, the client requests to see him again after the initial interview. In our opinion, his involvement has not created problems or hampered the program in any way. On the contrary, it has enhanced the services provided."†

* Susan Jan Hornstein, op. cit.
† From a letter appearing in the "Open Foum" section of *Victimology: An International Journal,* Vol. 2, 1978, Feb. 1978.

Mary Peterson, of the Solano Shelter for Battered Women, feels that in an effort to reach all women, we must reexamine our policies around male involvement in shelter operations: "To many black women, the exclusion of men from any program that is concerned with the family can seem to be a perpetuation of the breakup of the black family that has occurred in our country since slavery. Women should still dominate and control, but we need all the support we can get, including male support." The Solano shelter employs three males who have some contact with the residents.

Recently, funding sources have been asking whether or not males are part of shelter personnel. If you have male employees, then this is not a problem. If you are an all-female staff, however, this could create some difficulties. See the section on funding for tips on how to handle this. Further discussion on whether or not male therapists can or should work with battered women can be found in Chapter II.

Whether or not males should serve on shelter staff may be debatable, but the question of structuring the staff so that it has racial, economic, and cultural diversity is not. It is imperative that shelters commit themselves to strong affirmative-action efforts. Since it is now clear that abused women come from every conceivable background, it would be a disservice to them if the shelter staff that is trying to meet their needs did not reflect the diversity found among battered women themselves. Many shelters such as La Casa and Bradley-Angle House are committed not only to a multicultural representation but to maintaining as much heterogeneity as possible. Working out differences between older/younger, professionally trained/nonprofessional, gay/straight, nonwhite/white, and working/middle/upper-class women has been the most exciting, albeit the most difficult, part of La Casa's development. At Bradley-Angle House, the primary commitment is to hiring Third-World women. Since racism has been flourishing for thousands of years, it is clear that simply hiring nonwhite women will not automatically mean a well-diversified staff working in harmony toward common goals. But affirmative-action efforts with real teeth in them are a step in the right direction. They need to be followed up with regular consciousness-raising sessions designed to increase staff members' sensitivity and awareness.

In addition to making sure that your staff is sufficiently diverse, it is important to incorporate ex-residents into the staff when possible. Former battered women make committed and effective counselors. As new residents arrive, they will benefit from observing previously abused women who have not only succeeded in escaping the cycle of violence but have turned what was once a negative experience into something that is now positive, something that is working for, rather than against, them.

The manner in which your staff operates will be one of the more important decisions you make as you organize your program. Essentially, there are three models you may want to look at as you determine the work style best suited to your organization.

In the traditionally *hierarchical* work setting, lines of authority are clearly established. Policy is usually determined by the board of directors and implemented by the executive director. He or she manages the overall program, including the rest of the staff, who must answer to either him/her or an immediate supervisor whom he or she has designated.

Those who critize the traditional arrangement argue that almost all power and authority rest with "top staff," and lower-echelon staff members have little or no effect on decision making. Status and prestige are based not upon actual accomplishment but upon how high one has moved "up the ladder." Often, employees without credentials are locked into dead-end, low-paying positions regardless of how much knowledge and experience they acquire. Each employee has his or her area of "expertise," and little skill-sharing takes place. Rigid lines of authority frequently result in unequal relationships, which leads to power struggles and imbalances, intense personality clashes, lack of sufficient recognition or reward for achievement, and lack of employee motivation.

Those who favor the hierarchical work style feel that it results in the greatest efficiency. People have clearly designated roles and tasks, for which they can be held responsible. Accountability is therefore built in. Decisions can be made quickly and with a minimum of inconvenience. With precise lines of authority, the question "Where does the buck stop?" is easily answered. "Burnout" is minimized due to clearly delineated functions, which prevents everyone from trying to do everything.

At the Women's Transitional Living Center, the interoffice procedures reflect the traditional approach: "Employees report directly to their supervisor. If anyone other than the supervisor gives staff directions, check with your supervisor first. This includes the Executive Director and Board members. . . . Appropriate channels for staff to communicate are: through supervisor, through Executive Director, to Board of Directors."‡

At La Casa, the second model, which we will call the "pure" collective, is in effect:

> We will make decisions by consensus, not by majority vote. This means that if a decision cannot be agreed upon by everyone, we will reconvene a meeting with everyone present after a specified time period has elapsed; if agreement still cannot be reached, a mediator will be called in to help us come to agreement.
>
> In addition to being collective, we are also committed to being nonhierarchical. Everyone has always received the same pay. There has been no executive director. All skills are valued equally; maintenance and sanitation, child care, food shopping, advocacy, fund raising, typing, administration and counseling. All are seen as different but equal skills. No one skill receives or deserves more power or authority than any other.*

Those that support the "pure" collective model believe that it offers the only truly nonoppressive working environment for women. The principles of operating a collective are in direct opposition to those at work within the traditional setting. Value is placed on ability and willingness to learn, rather than on credentials or formal experience. Concerted efforts are made to value all functions equally, and skill sharing is incorporated as much as possible. Efforts are made to avoid specialization, and staff are committed to sharing the unpleasant tasks as well as the creative, rewarding ones. Since each member is accountable to the group, checks and balances are built in.

Some argue that the "pure" collective is great in theory but

‡ Sherry James and Susan Naples, op. cit.
* Hornstein, op. cit.

difficult to implement in practice. Consensus is required for all decisions, which is often cumbersome, emotionally draining, and time-consuming. Equal pay sounds fine, but some people need more money than others; and a person recently joining the staff should not receive as much salary as someone who has been working with the program for years. Collectivity can sometimes stifle leadership by the refusal to openly recognize differences in levels of ability and skill. Although attempts are made to share power equally, frequently those with the most verbal skills actually control the group. Often, this leaves low-income women, many times in the minority, at a disadvantage. Many women who are not particularly self-confident may feel overwhelmed and intimidated by the expectations that the collective places upon them; expectations that they might feel unable, at that time, to meet. If the collective is multicultural, major struggles can ensue when different value systems meet head on. These struggles are often left unresolved.

Many veterans of the women's movement have been through the "pure" collective model and have found that some of the obstacles described above dictate a new approach. Hence, the development of the third model, the "modified" collective. In this model, an attempt is made to encompass the best features of the other two, while at the same time discarding the most offensive (traditional) and most unworkable ("pure" collective).

There may be a director, but usually she involves the rest of the staff in important decision making. At the same time, she or others may make some decisions within agreed-upon principles without consulting everyone. Sometimes there is a "coordinating level" within the staff consisting of two or three people who are responsible for administering the program and who consider themselves accountable to each other. While it is true that there are "lower" staff levels, perhaps consisting of service-delivery positions (advocates, counselors) and support staff (secretaries, bookkeepers), every effort is made to see to it that training and upward mobility are built into all phases of program operation. All work is equally valued, but those with special skills and abilities are encouraged to develop them to their fullest as well as share them with others. Indigenous leadership is recognized and valued. Those with greater responsibility and/or history of work with the program may receive more money but not to the extent that huge gaps exist between salary levels. Although power imbalances do exist, those who favor this model argue that it is healthier to have them out in the open, where they can be dealt with. Frequently, the collective model establishes a screen that camouflages and hides serious power struggles. This camouflage often develops regardless of the level of sincerity and commitment on the part of those within the group.

The foregoing information is of course quite generalized. Probably there are "pure" collectives that don't have some of the problems described above. Perhaps there are traditionally run shelters that adequately meet the needs of staff and residents. And the "modified" collective may not really be as workable as it sounds. As you develop your operating philosophies and policies regarding shelter functions, you will of course need to explore further the options mentioned here. Firsthand checks with other shelters, additional reading, and consultation with the proposed client population will assist you in making a sound decision. Our thoughts on the subject are not intended to serve as a complete guide but, rather, as a base from which to develop your thinking.

Whether your staff is based on a traditional or a collective model, you will need to consider the kinds of services you wish to provide, and work to insure that they are available without duplication of effort or misunderstanding of roles. Whatever your approach, there are certain basic traits that are important to the optimal development and functioning of any domestic-abuse program: warmth, flexibility, a basic orientation to the needs and problems of women in general and of abused women in particular, a positive attitude toward the ability of women to be independent and self-actualizing, and the ability to make the necessary commitment of time, energy, and emotional and physical output that forms the basis of a dynamic, responsive, and effective staff.

Most probably, you will need to staff your shelter on a twenty-four-hour basis. Night-time coverage is, of course, essential for both the phones and the shelter facility. You may want to try rotating shifts among the staff so that the same people aren't always working at night.

Flexibility should be built into staff functions as much as possible. Often, a shelter resident will single out a particular staff person or volunteer that she feels comfortable with. Staff and volunteers should be apprised of this need and receive proper training in counseling techniques so that they feel comfortable with a fairly loose arrangement.

One *inflexible* part of shelter functioning should be the rule: no sexually intimate relationships between staff members and residents will be tolerated. Why? Joan Valenti, former National Communications Network chairperson, explains:

> . . . And I have seen too many times, women in pain, confusion and crisis being taken advantage of by staff who are working through the need to be a savior, someone's mainstay—staff whose sense of self-worth and ego depended on being "loved" by clients. And therefore the women became responsible not only for their own problems and mental health, but also for the staff member, who was allegedly there to give unconditional support without demanding certain returns. It is my very strong personal belief . . . that we must offer them at least once in their lives, love with no strings— and that it is unethical for staff—male or female—to promote emotional dependency in any fashion. . . .
>
> . . . there is a third piece to my and our thinking—we offer safe haven. A major part of that is the space to have one's self as the only concern—to not have "relationships"—to finally be clear and alone with self. . . . The stress and pain of new love struggling to find its realities, its trust level—the possibility of that "event" can be enormously threatening (even though sought as a remedy to present pain and loss). . . .†

Volunteers make up at least part of the staff of most programs and are considered an invaluable means of extending the limited resources available. They may perform many functions that you might not otherwise be able to afford. Use of volunteers also makes available the talents and energies of a wide range of community women who for various reasons are not able to commit to a full-time job.

† Joan Valenti, "Relationships in the Shelters," *A Newsletter of the Feminist Alliance Against Rape and the National Communications Network,* July/Aug 1978, pp. 53–54.

When selecting volunteers, careful screening is necessary. Some of the same criteria should be used as when hiring staff. An ability to relate well to all women is important, as well as enthusiasm, commitment, and the capacity to foster independence in others.

Since volunteers often do not have the same degree of commitment as paid staff, and since they may have varying or conflicting notions of the kinds of services they wish to perform, it is a good idea to have one person, task force, or committee to carry the overall responsibility for coordination of volunteer services.

Training is usually necessary for volunteers to become competent, skilled advocates and service providers.

The Pennsylvania Coalition Against Domestic Violence (PCADV) points out: "A new volunteer who has had related experience may be able to begin work with only a brief orientation. In most programs, a series of training sessions are run several times a year. All volunteers are expected to complete the series. The philosophy and policies of the agency, the resources in the community, techniques of support counseling, record keeping, and the duties of a volunteer are some of the topics which could be included in the training."‡

The Women Against Abuse Emergency Shelter, in Philadelphia, conducts a three-part training program for its volunteers, focusing on the development of legal-counseling and court-accompaniment skills.

Scheduling volunteers can be a problem. Often, they are not as available as they had originally expected to be. Thoughtful scheduling, along with careful checking by the volunteer coordinator is important. Just expecting volunteers to show up at the appointed time without a verifying phone call first can be risky, especially if you are depending on them to cover phones, etc.

It is important that volunteers receive recognition for the contributions they make to the program. Formal recognition can be helpful to the volunteer who is seeking employment, and a volunteer is much more likely to remain with the program if she knows that the work she is doing is appreciated.

Some programs pay their volunteers a token "honorarium." This enables the program to expect more from the volunteer than

‡ Rie Gentzler, op. cit.

an occasional stint at the phones. The quality of the volunteer's work is often better if she is being paid, even if it's a small amount; and she may assume a greater amount of responsibility. Whenever possible, volunteers should sit in on staff meetings. This helps them to feel that they are an integral part of the program's operation and demonstrates that their input is considered to be needed and valuable.

One way to increase volunteer effectiveness is to make sure that you have adequate resource materials on hand for their use. Lists of local agencies, organizations, and individuals that offer services to battered women are helpful. The Women Against Abuse Emergency Shelter has a good volunteer manual that you may want to look at as you develop your materials.

PCADV refers to the high dropout rate of volunteers and mentions that recruitment is an ongoing process. Many colleges and universities have programs in which students are required to have practical experience in agencies. This is an excellent source for recruiting volunteers with backgrounds in women's studies, psychology, and human services. PCADV also suggests advertising, word of mouth, personal contacts, and a hook-up with a volunteer-services agency if one exists in your area, as additional recruitment possibilities. They say: "The more kinds of jobs you can offer to volunteers, the wider range of women you might attract. One program has a group of professional women who have formed a speaker's bureau."*

A few words of caution regarding volunteers: Care should be taken to avoid the traditional practice of using women as perpetual volunteers without significant reward or conscious recognition of the importance of their work.

Be careful also that you don't end up with a predominantly white, middle-class volunteer staff. This can easily happen, as low-income women often don't have the time or opportunity to do volunteer work. If this does occur, you might be able to compensate by hiring more minority and low-income women as paid staff. In addition, perhaps minority and low-income ex-residents could help with court accompaniment, welfare advocacy, etc.

* Ibid.

One interesting use of volunteers is the arrangement established by Women Against Abuse and the Philadelphia District Attorney's Office. The shelter provides volunteers to counsel abused women who come to the District Attorney's Office to file criminal complaints. In this way, victims of domestic violence receive needed counseling, resource and referral information, and assistance in utilizing civil as well as criminal remedies.

Training for your program's staff will have a different focus from the volunteer training outlined earlier. In-service training programs should be periodically scheduled. Regular sessions will not only increase the effectiveness of the staff member's on-the-job performance, they will also provide her with additional skills that may be of value when she reenters the job market. In-service training can cover a variety of areas, including counseling skills, advocacy, the legal system, welfare and food stamps, resource development, accompaniment, information and referral, public speaking, fund raising, administrative functions—virtually all activities that take place under the shelter umbrella. The use of role playing and other training techniques as well as audiovisual equipment is recommended. PCADV suggests that the training resources of local colleges, universities, and social-welfare agencies be utilized.

Staff working together in close quarters under intensive emotional demands must work out adequate means of communication, develop an effective system of mutual support, examine the caliber of their work, and adapt and refine their services. You may wish to utilize outside consultants, formalized meetings with specific agendas, rap groups or any combination of these in an ongoing process of support. Regular staff meetings are a necessity for self-evaluation, sharing of feelings, increased skill development, and improvement of services.

One of the more common phenomena that occur within grassroots agencies is that of "burnout." Burnout results primarily from overwork due to the vast need that the program is trying to meet, combined with insufficient resources to adequately do the job. As time goes by, constantly overextended staff members find themselves increasingly unable to keep up with the rapid pace and hectic environment. Eventually, many of them have no choice but to leave.

One of the most important steps in preventing burnout is to recognize and accept the limits that available funds and energy place on the staff's ability to respond to the overwhelming demand for its services. Often, it is difficult if not impossible to accept the fact that there are going to be many that the program is unable to help. Saying no can be heartbreaking but very necessary for the survival of the program.

Guilt is another contributing factor to burnout. Lenore Walker writes that "All refuge members become saddened when a former member or child is killed, an event that happens far too often. They assume guilt, feeling if only they had done better, she might have stayed."†

In addition to guilt and overwork, frustration can play a role in the burnout syndrome. Accepting the inability of many battered women to leave the abusive relationship can be extremely difficult. Witnessing an abused woman's return to further violence is painful and depressing, even though the counselor may know that her client may leave the battering situation at some later date.

Another way to prevent burnout is for staff members to take proper care of themselves. Vacations, occasional days off, reasonable work weeks, and adequate salaries should be built into program operation. Staff should be encouraged to rotate jobs when practical, in order to provide change of pace and to gain broader knowledge of the entire program operation.

Although the tendency is to do just the opposite, instituting these measures is necessary if the program is going to survive for more than a few years. It is certainly tempting, for example, to pay everyone less money, which might free up enough to hire one more person. At the time, this may seem like a sound move, but in the long run you will find that inadequate compensation, no matter how committed the staff, leads to inability to sustain their participation on a long-term basis. People cannot live indefinitely on inadequate incomes. Ultimately, you will get much more for

† Walker, op. cit.

your money by providing employees with a real career base, rather than a short-term, exhausting work stint.

It is important that women learn to properly value their own work. Historically, women have provided unpaid labor to a variety of causes, usually without much reward or recognition. Sometimes it seems as if we tend to perpetuate some of these patterns ourselves. One does not have to be overworked and underpaid to be committed. As individuals working for a better world, committed women need to properly pace themselves so that they will be able to continue on, constantly improving their services as well as enjoying the sense of personal achievement so necessary to effective and meaningful work.

SERVICES

As your program takes shape, you will be determining which services you are best equipped to provide. To some extent, this will depend on your particular stage of organizational development as well as on available resources. Some groups may be planning to establish a shelter with a variety of built-in support systems. Others may simply be in a position to provide some minimal information and referral through a hotline or as part of a larger community agency or organization.

The following is a comprehensive list of services needed by battered women. Depending on your resources and the particular needs of abused women in your area, you may decide to provide all or some of these forms of assistance.

In an Emergency

Crisis Intervention: Volunteers and staff covering hotlines and shelter phones should receive basic crisis-intervention training, including suicide prevention. A number of publications related to crisis intervention are included in the Bibliography.

Shelter: Either in a refuge established specifically for battered women, in already existing shelters (Salvation Army, etc.), at local hotels, or through volunteer emergency housing.

Medical Care: Should be available in emergency rooms of most hospitals. Some shelters have physicians on call. Shelter staff should be trained in first aid.

Transportation: Needed by victims to escape the scene of an assault and reach safety or a medical facility.

Food and Clothing: Many communities have programs that make food and clothing available on an emergency basis. Local stores, churches, individuals, community centers, and social-service agencies are possible resources.

Emergency Resources Booklet: As soon as possible, your shelter should develop "survival kit" booklets, identifying critical emergency resources, to hand out to victims.

On an Ongoing Basis

Child Care and Children's Services: Should be provided in shelters. See Chapter V for descriptions of children's service programs in existing refuges.

Income Assistance: Aid in obtaining welfare, employment, or financial assistance from family members.

Hospital, Police, and Court Accompaniment: See "Accompaniment and Advocacy" portion of this chapter and Chapter III.

Establishing Support Groups: Ongoing group counseling for shelter residents, ex-residents, nonresidents, social-service-agency and mental-health-center clientele, and battered women in private therapy. (See Chapter II.)

Meditation Teacher: We agree with Terry Davidson that having on call someone who can teach meditation is a good idea. It can be useful for both staff and residents as a stress reducer and means of finding inner peace.‡

Services for Men: See Chapter VI.

Transportation: Should be provided by shelters for medical and other appointments and for hauling of personal possessions, household goods, etc.

Legal Aid: Assistance in obtaining legal representation, separation, or divorce; utilization of any legal remedies (peace bonds, protective petitions, eviction orders, temporary mental commitment). Advocacy and support during utilization of the crim-

‡ Terry Davidson, *Conjugal Crime,* (New York: Hawthorn Books, 1978).

inal-justice system (filing complaints, appearing in court). Legal advocacy programs are described in Chapter III.

Educational and Vocational Guidance: Assistance in career planning, skills development, and job finding. Development of educational, job-training, and work-experience opportunities.

Assistance in Utilizing Community Services: General advocacy and accompaniment to welfare offices, legal-service programs, social-security offices, etc. See Chapter I for related information.

Referral to Existing Social Agencies: See sections on "Organizing a Hotline" and "Resource Development" in this chapter.

Long-term Housing: See section on "Follow-up" in this chapter.

Survival-skill Development: Information and assistance related to basic money management, utilization of the public transportation system, parenting, nutrition, driving. Skills in escaping immediate violence, self-defense. (See Chapter I.)

EDUCATION AND OUTREACH

Contacts with the community through educational programs and publicity are ways of developing understanding and acceptance for your program. Given the deeply ingrained societal attitudes that support or at least tacitly condone violent behavior toward women, the public is in need of information to bring to light the magnitude of the problem and to counteract myths and misinformation. Community contacts are also aimed at reaching victims of domestic violence, to let them know they are not alone and to inform them of available sources of help. More important, educational programs will serve the vital function of *prevention*. Without a serious change in the national consciousness regarding sex-role stereotyping, violence against women will not cease. It is particularly important that we reach young people (perhaps through the schools) in order to create a new generation of men and women committed to redefining marriage as an equal partnership.

Educational programs may consist of speaking engagements, workshops, and seminars geared to civic and church groups or schools and various professionals. It is particularly important to reach persons who work with abuse victims, such as mental-health professionals, emergency-room employees, lawyers and law-enforcement personnel, all of whom may have difficulty understanding and dealing with the problem. As more and more battered women "come out of the closet," those within traditional agencies and institutions will need to acquire the skills, understanding, and techniques that are most conducive to developing the independence of the abuse victim.

Terry Davidson urges that shelter staffs announce through the local school systems the availability of anonymous telephone counseling for children of violent couples.*

Although it can be frustrating to devote valuable time to efforts that are not directly related to providing immediate assistance to victims of abuse, it is absolutely necessary if we are going to ensure that the effective treatment models developed by those already in the field become incorporated into the mainstream approach to the problem. Eventually, just as many, if not more, battered women will visit mental-health centers as come to shelters. Literally thousands are already turning to the criminal-justice system. It is our responsibility to do our share in making these systems responsive and effective.

Media coverage can provide wide audiences with information about domestic violence and about your program. TV and radio programs are excellent sources of publicity. Public-service announcements, which are free, can be used to advertise your activities. It is helpful to develop connections with journalists, since newspaper articles also reach large numbers of people. You might consider seeking coverage from some of the smaller, special interest or neighborhood newspapers as well as the large, established dailies. Letters to the editor are a free means of countering or protesting news stories that present distorted views of the issues.

A few words of caution about the media: Often, shelters and hotlines are used by the media as a source of victims for television and radio shows but not as a source of expertise. Traditional sources of information such as universities and social-service agencies are certainly appropriate, but the media must recognize that the grass-roots groups that have been working on the prob-

* Ibid.

lem for years have developed a wide range of skills and knowledge regarding the family-violence issue.

Maria Roy, executive director of Abused Womens Aid in Crisis (AWAIC), a counseling program for abused women, addresses the problems of dealing with the media: "Be on guard against media people who overemphasize 'visual impact.' They may say something like, 'Provide us with a victim or no show.' This puts the organization in a very compromising position. After all, the agency's function is not to be a talent agency for battered women. Do not let any media person exploit the many emotionally fragile battered women who come into your office for help. Occasionally, there will be some battered women who will not mind radio or TV coverage: they may have extricated themselves from their dangerous home life; their husbands are no longer a threat. These women will definitely be important success models for the other women tuning in."†

A facet of shelter work that requires particularly large doses of emotional resilience and verbal agility is work with hostile radio, television, and newspaper personalities and unfriendly audiences. They can give you a hard time at first, but not for long, for you will quickly catch on to the assertive stance that New York NOW's Susan Maurer and Enid Kelijik recommend:

1. Don't get angry.
2. Make the heckler repeat the hostility. It will be toned down.
3. Acknowledge that you hear the other viewpoint; pick out something you can deal with.
4. Then go on to mention the four to six points you want to get across.
5. Come prepared. It would be good to have documented several examples of the runaround battered wives received from the local systems which have displayed attitudes similar to those of the caller instead of giving the woman her legal right to protection. Point to dramatic proofs as to why the woman who wants to leave is, in fact, prevented from saving herself.
6. This is an argument for the most hardened antiwoman heckler:

† Maria Roy, "A Model for Services." In Maria Roy, ed., *Battered Women, a Psychosociological Perspective* (New York: Van Nostrand Reinhold, 1977).

A program to save battered women will also save the heckler and friends from another generation of violent teenagers—teenagers who, having learned that people consider wife beating acceptable, will extend the violence they learned at home to strangers.‡

One way of providing information about your program is through an attractive, well-designed brochure. Brochures can be distributed in waiting rooms, posted on bulletin boards, and mailed to social-service agencies. The brochure should provide a concise overview of the problem and a description of your services. Some brochures include a brief section of emergency information: what to do if in need of immediate medical attention, how to handle the police, how a victim can get out of the house in a hurry, and how to go about pressing charges. You could also include information on the need for contributions to your program and volunteer help.

Another useful outreach function is the publication of various materials relating to domestic violence and your program. General information on the problem, resource lists, and survival kits can all be of great help either to victims of abuse or others interested in addressing the issue.

RESOURCE DEVELOPMENT

The need for facilities and counseling for battered women and their children is overwhelming. You will undoubtedly be confronted with a "full house" most of the time, and much of the discouragement and frustration you will encounter will be the result of not being able to provide adequate services to all of the women who seek you out. For this reason, we urge you to develop contacts with other shelters (Salvation Army, etc.) and programs to try to handle your overflow. Establishing other forms of emergency housing can be helpful.

A well-maintained resource file is invaluable in providing you with necessary information. Ongoing contact and communication with other groups in your area will be helpful in sharing information and resources. It may be well worth your while to develop a

‡ Terry Davidson, op. cit.

contact person in the various agencies and organizations with which you work, to cut down red tape and facilitate communication. A good, cooperative working relationship with persons in health, welfare, housing, legal, educational, and other agencies will make your efforts in securing services much more effective. It is particularly important to develop this type of relationship with the police department and welfare officials. You will need to be able to count on the police to respond quickly if there is trouble at the shelter and to transport battered women to you. (This may necessitate a policy change within the department; see Chapter III.)

The majority of the women staying at the shelter will probably need some form of immediate financial assistance. A good relationship with the welfare department will ensure quick and courteous service and may even result in a willingness to bend rules and modify procedures to accommodate the needs of your residents.

PCADV makes an important point regarding resource development and referral: "It is the responsibility of the program, as much as it is possible, to monitor the agencies and individuals to whom they refer clients to ensure that they are knowledgeable about and sympathetic to the problems of the abused. A woman who is getting support and encouragement from you should not be sent to an agency where, either implicitly or explicitly, she gets the message that she should take the abuse she gets because it's her fault anyway. Successful monitoring requires knowledge about agencies and their personnel. Sometimes this can be obtained through word of mouth or reputation in the community. Another way is through an education program where you visit agencies and individuals to inform them about your program and indirectly find out what their attitudes are. The most painful way to get this information is from your mistakes, the feedback you get from a client who you sent for help and who got criticism and verbal abuse. In some situations, referral to a nonsympathetic agency may be unavoidable. If that is the situation, prepare the client before she goes so that the consequences may be less traumatic."*

* Rie Gentzler, op. cit.

When pulling your resource lists together, don't forget that local health and welfare councils frequently maintain directories of services, and you would do well to secure copies of these and any other appropriate listings.

Don't overlook other shelter programs as possible resources. Due to the need for many battered women to leave the geographic area in which they reside, in order to escape abusive husbands, shelters are now establishing an "underground railroad," so that abused women can find refuge in another state or city if necessary. At some time it will probably become important to establish working relationships with other shelters in your part of the country to ensure that abuse victims have the opportunity to relocate if necessary.

LOCATING A STRUCTURE

There are a number of factors to consider in locating a structure to house your facility. Size is frequently a problem, and many shelters have had to make do with overcrowded conditions in order to provide service to as many people as possible. Adequate cooking and bathroom facilities are important, as are physical security and easy accessibility for people coming to the shelter as well as for staff and residents traveling from the shelter to hospitals, welfare offices, and other frequently visited locations. One factor that requires consideration is that of whether to purchase or rent. Although owning the house can give you a good deal of freedom, it involves a long-term financial commitment, which can be risky, as most funding is provided on a short-term or nonrenewable basis. The purchase of a house is considered a capital expenditure, which is most often not a permissible use of government money, so that other sources of financing the building would have to be secured. On the other hand, if you are planning to rent, it is important to find a building owner in basic sympathy with your program, with whom you have a good relationship, so that you can avoid hassles or attempts to control or interfere with your activities.

Safety codes, labor and industry standards, zoning requirements, and public-health standards all have to be met in order to provide decent living conditions to residents as well as avoid jeopardizing your operation by failure to comply with legal requirements. Make sure that you know the limitations on the number of residents your facility will be permitted to house before you make any final decisions. Also, make certain that extensive renovations will not be required in order to comply with the rules and regulations. One of Del Martin's tips for shelter hunters is to find an insurance broker who will get you the best available coverage for the least amount of money (workmen's compensation, fire, auto, liability).

Often, there is important work to be done in overcoming community objections to the presence of a shelter, as many people have fears and misconceptions about what such a facility will "do to the neighborhood." It may be helpful to solicit a couple of people from the neighborhood to help drum up support.

Depending on your community, there may be a possibility of obtaining housing from the Department of Housing and Urban Development or from your municipal government. Often there is usable housing sitting around empty that is owned by one of the above. Political pressure may be needed to gain access to it.

Across the country, shelters can be found in YWCAs, women's centers, houses, and apartment buildings. Sometimes, shelter offices are in a separate location from the residence itself; sometimes they share the same space. When this is the case, it becomes a real challenge to provide the best services possible under the circumstances.

The Abused: Advocacy Programs for Abuse Victims gives minimum standards for shelter operations. The list, developed by the Pennsylvania Coalition Against Domestic Violence, focuses on staffing patterns and the minimum amount of services the shelter should provide. The list will need to be adapted to your particular locality and situation.

LEGAL MATTERS

Incorporation: Incorporating your organization is probably the first legal step you will take. A lawyer is necessary. In fact, you will need good legal representation on an ongoing basis, so select your lawyer carefully. Many nonprofit organizations have feminist or community-oriented lawyers working with their programs. They may donate their services, at least until funds are secured. Some large law firms do a certain amount of pro-bono (free) work. Frequently, these firms have influence with state governmental bureaucracies or with the Internal Revenue Service and can expedite your applications. If you don't have a lawyer already working with your group, you may want to investigate this as a possibility.

Tax-exempt Status: In order to be eligible for almost any grant, you will need to qualify as a nonprofit, tax-deductible organization under Section 501C3 of the Internal Revenue Code. Requirements and procedures for this step may be found in Pamphlet #557, available from the Internal Revenue Service. Again, you would be well advised to have a lawyer prepare your application.

Bylaws: The development of your bylaws is an important part of your organizational development. They require much thought. Since the bylaws spell out what your organizational framework will be, it is important that they accurately reflect your group's philosophy. If you need a set of bylaws fast (for a funding application, etc.), you could use a standard set for nonprofit organizations temporarily, until you have the time to develop the set under which your group will operate. Some of the issues your bylaws will probably address are membership, officers, committees, and the board of directors. You will need to determine how much power will rest with the board and how much with the staff. Lately, it has become common for staff members to sit on nonprofit boards. There are a number of good books dealing with organizational structure available.

FINANCES

Realistic budgeting is vital to the successful operation of your program. This is especially important when dealing with government funding. When operating under government grants, very little budget change can occur without a lot of red tape. So when your proposals are being developed, you should devise your budgets with care. Private foundations aren't quite as rigid about how their money is spent, but usually you will have to stay fairly close to the approved budget. Often, expenditures come up that were not anticipated when the original proposal was developed. So it is a good idea to leave as much flexibility in the budget as possible. The Pennsylvania Coalition has developed model budgets for hotlines and for small, medium, and large shelters.

Be careful not to jeopardize your program's funding by sloppy bookkeeping. Make sure that competent financial advice is available at all times. Many women certified public accountants in private firms are providing competent accounting services to nonprofit women's groups at reduced rates. Check this out. Hiring a competent bookkeeper is a good investment of your program's funds. She should be experienced in computing payroll taxes, social security, unemployment tax, and any state or city taxes. She should be familiar with the required tax returns and make payments on time and without error.

Be certain to pay into your state's unemployment fund. Many a nonprofit group has survived a funding crisis by having most or all of its staff on unemployment insurance and working on a temporary, volunteer basis until the funds come in.

There are several simplified bookkeeping systems available that are well worth the investment. They can make bill paying and balancing the books simple processes. In addition, the companies that manufacture the systems will train your staff in how to work with them. If you can't afford to hire someone to keep your books, we strongly recommend that you investigate these systems. With training, a staff member could keep the books with periodic monitoring by your C.P.A.†

RECORD KEEPING

Accurate records provide an important source of statistical data, which will justify the need for your services to funding sources. Such data also provide you with valuable information regarding your activities, such as how many people you serve, most

† Recommended bookkeeping systems are Safeguard Business Systems, Inc., McBee Systems, and Shaw-Walker. For further information, contact your state society of certified public accountants.

and least active referral sources, kinds of problems you are presented with and kinds of services needed to deal with them, and demographic information. Without such records, you will not be in a position to evaluate your program, and ongoing evaluation efforts are necessary to ensure that your program develops effectively. Individual records also provide a means of ensuring that communication is kept open and that staff members are aware of one another's activities. Good client information readily available will make for more effective services to individual women.

PCADV recommends the following:

When deciding what kind of information you are going to record there are several factors to consider. These include confidentiality, the individual file system, data which can be used to provide specific information about your program, and everyday communication.

It is extremely important that you protect your clients' right to privacy. However you set up your system, it must be done in such a way as to ensure this confidentiality. Clients' individual folders should be kept in a locked file. A coding system should be used for information not in the file. For example, each client could be given a number upon intake and that number instead of her name could be used. How careful you need to be depends upon your situation. You need to do as much as is necessary to protect your client.

You also need to get as much information as is possible about your client, in order to help her determine her options. Almost all operating programs have developed forms for this information. Some are relatively simple and others quite sophisticated. You will, of course, wish to develop forms which are going to meet your needs.

This brings us to another use of information—providing statistics about the clients, the program, and the problem of abuse. A great deal of data can be gathered when specific information is kept for each client and records are kept on the activities of the programs such as speaking engagements, outside contacts, phone calls, and volunteer and staff time.

While still protecting the identity of each client, figures can be compiled to give a picture of the situation. Demographic information about clients can include age, race, education, marital status, economic level, number of children, religion, and county of residence. Program data could include sources of clients, referrals made, agencies dealt with, number of phone calls, counseling sessions and groups, number of residents and length of stay, number of children, and level of client participation in activities [Author's note: Also include legal steps taken, whether a complaint was filed, how many court appearances, if accompaniment was provided, and outcome.]

Data specific to the problem would concern the type of abuse; duration of the problem; alcohol, drug or mental-health problems; the precipitating event; police, legal, and agency contacts; characteristics of the abuser; and resolution of the situation. Again, you may see no immediate need for all of this information, but if you use forms which include it you will have it when the need arises, to show the many services a shelter provides.

Providing these services usually involves more than one person, so it is necessary to have mechanisms to facilitate communication. Phone logs, activity logs, and records of client-staff interaction are some ways of doing this. Depending on the number of workers, your system can be loosely or tightly constructed. The methods which you evolve need to be able to provide each person with the information she needs to do a good job.‡

When organizing your record-keeping and data-collection components, don't overlook the possible role of volunteers. They can be helpful here.

And remember: although record keeping can be annoying and inconvenient, the resulting data will be *very* important for your grant applications and proposals.

ECONOMIC DEVELOPMENT

Planning

Ongoing planning is an essential process for ensuring the effectiveness of your organization and plays an important part in the development of a sound funding base. When responding to the needs of the battered women in your community, it is very likely that your program will start without much preplanning or forethought. Often, women who have organized support services for battered women have found it necessary to start providing service

‡ Rie Gentzler, op. cit.

long before they had originally anticipated, due to the demand. When this occurs, the staff finds itself operating on a day-to-day basis, often within a crisis framework and sometimes in ways that are far from the original program design. Catherine Lynch and Thomas Norris discuss this problem in their article "Services for Battered Women: Looking for a Perspective": "In many spouse-abuse programs there is no lead time for substantive preplanning. Instead, it is more accurate to characterize program planning as a 'during and after' process. As community concern for the battered woman emerges, so does the program, often in bits and pieces on a 'catch-can' basis. Learning is done strictly on the job, almost a planning-by-reaction. Program goals, structure and process seem to evolve in response to the often fickle and contradictory demands of external decision makers who control resources (staff, facilities, funds, referrals) and policy (e.g., needing permission from the zoning department to operate)."*

In order for your program to become a viable force within the community, capable of providing ongoing, effective services to victims of abuse, it will be necessary to take time out from the day-to-day operation of the program to plan your present and future course of action. One way to accomplish this is to schedule regular staff retreats, preferably away from the office and the ringing of phones, to sit down and evaluate current operation and to make plans. An essential part of the planning process is the constant refinement and reestablishment of goals. It will be absolutely necessary not only to think of your goals in terms of the immediate future but to look ahead five years and perhaps more in order to ensure the long-term life of your program. So even though it can be frustrating and annoying to take time out from providing direct service, we urge you to go ahead and plan and schedule your retreats or appropriate planning sessions so that your organization will have the proper amount of planning energy for its growth and development.

You may have wanted to consider using organizational development consultants or similar kinds of resources within your com-

* Catherine Lynch and Thomas Norris, "Services for Battered Women: Looking for a Perspective." In *Victimology: an International Journal,* Vol. 2, Spouse Abuse, 1977–78, Feb. 1978.

munity. While it is true that traditional organizational development consultation may not appeal to grass-roots service providers, there are many facets of organizational development that those who manage spouse-abuse programs should be in touch with. If you do decide to use such consultation, it is a simple matter to reject the more traditional ingredients, which may run counter to your own operating philosophy, while at the same time retaining those concepts and advice that will benefit your organization. Organizational development consultants are usually available on a free-lance basis through either universities or consulting firms.

The primary funding goal of any nonprofit organization that is providing direct service to victims of abuse should be the achievement of economic self-sufficiency. We strongly advise you to develop a five-year plan incorporating various funding approaches that will result in some measure of self-sufficiency at the end of that period of time. It is very easy to get bogged down in the day-to-day operation of the program and fail to put the proper amount of energy into funding and refunding, especially when a large grant has been awarded. The staff energy turns almost exclusively to providing direct service, particularly in view of the overwhelming demand for that service. We caution you not to let this happen to your program. You must specify a certain amount of staff time and energy to the organizational development process, including planning, fund raising, etc., from the very beginning. One full-time staff person (assuming you have a staff of more than five) should be assigned to the economic development process. Failure to do this will leave your organization in funding crisis after funding crisis as grants run out and no money has been secured prior to the expiration of funds. Many nonprofit grass-roots organizations have gone down the drain because of their failure and inability to raise money.

There are a variety of methods of achieving economic self-sufficiency, which we will discuss in this section.

Image

One of the issues that you will have to contend with almost from the beginning is what kind of image your program will have in the community. Many grass-roots service providers have an emphasis, as mentioned earlier, on the nonprofessional, volunteer approach. While this may be the most effective approach for your organization, it is not necessarily the image that is most conducive to raising funds. You may want to consider adopting a more "professional" image in order to court funding sources. Adopting such an image does not necessarily mean abandoning one's grass-roots approach; it simply provides the organization with an appropriate and effective fund-raising tool. Another image question revolves around the nature of the services you provide. In order to court more funds, you might consider adopting a "family" approach, as opposed to a "feminist" approach. The family approach is of course much more appealing to funding sources, which are conservative and cautious in nature. Once again, billing your services as family oriented does not necessarily mean that you must change your program agenda. It's a question of how you promote yourselves or advertise what you do. Acquiring the skills to reassure funding sources while at the same time maintaining your own agenda is an important means of ensuring the continuity and long life of the organization. Funding sources are threatened by terms such as "feminist" or proposals that discuss promoting the independence and growth of women as opposed to improving the "family" environment and preventing "domestic abuse."

Backing

Whom you have connected with your organization is important in terms of soliciting support from certain sections of the community and soliciting certain funding sources. By including influential and wealthy people and perhaps men whom you will have to wrestle on other issues, you will do much toward securing the immediate trust and confidence of a variety of funding sources. Other people to consider would be directors of banks, members of school boards, and members and officers of other influential institutions in your community who are well known and who are perhaps connected to certain funding sources such as foundations or corporations.

Linkages

Along the same lines as board membership, you will want to consider linkages with existing agencies, institutions, or organizations as a way of gaining credibility. Government funding sources may not want to fund your small, nonprofit organization by itself, but perhaps will fund a joint undertaking between your project and a larger institution such as a university. Of course, you will have to be careful about maintaining control of your functions and your part of any kind of joint undertaking, but since there is little doubt that established agencies and institutions will be garnering a large share of the funds that will be appropriated for the battered-women issue, it may be in your interest to explore possible linkages at this time.

Marketing

One of the problems that occurs within grass-roots agencies is that although a great deal of knowledge, skill, and expertise are developed that are unique on the part of those within those agencies, there is a tendency to give this knowledge and expertise away. Instead, we suggest that you find ways to market the knowledge and expertise that you are accumulating as you provide services to battered women. When outside agencies, institutions, universities, governmental groups, etc., approach you to learn about the problem and to acquire the skills necessary to work with victims of abuse, we strongly suggest that you provide this knowledge and these skills only in exchange for financial compensation. Of course, we are not suggesting that you charge other nonprofit agencies or women's groups for such services. We are suggesting that you charge those agencies that can afford it. You may even want to go so far as to get the help of a marketing consultant. There are some consultants who do nothing but help organizations market their products and skills. Once again, these consultants are available through free-lance sources of private consulting firms.

Coalition Building

An effective way of raising funds is to form a coalition with other groups in your area that provide similar services. Of course, these coalitions are already beginning to be built (see Resources). Often, funding sources may not want to fund a small, single organization but will be interested in funding an "issue." Through banding together with other organizations, some of which may be more established and already have developed positive reputations with some funding sources, you may have more clout. In addition, if the coalition itself can raise funds, you may be able to consolidate specific fund-raising functions within the coalition framework such as direct-mail campaigns, solicitation of wealthy individuals, and corporate fund raising. These are some of the fund-raising endeavors that many individual organizations do not have the time to undertake but that could be undertaken by staff hired by a coalition. In addition, coalition building will reduce competition for existing funds, so that the maximum amount of funds available for the issue can be used to the best interest of those needing services.

Institutional Organization

One way to make sure that you will be around ten years from now is to find the means to incorporate yourself into an already existing larger institution. Now, many grass-roots groups will be wary of an undertaking of this nature because of the issue of control. However, this has been successfully done, and grass-roots groups can in some instances institutionalize themselves and still maintain the autonomy of their organization. One good model for this is the Women in Transition program, in Philadelphia. Women in Transition existed for five or six years on a shaky basis, going through one funding crisis after another. Eventually, the staff, board, and volunteers began to pressure the mental-health/mental-retardation system to incorporate women in transition services into the existing MH/MR program for the Philadelphia region. Pressure was exerted through public hearings and personal contacts within the MH/MR hierarchy. As a result, a long series of delicate negotiations culminated in the Women in Transition program incorporated into the West Philadelphia Community Mental Health Consortium. What this meant was that at least two staff salaries would be picked up by the Consortium on a permanent basis. The staff members, however, continued to work within the Women in Transition center, which maintained its autonomy with a separate board of directors, etc. There were several areas that required some give and take on both sides. For example, the Consortium's guidelines require that a consulting psychiatrist be involved during the intake process for women who come into the small groups run by WIT. The way that WIT got around this was to agree to consult a psychiatrist on the Consortium's staff who routinely OK'd their recommendations regarding small-group admissions. Of course, a great deal of paperwork was necessitated by this change, which placed additional burdens on the staff. The important thing, however, was that for the women who came through the door there was no difference between the nature and quality of services provided before WIT's incorporation into the Consortium and after.

Business

Another means of achieving economic self-sufficiency might be to start a business. If your organization considers this, it should take care to see to it that the business is as closely related to the operation of the program as possible. One possibility for those providing services to battered women would be getting involved in real estate. This may be a very effective way of getting revenue for the program as well as establishing second-stage and third-stage housing for battered women. Buying and operating apartment buildings with perhaps limited numbers of units within them in neighborhoods where property values are on the rise could be a very profitable undertaking for the organization. Clients could be equipped with the skills to renovate and repair buildings, which would provide them with temporary employment and future job opportunities. Initial funds needed may be somewhat large, but it is possible that they could be raised through foundation grants or through contributions from wealthy individuals or concerned people within the community. Perhaps if enough money were raised for the down payment on one building, that would eventually generate enough income to buy additional buildings. Some other possible business might be an answering service, a grocery store near the shelter, a catering service, etc.

Grantsmanship

One essential element of grantsmanship is proposal writing. We will not go into the technical aspects of developing proposals

here. There are several good books available on the subject; they
are listed in the Bibliography. We suggest that you acquire one
before you develop your proposal. In general, your proposal will
contain a statement of the problem, documentation of the need
for the services that you propose to provide, a description of those
services, how you propose to provide them, how much it will cost
to accomplish the provision of such services, and how you will cooperate with the existing agencies and institutions. Many proposals will contain a variety of appendixes such as letters of support from existing institutions, copies of bylaws, statement of
tax-exempt status, list of your board of directors, etc. The main
thrust of the proposal consists of the documentation of the need, a
listing of goals and objectives and the methodology for achieving
the stated goals. Once again, the question of image comes up. The
proposal should look "professional"; it should be polished, and it
should use the kind of language that appeals to funding sources.
Be careful not to lock yourselves into delivery of services you may
not be able to provide, given the realities of operating a direct-
service program. Although you will need to provide information
as to how you will accomplish your objectives, the more vague
you remain in terms of specifics the more leeway you will have
once the money does come through, provided, of course, the
money does come through. Del Martin has written an important
piece on the availability of funds through private and governmental sources for women's programs. We suggest that you read
carefully this section of her book. It will provide you with important information on the lack of priority given to women's programs by traditional funding sources. Ms. Martin discusses the
reasons for this, as well as a variety of options for coping with it.

Connections
No matter how much knowledge you may acquire about grantsmanship during the life of your program, the most important key
to raising money is *connections*. Whether you are looking for private money or government money, whether you are conducting
mail campaigns or approaching corporations, having personal or
business contacts with individuals who have influence with any of
these funding sources will do more to bring funds in your direc-

tion than any other single factor. This is not to say that skill and knowledge aren't necessary and won't be helpful as you develop your economic plan; however, unfortunate as it may be, the truth of the matter is that who you know is probably more important than anything else. Bearing this in mind, let's take a look at several methods for raising funds:

MAIL CAMPAIGNS

Solicitation by direct mail is an excellent way to build a permanent, ongoing source of income. We will not provide you with the details as to how to conduct these campaigns. Literature is available and is included in the Bibliography. The important thing to remember about solicitation by direct mail is that the first couple of years may not bring you much; however, you will be building a solid mailing list, so that by the time you have conducted this campaign four or five times it should be bringing in substantial amounts of money. A good way to build a list for direct-mail campaigns is to use your own mailing list combined with a mailing list of other women's groups. If such a mailing list is not available, other lists can be purchased and used for a fee from major magazines, other organizations such as the American Civil Liberties Union, etc. Direct-mail solicitation may be difficult for a small nonprofit group to undertake on its own. This would be a good undertaking for a coalition of women's groups.

Corporations

Approaching corporations is difficult for individual groups, particularly since corporation donations do not amount to large amounts of money. Three to five thousand dollars, perhaps ten thousand dollars, is a typical contribution. If, however, you band together with other nonprofit organizations and approach the corporations as a body, you may be able to raise up to as much as fifty to one hundred thousand dollars a year in your community. This money could then be divided among the participating organizations. It is very important to utilize whatever influential friends and supporters you may have.

Individual Contributions

This is another good source of continuing income although perhaps not in major amounts. This money will not dry up. Individuals who contribute one year are very likely to contribute the next. The ideal would be to induce somebody to write the organization into her or his will for an ongoing endowment that would continue indefinitely. Using the local who's who and other social directories, you can begin to approach women and men who have the resources and who may be interested in your program. Remember: battered women come from every economic class. One direction that La Casa de las Madres took was to establish a group called Friends of La Casa, made up of either individuals with resources of their own or people who could influence others to make significant contributions. This group provides an ongoing source of funds and support for La Casa.

Bake Sales

Of course, there are always the traditional methods of raising small amounts of money—perhaps as your group is just starting out—such as bake sales, rummage sales, car washes, etc. In addition, don't forget the free food, clothing, and other goodies that may be available through charitable institutions, agencies, or organizations.

GOVERNMENT FUNDS

As you develop your fund-raising plans, you will need to make decisions as to what directions in which to best channel your energies. Del Martin quotes Marilyn Prosser, who heads a consulting firm in Sacramento, California, that supports consumer-sponsored organizations in program development and funding, on why she prefers to go after federal monies:

(1) Duration of the grant period is usually longer. Federal projects range from 36 to 54 months, and sometimes beyond seven years, whereas local grants rarely exceed one or two years. (2) Program and fiscal audits are less frequent. Federal agencies are more

business-oriented, but local agencies have a tendency to move in and interfere with day-to-day operation. (3) Grants made by the federal government are larger and can amount to hundreds of thousands of dollars. Local grants of $30,000 are atypical; they rarely exceed $10,000. In the case of revenue-sharing funds, $88,000 would be high. (4) Federal grants can escalate from the first year to the third to reflect the growth of the project. But in a two-year local grant the maximum amount would be allotted for the first year, with the expectation that funding develops other more stabilized sources for ongoing funding.†

The Women's Bureau of the Department of Labor says the following about applying for government money: "Organizations looking to the federal government for funding should realize that discretionary funds are much more limited than they were previously. Most monies are now channeled to State and local governmental units under the system of revenue sharing. . . . It may be advisable to first direct your efforts to getting the program funded by the State legislature or local council as an ongoing responsibility. The State legislature of Montana, for example, has authorized funds for a shelter. If the State or local legislative body assumes the funding responsibility, it is less likely that the program will be phased out after a year or two. On the other hand, if you seek funds for an experimental and demonstration program, there is always the possibility that the project, no matter how worthy, will be terminated for lack of funding. Of course, demonstration programs have advantages too, in that they offer opportunity to try innovative program ideas."

The Department of Labor also suggests that before drafting your funding proposal, carefully research what services are available that could be used for battered women. Then, as a component of your proposal, devise an effective system of referral to those resources.

The Center for Women Policy Studies points out: "All communities receive General Revenue Sharing money yearly and there are virtually no restrictions on what the community can do with these funds. The Federal government does not require either

† Del Martin, *Battered Wives* (San Francisco, New Glide Publication, 1976).

prior approval of expenditures or the existence of a local plan as do most block grant programs. General Revenue Sharing funds are usually considered part of the local government budget and must be investigated from the local level. To find out how your community uses GRS funds, get in touch with your local government. Several shelters in California started with an initial GRS grant. For more information on how one obtained funds, write: Women's Transitional Living Center, Inc., P. O. Box 6103, Orange, California 92667."‡

What follows is a list of government agencies with summaries of programs that could fund services for victims of family violence. The list was compiled primarily from information from the Center for Women Policy Studies; the periodical *Spouse Abuse Northeast News;* the Department of Labor's *Information Kit on Battered Women,* published by the Women's Bureau; and the National League of Cities. Although some of these agencies are not at this moment committing funds for these services, it is quite possible that they will be in the near future, particularly since their federal mandates could be interpreted to permit funding this type of service.

The Center for Women Policy Studies notes that those "seeking Federal funds should remember that in most instances decisions are made at the local level. That is, Federal agencies maintain state or community offices to administer their programs, and requests for funds should be made to these offices. To find the address of your local or regional office and learn who administers allocations for the programs in which you are interested, write the national office in Washington, D.C."

U. S. Department of Health, Education, and Welfare (HEW)

Title XX, a 1975 amendment to the Social Security Act, is a $2.5-billion federal program that provides for the allocation of monies to states for a variety of social services. The program is administered nationally by the Department of Health, Education, and Welfare. Funds are appropriated to states on a 75-per cent-federal/25-per cent-state matching basis, according to a formula

‡ *Response,* newsletter published by the Center for Women Policy Studies, Washington, D.C., Dec. 1977.

based on population. The program's national goals include: the achievement and maintenance of self-sufficiency and of economic self-support, the prevention or remedying of neglect, abuse, or exploitation of children and adults unable to protect their own interests, and preserving, rehabilitating, or reuniting families.

In each state, Title XX can be broken up into various areas or components. The "Protective Services" component is the one under which funds may be allocated for shelters and services for battered women and their children who may be subject to abuse. Services for battered persons and their dependent children may include individual and family counseling, advocacy and legal services, and shelter. "In those instances where shelter is obviously necessary for the protection of the individual, room and board expenses are allocated as necessary, integral, but subordinate to the service objectives."

An agency is designated in each state (usually the Department of Human Services, Welfare Department, or equivalent state agency) to administer Title XX funds for that state. States design their own programs ("state plans") to meet the needs of their communities, and there is considerable latitude allowed to design whatever kind of program each state feels would best meet the broad goals of the program. In many states, local Title XX agencies (usually the Welfare Department) assist with the development of the state plan and the distribution of Title XX funds for that particular area.

States must publish and make generally available an annual "program plan" three months prior to the start of the program year. A period of forty-five days is required by law for public review and comment (via public hearings and written comment) between the publication of the proposed plan and that of the final plan. The needs and priorities of the public can be expressed at that time and have an impact on the state plan.

Public agencies and private organizations are designated to provide services on a contract basis. They receive contracts, from state or local Title XX agencies, for services and are reimbursed after these services are provided. Interested agencies can contact their state or local Title XX agency for information concerning application for designation as a service provider for the coming year; it is preferable to do so as early in the planning process as possible. The program provides for citizen input so organized efforts to exert pressure can influence funding decisions.

There are several publications available that explain Title XX and how to apply for its funds. They are listed in the Bibliography.

Action—Agency for Volunteer Service

Women's centers, shelters, and hotlines that utilize the services of community volunteers can increase their staff component through Action programs. Vista volunteers can be assigned as staff members for up to one year of full-time work. University Year for Action and the Retired Senior Volunteer Program, other programs within Action, are also able to supplement staffs by placing volunteers for a given period of commitment.

Action also has a limited direct-grants program. Through its Mini-Grants program, up to five thousand dollars can be given to a project, but every dollar over two thousand must be matched by the project. The funds are to be used to stimulate volunteerism in the project's effort to "meet basic human needs" in the community. To qualify for Action's grant programs, a group must be tax-exempt under Section 501C3 of the Internal Revenue Code.

Recently, Action funded one national technical assistance center on family violence, along with ten regional centers. Their function is to disseminate information related to family violence and technical assistance to those working in the field. In addition, they are developing a national communication network to promote the sharing of accurate knowledge among grass-roots domestic violence organizations, professionals, and the public.

The national center is a program of the Domestic Violence Project of Ann Arbor, Michigan. The Women's Resource Network serves as the technical assistance center for Region III, which consists of Delaware, Maryland, Pennsylvania, Virginia, West Virginia, and the District of Columbia.

The other nine centers are

Region I: CT, ME, MA, NH, RI, VT
Domestic Violence Technical Assistance Project
(DVTAC)
342 Shawmut Avenue
Boston, MA 02118
(617) 266-4305, Ms. Renae Scott

Region II: NJ, NY, PR
Volunteers Against Violence
Technical Assistance Program (VAVTAP)
c/o American Friends Service Committee
15 Rutherford Place
New York, NY 10003
(212) 777-4600, Ms. Yolanda Bako

Region IV: AL, FL, GA, KY, MS, NC, SC, TN
Technical Assistance Center (TAC)
c/o Wife Abuse Crisis Service, Inc.
499 South Patterson
Memphis, TN 38111
(901) 324-3862, Ms. Gloria Pyne

Region V: IL, IN, MI, MN, OH, WI
Technical Assistance Center (TAC)
c/o Community Crisis Center, Inc.
600 Margaret Place
Elgin, IL 60120
(312) 697-2380, Ms. Gretchan Vapnar

Region VI: AR, LA, NM, OK, TX
Technical Assistance Center (TAC)
c/o Houston Area Women's Center
Council for Abused Women
P. O. Box 20186, Room E 401
Houston, TX 77025
(713) 792-4403, Ms. Susan Eggert

Region VII: IA, KS, MO, NB
Rural Domestic Violence
Technical Assistance Project (RDVTAC)
105 Wedgewood, Suite 6
Lincoln, NB 68510
(402) 483-4019, Ms. Karalyn Schmidt

Region VIII: CO, MT, ND, SD, UT, WY
Technical Assistance Center (TAC)
c/o Colorado Association for Aid to Battered Women
CWC-Box 136, Montview & Quebec
Denver, CO 80220
(303) 355-7080, Ms. Loyce Rulon

Region IX: AZ, CA, HI, NV, GU
Technical Assistance Center (TAC)
c/o Southern California Coalition on Battered Women
P. O. Box 5036
Santa Monica, CA 90405
(213) 396-7744, Ms. Barrie Levy

Region X: AK, ID, OR, WA
Technical Assistance Center
c/o Women's Support Shelter, YWCA
405 Broadway
Tacoma, WA 98402
(206) 272-0354, Ms. Carol Richards

Action's programs are processed through its state offices. For a list of these offices and more information about the programs, write: Action, 806 Connecticut Avenue NW, Washington, DC 20525.

U. S. Department of Housing and Urban Development (HUD)
The Housing and Community Development Act of 1974 set up a program under Title I called Community Development Block Grants (CD). This program provides grants to city, county, and,

to a very limited extent, state governments for a wide variety of community-development activities. Priorities for the use of these funds are determined at the local level. Thus, the first step in obtaining HUD funding is contacting your elected city, county, or state representative for his/her support of your program.

The types of projects that may be eligible for CD funds are the acquisition, construction, or rehabilitation of publicly or privately owned social-service centers. (Private residences are excluded.) Also, provision of social services such as counseling, legal aid, or health services administered by public or private agencies is eligible but under very restrictive conditions. The director of the community planning and development division of the HUD area office serving your jurisdiction can help you determine whether a particular project qualifies.

HUD guidelines have recently been modified to allow HUD funds to be used for the purchase of emergency shelters.

The Harriet Tubman Shelter, P. O. Box 7026, Powderhorn Station, Minneapolis, MN 55607, is one shelter that has already received HUD monies by applying through its area office. For a list of area offices, write U. S. Department of Housing and Urban Development, Washington, DC 20410; and for a guide on how to monitor your community's block-grant money, write Center for Community Change, 1000 Wisconsin Avenue NW, Washington, DC 20007.

U. S. Department of Labor

Through the Comprehensive Employment and Training Act (CETA), the Department of Labor has funded a number of projects to assist battered women. Under CETA Title I, project components have been funded to provide employment counseling, training, and related supportive services. Under Titles II and VI (CETA's economy-stimulus package), staff positions in shelters and community shelters themselves have been funded.

The agents for administering these CETA programs are those state and local governments that have been designated prime sponsors. Cities with populations of more than one hundred thousand, are direct prime sponsors, and cities of between fifty and one hundred thousand can form consortia to receive prime-sponsor status. The remaining areas come under the state prime sponsor. Prime sponsors maintain local staffs that are responsible for the allocation of CETA funds; they are the people who should be contacted to request a grant.

Several restrictions on CETA monies make them a temporary funding measure, rather than a solution to funding problems. These restrictions include a one-year limit on funding, with a possible extension for another six months, and stipulate that the person hired be unemployed. To find the prime sponsor in your area and the names of projects that are utilizing CETA funds, write Women's Bureau, U. S. Department of Labor, 200 Constitution Avenue NW, Washington, DC 20210. The Women's Bureau also has a free booklet, *A Guide to Seeking Funds from CETA,* to assist individuals and organizations in applying for CETA monies.

Community Services Administration (CSA)

Community Action Agencies (CAAs) are the primary grantees of the CSA, and they provide advocacy and social-service delivery through a grants program called Community Action Programs (CAP). There are 879, CAA offices, covering 2,293 of the 3,141 counties in the country. Using the existing networks that these offices have established in the local communities, CAAs are capable of providing services or appropriate referrals to families or family members in crisis situations.

In fiscal year 1979, CSA is planning to fund one or two pilot family crisis centers to be operated by CAAs in five cities. Each center will be open twenty-four hours a day and will provide services to an entire family in time of personal crisis. The centers will offer medical care, emergency shelter and food, and referral services to other agencies. They will also provide on-site social-welfare and Supplemental Security Income eligibility determination.

Shelters and counseling programs in several areas have already applied for and received CAA funds under the CAP program. An example is the Bergen County Community Action Program, 9090 Main Street, Hackensack, NJ 07601, which recently opened its shelter. To find out where your local CAA is located, write Community Services Administration, 1200 Nineteenth Street, NW,

Washington, DC 20036. In addition, two state coalitions have obtained CSA grants to provide technical assistance to family violence programs.

Law Enforcement Assistance Administration (LEAA)

Since 1974, LEAA has funded approximately thirty-five programs that give direct services to victims of domestic violence or offer a court mediation program. For 1977–78, LEAA's allotment for domestic violence went to four shelters for women and their children and to one technical-assistance project for dissemination of information and technology to community groups through a newsletter and clearing house on sensitive crimes.

The LEAA has also funded twenty programs in either police crisis-intervention training or court diversion that encompass domestic violence as well as other specialized areas.

In September of 1977, LEAA announced a family-violence funding initiative to develop and test models of comprehensive programs aimed at the prevention or reduction of family violence.

Financial support is divided among several demonstration projects to test the effectiveness of a community-wide effort to intensify the various points of intervention for family violence and plan specific criminal-justice and community programs to make the interventions effective.

The program is particularly aimed at improved police response, more effective prosecution, prevention or reduction of community violence, and provision of a broad range of mental-health and social services for families in which violence occurs. Information on LEAA-funded programs and proposal applications can be obtained through Jeannie Santos, LEAA, Department of Justice Office at Regional Operations, 633 Indiana Ave. N.W., Washington D.C. 20531.

Federal Funds for Research Projects

Department of Health, Education, and Welfare (HEW)

A. *Office of Human Development*—Has funded a survey of existing programs through its Office of Planning, Research, and Evaluation.

B. *Administration on Children, Youth, and Families*—Twenty demonstration treatment centers for abused and neglected children provide some services that are directly or indirectly related to abused spouses.

C. *National Center for Health-services Research*—Contemplates awarding a grant to explore the use of the hospital emergency department as a case-finding site and to identify the relationship between spouse beating and drug abuse, alcoholism, and suicide.

D. *National Institute of Mental Health (NIMH)*—Has funded pioneering studies in the family-violence field conducted by Richard Gelles, Suzanne Steinmetz, and Murray Straus.

The best way to obtain information on research and demonstration projects, which are awarded funds directly by the federal government, is to read the announcements in *Commerce Business Daily*. All government requests for proposals (RFPs) are announced in *Commerce Business Daily*. Normally, you must be associated with a qualified research organization or university.

During 1977–78 the White House convened two meetings of concerned persons from federal agencies and communities and organizations concerned with the family-violence problem to focus attention on problems posed by the emerging needs of social programming for domestic violence. The meetings have resulted in heightened awareness by agency personnel of the problems people in the community face when seeking federal funding.

FOUNDATIONS

There are a number of small "progressive" foundations that are particularly interested in funding grantees that are working for social change. These foundations might be good places to initiate your fund-raising activities. Among them are the Ms. Foundation, the Max and Anna Levinson Foundation, and Joint Foundation Support.* Actually, JFS is an association, of nine foundations and

* The Ms. Foundation, Room 412, 370 Lexington Avenue, New York, NY 10017. Contact person: Rochelle Korman, associate director, (212) 689-. 3475. The Max and Anna Levinson Foundation, 95 State Street, Suite 405, Springfield, MA 01103, (413) 737-1441. Contact person: Sidney Shapiro, executive director. Joint Foundation Support, 1 East Fifty-third Street, New York, NY 10022. Contact person: Patricia Hewitt, executive director, (212) 755-6023.

individuals that fund women's groups as well as other types of projects. JFS staff do the investigation and evaluation of grant proposals and make recommendations to the nine member foundations. In addition, the staff may also help grantees prepare their proposals and refer them to other possible funding sources. They offer small grants to projects that deal with wife abuse on a national level.

The Foundation Center can offer assistance as to how to go about applying for funds from a foundation. The Center's collection of source materials on foundations includes standard reference works and public records such as annual reports of many national foundations and a list of over twenty-six thousand grant-making foundations. For a fee of $3.00 it is possible to order a microfiche printout of a list of grants made by private foundations in 1976 in such subject areas as "Women" and "Crime and Deliquency." The Foundation Center has regional collections in almost every state. For a listing of the collections, write to the Foundation Center, 1001 Connecticut Avenue, NW, Washington, DC 20036. See the Bibliography for other publications related to foundations.

One source of technical assistance and information is the Women's Action Alliance.† Situated in New York, the alliance will provide you with helpful information and assistance in the fund-raising area. They also serve as a national clearinghouse for women's organizations. They have published a list of foundations that have funded woman-abuse projects.

A very valuable source of information and technical assistance is Women's Resources of Philadelphia. Designed to enable women's organizations to strengthen their impact, Women's Resources provides management consultation, proposal-writing instruction, fund-raising assistance and program evaluation/data collection. Write: 613 Lombard St., Philadelphia, PA 19147.

Where to Find Foundation Money for Women's Projects, a directory of foundations that are interested in funding women's groups, is available from the Independent Women's Press, 34 R Prospect Street, Room B154, Yonkers, NY 10701. An extensive

† Women's Action Alliance, 370 Lexington Avenue, New York NY 10017, (212) 532-8330.

listing, the directory includes hundreds of foundations that have funded projects related to women, including some that have granted funds specifically in the area of wife abuse.

We will not attempt to provide you with detailed information on raising money from foundations. There are several publications available that contain such information. A particularly good one, published by the Women's Action Alliance, is called *Getting Your Share: An Introduction to Fundraising*. The booklet is designed to take nonprofessional grant seekers through all the steps of foundation fund raising—from writing a proposal, researching foundations, and making contact with the foundation, to what to do when you do or do not receive a grant. Also, see Kathy Fojtik's *The Bucks Start Here*.

FUND-RAISING TIPS

1. Make sure that your funding sources are as varied as possible. The more numerous your source of funds, the less control any one funding source can exercise over your program's operation. If your funding sources are varied, then losing one of two of them will not mean the end of your program.

2. Remember that in order to be eligible for any foundation grant, you must have been granted tax-exempt status from the Internal Revenue Service. Publications on obtaining this status are included in the Bibliography.

3. Keep in mind that, once you have succeeded in obtaining funds, it is only the beginning. Grant management and refunding must be ongoing, integral parts of program operation.

4. The women of the Pennsylvania Coalition Against Domestic Violence recommend that you find out who is funding other social-service projects in your area; consult with officials in local, state, and federal agencies that might logically be able to help you locate money; request information from your federal and state legislators; consult the Catalogue of Federal Domestic Assistance, which contains a fairly current cross-reference list of government agencies and grant programs and should be available at the public library.

5. Purchase-of-service agreements can provide an important source of income. Under such an agreement, an agency that refers

clients to you pays a stipulated cost for your services. The more such agreements you obtain, the better.

6. If certain funding sources are concerned about reverse discrimination, they may require that you either provide services to males (abusers or so-called battered husbands) or that you include males on your staff. A couple of suggestions as to how to get around this:

a) Offer to provide services to abused men. The likelihood of any men making genuine attempts to utilize your services is small, and you could line up one or two sympathetic male volunteers to provide shelter and/or counseling, just in case.

b) Offer to have male consultants on your staff. They would not have to come into actual contact with the women you serve.

EVALUATION

In addition to obtaining data through follow-up procedures (which will help you determine the effectiveness of your program), we suggest that you provide for ongoing evaluation of the shelter program by the residents both during their stay and when they leave. Their feedback will be the most important determinant in refining and improving your services.

You may also want to conduct an annual evaluation through your board of directors or funding source or both. There are pros and cons to having a funding source or other outside agency conduct an evaluation of your program. A more traditional outside party may want to structure evaluative mechanisms that ask the wrong kinds of questions or set up the wrong kinds of measures. For example, a finding that marital violence was reduced after a couple had undergone joint counseling does not necessarily indicate that there were positive results from the couple's interaction with counseling services. Without knowing what factors led to the reduced violence, one cannot assume that the reduction was not accomplished through less-assertive behavior on the part of the wife, rather than on reduced aggression on the part of the husband.

Although some negative factors could develop through an evaluation by an outside source, it is also true that an outside party may be able to observe things that you cannot see because you are too close. If you do decide to have an outside party evaluate your progress, it is important that you work together on the development of procedures and mechanisms.

When conducting an evaluation, it is helpful to return to the original program goals to see if they are being met. If they are, then the next step is to determine where to go from there. If you are having difficulty reaching the original goals, there are a variety of questions you need to ask:

1. Were the goals realistic? Often, those of us who work for social change tend to bite off more than we can chew, and sometimes less lofty goal setting needs to take place after unforeseen obstacles and stumbling blocks are encountered.

2. Is the program design conducive to reaching the original goals? Perhaps your program has been so swamped that the staff is finding itself reacting on a day-to-day crisis level, rather than following a predetermined course of action. When this happens, it becomes necessary to develop more control over your program, as opposed to the other way around.

3. How smooth and efficient is the operation? Once again, when the need for services far exceeds the ability of the program to respond, general chaos and confusion can result. Ensuing "burnout" and staff turnover can contribute to less-effective program operation than originally envisioned.

Asking yourselves these and other questions can help to pinpoint the areas in which effective goal implementation is breaking down, so that you can begin to initiate remedial measures.

FOLLOW-UP

Leaving a shelter can be traumatic for the victim of domestic violence. She can find herself without the support community that has sustained and nurtured her for the past several days or weeks. If she relocates out of her old neighborhood, she is isolated and on her own. Most likely, her future is uncertain and may look pretty bleak if she has no job skills or educational credentials. Although she may be determined to make it, she is vulnerable and susceptible to returning to her husband if he finds her.

Most shelters recognize the need for continued contact, assistance, and support for the woman who has left the refuge. Usually, ongoing rap groups exist for former residents. Some shelters set aside special nights for potluck suppers and informal get-togethers. Although these efforts are helpful, it is clear to those in the field that they are not enough.

In order for the battered women to become truly independent, it will probably be necessary to establish networks of former abused women who can offer each other the ongoing support, companionship, and caring necessary to permanently break the cycle of violence.

Of course, help should be provided, as the woman leaves the shelter, in securing permanent housing, obtaining furniture, moving in, etc. If she is relocating out of her neighborhood, information on resources and activities in the new community should be available to her. One step that may be helpful to former residents is to put pressure on public-housing and other officials in your community to free up space for your clients.

In England, a network of second-stage houses has come into existence. Lenore Walker describes the transition process developed by Chiswick Women's Aid, which encourages women to leave the shelter for second-stage housing as soon as possible. Under this system, battered women are eligible for financial assistance under the welfare system and may stay in the house until they feel ready to leave. For those women who choose to continue in this communal living style indefinitely, third-stage housing has been arranged.‡ In time, the shelter community in this country may be in a position to develop similar alternatives for their former residents.

Information gathered through follow-up efforts is extremely useful to an ongoing assessment of your program. Ascertaining the kinds of living situations women go to when they leave the shelter, the kinds of life-altering decisions they do or do not make, problems they encounter, whether or not they return to abusive relationships—these and other factors can help you to look at how effectively you have worked toward your goals and objectives. Again, such data can also serve to objectively demonstrate and justify your group activities to funding sources, as well

‡ Walker, op. cit.

as serving as the basis for further research, should you choose to become involved in that.

Finally, working with battered women can be frustrating and emotionally draining, and you need all the positive reinforcement you can get. In the instances in which follow-up shows that a woman has really gotten herself together, you deserve the reward of knowing that.

ORGANIZING A HOTLINE

Frequently when a woman is battered, her first step in seeking help consists of a phone call. Traditionally, she has called the police, a minister or priest, a relative, or a friend. Today she may call one of the hundreds of hotlines and telephone referral systems currently set up to provide her with support and assistance.

A hotline is often the very first service that is initiated when a group of concerned individuals decide to develop support services for victims of abuse. Sometimes a hotline remains the primary service-delivery model. Often, it is later incorporated into a shelter. Whatever the eventual status of the project, hotlines should include:

1. Twenty-four-hour staffed telephone service.
2. Immediate peer and option counseling.
3. Staffing by trained counselors.
   Training should include:
   a) Education about the problems of domestic violence in accordance with woman-oriented goals and principles.
   b) General counseling skills, including active listening, role playing, communication techniques, problem solving, goal setting, and value clarification.
   c) In-depth knowledge and skills concerning option counseling and referral, i.e., legal, welfare, housing, health counseling, and other appropriate services.
   d) Crisis intervention, including:
      1) Contact on a *feeling,* rather than factual, level.
      2) Immediate exploration of the problem.
      3) Mutual agreement on the definition of the problem.
      4) Focus on most pressing part of problem—immediate action with likelihood of results.

     5) Exploration of resources.
     6) Contracting of and agreement on plan of action and
        goals.
   e) Knowledge about procedures of legal, welfare, and medical
     systems in local service area.

Some general tips for running a hotline:

1. Services must be free and confidential.
2. Maintain a file of information and referral sources for your service area covering legal, welfare, housing, health, and counseling data.
3. Statistics should be kept on all calls.
4. Services should be publicized, on an ongoing basis in local service area, including name, phone number, hours, and services offered.*

Referrals are a key part of any hotline operation. Again, we turn to the Pennsylvania Coalition for advice:

"This is the basic information component of counseling and requires a knowledge of what options and services are available in the community. They include hospitals and doctors, police, legal services, welfare agencies, counseling and guidance services, housing and rental agencies, employment agencies, and child-care facilities. Sometimes a client has already sorted through her options, made a decision, and needs only some information on how to carry out her decision. For example, she may have decided that the best avenue for her to take at this time is to see a marriage counselor. What she needs now is the names of competent, sympathetic people in that field. Perhaps that will be her only contact with your program or perhaps she may need additional help at a later time. In other cases referral information is only part of the counseling process and may include accompaniment and shelter."†

Often when a woman calls a hotline or other service program, she just needs to talk. At other times, concrete resource and survival information is called for. And on other occasions she may need intensive counseling. Part of the counselor's function is to

---

* Most of the above information came from hotline guidelines established by PCADV and published in Rie Gentzler, *The Abused: Advocacy Programs for Abuse Victims* (Lancaster, PA: Pennsylvania Coalition Against Domestic Violence, 1977).

† Rie Gentzler, op. cit.

get a feel for the woman's needs and to move in the direction that best meets those particular needs. This requires sensitivity and skill, and cannot be accomplished in a five-minute phone conversation. We urge you to read Chapter II, "Working with the Victim," for information and insight on the ins and outs of telephone counseling for battered women.

IF YOU ARE WITHIN AN EXISTING AGENCY

Most of the information contained in this section is directed toward newly forming private, nonprofit corporations. But perhaps you are within an already existing agency or organization and seek to expand your services to battered women either through establishing a shelter, developing support groups, providing temporary housing, or lending other forms of assistance.

If this is the case, we strongly urge you to connect with the existing women's group or groups in your area that are already concerned with the issue. We feel that it is vital that the women who have created the climate of concern for the problem and provided the initial response be in a position to significantly influence the design and implementation of programs for battered women. All too often, those that labor long and hard to see to it that their constituents get a better break are left out in the cold, once the subject is considered "in" by the powers that be and the funds begin to flow. Let's try to make sure that this doesn't happen to the battered women's movement.

If there is no organized group concerned specifically with abused women in your community, we suggest you contact the closest chapter of the National Organization for Women, which has a task force of battered women. Through touching base with others in the community who are working on or have an interest in the issue, it may be possible to plan a total-community approach to the problem. Cooperation between grass-roots service providers, mental-health and family-service agencies, the criminal-justice system, the Department of Public Welfare, and housing officials and employment groups could lead to the development of a comprehensive, multifaceted effort that addresses the whole issue of family violence. Along these lines some communities are forming family-violence task forces.

As professionals and paraprofessionals—whether lawyers and legal workers, social workers, counselors, health-care workers, welfare workers, ministers, priests, and rabbis, employment counselors, academics, business people, teachers, or child-care workers —you should follow the seven general guidelines below for aiding the abused woman:

1. Take her seriously. As in your treatment of all other clients, *respect* for her is the key element in a constructive professional approach.
2. Remind yourself and your staff frequently that your job is *not* to rescue or take care of a battered woman. Instead, your job is to reinforce her capacity to take care of herself, her self-respect, her understanding of her options, and her initiative.
3. Examine carefully and critically your own feelings about battered women. Given the culture all of us have been shaped in, it would be a major miracle for any of us—no matter what credentials we hold—to have escaped internalizing the patriarchal assumptions underpinning our mores, myths, and professional training. Enroll in sensitivity sessions and training on the counseling of battered women run by women's groups experienced in the subject.
4. *Refer on* a battered woman to another counselor more experienced with the problem if you find yourself angry at the victim or if you experience any excessive feelings about her. Know your limits. *Not everyone* can counsel battered women.
5. Keep yourself and your staff updated on the services available to battered women in your community. Display cards and brochures from these services in visible and readily accessible areas.
6. Consult with women's groups focused on battered women and with family-violence task forces.
7. Give reading and reflecting time to feminist discussions of serving battered women.

In addition to these general statements, directed to all professionals and paraprofessionals working within traditional agencies, we offer some specific information for particular service workers.

DOCTORS, NURSES, HEALTH PARAPROFESSIONALS

Staffs of hospital emergency rooms, clinics, private practices, and company medical and counseling departments should be on the alert for signs of battering. Lenore Walker discusses several areas of consideration for hospital emergency rooms, private physicians and clinics, and company medical and counseling departments. The following list represents a summary of her thoughts:

HOSPITAL EMERGENCY ROOMS

1. Often, emergency-room doctors do not have the time to question the origin of injuries, even when they seem suspicious.
2. Nurses have the most ongoing contact with abuse victims.
3. The battered woman's chart should be tagged to alert staff members.
4. The woman should be examined and interviewed alone.
5. She should be asked directly if the injuries are the result of a beating.
6. She should be given resource information.
7. Whenever possible, a battered woman should be admitted to the hospital, since it provides a safe refuge.

PRIVATE PHYSICIANS AND CLINICS

1. Private physicians and clinics see a smaller number of battered women.
2. Battered women often seek medical help for symptoms related to stress.
3. Many battered women come to the notice of medical personnel during pregnancy (often, the batterer's violence escalates during pregnancy).

COMPANY MEDICAL AND COUNSELING DEPARTMENTS

1. Many abusers are well known to their wives' co-workers.
2. The abuse victim will often seek medical assistance or counseling through her company. This keeps the abuser from knowing that she is seeking help.
3. Frequently, an abused woman stays absent from work for several days after a severe battering incident (she waits until makeup can cover the bruises).
4. Some large companies will place battered women on disability while suggesting referral sources for psychotherapy.

Another valuable resource for medical practitioners is a medical school thesis written by Anne Flitcraft, a student at Yale Medical School. The paper provides substantial information about battered women who seek emergency-room treatment, and should be read by any practitioner who is likely to come in contact with abuse victims within a hospital setting.

Some of the important points contained in the paper are the following:

1) During the early phases of an abusive relationship, battered women may come to the emergency room for primary intervention in the abusive relationship, rather than medical attention for an injury per se.

2) It has been documented that as a relationship continues, the battering escalates rather than declines. As a result, physicians should take care not to ignore the real risks battered women face, and understand the severity of injury that is likely to occur if intervention is not available.

3) Pregnancy appears to be related to battering.

4) Battered women are most likely to have injuries to the head, face, chest, abdomen, and breasts.

5) Although battered women are more frequently referred for psychiatric care, they have no greater history of psychiatric disturbance than nonbattered women.

6) Physician-patient interaction may well be the sole confidential contact that many battered women find possible.

7) Battered women may account for up to 18 per cent of all emergency-room treatment.

8) Many battered women that are treated at the emergency room will express concern about child abuse.‡

SOCIAL WORKERS AND COUNSELORS

(See also Chapters II and VI.)

Family caseworkers, according to Beverly Nichols, are often reluctant to examine the possibility of divorce for an abused

‡ Anne Flitcraft, "Battered Women: an Emergency Room Epidemiology with a Description of a Clinical Syndrome and Critique of Present Therapeutics," Yale Medical School thesis, 1977, unpublished.

woman. Yet divorce, ". . . as a viable option in cases where abuse is chronic and flagrant, should be actively explored. Existing divorce counseling, as an independent focus in family service agencies, is a welcome recognition of a long-neglected need."*

Nichols also urges those who staff family service agencies to refer women to consciousness-raising groups as an addition to ongoing therapy. Assertiveness training is another option to have the woman consider.

Clearly, advocacy is another function social workers should take on. To act as advocates, you have to be familiar with relevant laws and with police response to abused women's calls for help. Additionally, social workers could develop training and consulting programs for the police.

On a policy-formulation level, social workers can also address the problems that battered women face.

Lenore Walker points out that social welfare agencies can find ways to provide immediate financial assistance to battered women, particularly in the form of rent assistance. She mentions that states could be reimbursed for this type of assistance through Title XX of the Social Security Act. She also suggests that social service departments or state health departments be required to keep "anonymous statistical data on the incidence of battered women."

WELFARE WORKERS

Welfare workers have a pivotal role in making sure battered wives get services they deserve and need. The West Virginia Department of Welfare was one of the first to determine that battered wives are immediately eligible for welfare benefits. You can actively lobby from within your departments to make abused women an eligible group for welfare payments in your regions.

LAWYERS AND LEGAL WORKERS

We see three major areas in which you can be helpful to the battered woman: You can be a source of technical information

* Beverly Nichols, "The Abused Wife Problem," *Social Casework,* Jan. 1976, p. 30.

for her. You can provide emotional support as a professional or paraprofessional assisting her over the official hurdles. And finally, you can be an advocate pressing to expand her choice of options.

The Brooklyn Legal Services handles these three functions as follows:

If the client has a visible injury, we ask "when (how) did your husband do that to you?" We break the ice by telling her how terrible it is that so many women are beaten by their husbands and cannot get help. Frequently, those to whom she has previously turned for assistance did not believe her account of the brutality she suffered. Or, if they did believe her, they blamed her for provoking the attacks, and minimized her injuries. Often we find that we are the first helping agency to unreservedly disapprove of her husband's violence. This support overcomes the clients reticence and enables her to tell the whole story. We ask all the details of each beating:

Date; day of the week; time of day; place, room of house or building; weapons? other instruments? (electrical cords, chairs, bottles?) closed fist? open hand? choking? stomping? duration of incapacity; medical treatment; name of physician or hospital; address of physician or hospital; medications, medical or surgical procedures; repeated medical treatment or visits; police called; court appearances; court disposition; witnesses' names and addresses; client's feelings and reactions; aftereffects (loss of appetite, sleeplessness, headaches, nausea, menstrual cramps?); husband's height and weight; client's height and weight; husband's knowledge of martial arts; client's military training.

Getting this information serves three purposes. The beatings tend to be at night, in the marital home, when no one else is present. Women often fail to seek medical attention because they are ashamed that their husbands have injured them. If children are witnesses, courts refuse to hear them because they do not want the children involved in their parents' dispute. To preserve evidence we have a camera in the office to photograph injuries. We get the names and addresses of friends or relatives who saw the client shortly after the beating, and can describe her physical appearance and general condition. Corroboration of any type strengthens the case.

Framing the relief in cases in which the client has suffered physical brutality or harassment is often less a question of finances than of the client's safety. We encourage a battered wife to move away from the marital home. She is not safe in the house in which her assailant lived or still lives. We seek partition and sale if the property is jointly owned.

When moving is not feasible, exclusive use and occupancy of the family home should be requested. This relief is necessary whether the residence is owned or rented, is held jointly or by one party, or is public or private housing. (In jurisdictions which provide for equitable distribution of marital property and transfer of title, it should be sought in the alternative.) Even when the wife owns or rents the home solely in her name, a court order may be the only way to exclude the abusive husband, and secure a safe residence for the wife and children. It may be argued that such relief saves the children from the additional trauma of moving away from home and friends. It may be the least expensive home possible when mortgage payments are low. Exclusive possession is a double-edged sword. It allows a woman to keep "her home," but makes her vulnerable to continued attacks.

Obtaining denial of visitation is difficult. Even in cases of physical cruelty courts grant unsupervised visitation to violent husbands. Judges believe that men who beat their wives probably have been provoked, and that such men are therefore no danger to their children. This prejudice ignores the facts that some children who have witnessed their fathers beating their mothers are afraid of their fathers, and that there is a high correlation between wifebeating and alcoholism.

We interview the children, alone, one at a time, when visitation or custody is in issue. Depending upon their ages, we may distract them with toys or plants. We talk about school, siblings and friends. We ask questions, trying not to suggest answers. We never tell children what do say, but urge them to tell us and the judge how they feel. We tell them that only by means of their telling the judge their wishes with regard to custody and visitation will the judge be able to give them what they want.

It is difficult to overcome the fact that we represent their mother and that she brought them to our office. But even under these conditions, children frequently tell us that they want to visit with their father. For those who are afraid or abused, these interviews enable us to prepare their cases. The interviews protect the children, and prevent us from vindicating a client's desire for revenge, or sense of possessiveness.

Protecting the Client

The final item in the initial interview of a battered wife is the problem of her safety during the divorce action. We suggest that she and the children stay with relatives or friends, or at a refuge for battered women, if she is in danger. These refuges have been established by women's groups, often with local government or church help, in many cities. Service of a divorce summons or notice of appearance may cause the abusive husband to attack his wife for daring to oppose his authority. In crowded urban jurisdictions most forms of pendente lite relief are too slow to be used in emergencies. If the trial calendar moves quickly there is no reason to make pendente lite motions, which, with adjournments and time lags for decisions and entry of orders, are concluded at the same time the case is reached for trial. Where pendente lite motions receive prompt hearing and decision, or delays are incurred on the trial calendar, requests for custody, child support, alimony, exclusive possession, and denial of visitation, or supervised visitation, should be made when the summons or notice of appearance is served.

Many women believe that their husbands will litigate a divorce. Husbands may threaten or inflict additional violence, but most wife beaters do not even appear in the action. If issue is joined we then interview the witnesses, get medical records, review criminal, civil and family court files, and talk to children to prepare for negotiation and trial.†

Be sure to turn to Chapters III and IV for more information on legal aspects of battering.

MINISTERS, PRIESTS, AND RABBIS

The tradition of the Good Samaritan is one the church has strongly reemphasized in the chaos of contemporary postindustrial societies. We highlight Terry Davidson's words in an effort to encourage church leaders and members to back up Christian words with action:

> I call upon your churches—where the acceptance of wifebeating has been fostered—to realize that even today the churches have not been in the vanguard of the anti-wifebeating movement. Determine

† Marjory D. Fields, "Representing Battered Wives, or What to do Until the Police Arrive," *The Family Law Reporter*, Vol. 3, Apr 5, 1977.

to form a group of volunteers from within the congregations (perhaps banding together with other congregations to ensure anonymity and security) who will give emergency overnight shelter to a battered woman and her children fleeing from marital violence. As a start, to interest volunteers invite a women's group offering services to battered wives—legal advocacy with courts, counseling, or workshop. Your local chapter of NOW could undoubtedly direct you to these groups. . . .

Concerned clergymen might preach a sermon verifying that Christ did not endorse wifebeating and neither does he. Speak out from the pulpit and face to face that wifebeating is sinful. And when a battered wife comes to you, don't exclude her husband from your pastoral counseling.

Guarantee help for the offspring of wifebeating unions. Publicize a phone number such that a child can call and be assured anonymity if desired, and confidentiality, where the child can unburden itself about the horrors in its household. The daily nightmare will be somewhat eased if there is a nurturing, trustworthy adult the child can talk to—and be believed by.

. . . The church can hardly avoid taking a second look at the facade of Christian caring it extended to the battered wife. Of the thirty pastors known to be responsive to social issues, first contacted by the American Friends Service Committee (AFSC) Clergy Outreach, only seven were caring enough to respond. The greatest potential would be realized if the church revived its ancient tradition of safe refuge on behalf of the fleeing victim and her children.‡

We recommend Ms. Davidson's book for anyone interested in working on the battered-woman issue.

MANDATORY REPORTING

A serious difference of opinions exists around the question of mandatory reporting of battering incidents that may be detected by service professionals. One camp argues vigorously for legally requiring such reporting, with or without the abused woman's consent.

Though we can understand the reasons why people make that argument, we oppose mandatory reporting, because it strips from

‡ Davidson, op. cit.

the victim her power and right to choose whether to go to the authorities or not. Battered women are adults, fully able to make such decisions for themselves. The battered woman knows the risks and costs involved with contacting officials. She is better able to judge the wisdom of such a course of action. Her history as a battered woman is one of coercion at the hands of external forces. The very last thing her professional supporters should do is to add official coercion to that which she has already experienced.

ACCOMPANIMENT AND ADVOCACY

There are some occasions when a victim will want someone with her to help her through procedures that are foreign to her or particularly difficult for her. Trips to the hospital, doctor's office, police station, welfare department, courtroom, or lawyer's office are events during which accompaniment and advocacy may well reinforce a battered woman's self-respect and confidence. Advocates may be staffers or they may be other battered women experienced in the ways of the agency or institution a victim must deal with. For whoever accompanies the woman, the primary guideline to follow is to be present to support a battered woman as *she* takes as active and as central a role as possible. An advocate must establish a very low profile while the *victim* handles the officials, forms, procedures, and bureaucracies. The job of the advocate is to offer emotional support and feedback to the victim as she makes her way through official and professional mazes.

Though the battered woman and her advocate must evaluate each situation separately in deciding how to proceed, these useful general principles for hospital and police accompaniment, developed by the Marital Abuse Project, of Delaware County, Pennsylvania, should be kept in mind:

HOSPITAL PROTOCOL

1. When on call for hospital accompaniment, be prepared to come to any hospital if notified by the victim or by the hospital or police with the permission of the victim.
2. Introduce yourself to the Emergency Room person as a volunteer from your organization. Then introduce yourself to the victim and

to anyone who has accompanied her to the Emergency Room (family, friends, police).

3. Remain with the victim in a supportive role in the examining room—only one volunteer. Assist the doctor and nurse during the examination if requested. Handle no evidence! Do not take samples to the lab, even if asked by the hospital staff. Politely explain that you can't.

4. Have change in your pocket and offer to get coffee, etc., for the victim. (No coffee in the examining room.)

5. Do not attempt to elicit information about the abuse from the victim if she is not inclined to talk about it, but act as an attentive and supportive listener if she does want to talk.

6. Answer any questions she has about her options, and explain to her the importance of having a hospital report of her injuries. Encourage her to be sure that the cause of her injuries is written on the hospital report.

7. Find out if the police have been notified, and request that this be done if the victim wants them. Explain that a police report may also be valuable.

8. Remember the importance of privacy—answer immediate questions, but suggest holding more detailed discussion of her situation until later when there is more privacy and she is less upset. Do not fill out any intake or other forms in the Emergency Room.

9. Tell the victim about our services and give her a brochure. (If it is not safe for her to take this with her, try to be sure she has the hotline number at least.) Discuss her immediate safety and arrange for follow-up.

10. If the victim wants no further assistance or follow-up, ask her to write her name and phone number for you.

11. Give her a card with a name on it, and tell her to refer to this number when she calls the office, in order to ensure confidentiality.

POLICE PROTOCOL

1. Introduce yourself at the desk as a volunteer from your organization and ask to see the victim.

2. Knock if the door is closed and wait for an invitation to enter.

3. If you are asked to sit in on the interrogation, explain that you can do so with the permission of the victim, but you cannot participate in the questioning. Explain that your role is emotional support of the victim.

4. If the police are talking to the victim, ask her if she would like you to stay. If she wants you there, stay as her friend. Also ask police if you may stay.

5. They may ask if she told you anything about the assault. Explain that your role is emotional support, and do not repeat what she has told you. Encourage her to make a complete report to police. If there is a difference between what she told you and what she tells the police, discuss this with her later in private.

6. Do not write anything down in the presence of police or the victim. Arrange for her to give you her phone number.

7. Be familiar with the remedies available to police and suggest to the woman that she ask them to use these remedies if appropriate. What they are *willing* to do will differ from district to district. Be sure to report to the office about your interaction with the police.

8. If decisions need to be made about what she should do next, ask if there is a place where you can talk to her alone. Perhaps you could go out to your car if there is no private place in the police station. Discuss her options and her safety, decide whether to go to the hospital for a hospital report, tell her about our services, and decide on the next step.

9. Be sure she has a brochure (or at least the hotline number) and give her a card with a number on it. Tell her to refer to the number to insure her confidentiality when she calls the office.

10. Try to get the police to drive her to wherever she is going next.

11. If the police are taking her to her house to get her things, or are going to her house for any other reason, make it clear that you are not allowed to go to the house, and arrange for them to meet you nearby, out of sight of the house.

12. If the victim wants no further assistance or follow-up, ask if you may call her in a few days to see if she is OK. If she agrees, ask her to write her name and phone number for you.

RELATING TO POLICE AND HOSPITAL PERSONNEL

1. Listen carefully to everything that is going on.

2. Learn the names of the people you are dealing with. You may see them again. Let the office know which people were helpful in the situation and which were uncooperative.

3. When you identify yourself, do it quietly. Do not draw attention to the victim in the Emergency Room or the police station.

4. Try not to get in the way in the Emergency Room or the police

station. Everybody is busy with their own job. We are only one of many.

5. Do not argue with police or hospital personnel. Be diplomatic and polite, while keeping the victim's best interests in mind.

6. Do not let anyone draw you into making judgments about the case. Someone may say, "I don't know about this woman, she was drinking," "I don't think she was really hurt," "She's an hysterical type." Just smile and be noncommittal, or say something like, "I don't understand."

7. You may have suggestions the police or hospital may take in behalf of the victim. Usually, you should suggest this to her, and let her suggest it to the police or hospital.

8. If the victim is going into emergency housing, she may use your organization's office address as her mailing address while she is there. Her home address will still be on police and hospital records also, but her future address should be the office, not the actual place where she will be staying.

9. You are there for support of the victim. Avoid using the time for social conversations. You may be asked questions about our services. Be open to this, and give information asked for, but try not to spend more time than necessary. It will take your time away from the victim.

10. If you discover people on the staff who are unaware of our services, or if you feel in general the staff is a problem, make a note of it in your report.

11. Compliment the hospital staff and police officers when a job is well done.

12. Don't talk to reporters. Refer them to the office.

VICTIM RELATIONS

1. Remember all information is confidential.

2. Don't make judgments.

3. All victims are different; treat each one as such. *Don't assume* you know what she will say or what she is thinking.

4. Don't write down anything! Wait until you get home or in your car.

5. If the victim is in the waiting room, introduce yourself, give her a card. Eye contact is very important. Help her to feel that you are there for her—only. Ask her if she would like you to stay with her.

6. If she is already in the examining room, get permission at the

desk, knock on the door, enter and introduce yourself and again ask if she would like company.

7. A good opener would be, "How do you feel?" Then, "Would you like me to explain the purpose of the hospital report?" She may want to hold your hand—offer it.

8. If she asks for something to drink, ask the nurse if it is O.K.

9. Be a good listener.

10. Do not tell a woman what she ought to do. Offer alternatives and let her make her own decision.

11. Crisis will cause a person to become confused. She may not make sense when she tells you what happened. Listen. Don't make judgments. She probably hasn't gotten her thoughts together yet.

12. She is probably feeling guilty. "Why me?" is a question indicating guilt. Explore this and try to say, "It's not your fault." Whatever she may have done in the marriage, it does not justify violence.

13. If you sense she is feeling something but not saying it, you could say, "You sound like you are more concerned about your husband than yourself," or "You sound like you think you should have done more in the situation." Get those feelings out and help her to clarify them.

14. Find out who brought her. If family members are there, offer to talk to them while she gets dressed, to let them know she is O.K.

15. Tell her, as soon as she can, write everything down and keep it. She may need to know the order of events later.

16. Always make sure that you tell her about our services and make plans to follow through on whatever support and services she wants. Be sure she has the hotline number, if nothing else. If she wants nothing more from us now, be sure to ask whether you can call her back later to see how she is.

17. Don't feel useless. Just being there helps.*

COALITION BUILDING

A national movement of women working against wife abuse has coalesced over the past two years: the National Coalition Against Domestic Violence (NCADV). Starting in Houston at the November 1977 National Women's Conference, battered-women's-movement activists from many states acted on the need to mount

* Marital Abuse Project, Delaware Cty. In Rie Gentzler, op. cit.

a national attack against a national epidemic by formally joining together in a coalition.

The next stage in the NCADV unifying process was the January 1978 United States Civil Rights Commission Consultation on Domestic Violence, in Washington, DC. There, representatives from grass-roots groups and state coalitions formed task forces.

Participants in the D.C. Consultation meeting also proposed a structure and working guidelines for the National Coalition.

Tentatively, the NCADV has come up with some working principles. The Third Meeting of the Steering Committee agreed that:

> The NCADV is comprised of people dealing with concerns of the battered woman and her family. The member organizations are women-controlled, independent, community-based groups dedicated to a philosophy of nonviolence, equality and empowerment of women. We represent different racial, social, sexual, economic, age groups and geographical areas.

The NCADV will work to:

facilitate communication among members

facilitate sharing of resources and skills among members

aid in developing and/or securing national resources for members

educate the public to a nonacceptance of violence

monitor and impact legislation relating to domestic violence

provide consulting to government and private social-services, criminal-justice, health and welfare agencies

aid in the developing of state and regional coalitions

provide battered women access to a National Network of shelters (underground railroad)

develop guidelines and models demonstrating sound fiscal management, program-based research and consumer involvement

support and initiate change in sex role expectations for men and women

effect change within human service organizations to bring about a recognition of individual rights within a relationship.†

† Unpublished guidelines, National Coalition Against Domestic Violence, Portland, OR, 1977.

While national coalition work solidifies, regional and state efforts continue.

The Pennsylvania Coalition Against Domestic Violence, for example, is an organization composed of a number of grass-roots groups throughout the state that provide services and advocacy for victims of domestic violence.

Founded in 1976, the Coalition's working philosophy is based on the belief that programs designed to meet the needs of battered women should be self-governing and controlled by women. The Coalition is committed to providing services to the victims of domestic violence, exposing the roots of domestic violence in the institutionalized subservience of women in this culture, and providing quality services statewide through cooperative, noncompetitive means.

The West Coast states coalitions have banded together to form the Western State Shelter Network. Meanwhile, representatives to NCADV from New York, New Jersey, and Pennsylvania agreed to the following tentative list of principles of unity:

a. We will work collectively and non-competitively.

b. We will work against violence in the media.

c. We recognize that violence against women is integral to the maintenance of American culture, particularly the control and subservience of women.

d. We are working for systematic change to eradicate the need for our work.

e. Members of Region I shall be representative of and/or community-based groups providing services and/or advocacy for battered women.

f. We shall work against racism, classism, sexism, ageism, and homophobia in this movement.

g. We are committed to a feminist analysis of abuse against women and the empowering of all women.‡

Should your group be interested in establishing contact with the National Coalition, the following individuals represent the Coalition around the country.

‡ "Summary of Third Meeting of the NCADV Steering Committee," *A Newsletter of the Feminist Alliance Against Rape and the National Committee Communications Network,* July/Aug. 1978.

NATIONAL COALITION AGAINST DOMESTIC VIOLENCE
STEERING COMMITTEE MEMBERS

	Name	Organization	Phone(s)
Chairperson	Cynthia Dames P. O. Box 1501 Santa Fe, NM 87501	Battered Women's Project Counseling & Resource Ctr.	505-982-8516 505-988-9731
First Alternate Chairperson	Bobbi Spicer 1426 Pierce St. Lakewood, CO 80216	Women in Crisis (Denver)	303-234-1494 9–5 days 303-232-0996 nights
Second Alternate Chairperson	Kathleen Fotjik 1917 Washtenaw Ave. Ann Arbor, MI 48104	Domestic Violence Project	313-995-5460 (work) 313-995-2532 (home)
Secretary	Tillie Black Bear 926 Katherine Vermillion, SD 57069	Indian Education Office School of Education U. of South Dakota	605-677-5453 605-624-9335
Treasurer	Anna Kuhl 1017 Garland Ave. W. Spokane, WA 99205	Wash. State Shelter Network 829 Broadway Ave. W. Spokane, WA 99201	509-328-6542 509-326-5515 509-624-8555
Member	Jean MacKenzie Simmons Lake Dr. Johnston, RI 02919		401-942-2094

	Name	Organization	Phone(s)
Member	Joani Kamman RFD #1 Shelburn Falls, MA 01370	NELCWIT 310 Main St. Greenfield, MA 01301	413-772-0806 413-625-6768
Alternate	Betsy Karl 29 Hill Farm Rd. Bloomfield, CT 06002		203-242-0530
Member	Yolanda Bako 3002 Wilson Ave. Bronx, NY 10469	New York Coalition for Battered Women	212-655-0877
Member	Barbara Hart, Esq. Reading, PA 19601	Pennsylvania Coalition Against Domestic Violence	215-376-8656 (work) 215-373-5697 (home)
Member	Virginia Sanchez-Tovar Fairfax Co. Women's Shelter P. O. Box 1174 Vienna, VA 22184		
Member	Lin Calpsaddle 5807 Taylor Rd. Riverdale, MD 20840		301-277-3927 301-628-1227
Member	Leslie Bennett 2116 E. Central Orlando, FL 32803	Spouse Abuse Inc. P. O. Box 6276 Orlando, FL 32803	305-420-3751

	Name	Organization	Phone(s)
Member	Dee Hahn-Rollins 1100 W. 42nd St. Indianapolis, IN 46208	Domestic Violence Project	317-251-5541
Alternate	Barbara McKeand-Stevenson 1771 Dix Hwy Lincoln Park, MI 48146		313-389-2200
Member	Helen Sklar 1043 Jennifer Madison, WI 53703	Dane Co. Advocates for Battered Women	608-255-4209
Member	Deborah Neas 34118 Delafield Oconomowoc, WI 53066		414-444-2333 (work) 414-646-3939 (home)
Alternate	Kenyari Bellfield 300 Oakland Ave. S. St. Paul, MN 55407	Harriet Tubman House	617-827-2841
Member	Karen Waller 4417 Abbott Rd. Lincoln, NB 68516		402-423-6779
Member	Virginia Martinez 343 S. Dearborn #910 Chicago, IL 60608	Chicago Coalition on Battered Women	312-427-9353 312-829-5920
Member	Linn Bendsley c/o Women's Haven	Women's Haven P. O. Box 14664 Fort Worth, TX 76117	817-336-1711

	Name	Organization	Phone(s)
Member	Dr. Amelia Medina 1106 Alexandria Dr. Corpus Christi, TX 78412	Women's Shelter P. O. Box 3368 Corpus Christi, TX 78404	512-881-8888 (24 hours) 512-991-1472
Member	Bonnie Tinker 6243 NE 19th Ave. Portland, OR 97211	Oregon Coalition ADV P. O. Box 40132 Portland, OR 97240	503-284-2500
Member	Mary Peterson 937 Tabor Ave. P. O. Box 2051 Fairfield, CA 94533	Solano Center for Battered Women	707-425-9768
Alternate	Ruth Slaughter P. O. Box 2007 Pasadena, CA	Haven House	
Alternate	Bev Monasmith 6180 Canterbury Dr. #337 Culver City, CA 90230		213-731-7384
Alternate	Sally Amsden 1423 Cabrillo #c Venice, CA 90291		213-392-6089 (work) 213-731-7384 (home)

Should your group be interested in forming a state or regional coalition, the following article, reprinted from the *Oregon Coalition Against Domestic Violence Newsletter* should be helpful.

HOW TO ESTABLISH A COALITION*

From June Kuehn in Ocean Springs, Mississippi, the Coalition for Battered Women has received a letter "requesting information concerning the establishment of a Coalition for Battered Women here on the (Mississippi Gulf) Coast."

The Coalition was started in Oregon more than two years ago when B.A. [Bradley-Angle] House, the Family Law Center, Community Law Project, Crime Prevention Bureau and interested individuals met to discuss how information about services for battered women could be publicized, how myths that kept women trapped in violent relationships could be talked about and how groups already working on the problem (social service agencies, churches, law enforcement agencies, shelter homes) could share their information.

The first project planned was a public conference on the issue of household violence. Money was raised for air fare for Del Martin, co-chair of NOW's task force on Household Violence and author of *Battered Wives* to come up and keynote our conference. Four workshops were presented: legal rights of battered women (in getting police help, criminal prosecution, restraining orders and divorces), counseling (by paraprofessionals and peers, women who had left the cycle of dependency and violation), a women's only personal sharing workshop, and what shelters provide and need (focusing on the local shelters in Portland and spending time discussing how to get one started). A lot of effort was spent reaching the media and a preconference press conference with Del Martin and local women was well attended.

At the end of the day-long conference, a general session was held and those attending were urged to sign up for task forces to deal with public speaking engagements and legislation and other areas. As people came to the conference, informational packets were given out with a reprint of Betsy Warrior's excellent article on "Battered Women," a bibliography, a reprint of a speech by a Detroit policeman, and a list of local resources and hotlines. The names and addresses of everyone who came became the nucleus of a mailing

* *Oregon Coalition Against Domestic Violence Newsletter,* May 15, 1978.

list. A conference fee of $3 was collected and used to start up a newsletter. All succeeding conferences have emphasized ability to pay and have provided child care and inexpensive food in order to make the conference accessible. The local Women's Resource Center was paid back for a small loan it had given to start the conference.

In the organizing a balance was constantly forged: women who had emerged or were still in battering relationships were given a lot of support for being where they were at, offered support for making changes and brought into the planning of the conferences and onto the working committees and coalition meetings. At the same time influential people such as sympathetic reporters and legislators were talked to and brought into the Coalition. A legislative session started two months after the conference and the Oregon Women's Political Caucus had a statewide conference in Salem emphasizing workshops on issues that the legislature should address. Members of the Coalition put on an excellent workshop with three battered women speaking, and members of legal aid and the task force that had drafted new laws sponsored by women legislators to (1) fund shelter homes and (2) change the procedure for arrest in criminal domestic assaults to make arrest mandatory and (3) widen the accessibility to restraining orders for unmarried people and people not filing for divorce and give restraining orders enforceability by requiring the police to make arrests for violations.

The Oregon Women's Political Caucus is composed of a lot of professional women and long-time political activists as well as students. At the end of a workshop a poll was taken of the women in the room as to whether they had ever been beaten or threatened; the panel was composed of mostly low-income women and had two Chicana women; the audience was all white. In a room of 70 or 80 women all but a dozen raised their hands. A real feeling of solidarity and support emerged from that meeting. Because the realities of limited income and racism create more barriers for battered women, an active policy of working with minority women and making political and cultural events accessible to women on limited income has been initiated and continued. Child care, transportation and meeting in decentralized groups all around the state are important means to this end.

During the hearings at the legislature, emphasis was given to women testifying to their own experiences, bringing their reality to legislators in addition to technical discussion of legal points by lawyers and social workers.

In organizing the Coalition throughout the state, follow-up to conference meetings in Portland included visiting other towns and cities in the state to give support, presentations, workshops and technical assistance regarding funding to new shelters and groups: Astoria on the coast, Ashland in Southern Oregon, Bend in Eastern Oregon. Groups working in shelters and hotlines in Oregon were brought into the Western States Shelter Network, a coalition of West Coast shelters that has been meeting regularly since a large conference in San Francisco in December 1976. We are also now linked to the newly formed National Coalition Against Domestic Violence.

The Coalition works closely with shelters, helping to deal with agencies such as welfare, the public (speaking engagements) and monitoring the work of the police and district attorney and new laws before state and federal government. Legal answers to the problem will not be the ultimate way of solving woman battering; we have always kept an eye on the solution of freeing women by returning their power to them: bringing them into decision-making and organizing, supporting them through personal sharing, finding housing and jobs.

So how do you start a Coalition? Find all those who are currently working or living in the situation of domestic violence. Arrange meetings, work through women's groups. Avoid sectarianism and elitism by working in a collective, task oriented fashion. Find friendly media and legislators and activists. Especially now that battered women are an "in" issue, make sure that social service agencies don't co-opt the group. Emphasize the need to bring attention to the women most sorely affected, the battered women. Resist attempts to turn battered women into a "law and order" issue; channeling convicted men into work release centers and mandatory counseling by anti-sexist professionals and paraprofessionals is also important.

Networking is very important, maintaining contacts throughout the region. Keep meetings to a necessary minimum; there is so much to do that that should be the focus. From the beginning some provisional basis of unity should be worked out, especially in a shelter network group. It has been our experience that debates over rhetoric can delay action, but that tactical decisions need to always keep in mind ultimate goals and fair process. Going around the room at every meeting identifying everyone and why they are there and constructing agendas from what people bring up allows new people to become part of the group and know one another and to put new areas of interest before the group. It is a very good process.

FOR SHELTER AND BEYOND

For battered women, battered
by the fist of your keeper,
by the nailed boots of the man
drunk on the bottle or the booze of his will,
by the angry man, by the selfpitying man,
by the man kicked by those who can afford
to pass on rage.

For battered women, battered
by hunger, by poverty, by bills coming
in with the old bills unpaid and the phone
turned off and the children with no
shoes to wear to school.
For battered women, battered
by the rapist in the street,
by the rapist you thought your friend,
by the rapist your uncle, the rapist
in every man who uses women
like something he can wipe himself on.

For battered women, battered
by birthing methods invented for doctors'
profits, with your baby
yanked out of you strapped down,
battered by social workers prying,
battered by jail, battered by divorce
court, battered by electroshock,
battered with drugs that slow your body
and snuff your mind.

For battered women, battered
by insults on the corner and on the job,
by the lack of love, by the loss of love,
by the rancid garbage abuse that comes

to the aged, by the death of children,
by the death of respect for you
and who you are
battered but alive,
woman ready to give birth again to hope,
ready to midwife hope
for other bleeding women.

Marge Piercy

RESOURCES

A comprehensive "Family Violence Resource Kit," which serves as a supplement to *Stopping Wife Abuse,* is available through the Women's Resource Network. This package was originally developed as an appendix to this book, but limited space precluded its inclusion.

The kit contains a wide selection of materials designed to provide additional help to those seeking to implement the suggestions and recommendations detailed earlier in the book. The kit is divided into eight sections, each of which corresponds to one of the eight preceding chapters.

The following is a sample listing of the kit's contents.

Information on:
Self-defense
Common-law Marriage
Housing
Child Care
Finding and Choosing Lawyers and Therapists
Separation
Divorce
Support

Child Custody
Property
Living on Welfare
Employment
Continuing Education
Guidelines for Providing Crisis Counseling
State Legislative Contacts (useful when working to enact state spouse-abuse legislation)
Description of The Children's Program at La Casa de las Madres Shelter, San Francisco, California
List of Social Scientists That Are Currently Conducting Wife-beating Research
Report on Domestic-violence Problem in Rural Areas
Sample Forms for Those Providing Shelter and Support Services:
Intake Forms
Monthly Report Forms
Data-collection Forms
Client-information Forms
Shelter Out-take Forms
Sample Shelter Bylaws
Guidelines on Documenting the Incidence of Wife Assault
Sample Standards for the Operation of Shelters
Sample House Rules
Sample Shelter Organizational Charts
Sample Shelter Histories
List of Resources Needed to Establish Programs for Battered Women
Information on Organizing Volunteer Emergency Housing for Battered Women
Model Budgets for Shelters and Hotlines
Courtroom Advocacy Guidelines
"The Nuts and Bolts of Advocacy"
Organizational Development Information
Program Management Information
Fund-raising Information
Developing Your Volunteer Program
Sample Manuals and Brochures

Since more than adequate resource information is contained in the Bibliographies at the end of the book, we have not included an additional resource list. See footnotes throughout chapters for additional resource information.

LIST OF PROGRAMS PROVIDING SERVICES TO BATTERED WOMEN

This is a recently compiled list of every known project working in the interests of battered women. The list was compiled by the Center for Women Policy Studies under a grant awarded by the Law Enforcement Assistance Administration. Completed in April 1978, the list was developed by Susan Bancroft and produced by Diane Hamilton.

ALASKA
Shelters
Abused Women's Aid in Crisis (AWAIC)
P. O. Box 4-819
Anchorage, AK 95509
(907) 272-0100–Crisis
(907) 276-6935–Office
   Services: Legal aid ($5 per family, sliding scale), counseling, referral, hotline (24 hrs.), children's activities 4 hrs. per day, housing (max. capacity 34, limit 30 days, will take children)
   Funding: State legislature

ARIZONA
Shelters
Rainbow Retreat, Inc.
4332 N. 12th St.
Phoenix, AZ 85014

(602) 263-1113

> Services: Counseling, referral, hotline (24 hrs.), child care, housing (sliding donation scale, max. 10 women, children welcome, time limit 1–2 weeks), nutrition program
>
> Funding: City, CETA, donations, Presbyterian church, fund raising

Other Services

Citizen Participation and Support Project

7012 North 58th Dr.

Glendale, AZ 85301

(602) 931-5593

> Services: Counseling, referral, hotline (24 hrs.), child care and housing purchased for client
>
> Funding: City of Glendale

New Directions for Young Women

246 S. Scott

Tucson, AZ 85701

(602) 623-3677

> Services: Counseling, referral, child care (1–3 P.M.), advocacy groups, general education diploma for all females 12–18 years of age
>
> Funding: LEAA

ARKANSAS

Shelters

Northwest Arkansas Project for Battered Women and Their Families

P. O. Box 1168

Fayetteville, AR 72701

(501) 521-1394

> Services: Referral, hotline (24 hrs.), housing, counseling
>
> Funding: CETA, County Quorum Court, Washington County EOA, private donations

Other Services

Advocates for Battered Women

700 N. Polk

Little Rock, AR 72205

(501) 664-8834–Crisis

(501) 664-8834–Office

> Services: Legal aid, counseling, referral, hotline (24 hrs.)
>
> Funding: Volunteer at present time

CALIFORNIA

Shelters

La Casa de las Madres

P. O. Box 15147

San Francisco, CA 94115

(415) 626-9343–Crisis

(415) 626-7859–Office

> Services: Legal aid, counseling, referral, child care, housing (maximum 30, children welcome)
>
> Funding: Vanguard, Colman Youth Services, San Francisco Foundation

Haven Hills, Inc.
P. O. Box 66
Canoga Park, CA 91305
(213) 887-6589–Crisis
(213) 340-2632–Office
  Services: Legal aid, counseling (sliding scale), referral, hotline (24 hrs.), housing (max. 30 days, max. capacity 15, children welcome)
  Funding: City Revenue Sharing, State Health Dept., community resources, private foundations

Rosasharon
P. O. Box 4583
North Hollywood, CA 91607
(213) 769-4237, 781-2722–Crisis
(212) 985-2006–Office
  Services: Counseling, referral, hotline (24 hrs.), child care, housing (max. 30–45 days, max. capacity 30–40, children welcome)
  Funding: City of Los Angeles

Sojourn c/o Ocean Park Community Center
245 Hill St.
Santa Monica, CA 90405
(213) 399-9228
  Services: Counseling, referral, hotline (24 hrs.), child care, housing (max. 30 days, max. capacity 4, children welcome)
  Funding: Private donations

Berkeley Women's Refuge
2134 Allison Way
Berkeley, CA 94704
(415) 849-2314–Crisis
(415) 845-9256–Office
  Services: Counseling, referral, hotline (24 hrs.), housing (max. 7–10 days, max. capacity 23, children welcome)
  Funding: Revenue sharing city/county, ACAP, private donations

Harbor Area YWCA Refuge and Services for Victims of Domestic Violence
437 W. 9th St.
San Pedro, CA 90731
(213) 547-9343–Crisis
(213) 547-0831–Office
  Services: Counseling, referral, hotline, housing (max. 14 days, max. capacity 10, children welcome)
  Funding: YWCA, churches, CETA, individuals

Haven House, Inc.
P. O. Box 2007
Pasadena, CA 91107
(213) 681-2626
  Services: Legal aid (sliding scale), counseling, referral, hotline (24 hrs.), child care, housing (max. 30 days, max. capacity 35, children welcome)
  Funding: L. A. County-General Revenue Sharing

Marin Abused Women's Services
P. O. Box 2924
San Rafael, CA 94901
(415) 924-6616–Crisis
(415) 457-4413–Office
  Services: Legal aid, counseling, referral, hotline (24 hrs.) child care
  (hours by arrangement), housing (max. 28 days, max. capacity 10,
  children welcome)
  Funding: Private donations

Mother's Emergency Stress Service
2515 J St.
Sacramento, CA 95816
(916) 466-7811–Crisis
(916) 446-2791–Home
  Services: Legal aid, counseling, referral, hotline (24 hrs.), housing
  (max. 60 days, max. capacity 15, children welcome), prechild-
  abuse and child-abuse counseling
  Funding: County (for crisis line only)

Coalition for Alternatives to Domestic Violence
P. O. Box 910
Riverside, CA 92502
(714) 686-HELP
  Services: Legal advice (sliding scale), counseling, referral, hotline (24
  hrs.), some child care, housing (max. 14 days; fees: $1.00 for women,
  $.50 for children, sliding scale)

Violence in the Family Project, Community Action Commission
735 State St.
Santa Barbara, CA 92102
(805) 968-2556–Crisis
(805) 963-1526–Office
  Services: Legal aid (sliding scale), referral, hotline (24 hrs.), housing
  (client advocate, small demonstration shelter)
  Funding: CETA, Title VI

Women's Resource Center, Inc.
4070 Mission Ave., Room 220
San Luis Rey, CA 92068
(714) 757-3500–Crisis
(714) 757-3500–Office
  Services: Counseling, referral, hotline, housing (max. 1 day, max. capacity 15, children welcome)
  Funding: County Revenue Sharing, contributions, and United Way

Women's Shelter
P. O. Box 4222
Long Beach, CA 90804
(213) 437-4663
  Services: Counseling, referral, hotline, child care (for residents), hous-
  ing (max. 28 days, max. capacity 21, children welcome)
  Funding: Long Beach, CETA, Second Community Service Fund, and
  private donations

San Francisco Women's Center
63 Brady St.
San Francisco, CA 94103
 (415) 431-1180
   Services: Legal aid, referral, housing
   Funding: Grants, private donations, membership dues

Solano Center for Battered Women
P. O. Box 2051
Fairfield, CA 94533
(707) 429-HELP–Crisis
(707) 425-9768–Home
   Services: Counseling, referral, hotline (24 hrs.), max. capacity 6, children welcome
   Funding: County and city monies, CETA

WOMA—The Women's Alliance
1509 E. Santa Clara St.
San Jose, CA 95116
(408) 251-6655
   Services: Legal aid, counseling, referral, hotline, housing
   Funding: CETA, State Health Dept., private foundations and private industry

Womanspace Shelter for Battered Women
P. O. Box 106994
Sacramento, CA 95816
(916) 466-7811–Crisis
(916) 446-2791–Office
   Services: Legal aid, counseling, referral, hotline (24 hrs.), child care, housing (max. 56 days, max. capacity 15, children welcome)
   Funding: Community support

Women Encouraging Enterprise and Development (WEED)
Station A., Box 111
Auburn, CA 95603
(916) 885-8406
   Services: Legal aid, counseling, referral, hotline (24 hrs.), housing, children welcome

Women's Transitional Living Center, Inc.
P. O. Box 6103
Orange, CA 92667
(714) 992-1931
   Services: Counseling (donation requested), referral, child care, housing ($1.00 for women, $.25 for children, max. 30 days, max. capacity 18)
   Funding: Revenue sharing, private donations

Women United Against Battering
P. O. Box 893
Placerville, CA 95667
(916) 622-1235
(916) 626-0338

Services: Counseling, referral, hotline, child care, housing (max. 5 days, children welcome)
Funding: County donation

YWCA Women Against Domestic Violence
P. O. Box 1362
Monterey, CA 93940
(408) 649-0834
Services: Referral, hotline (10 A.M.–10 P.M.), housing (max. 14 days, max. capacity 30, children welcome, sliding scale)
Funding: Service clubs, donations, YWCA, revenue sharing

Other Services
The Battered Women's Project
2187 Ulric St., Suite D
San Diego, CA 92111
(714) 565-7197–Crisis
(714) 565-7198–Office
Services: Legal aid, counseling, referral, hotline (24 hrs.)
Funding: CETA

Legal Aid Foundation of Long Beach
4790 E. Pacific Coast Hwy.
Long Beach, CA 90804
(213) 434-7421
Services: Legal aid, counseling, referral
Funding: Legal Services Corporation

Santa Monica Hospital Medical Center
1225 Fifteenth St.
Santa Monica, CA 90404
(213) 451-1511
Services: Counseling, referral, medical care
Funding: Self-supported

Mountain Sisters Collective
Box 426, Old Bank Mall
Angels Camp, CA 95222
(209) 736-2723–Crisis
(209) 736-4801–Office
Services: Counseling, referral, community education
Funding: Private funding

Women's Crisis Support
640 Capitola Rd.
Santa Cruz, CA 95062
(408) 425-2058
Services: Counseling, referral, hotline (24 hrs.)
Funding: CETA and county revenue sharing

Women's Litigation Unit—Neighborhood Legal Assistance
1095 Market St.
San Francisco, CA 94103
(415) 626-3819

Services: Legal aid (residence and low-income requirement)
Funding: Legal Services Corporation

Cumings, Jordan, and Morgan
96 Jessie St.
San Francisco, CA 94105
(415) 495-4495
Services: Legal aid (charge involved)
Funding: Private law office

YWCA Women's Emergency Shelter
P. O. Box 3506
Santa Rosa, CA 95402
(707) 546-1234–Crisis
(707) 546-1477–Office
Services: Legal aid, counseling, referral, hotline, child care
Funding: Revenue sharing, State Health Dept., community fund raising, churches, private donations

COLORADO
Shelters
Battered Women Services
12 N. Meade
Colorado Springs, CO 80907
(303) 633-4601–Crisis
(303) 471-HELP–Evenings and weekends
Services: Counseling, referral, hotline (24 hrs.), housing (private homes, children welcome)
Funding: CETA, donations

Battered Woman Project c/o Women's Resource Center
4th and Rood
Grand Junction, CO 81501
(303) 243-0190
Services: Counseling, referral, hotline (24 hrs.), housing (max. 14 days, max. capacity 4 women, sliding scale, children welcome)
Funding: Individual contributions

Brandum Guest House
1260 Pennsylvania
Denver, CO 80203
(303) 832-7826
Services: Counseling, referral, hotline (24 hrs.), child care, housing (max. 28 days, max. capacity 50, children welcome)
Funding: United Way and CETA

Columbine Center
1331 Columbine
Denver, CO 80206
(303) 399-0082–Crisis
(303) 399-4554–Office
Services: Legal aid (sliding scale), counseling (sliding scale), referral, hotline (24 hrs.), child care, housing (max. 30 days, max. capacity 25–30, children welcome)

Women in Crisis
P. O. Box 1955
Evergreen, CO 80439
(303) 232-0996–Crisis
(303) 674-5504, 234-1494–Home
    Services: Legal aid (sliding scale), counseling, referral, hotline (24
    hrs.), child care, housing (max. capacity 40, children welcome)
    Funding: CETA, private foundations, Dept. of Social Services

Women in Crisis
1426 Pierce St.
Lakewood, CO 80214
(303) 232-0996–Crisis
(303) 234-1494–Office
    Services: Legal aid, counseling, referral, hotline (24 hrs.), housing
    (sliding scale, max. 28 days, max. capacity 40, children welcome)
    Funding: CETA, Piton Foundation

Safe House
1264 Race St.
Denver, CO 80206
(303) 338-4703
(303) 388-4268
    Services: Legal aid, counseling, referral, hotline (10 A.M.–5 P.M.),
    child care, housing (max. 90 days, max. capacity 30, children wel-
    come)
    Funding: LEAA, Denver Dept. of Social Services, private donations,
    Denver Anti-Crime Council

York Street Center
1632 York St.
Denver, CO 80206
(303) 333-5626–Crisis
(303) 321-8191–Sexual assault only
(303) 388-0834–Office
    Services: Legal aid, counseling, referral, hotline (24 hrs.), child care
    (daytime only), housing (max. 14 days)
    Funding: LEAA

Other Services
Boulder County Women's Resource Center
1406 Pine St.
Boulder, CO 80302
(303) 447-9670
    Services: Counseling, referral
    Funding: CETA, city, county, United Way, private donations

CONNECTICUT
Shelters
New Haven Project for Battered Women
P. O. Box 1329
New Haven, CT 06505
(203) 789-8104

Services: Counseling, referral, hotline (9 A.M.–5 P.M. and some evenings), child care, emergency housing
Funding: City and grants

Prudence Crandall Center for Women
37 Bassett St.
New Britain, CT 06051
(203) 225-6357, 229-6939
Services: Counseling, referral, child care, housing (max. 60 days, max. capacity 10 women, children welcome)
Funding: CETA, various churches

Yale/New Haven Hospital Rape Counseling Team
Emergency Services/Yale New Haven Hospital
789 Howard Ave.
New Haven, CT 06510
(203) 436-1960
Services: Counseling, referral, housing (max. 7 days, max. capacity 15, children not accepted)
Funding: Hospital

Other Services
Catholic Family Services
90 Franklin Sq.
New Britain, CT 06051
(203) 225-3561
Services: Counseling (sliding scale), referral
Funding: United Way, fees, grants

New Haven Legal Assistance Association
399 Temple St.
New Haven, CT 06511
Services: Legal aid, counseling, referral
Funding: Legal Services Corporation, Title XX, United Way

Stand, Inc.
246 Main St.
Derby, CT 06418
(203) 735-9553
Services: Counseling, referral
Funding: Dept. of Mental Health, United Way, TEAM, New Haven Foundation, Connecticut Foundation for the Fine Arts

YWCA of Greater Bridgeport
1862 East Main St.
Bridgeport, CT 06610
(203) 334-6154
Services: Legal aid, counseling (sliding scale), referral, hotline (24 hrs.)

DISTRICT OF COLUMBIA
Shelters
House of Ruth
1215 New Jersey Ave., N.W.
Washington, DC 20001

(202) 347-9689
  Services: Legal aid (emergency basis), counseling, referral, hotline (24
  hrs.), housing (overnight stay, max. capacity 30, children welcome)
  Funding: Community, churches, business groups, social organizations

House of Imogene
214 P. Street, N.W.
Washington, DC 20001
(202) 797-7460
  Services: Counseling, referral, housing (max. 7 days, max. capacity 25,
  children not accepted)
  Funding: Individual contributions

Other Services
 Citizen's Complaint Center/U. S. Attorney's Office
601 Indiana Avenue, N.W., first floor
Washington, DC 20004
(202) 376-2568
  Services: Legal aid, counseling, referral
  Funding: Dept. of Justice

Families and Children in Trouble (FACT)
c/o Box C, 1690 36th Street, N.W.
Washington, DC 20007
(202) 628-FACT–Crisis
(202) 965-1900–Office
  Services: Phone counseling, referral, hotline (24 hrs.)
  Funding: Dept. of Human Resources, Bureau of Social Services, private grants and donations

DELAWARE
  Shelters
  People's Place
  121 S. Walnut
  Milford, DE 19963
  (302) 422-8011
    Services: Legal aid, counseling, referral, hotline (24 hrs.), housing
    Funding: Self-supporting

  YWCA Women's Center
  Arden Center/2210 Swiss Lane
  Ardentown, DE 19810
  (302) 475-8424
    Services: Legal aid, counseling, referral, child care, housing (max. 14
    days, max. capacity 8, children welcome)
    Funding: United Way

FLORIDA
  Shelters
  Domestic Assault Shelter
  c/o YWCA, 901 South Olive
  West Palm Beach, FL 33401
  (305) 588-1121
  (305) 833-2439

Services: Counseling, referral, hotline (24 hrs.), child care (sliding scale), housing (sliding scale, max. 21 days, max. capacity 6, children welcome
Funding: Private donations and state grant

Hubbard House
1231 Hubbard St.
Jacksonville, FL 32206
(904) 354-3114–Crisis
(904) 354-3114–Office
Services: Legal aid, counseling, referral, hotline (24 hrs.), child care, housing ($1.00 per day, max. 21 days, max. capacity 25 women, children welcome)
Funding: Public contributions, private foundations, businesses, CETA

Spouse Abuse, Inc. c/o We Care, Inc.
112 Pasadena Pl.
Orlando, FL 32803
(305) 628-1227 (24 hrs.)
(305) 425-2624 (8 A.M. to midnight)
Services: Legal aid, counseling, referral, hotline (24 hrs.), child care (referrals), housing (max. 21 days)
Funding: LEAA, Orange County, donations, Community Mental Health Board, United Way

The Spring, Inc.
P. O. Box 11087
Tampa, FL 33610
(813) 251-8620
Services: Legal aid, counseling, referral, hotline (24 hrs.), child care, housing (max. 14 days, max. capacity 10, children welcome)
Funding: Private donations, volunteers

Safespace: Battered Women's Shelter
P. O. Box 186
(305) 576-6161–Crisis
(305) 579-2915–Office
Services: Legal aid, counseling, referral, hotline (24 hrs.), housing ($1.25 per day, max. 21 days, max. capacity 30, children welcome)
Funding: LEAA, Dade County

YWCA of Jacksonville
325 E. Duval St.
Jacksonville, FL 32202
(904) 354-6681
Services: Counseling, referral, job training and placement, housing ($30 per week, max. 60 days, max. capacity 86, children welcome)
Funding: Manpower

Other Services
Victim Advocate Program
Ft. Lauderdale Police Dept.
1300 W. Broward Blvd.
Fort Lauderdale, FL 33312
(305) 761-2143

Services: Counseling, referral, hotline (24 hrs.)
Funding: City of Fort Lauderdale

Citizen Dispute Settlement Center
1351 NW 12th St.
Miami, FL 33125
(305) 547-7062
Services: Referral, mediation (domestic and neighbor)
Funding: LEAA and Dade County

Domestic Assault Project
Pan Am Bldg., 307 N. Dixie Hwy.
West Palm Beach, FL 33402
(305) 588-1121–Crisis
(305) 837-2418–Office
Services: Counseling, referral, hotline (24 hrs.)
Funding: LEAA, state and county

Pensacola YWCA
1417 N. 12th Ave.
Pensacola, FL 32504
(904) 438-2171
Services: Referral
Funding: Self-supporting

GEORGIA
Shelters
Council on Battered Women
45 11th St., NE
Atlanta, GA 30309
(404) 572-2626–Crisis
(404) 873-1766–Office
Services: Legal aid, counseling, referral, hotline (weekends and after
five), child care, housing (max. 30 days, max. capacity 36, children
welcome)
Funding: Contributions

YWCA Crisis Center
48 Henderson St.
Marietta, GA 30064
(404) 973-8890
Services: Referral, housing (max. 5 days, max. capacity 3 adults, children accepted, sliding scale of fees)
Funding: Donations from YWCA and community

IDAHO
Shelters
The Woman's Advocates
454 North Garfield
Pocatello, ID 83201
(208) 232-HELP–Crisis
(208) 232-9169–Answering service

Services: Counseling, referral, hotline, child care, housing (max. 3 days, max. capacity 1, children welcome)
Funding: YWCA, volunteers

Emergency Housing Services, Inc.
P. O. Box 286
815 N. 7th St.
Boise, ID 83701
(208) 343-7541
Services: Referral, housing (max. 14 days, max. capacity 18, children welcome)
Funding: Private donations

ILLINOIS
Shelters
A Woman's Place
505 W. Green
Urbana, IL 61801
(217) 384-4390–Crisis
(217) 384-4390–Office
Services: Counseling (peer), referral, hotline (24 hrs.), housing (sliding fee scale, max. 21 days, children welcome)
Funding: United Way, Champaign Cty. Mental Health Board, revenue sharing, Peoria Catholic Diocese, donations, fees

Community Crisis Center
600 Margaret Pl.
Elgin, IL 60120
(312) 697-1093
Services: Legal aid, counseling, referral, hotline (24 hrs.), child care, housing (max. 21 days, max. capacity 10, children welcome)
Funding: CETA, Dept. of Children and Family Services, private foundation, township revenue sharing

Gospel League
955 W. Grand Ave.
Chicago, IL 60622
(312) 423-2480
Services: Legal aid, referral, hotline, child care, housing (max. capacity 40, children welcome)
Funding: Individuals and groups

R. I. County Council on Alcoholism (New Hope League)
R. R. 2, P. O. Box 288
East Moline, IL 61244
(309) 797-4220–Crisis
(309) 792-0292–Office
Services: Counseling, referral, hotline (24 hrs.), child care, housing (max. capacity 18, children welcome)
Funding: State Dept. of Mental Health, R. I. County Mental Health Board, United Way, private contributions

Sojourn Women's Center, Inc.
915 N. 7th St.
Springfield, IL 62702
(217) 544-2484–Crisis
(217) 525-0313–Office
   Services: Counseling, hotline (24 hrs.), housing (max. 14 days, max.
   capacity 8, children welcome)
   Funding: Individual donations, private organizations, religious groups,
   city revenue-sharing funds, CETA

Salvation Army Emergency Lodge
800 West Lawrence Ave.
Chicago, IL 60640
(312) 275-9383–Crisis and office
   Services: Legal aid, counseling, referral, housing (max. days negotia-
   ble, children welcome, max. capacity 125)
   Funding: United Way, Salvation Army

Women's Center
408 W. Freeman
Carbondale, IL 62901
(618) 457-0346
   Services: Legal aid, counseling, referral, hotline (24 hrs.), housing
   Funding: City, United Way, 708 Mental Health Board, individual contributions

Women's Crisis Service
1101 Main St., #306
Peoria, IL 61606
(309) 674-4443–Crisis
(309) 676-0200–Office
   Services: Counseling, referral, hotline, housing (max. 21 days, max. capacity 6, children welcome)
   Funding: Human Service Center, CETA, private donations

Other Services
Cook County Legal Assistance Foundation, Inc.
19 S. LaSalle, Suite 1419
Chicago, IL 60603
(312) 263-2267
   Services: Legal assistance, legal counseling, referral
   Funding: Legal Services Corporation

Des Plaines Valley Community Center
612 S. Archer Rd.
Summit, IL 60501
   Services: Legal assistance, counseling, referral, hotline (9 A.M.–9 P.M.),
   child care (sliding scale, 6 A.M.–6 P.M.)
Emergency Department/Illinois Masonic Medical Center
836 Wellington
Chicago, IL 60657
(312) 525-2300
   Services: Counseling, referral
   Funding: Hospital/patient revenues

Women's Services Department/Loop YWCA
37 S. Wabash, 3rd floor
Chicago, IL 60603
(312) 372-6600
　Services: Legal advice, consultation, referral (sliding scale)

INDIANA
Other Services
Women's Shelter Advisory Committee of YWCA
802 N. LaFayette Blvd.
South Bend, IN 46601
(219) 232-3344–Crisis
(219) 233-9491–Women's Center
　Services: Legal aid, counseling, referral, hotline
　Funding: Self-supporting

YWCA Shelter for Women Victims of Violence
P. O. Box 5338
Fort Wayne, IN 46805
(219) 424-2554–Crisis
(219) 424-2621–Office
　Services: Counseling, referral, hotline (24 hrs.), child care, housing
　(max. capacity 30, children welcome)
　Funding: CETA, UNITED WAY

IOWA
Other Services
Legal Services Corporation
315 East Fifth
Des Moines, IA 50309
(515) 243-2151
　Services: Legal aid
　Funding: National Legal Services Corporation

Story County Sexual Assault Care Center
P. O. Box 1150, ISU Station
Ames, IA 50010
(515) 292-1101–Crisis
(515) 292-2305–Office
　Services: Counseling, referral, hotline (24 hrs.), housing (3 days, chil-
　dren welcome, in community member homes
　Funding: city, county revenue sharing, Iowa State University (Office of
　Student Affairs), private donations, fund raising

KANSAS
Shelters
Wichita Women's Crisis Center
1158 N. Waco
Wichita, KS 67203
(316) 263-9806–Crisis
(316) 263-6520–Office
　Services: Legal advice, counseling, referral, hotline (24 hrs.), housing
　(max. 21 days, max. capacity 15, children welcome)
　Funding: HUD, CETA

Women's Transitional Care Services
P. O. Box 633
Lawrence, KS 66044
(316) 864-3506, 841-2345
    Services: Legal aid, counseling, referral, hotline (24 hrs.), housing
    (max. 21 days, children welcome)
    Funding: Church grants, community donations

Other Services
Margaret W. Jordan
2515 W 91st St.
Leawood, KS 66206
(913) 649-7691
    Services: Legal aid, counseling, referral
    Funding: Private attorney's office

Pawnee Mental Health Center
320 Sunset
Manhattan, KS 66502
(913) 539-5337
    Services: Counseling (sliding scale), referral
    Funding: HEW, county and state monies, fees

Wyandot Mental Health Center
Eaton at 36th Ave.
Kansas City, KS 66103
(913) 831-9500
    Services: Counseling (fee), referral, hotline (24 hrs.)
    Funding: County and state monies, fees

KENTUCKY
    Shelters
    Mission House
    1305 W. Market St.
    Louisville, KY 40203
    (502) 584-4024
        Services: Referral, housing (max. 5 days, max. capacity 8, children
        welcome)
        Funding: Donations, agencies

Spouse Abuse Center
YWCA, 604 S. 3rd St.
Louisville, KY 40202
(502) 585-2331–Crisis
(502) 585-2331–Office
    Services: Legal aid, counseling, referral, hotline (24 hrs.), child care
    (Mon.–Fri., 9 A.M.–5 P.M.), housing (max. 30 days. max. capacity 15,
    children welcome), sliding scale
    Funding: CETA

Green River Comprehensive Care Center
P. O. Box 950
Owensboro, KY 42301

(800) 482-7972–Crisis
(502) 683-7277–Office
  Services: Counseling (sliding scale), referral, hotline (24 hrs.), housing
  Funding: Reimbursement for services provided

Other Services
Battered Women's Unit of Legal Aid
317 S. 5th St.
Louisville, KY 40202
(502) 637-5301–Crisis
(502) 637-5301–Office
  Services: Legal aid, referral
  Funding: Legal Services Corporation

Northeast Kentucky Legal Services
P. O. Box 679
320 E. Main St.
Morehead, KY 40351
(616) 784-8921
  Services: Legal aid, referral
  Funding: Legal Services Corporation

LOUISIANA
  Other Services
  YWCA Battered Women's Program
  3433 Tulane Ave.
  New Orleans, LA 70119
  (504) 486-0377–Crisis and office
    Services: Counseling, referral, hotline (24 hrs.)
    Funding: Title XX, donations

MARYLAND
  Shelters
  Battered Partners Program—Carroll County Department of Social
  Services
  95 Carroll St.
  Westminster, MD 21157
  (301) 848-5060
    Services: Counseling (sliding scale), referral, child care (fee), housing
    (fee, max. 14 days, children welcome, Carroll County residents only)
    Funding: Department of Social Services

  Good Neighbors Unlimited
  208 Duke of Gloucester St.
  Annapolis, MD 21401
    Services: Legal aid, counseling, referral, child care, housing (max. 10
    days, max. capacity 12, children welcome. Must be referred through
    Police Department)
    Funding: Private donations

  House of Ruth, Baltimore
  2402 N. Calvert St.
  Baltimore, MD 21218

(301) 889-RUTH
  Services: Counseling (sliding scale), referral, housing (max. capacity 15, children welcome)
  Funding: Private contributions

Maryland's Children's Aid and Family Services Society
22 N. Court St.
Westminster, MD 21157
(301) 876-1233–Office
(301) 848-3111–Crisis referral
  Services: Counseling, referral, housing (children welcome)

Passage Crisis Center
8500 Colesville Rd.
Silver Spring, MD 20901
(301) 589-8608–Crisis
(301) 565-7729–Office
  Services: Counseling, referral, hotline (24 hrs.), housing (max. 3 days, max. capacity 8, children welcome)
  Funding: Montgomery County Health Department

Women's Refuge
Seton Plaza, Suite 201
952 Seton Dr.
Cumberland, MD 21502
(301) 777-1509
  Services: Counseling, referral, housing (max. 6 days, children accepted)
  Funding: CETA and community donations

YWCA Women's Center
167 Duke of Gloucester Rd.
Annapolis, MD 21401
(301) 268-4393
  Services: Counseling, referral, child care (at shelter), housing (max. 10 days, max. capacity 6)
  Funding: Donations

Other Services
A Woman's Place
150 Maryland Ave.
Rockville, MD 20850
(301) 279-8346
  Services: Legal aid, counseling, referral
  Funding: County funds

Violence Clinic/Department of Psychiatry
University of Maryland Hospital
645 West Redwood St.
Baltimore, MD 21201
(301) 528-6475
  Services: Counseling (psychiatric evaluation), referral (fee)
  Funding: Hospital revenues

MASSACHUSETTS

Shelters

Elizabeth Stone House
108 Brookside Ave.
Jamaica Plain, MA 02130
(413) 522-3417
  Services: Counseling, housing (max. 180 days, max. capacity 6)

Casa Myrna Vasquez c/o Pat Quintant
425 Shawmut Ave.
Boston, MA 02118
(617) 262-9581
  Services: Legal aid, counseling, referral, hotline (24 hrs.), housing
  (max. capacity 25, children welcome, Spanish-speaking)
  Funding: Private donations

New England Learning Center for Women in Transition
310 Main St.
Greenfield, MA 01301
(413) 772-0125
  Services: Legal aid, counseling. referral, child care (Mon.–Fri., 9
  A.M.–4 P.M.), housing (max. 30 days, max. capacity 10, children welcome), support groups, transportation, advocacy, crisis intervention
  Funding: CETA, Department of Mental Health, fund raising, donations

Respond
1 Summer St.
Somerville, MA 02143
(617) 623-5900
  Services: Legal aid, counseling, referral, child care, housing (max. capacity 4, children welcome)
  Funding: Community development, foundations

Transition House, c/o Women's Center
46 Pleasant St.
Cambridge, MA 02138
(617) 661-7203–Crisis
(617) 354-6394–Office
  Services: Legal aid, counseling, referral, hotline, child care, housing
  ($1.50 per day, max. 28 days, children welcome)
  Funding: CETA, donations, private foundations, Department of Mental
  Health

Women's Services Center of Berkshire County
33 Pear St.
Pittsfield, MA 01201
(413) 443-0089–Crisis
(413) 442-9458–Office
  Services: Counseling (sliding scale), referral, hotline (24 hrs.), child
  care, housing (emergency shelters, children welcome)
  Funding: Community Development Block Grant, Campaign for
  Human Development

YWCA Women Against Violence
Natick, MA 01760
(413) 872-6161, 369-6112–Crisis
(413) 653-4464–Office
   Services: Legal aid, counseling, referral, hotline (24 hrs.), child care,
   housing (pay for food)
   Funding: Government grant

Other Services
Boston College Legal Assistance Bureau
21 Lexington St.
Waltham, MA 02154
(617) 893-4793
   Services: Legal aid ($1.00 fee), referral
   Funding: Boston College Law School, City of Waltham

Cambridge-Somerville Legal Services
24 Thorndike St.
East Cambridge, MA 02141
(617) 492-5520
   Services: Legal aid, referral
   Funding: Legal Services Corporation

Gardner Women's Center
175 Connors St.
Gardner, MA 01462
(617) 632-5150
   Services: Legal aid, referral, counseling, hotline (9 A.M.–4 P.M.)
   Funding: CETA

Lynn District Court Clinic
580 Essex St.
Lynn, MA 01907
(617) 598-5200
   Services: Legal aid, counseling, referral, hotline (9 A.M.–4 P.M.)
   Funding: Department of Mental Health

Social Service Department—St. Luke's Hospital
101 Page St.
New Bedford, MA 02740
(617) 997-1515, ex. 371–Office
   Services: Counseling, referral
   Funding: Private, nonprofit organization

Suffulk County District Attorney's Office
503 Washington St.
Dorchester, MA 02124
(617) 287-1195
   Services: Legal aid, counseling, referral
   Funding: LEAA

Women's Law Collective
678 Massachusetts Ave.
Box 125
Cambridge, MA 02139

(617) 492-5110
    Services: Legal aid (sliding scale), referral
    Funding: Self-supporting

Womanspace: Feminist Therapy Collective, Inc.
636 Beacon St. •
Boston, MA 02215
(617) 267-7992
    Services: Counseling (fee negotiable), referral
    Funding: Contributions, fees, sale of bibliographies

MICHIGAN
Shelters
Assault Crisis Center
561 N. Hewitt
Ypsilanti, MI 48197
(313) 668-8888–Crisis
(313) 434-9881–Office
    Services: Counseling, referral, hotline (24 hrs.), housing (max. 3 days,
    children welcome)
    Funding: LEAA and local grant

Project Shelter
Women's Center
Marquette, MI 49855
(616) 227-2219
    Services: Legal aid, counseling, referral, housing (max. 3 days, max.
    capacity 10, children welcome)
    Funding: Non-funded, staffed by volunteers

Rape/Spouse Assault Crisis Center
29 Strong Ave.
Muskegon, MI 49441
(616) 722-3333–Crisis
(616) 726-4493–Office
    Services: Legal aid, counseling, referral, hotline (24 hrs.), child
    care (daytime), housing (max. 21 days, max. capacity 10 families)
    Funding: Kalamazoo Foundation

Other Services
Domestic Violence/Victim Assistance Project
1917 Washtenaw Ave.
Ann Arbor, MI 48104
(313) 995-5444–Crisis
(313) 995-5460–Office
    Services: Referral, hotline (24 hrs.)
    Funding: HUD, CETA, VISTA, United Way, private foundations, and
    donations

Every Woman's Center
310 E. 3rd St.
Flint, MI 48503
(313) 238-7671

Services: Counseling (sliding scale), referral
Funding: Mott Foundation, Junior League

Sisters for Human Equality (SHE)
1320 S. Washington
Lansing, MI 48910
(517) 374-0818–Crisis
(517) 484-1905–Office
Services: Legal aid, referral
Funding: Legal Services Corporation, City of Ann Arbor AAA, CETA

Women's Justice Center
651 E. Jefferson
Detroit, MI 48226
(313) 961-7073
Services: Legal referral, counseling
Funding: UCS, private donation

Women's Survival Center
70 Whittemore
Pontiac, MI 48058
(313) 335-1520–Crisis
(313) 335-2685–Office
Services: Counseling, referral, hotline (9 A.M.–5 P.M.)
Funding: Churches, CETA

Women in Transition
218½ Washington St.
Grand Haven, MI 49417
(616) 842-7970, 842-6310
Services: Counseling, referral, public education

MINNESOTA
Shelters
Northeastern Coalition for Battered Women, Inc.
2 East Fifth St.
Duluth, MN 55805
(218) 722-0222–Crisis and office
Services: Counseling, referral, hotline (24 hrs.), child care, housing
(max. capacity 12, children welcome)
Funding: State funds, private grants

St. Joseph's House
2101 Portland Ave.
Minneapolis, MN 55404
(612) 874-8867
Services: Legal aid, referral, hotline (24 hrs.), housing (max. 30 days,
max. capacity 15, children welcome)
Funding: Donations, churches, individuals

Harriet Tubman Shelter
3001 Oakland
Minneapolis, MN 55414
(612) 827-2841

Services: Legal aid, counseling, referral, hotline (24 hrs.), child care (8:00 A.M.–5 P.M.), housing (max. capacity 30, children welcome)
Funding: Private foundation, HUD, Minneapolis Housing Authority

Victim's Crisis Center/Freeborn Mowe Mental Health Center
908 N.W. 1 Dr.
Austin, MN 55912
(507) 437-6680
Services: Legal aid, counseling, referral, hotline, child care, housing (children welcome)
Funding: Minnesota Department of Corrections, Victim Services Division

Woman's Advocates
584 Grand Ave.
St. Paul, MN 55103
(612) 227-8284
Services: Legal aid, counseling, referral, hotline (24 hrs.), housing
Funding: State Welfare Department, County Mental Health Board, private foundation

Other Services
Community Planning Organization
333 Sibley, #503
St. Paul, MN 55101
(612) 291-8323
Services: Information and referral
Funding: Foundation grants, corporate grants, membership fees

South Suburban Family Service
633 S. Concord
South St. Paul, MN 55075
(612) 451-1434–Crisis
(612) 451-1434–Office
Services: Counseling (fee), referral
Funding: United Way

Walk-In Counseling Center
2421 Chicago Ave.
Minneapolis, MN 55404
(612) 870-0565
Services: Counseling and referral
Funding: County Mental Health Board

MISSOURI
Shelters
St. George's Home for Women
1600 E. 58th St.
Kansas City, MO 64110
(816) 444-4750
Services: Counseling, housing (max. 90 days, max. capacity 16, children welcome)
Funding: Churches, private foundations, state support

Women's Self-Help Center
27 N. Newstead
St. Louis, MO 63108
(314) 531-2033, 534-7273–Crisis
(314) 531-2003–Office
 Services: Legal aid, counseling, referral, hotline (24 hrs.), housing
 (approx. 7 days, max. capacity 30, children welcome, housing is in individual homes)
 Funding: CETA, Manpower, private foundations, Legal Aid Society,
 United Way

Other Services
Crisis Intervention, Inc.
P. O. Box 585
Joplin, MO 65801
(417) 623-8310
 Services: Referral, hotline (24 hrs.)
 Funding: Local contributions

Child Center of Our Lady of Grace
7900 Natural Bridge
St. Louis, MO 63121
(314) 383-0200
 Services: Counseling (fee), child care
 Funding: United Way, client fees

Legal Services of Eastern Missouri, Inc.
607 N. Grand
St. Louis, MO 63103
(314) 533-3000
 Services: Legal advice, counseling, referral
 Funding: Legal Services Corporation, United Way

Women's Counseling Center
6808 Washington
St. Louis, MO 63130
(314) 725-9158
 Services: Counseling (sliding scale), referral
 Funding: Client fees, donations

Linda Cobb, Social Service Department
c/o Malcolm Bliss Mental Center
1420 Grattan
St. Louis, MO 63110
 Services: Counseling, workshops for community organizations

MONTANA
 Shelters
Great Falls Mercy Home
P. O. Box 6183
Great Falls, MT 59406
(406) 453-6511–Crisis
(406) 761-6538–Office

Services: Counseling, referral, hotline (24 hrs.), housing (time limit flexible, max. capacity 13, children welcome)
Funding: Churches, social services groups, donations

Glendive Task Force Against Spouse Abuse
Hegenston Building
Glendive, MT 59330
(406) 365-2412–Crisis
(406) 365-3364–Office
Services: Counseling, referral, hotline, housing
Funding: CETA, Action for Eastern Montana

Community Resources
1937 Florida
Butte, MT 59701
(406) 792-2616–Crisis
(406) 792-2616–Office
Services: Legal aid (donation), counseling, referral, child care, housing (max. capacity 8, children welcome)
Funding: Self-supporting

Other Services
Woman's Place
1130 W. Broadway
Missoula, MT 59801
(406) 543-7606
Services: Counseling, referral, hotline (24 hrs.)
Funding: Donations, grants

Billings Rape Task Force
1245 N. 29th St., Rm. 218
Billings, MT 59101
(406) 259-6506
Services: Counseling, referral, hotline (24 hrs.)
Funding: United Way, city revenue sharing funds

NEBRASKA
Shelters
People's City Mission
124 S. 9th St.
Lincoln, NE 68508
(402) 432-5329
Services: Counseling, referral, housing (max. capacity 10 families, children welcome)
Funding: United Way, churches, fees, grants, donations

Salvation Army
511 N. 20th St.
Omaha, NE 68102
(402) 346-5155
Services: Referral, housing (max. 14 days, max. capacity 30, children welcome)
Funding: United Way, Douglas County Social Services

Shiloh Youth Revival Center
1045 N. 34th St.
Omaha, NE 68131
(402) 553-3947
  Services: Counseling, hotline, housing (max. 3 days, max. capacity 10, children not accepted)
  Funding: Self-supporting

Siena House
804 N. 19th St.
Omaha, NE 68102
(402) 341-2642–Crisis
(402) 341-1821–Office
  Services: Referral, child care, housing (max. capacity 30, children welcome)
  Funding: Private donations

Other Services
Community Social Services
303 W. 4th St.
Hastings, NE 68901
(402) 463-2112
  Services: Counseling ($5 per visit), referral
  Funding: United Way, Catholic Church

Immanuel Medical Center
6901 North 72nd St.
Omaha, NE 68122
(402) 572-2225–Crisis
(402) 572-2259–Office
  Services: Counseling, referral, hotline (24 hrs.)
  Funding: Grants and hospital revenues

Operation Bridge, Inc.
3929 Harvey St., Suite 124
Omaha, NE 68131
(402) 346-7102
  Services: Counseling

Mayor's Commission on Women
1819 Farnam St., ℁501
Omaha, NE 68102
(402) 444-5032
  Services: Legal advocacy, crisis intervention, referral
  Funding: CETA

NEW JERSEY
  Shelters
  Atlantic County Women's Center
  Box 84B, R. D. 3
  W. Hickory St.
  Mays Landing, NJ 08330
  (609) 653-8411

Services: Counseling, referral, hotline (24 hrs.), housing (max. 30 days, max. capacity 20, children welcome)
Funding: Donations

Bergen County Community Action Program
215 Union Street
Hackensack, NJ 07601
(201) 487-8484–Crisis
(201) 487-8446–Home
Services: Counseling, referral, hotline (24 hrs.), child care, housing, (max. 28 days, max. capacity 12, children welcome, currently using motels and private residences)
Funding: CETA, Bergen County monies

Hudson County Coalition for Battered Women
Jersey City YWCA
111 Storms Ave.
Jersey City, NJ 07306
(201) 333-5702, 333-3045, 339-7676–Crisis
(201) 333-5703–Office
Services: Legal aid, counseling, referral, hotline (24 hrs.), child care, housing (max. 28 days, max. capacity 15, children welcome)
Funding: Private contributions

Shelter Our Sisters
133 Cedar Ave.
Hackensack, NJ 07601
(201) 342-1185
Services: Legal advice, counseling, referral, hotline (24 hrs.), child care, housing (max. 90 days, children welcome)
Funding: Self-supporting

Women's Resource and Survival Center
57 W. Front St.
Keyport, NJ 07735
(201) 264-4111
Services: Legal aid, counseling, referral, hotline (24 hrs.), child care, housing (3 days max.)
Funding: HEW, NIMH, county, state and local monies

Other Services
Camden Regional Legal Services
11 W. Union St.
Burlington, NJ 08016
(609) 386-6660
Services: Legal aid, referral
Funding: Legal Services Corporation

NEW YORK
Shelters
Henry Street Settlement Urban Life Center
265 Henry St.
New York, NY 10002

Services: Legal aid, counseling, referral, child care, housing (max. 6 months, max. capacity 18 families)
Funding, LEAA, N. Y. Dept. of Social Services, Robert Sterling Foundation

Long Island Women's Coalition, Inc.
P. O. Box 183
Islip Terrace, NY 11752
(516) 589-1658, 581-5179, 757-7797
Services: Legal aid, counseling, referral, hotline, housing (temp. in home, max. capacity 6 women with children)
Funding: Donations, private foundations, NOW

Project Green Hope: Services for Women, Inc.
448 E. 119th St.
New York, NY 10035
(212) 369-5100
Services: Counseling, referral, housing (max. 6 months, no children), parenting education program
Funding: LEAA, CETA, corporate donations

Tompkins County Task Force for Battered Women
c/o Suicide Prevention and Crisis Service
Women's Community Building
Ithaca, NY 14850
(607) 272-1616–Crisis
(607) 272-1505–Office
Services: Counseling, referral, hotline (24 hrs.), child care, housing (max. 3 days, children welcome)
Funding: Private contributions

Victims Information Bureau of Suffolk, Inc.
501 Rte. 111
Hauppauge, NY 11787
(516) 360-3606–Crisis
(516) 360-3730–Office
Services: Legal aid, counseling, referral, hotline (24 hrs.), child care, housing (max. 30 days, max. capacity 20 children welcome)
Funding: LEAA, private contributions

Women's Survival Space
P. O. Box 279
Bay Ridge Station
Brooklyn, NY 11220
(212) 439-7281–Crisis
(212) 439-4612–Office
Services: Legal aid, counseling, referral, hotline (9 A.M.–5 P.M.), child care, housing ($5 per day, sliding scale, max. 42 days, max. capacity 40, children welcome)
Funding: Self-supporting, grant

Women's Resource Center of the Jamestown Girls Club
532 E. 2nd St.
Jamestown, NY 14701

(716) 484-1820
   Services: Counseling, legal information, referral, hotline (9 A.M.–5 P.M.), housing (7 days max., max. capacity 5 families, children welcome)
   Funding: CETA

Young Women's Christian Association of Binghamton
Hawley and Exchange St.
Binghamton, NY 13901
(607) 772-0340
   Services: Counseling, referral, child care (mornings only), housing (max. 3 days, max. capacity 3, children welcome)
   Funding: Interfaith Action Council

YWCA Battered Women's Project
44 Washington Ave.
Schenectady, NY 12305
(518) 374-3394
   Services: Legal aid, counseling, referral, hotline (24 hrs.), child care (mornings only), housing
   Funding: CETA

YWCA of the Tonawandas
49 Tremont St.
Tonawanda, NY 14120
(716) 692-5643–Crisis
(716) 692-5580–Office
   Services; Legal referral, counseling referral, hotline (24 hrs.), child care, housing (max. 1 day, max. capacity 2, children welcome)
   Funding; United Methodist Women's Conference, YWCA

New York City Human Resources Administration/Battered Womens' Shelter
250 Church St., 13th floor
New York, NY 10013
(212) 581-4911–Crisis
   Services: Legal referral, counseling referral, hotline (24 hrs.), child care (9 A.M.–5 P.M.), housing (max. capacity 87, children welcome)
   Funding: Muncipal Agency

Other Services
Abused Women's Aid in Crisis, Inc.
P. O. Box 1699
New York, NY 10001
(212) 686-1676–Crisis
(212) 686-3628–Office
   Services: Referral, counseling, hotline
   Funding: Private foundations, contributions

Abused Spouse Center
29 Sterling Ave.
White Plains, NY 10606
(914) 948-3400–Crisis

(914) 949-1741–Office
  Services: Legal aid, counseling, referral, hotline
  Funding: CETA

Afterhouse Committee of the Task Force for Victims of Domestic Violence
70 Harvard Pl.
Buffalo, NY 14209
(716) 886-7359
  Services: Legal aid, counseling, referral, hotline (9 A.M.–5 P.M.)
  Funding: Self-supporting

Brooklyn Legal Services Corporation B
152 Court St.
Brooklyn, NY 11201
(212) 855-8029
  Services: Legal aid, referral
  Funding: Federal

Outreach
41 Sussex
Port Jervis, NY 10940
(212) 856-5800
  Services: Counseling, referral
  Funding: Self-supporting

Litigation Coalition for Battered Women
759 10th Ave.
New York, NY 10019
(212) 581-2810
  Services: Legal aid
  Funding: Legal Services Corporation, New York Foundation, New York Community Trust

Rape Crisis Center
66 Chenango St.
Binghamton, NY 13901
(607) 722-4256
  Services: Counseling, referral, hotline (24 hrs.), community education
  Funding: LEAA, CETA, local funding

Battered Women Assistance Program
26 North St., Rm. 54
Middletown, NY 10940
(914) 343-3750
  Services: Legal aid, referral, advocacy, community education

Victim/Witness Assistance Project
50 Court St.
Brooklyn, NY 11201
(212) 834-7444–Crisis
(212) 834-7450–Office
  Services: Counseling, referral, hotline, in-court assistance
  Funding: LEAA

Battered Women Assistance Project
26 North St. Rm. 54
Middletown, NY 10940
(914) 343-3750
  Services: Legal aid, counseling, referral
  Funding: CETA

Battered Women's Law Project
2 Cannon St., Rm. 308
Poughkeepsie, NY
(914) 473-4818
  Services: Legal aid, referral, community education

Coalition for Abused Women
P. O. Box 94
East Meadow, NY 11554
(516) 542-2594–Crisis
(516) 542-2846–Office
  Services: Legal aid, counseling, referral, hotline (24 hrs.), community
  education
  Funding: CETA

Children & Youth Development Services
262 9th St.
Brooklyn, NY 11215
(212) 788-4800
  Services: Counseling, referral, hotline (Mon.–Fri., 9 A.M.–5 P.M.)
  Funding: Self-supporting

Caren Delrow
116 Benedict Ave.
Syracuse, NY 13210
(315) 478-4910
  Services: Legal advice, referral
  Funding: Private law office

Eastern Women's Center
14 East 60th St., 8th floor
New York, NY 10022
(212) 832-0099–Crisis
(202) 832-0033–Office
  Services: Counseling, referral, hotline (24 hrs.)
  Funding: Private donations

Family Abuse Project, Manhattan Family Court
60 Lafayette St. Rm. 4E22
New York, NY 10013
(212) 766-9588, 766-9587
  Services: Legal aid, counseling, referral
  Funding: LEAA

Hudson Guild Family Life Center
441 W. 26th St.
New York, NY 10001

(212) 760-9844
Services: Counseling, referral
Funding: Title XX

NORTH CAROLINA

Shelters

Rape, Child, & Family Crisis Council of Salisbury
211 N. Church St.
Salisbury, NC 28144
(704) 636-9222
Services: Counseling, referral (fee), 24 hrs., housing (not always available, fee)
Funding: Donations

Switchboard—Battered Women's Project
312 Umstead St.
Durham, NC 27707
(704) 688-1140
Services: Legal aid, counseling, referral, hotline (24 hrs.), housing

Women's Aid: Services for Abused Women
P. O. Box 1137
Greensboro, NC 27402
(919) 275-0896
Services: Legal aid, counseling, referral, hotline (24 hrs.), child care, housing (children welcome)
Funding: Title I of Higher Education Act for administrative expenses

Battered Women's Crisis Line at Hasslehouse
1022 Urban Ave.
Durham, NC 27701
(919) 688-4353
Services: Legal aid, counseling, referral, hotline (24 hrs.), housing

Other Services

Greensboro Legal Aid Foundation
917 Southeastern Bldg.
Greensboro, NC 27401
(919) 272-0148
Services: Legal aid, referral
Funding: Legal Services Corporation, United Way

Halifax County Mental Health Center
P. O. Box 757
Roanoke Rapids, NC 27870
(919) 537-2909–Crisis
(919) 537-6174–Office
Services: Counseling (fee), referral, hotline (24 hrs.)
Funding: State and county monies

Wake County Women's Aid: Services for Abused Women
YWCA, 1012 Oberlin Rd.
Raleigh, NC 27605
(919) 828-3205
Services: Referral

NORTH DAKOTA

Shelters

Women's Abuse/Children's Village Family Service
1721 S. University Dr.
Fargo, ND 58102
(800) 472-2911–Crisis
(701) 235-6433–Office
 Services: Counseling, referral, hotline (7 A.M.–1 A.M.), housing
 Funding: CETA, United Way, Stern Foundation, donations

Fargo/Moorhead YWCA
411 Broadway
Fargo, ND 58102
(701) 232-2546
 Services: Counseling, referral, housing ($7 per night, max. capacity 14,
 children welcome)
 Funding: Churches, memberships, United Way

Other Services

Legal Assistance of North Dakota
420 N. 4th St., ⚹324
Bismarck, ND 58501
(701) 258-4270
 Services: Legal aid (fee in some cases)
 Funding: Legal Services Corporation

OHIO

Shelters

Arkron Task Force on Battered Women
146 S. High St.
Akron, OH 44305
(216) 762-6685
 Services: Legal aid, counseling, referral, hotline (Mon.–Fri., 10 A.M.–6
 P.M.), child care, housing (max. capacity 3, children welcome).
 Funding: Fund raisers, honorariums, self-supporting

Butler County Women's Crisis Shelter
5021 Fairfield Circle
Fairfield, OH 45014
(513) 874-3690
 Services: Legal aid, counseling (sliding scale), referral, hotline (24
 hrs.), housing (sliding scale, max. 5 days, max. capacity 12, no children)
 Funding: Private donations

Furnace Street Mission
P. O. Box 444
Akron, OH 44309
(216) 923-0174
 Services: Counseling, referral, hotline, housing (max. 7 days, children
 welcome)
 Funding: Donations

Green County Crisis Center
53 N. Collier St.
Xenia, OH 45385
(513) 376-2993, 426-2302–Crisis
(513) 376-9471, 426-0020–Office
    Services: Counseling (sliding scale), referral, hotline (24 hrs.), housing
    (max. 2 days, children welcome)
    Funding: Green-Clinton Mental/Retardation Board

Heidi House
P. O. Box 8053
Columbus, OH 43201
(614) 294-2720
    Services: Legal aid, counseling, referral, child care, housing ($1.50 per
    day, max. 6 months, max. capacity 4, children welcome)
    Funding: Local donations, churches, revenue sharing, City Council,
    local foundations

Project Woman
22 E. Grand
Springfield, OH 45506
(513) 325-3707
    Services: Counseling, referral, hotline (24 hrs.), housing (max. 7 days)
    Funding: Memberships, donations, church organizations

Alice Paul House/YWCA
9th and Walnut St.
Cincinnati, OH 45202
(513) 381-5610–Crisis
(513) 381-6003–Office
    Services: Counseling, referral, hotline (24 hrs.), housing (max. 30
    days, max. capacity 17, children welcome)
    Funding: LEAA, CETA, Title XX, private foundations

Women Together, Inc.
P. O. Box 6331
Cleveland, OH 44101
(216) 961-4422–Crisis
(216) 631-3556–Office
    Services: Legal aid, counseling, referral, hotline (24 hrs.), child care,
    housing (max. capacity 8, children welcome)
    Funding: Self-supporting

Other Services
Witness/Victim Service of Cuyahoga County
Justice Center
1215 W. 3rd St.
Cleveland, OH 44113
(216) 623-7345
    Services: Legal aid, counseling, referral, child care
    Funding: LEAA

YWCA of Clermont County
55 South 4th St.
Batavia, OH 45103
(216) 732-0450
  Services: Counseling, referral
  Funding: CETA

OKLAHOMA
Shelters
Women's Resource Center/Norman, Oklahoma, Task Force for Battered
  Women
P. O. Box 474 (Peters & Gray)
Norman, OK 73070
(405) 364-9424
  Services: Counseling, referral, hotline, housing (max. 3 days, children
  welcome)
  Funding: CETA, County Mental Health Association

YWCA Women's Resource Center
3626 N. Western Ave.
Oklahoma City, OK 73118
(504) 528-5440
  Services: Counseling, referral, hotline (daytime hours only), housing
  (max. 3 days, children welcome)
  Funding: Self-supporting

Other Shelters
Tulsa Task Force for Battered Women, Inc.
524 S. Boulder, Rm. 206
Tulsa, OK 74103
(918) 622-2345–Crisis
(918) 585-8917–Office
  Services: Counseling, referral, hotline (24 hrs.), child care (limited)
  Funding: General revenue sharing, donations

OREGON
Shelters
Bradley/Angle House
P. O. Box 40132
Portland, OR 97240
(503) 281-2442–Crisis
(503) 281-8275–Office
(503) 249-8117–Child program
  Services: Legal aid, counseling, referral, hotline, (24 hrs.), child care,
  housing (max. capacity 15, children welcome)
  Funding: CETA, private foundations, donations, resident fees

Womanspace
P. O. Box 3030
Eugene, OR 97403
(503) 485-6513

Services: Counseling, referral, hotline. housing (sliding scale, children welcome)
Funding: CETA, donations, city/county revenue sharing

Salem Women's Crisis Service for Battered Women
P. O. Box 851
Salem, OR 97308
(503) 399-7722
(503) 378-1572
Services: Legal aid, counseling, referral, hotline (24 hrs.), housing (max. 3 days, no children)
Funding: CETA, city revenue sharing

Women's Resource Center of Lincoln for Battered Women
908 SW Hurbert
Newport, OR 97365
(503) 265-2491–Crisis
(503) 265-7551–Office
Services: Counseling, referral, hotline (24 hrs.), housing ($1 per night, max. capacity 10, children welcome)
Funding: CETA, county monies

BEWARE
276 E. Main
Hillsboro, OR 97123
(503) 640-1171
Services: Counseling, referral, housing
Funding: CETA

Other Services
Rape Relief Hotline
522 SW 5th, 6th floor
Portland, OR 97202
(503) 235-5333–Crisis
(503) 224-7125–Office
Services: Counseling, referral, hotline (24 hrs.)
Funding: CETA, foundations, private corporations

PENNSYLVANIA
Shelters
A Woman's Place
108 Main St.
Sellersville, PA 18960
(215) 257-0188
Services: Counseling, referral, hotline (24 hrs.), housing (max. 14 days, $2.50 per day, max. capacity 6, children welcome)
Funding: Philadelphia Foundation, Douty Foundation

Hospitality House
205 Myrtle St.
Erie, PA 16507
(814) 454-1963
Services: Counseling, referral, hotline (24 hrs.), housing (max. 5 days, children welcome)
Funding: State and private donations

Women Against Abuse
P. O. Box 122233
Philadelphia, PA 19144
(215) 843-2905–Crisis
(215) 843-2438–Office
  Services: Counseling, referral, hotline (8 A.M.–6 P.M.), child care
  (mornings only), housing ($1.00 per day, max. 30 days, max. capacity
  30, children welcome)
  Funding: Governor's Justice Commission (LEAA), Philadelphia Foundation, United Way

Women's Center of Beaver County
1305 Third Ave.
Beaver Falls, PA 15010
(412) 843-6440
  Services: Legal aid, counseling (fee), referral, hotline (24 hrs.), housing ($2 per day, max. 14 days, max. capacity 14, children welcome)
  Funding: Beaver Butler Presbyterian Church, donations

Women's Center
1000 S. Market St., Box 221
Bloomsburg, PA 17815
(717) 784-6631
  Services: Counseling, referral, hotline (24 hrs.), housing (max. 5 days,
  max. capacity 3, children welcome)
  Funding: Donations and contributions

Women's Center and Shelter of Greater Pittsburgh
616 N. Highland Ave.
Pittsburgh, PA 15206
(412) 661-6066
  Services: Counseling, referral, hotline (24 hrs.), child care, housing
  (max. 6 days, max. capacity 19, children welcome, $2.00 per night)
  Funding: Self-supporting

Women in Crisis
4th and Market St.
Harrisburg, PA 17101
(717) 238-1068
  Services: Legal aid, counseling, referral, hotline (24 hrs.), child care
  daytime hours only), housing ($2.00 per night, max. 30 days, max.
  capacity 7, children welcome)
  Funding: Public Health Trust of Pennsylvania, Tri-County United
  Way, payments

Women's Resource Center of Chester County
YWCA, 123 N. Church St.
West Chester, PA 19380
(215) 431-1430
  Services: Referral, hotline (24 hrs.), counseling, child care (daytime),
  housing (14 days max., children welcome)
  Funding: YWCA, donations

Wise Options for Women
YWCA 815 W. 4th
Williamsport, PA 11754
(717) 322-4714
  Services: Counseling, referral, hotline (24 hrs.), child care (daytime),
  housing (max. 30 days, max. capacity 8, children welcome)
  Funding: CETA, United Way, Williamsport Foundation

Other Services
Berks Women in Crisis
c/o Jacque Melton, 1045 Moss St.
Reading, PA 19604
(215) 372-7273
  Services. Counseling, referral, hotline (24 hrs.)
  Funding: Methodist Social Concern Committee, contributions

Women's Resource Center, Inc.
407 Connell Bldg., North Washington Ave.
Scranton, PA 18503
(717) 346-4671
  Services: Legal information, counseling, referral, hotline (24 hrs.)
  Funding: LEAA, Lackawanna County Drug & Alcohol Commission

Women's Resource Network
4025 Chestnut St.
Philadelphia, PA 19104
(215) 387-0420
  Services: Legal aid, counseling, referral
  Funding: Local and National foundations

Women in Crisis/YWCA
8th and Washington St.
Reading, PA
(717) 372-7273
  Services: Legal aid, counseling, hotline (24 hrs.)
  Funding: Ms. Foundation, Levinson Foundation

Marital Abuse Project of Delaware County, Inc.
P. O. Box 294
Wallingford, PA 19086
(215) 565-4590–Crisis
(215) 565-6272–Office
  Services: Counseling, referral, hotline
  Funding: LEAA

Central Pennsylvania Legal Services
524 Washington St.
Reading, PA 19604
(215) 376-8656
  Services: Legal advice, counseling, referral

Pennsylvania Coalition Against Domestic Violence
110 N. Lime St.
Lancaster, PA 17602

Services: Legal aid, counseling, referral, hotline
Funding: Ms. Foundation, Levinson Foundation

Susquehanna Valley Women in Transition, Inc.
P. O. Box 502
Sunbury, PA 17801
(717) 379-9625
Services: Legal aid, counseling, referral, hotline
Funding: CETA

Women's Aid Center, Inc.
67 N. Church St., 3rd floor
Hazleton, PA 18201
(717) 455-9971
Services: Counseling, referral, hotline (9 A.M.–midnight)
Funding: CETA, United Church of Christ, AAUW

Womencenter
Box 621
Wilkes Barre, PA 18703
(717) 829-7868
Services: Legal aid, counseling, referral, hotline
Funding: CETA

Women in Transition
3700 Chestnut St.
Philadelphia, PA 19104
(215) 382-7016–Crisis
(215) 382-7019–Office
Services: Legal aid, counseling (sliding scale), referral, hotline (10 A.M.–12 noon, 2 P.M.–4 P.M.)
Funding: CETA, Mental Health of County, Philadelphia Foundation

PUERTO RICO
Other Services
Ona Lara Porter, Consultana
P. O. Box 74
Punta Borinquen, PR 00604
(809) 891-1510, ex. 5141
Services: Counseling, referral
Funding: Self-supporting

RHODE ISLAND
Shelters
Women's Center of Rhode Island, Inc.
37 Congress Ave.
Providence, RI 02907
(401) 781-4080–Crisis
(401) 781-4480–Office
Services: Legal aid, counseling, referral, hotline (24 hrs.), child care, housing (max. 14 days, max. capacity 20, children welcome)
Funding: United Way, CETA, R. I. Foundation, Providence Christian Center

Sojourner House, Inc.
P. O. Box 5667, Weybosset Hill Sta.
Providence, RI 02903
(401) 751-1262
  Services: Legal aid and advocacy, counseling, referral, hotline (24
  hrs.), housing ($1.50 per day, max. capacity 12, children welcome)
  Funding: Contributions

Other Services
Rhode Island Legal Services, Inc.
77 Durance St.
Providence, RI 02903
(401) 274-3140
  Services: Legal aid, referral
  Funding: Legal Services Corporation

SOUTH CAROLINA
Other Services
Women in Crisis/Family Counseling Services
P. O. Box 10306
(803) 271-0220–Crisis
(803) 232-2434–Office
  Services: Legal aid, counseling (sliding scale)
  Funding: United Way, local groups

SOUTH DAKOTA
Shelters
Brookings Women's Center
802 11th Ave.
Brookings, SD 57006
(605) 692-4359–Crisis
(605) 688-4518–Office
  Services: Counseling, referral, housing ($4 per day, children welcome)
  Funding: Donations, membership, grants

South Central Community
Box 6
Lake Andes, SD 57356
(605) 487-7634
  Services: Legal aid, counseling, referral, hotline (24 hrs.), housing
  (max. capacity 14, children welcome)

TENNESSEE
Other Services
Wife Abuse Crisis Service
4995 Patterson
Memphis, TN 38111
(901) 458-1661–Crisis
(901) 324-5969–Office
  Services: Counseling, referral, hotline (9 A.M.–5 P.M.), limited child
  care
  Funding: CETA, donations

Services for Women in Crisis, Inc.
Box 3240
Nashville, TN 37219
(615) 254-1168
  Services: Job training, advocacy
  Funding: CETA, Governor's discretionary funds

TEXAS
Shelters
Center for Battered Women
P. O. Box 5631
Austin, TX 78763
(512) 472-HURT–Crisis
(512) 472-4879–Office
  Services: Legal aid, counseling, referral, hotline (24 hrs.), child care, housing (max. 28 days, max. capacity 14, children welcome)
  Funding: Travis County, City of Austin, Hogg Foundation, Austin-Travis County Mental Health

Women's Shelter, Inc.
P. O. Box 3368
Corpus Christi, TX 78404
(713) 881-8888
  Services: Counseling, referral, hotline (24 hrs.), child care, housing (max. capacity 16, children welcome)
  Funding: CETA, private gifts, County Commissioner's Court

Houston Area Women's Center, Inc.
P. O. Box 20186, Rm. E401
Houston, TX 77025
(713) 527-0718–Crisis
(713) 792-4411–Office
  Services: Counseling, referral, hotline, child care, housing (max. capacity 11, children welcome)
  Funding: Local foundations, private sources

Women's Haven, Inc.
P. O. Box 12180
Fort Worth, TX 76116
(214) 336-3355–Crisis
(214) 336-1711–Office
  Services: Legal aid, counseling, referral, hotline (24 hrs.), child care, housing (max. capacity 20, children welcome), job assistance
  Funding: CETA, Capitol Cities Foundation, Sid Richardson Foundation, individual contributions, churches, organizations

Other Services
TRIMS, Attn.: Mary Beth Holley
1300 Moursund
Texas Medical Center
Houston, TX 77030
(713) 797-1976

Services: Counseling, referral
Funding: Texas Department of Mental Health

Women's Help, Inc.
P. O. Box 11449
Dallas, TX 75223
(214) 827-5260–Crisis
(214) 827-5261–Office
Services: Counseling, referral, hotline (24 hrs.)
Funding: Private donations

UTAH
Other Services
Rape Crisis Center, Inc.
776 W. 200 North
Salt Lake City, UT 84116
(801) 532-RAPE–Crisis
(801) 532-7286–Office
Services: Legal aid, counseling, referral, hotline (24 hrs.)
Funding: Title XX, donations

VERMONT
Shelters
Umbrella of St. Johnsbury, Inc.
79 Railroad St.
St. Johnsbury, VT 05819
(802) 748-8645
Services: Referral, hotline (daytime only), child care (emergency), housing (max. 14 days, max. capacity 12, children welcome)
Funding: Community donations

Women's Crisis Center
14 Green St.
Brattleboro, VT 05301
(802) 254-6954
Services: Legal aid, counseling, referral, hotline (24 hrs.), child care, housing ($10 per week, max. 60 days, max. capacity 4, children welcome)
Funding: LEAA

Other Services
Vermont Legal Aid, Inc.
3 Summer St.
Springfield, VT 05156
(802) 885-5181
Services: Legal aid, referral
Funding: Legal Services Corporation, private contributions

VIRGINIA
Shelters
CEASE (Community Effort for Abused Spouses)
8119 Holland Rd.
Alexandria, VA 22306

(703) 360-6910
Services: Legal aid, counseling (fee), referral, hotline (24 hrs.), child care, housing (motel, max. stay several days, children welcome)
Funding: LEAA

Fairfax County Women's Shelter
P. O. Box 1174
Vienna, VA 22180
(703) 527-4077–Hotline
(703) 827-0090–Shelter
Services: Counseling, referral, hotline (24 hrs.), child care (24 hrs.), housing (max. 14 days, max. capacity 8, children welcome)
Funding: CETA, Fairfax County, private donations

Mahala, Inc.
7089 Crown Rd.
Roanoke, VA 24018
Services: Legal aid, counseling, referral, hotline, child care, housing (max. 25 people, children welcome)
Funding: Self-supporting

Women's Resource Center
203 Phlegar St.
Christiansburg, VA 24073
(703) 382-6553
Services: Counseling, referral, hotline (24 hrs.), child care, housing (max. 7 days, max. capacity 8, children welcome)
Funding: Community Services Administration, CETA

Other Services
Connections Social Services
2800 N. Pershing Dr.
Arlington, VA 22201
(703) 528-3200
Services: Legal aid, counseling, referral, hotline (24 hrs.)

Woman to Woman
420 E. Market St.
Harrisonburg, VA 22801
(703) 434-1231–Crisis
(703) 434-1766–Office
Services: Counseling, referral, hotline (12 noon–12 midnight)
Funding: Volunteers

WASHINGTON
Shelters
ALIVE (Alternatives to Living in Violence)
611 Highland
Bremerton, WA 98310
(206) 946-0329
Services: Legal aid, referral, counseling, hotline (24 hrs.), housing (max. 21 days, children welcome)
Funding: Community donations

Catherine Booth House
The Salvation Army
925 N. Pike St.
Seattle, WA 98122
(206) 322-7959
 Services: Counseling, referral, hotline (24 hrs.), housing (max. capac-
 ity 16, children welcome)
 Funding: United Way, donations

Dawson House
15 N. Naches Avenue
Yakima, WA 98902
(509) 248-7796
 Services: Legal aid, counseling, referral, hotline (24 hrs.), child care
 (daytime only), housing (max. 14 days, max. capacity 9, children welcome)
 Funding: United Way, donations

New Beginnings
217 9th Ave.
Seattle, WA 98109
(206) 622-8194
 Services: Counseling, referral, housing (sliding scale, max. 30 days
 max. capacity 10, children welcome)
 Funding: Self-supporting

Survival Center of Snohomish County
5205 S. 2nd
Everett, WA 98203
(206) 25A-BUSE–Crisis
(206) 258-3543–Home
 Services: Counseling, referral, hotline (24 hrs.), child care, housing
 (children welcome)
 Funding: CETA, revenue sharing, private foundations, donations

Women's Resource Center/Seattle King County YWCA
1118 5th Ave.
Seattle, WA 98101
(206) 447-4882
 Services: Counseling, referral, housing (max. 14 days, max. capacity
 14, children not accepted)
 Funding: United Way, Cooper Levy Foundation

YWCA Emergency House
1012 W. 12th
Vancouver, WA 98660
(206) 695-0501
 Services: Counseling, referral, hotline, housing (sliding scale, max. 21
 days, max. capacity 13, children welcome)

YWCA Women's Support Shelter
405 Broadway
Tacoma, WA 98402

(206) 383-2593—Crisis
(206) 272-4181—Office
 Services: Counseling, referral, hotline (24 hrs.), child care, housing
 (max. 6 months, max. capacity 37 rooms, children welcome)
 Funding: CETA, United Way, revenue sharing, Title XX, Title XIX,
 rent and counseling fees

Other Services
Community Service Officers Section—Seattle Police
1810 E. Yesler
Seattle, WA 98122
 Services: Counseling, referral
 Funding: City general fund, unit of the Seattle Police Department

Evergreen Legal Services
171½ Howitt
Everett, WA 98201
(206) 258-2681
 Services: Legal aid, counseling, referral
 Funding: Legal Services Corporation

Evergreen Legal Services
618 2nd Ave.
Seattle, WA 98104
(206) 464-5911, 464-5964
 Services: Legal aid, counseling, referral
 Funding: Soroptimists International, Seattle Metro Chapter

Inc. Spot Counseling Center—Youth Services
P. O. Box 171
17516 Bothell Way, NE
Bothell, WA 98011
(206) 485-6541
 Services: Counseling (initial $20 fee, free thereafter), referral, hotline
 Funding: County human services/United Way

People Assistance Team
P. O. Box 1995
Vancouver, WA 98663
(206) 696-8226—Crisis
(206) 696-8292—Office
 Services: Counseling, referral
 Funding: LEAA, local monies

Vancouver Women's Resource Center
602 W. Evergreen Blvd.
Vancouver, WA 98663
(206) 695-6386
 Services: Counseling, referral
 Funding: Donations

Women's Association of Self-Help
11100 NE 2nd St.
Bellevue, WA 98008

(206) 445-9274
  Services: Counseling, referral
  Funding: Donations

Women's Resource Center/YWCA
829 Broadway Ave. W.
Spokane, WA 99201
(509) 838-4428–Crisis, evenings, & weekends
(509) 327-1508–Office
  Services: Counseling, referral, hotline
  Funding: United Way, LEAA
Washington State Women's Council
15th & Columbia
Olympia, WA 98504
(206) 753-2870
  Services: Information and education services

Women's Shelter & Support Services Program
220 E. Union
Olympia, WA 98502
(206) 352-0593
  Services: Counseling, referral
  Funding: YWCA, Inter-Governmental Human Resources Advisory
  Council

YWCA/Pasada
1026 N. Forest
Bellingham, WA 98225
(206) 734-4820
  Services: Counseling, referral
  Funding: CETA

WEST VIRGINIA
  Shelters
  Rape Information Service, Inc.
  221 Willey St.
  Morgantown, WV 26505
  (304) 292-2121–Crisis
  (304) 292-5015–Office
    Services: Counseling, referral, hotline, child care, housing (max. 14
    days, children welcome), transportation, advocacy
    Funding: CETA

  Other Services
  Domestic Violence Center
  31 Hillcrest
  Charleston, WV 25303
  (304) 345-0848–Crisis
  (304) 346-9471, ex. 283–Office
    Services: Legal aid, counseling, referral
    Funding: CETA

WISCONSIN
Shelters
Waukesha County Battered Women's Task Force (Kathryn Espeseth, co-ordinator)
1303 Fleetfoot Dr.
Waukesha, WI 53186
(414) 547-3388–Crisis
(414) 691-3200, ex. 366–Office
  Services: Counseling, referral, hotline, housing (private)
  Funding: Gratuities from speaker's bureau, Community of the Living Spirit

Task Force on Abused Women, Mental Health Association of Portage County
945 A Main St.
Stevens Point, WI 54481
(715) 344-5759
  Services: Counseling, referral, housing (max. 2 days, max. capacity 3, children welcome)
  Funding: Mental Health Association/United Way, donations

National Organization for Women, North Central Wisconsin Chapter
Box 793
Wausau, WI 54401
(715) 842-7636
  Services: Counseling, referral, hotline, child care, housing

Women's Horizons, Inc.
1630 56th St.
Kenosha, WI 53140
(414) 652-1846
  Services: Legal referral, counseling, hotline (24 hrs.), child care, housing
  Funding: CETA, Kenosha Comprehensive Board

Women's Service Center Domestic Violence Project
102 N. Monroe
Green Bay, WI 54301
(414) 432-4244
  Services: Counseling (sliding scale), referral, hotline (24 hrs.), child care, housing (max. 30 days, max. capacity 16, children welcome)
  Funding: CETA, VISTA, local monies

Other Services
Abused Women's Project
1100 Lake View Dr.
Wausau, WI 54401
(715) 842-1636
  Services: Counseling, referral, hotline (24 hrs.)
  Funding: Marathon County Human Services Board

Dane County Advocates for Battered Women
P. O. Box 1145
Madison, WI 57301

(608) 251-4445
   Services: Counseling, referral, hotline (9 A.M.–5 P.M. weekdays only),
   help in finding short-term housing in some cases
   Funding: Unified Mental Health Board, CETA, donations

Hotline
P. O. Box 221
Green Bay, WI 54301
(414) 437-9008–Crisis
(414) 468-3479–Office
   Services: Legal aid, counseling, referral, hotline (24 hrs.)
   Funding: Unified Mental Health Board, CETA, private donations

Family Service
214 N. Hamilton St.
Madison, WI 53703
(414) 251-7611
   Services: Counseling (fee), referral
   Funding: United Way

Lakeshore Association for Abused Women
P. O. Box 398
Manitowoc, WI 54220
(404) 684-5770
   Services: Counseling, referral, hotline
   Funding: CETA

Women's Resource Center
2101 A Main St.
Stevens Point, WI 54481
(715) 346-4851
   Services: Referral, hotline (9 A.M.–9 P.M.)

ADDITIONAL LISTINGS

Friends of the Family
P. O. Box 4042
Scottsdale, AZ 85258
(602) 949-7256–Office
   Services: Legal aid, counseling, referral, hotline, child care, housing,
   (sliding scale, max. 45 days, max. capacity 15, children welcome)

Emergency Shelter Program, Inc.
24518 Mission Blvd.
Hayward, CA 94544
(415) 881-1244–Crisis
(415) 881-1246–Office
   Services: Counseling, referral, hotline (24 hrs.), housing (max. 10 days,
   max. capacity 23, children welcome, bilingual shelters)
   Funding: Revenue sharing, private donations

Battered Woman Project
205 N. 4th
Grand Junction, CO 81501

(303) 242-0190–Crisis
Services: Counseling, referral, hotline (24 hrs.), child care, housing (max. 14 days, children welcome)

Washtenaw County Legal Aid Society
212 E. Huron
Ann Arbor, MI 48104
(313) 665-6181–Office
Services: Legal aid, referral
Funding: Legal Services Corporation, City of Ann Arbor, AAA, CETA

YWCA of Pontiac/North Oakland Domestic Crisis Shelter
269 West Huron Street
Pontiac, MI 48053
(313) 332-HELP–Crisis
(313) 334-0973–Office
Services: Counseling, referral, hotline (24 hrs.), child care, housing (max. 21 days, max. capacity 11, children welcome)

Bozeman Help Center
323 S. Wall
Bozeman, MT 59715
(406) 586-3333–Crisis
Services: Counseling, referral, hotline
Funding: Private contributions

Night Prosecutor's Program
City Hall Annex
67 North Front St.
Columbus, OH 43215
(614) 222-7483–Crisis
Services: Counseling, referral, hotline (8 A.M.–12 midnight), mediation
Funding: City budget

Phoenix House
P. O. Box 8323
Columbus, OH 43201
(614) 294-3381–Crisis
(604) 294-7876–Office
Services: Legal aid, counseling, referral, hotline (24 hrs.), child care, housing (max. 28 days, max. capacity 12, children welcome)
Funding: Private foundations, CETA, Title XX, donations, fees

Lancaster Shelter for Abused Women
110 North Lime St.
Lancaster, PA 17602
(717) 299-1249–Crisis
Services: Legal aid, counseling, referral, hotline, child care, housing (max. capacity 20, children welcome)
Funding: Community Services Administration, federal, Title XX, local monies

Victim Advocacy/District Attorney's Staff
107 Cumberland Ave.
Ashland City, TN 37015
(615) 292-9623–Crisis
(615) 292-4404–Office
  Services: Legal aid, counseling, referral, hotline
  Funding: LEAA

Women's Resource Center of the YWCA
740 College Ave.
Racine, WI 53403
(414) 633-3233–Crisis
(414) 633-3233–Office
  Services: Counseling, referral, hotline (24 hrs.), housing (max. 14
  days, children welcome)
  Funding: United Way, private foundations, CETA, gifts from community groups and individuals

BIBLIOGRAPHY

DOMESTIC VIOLENCE BIBLIOGRAPHIES

This Bibliography was published in November 1978 by the National Technical Assistance Center on Family Violence, c/o Domestic Violence Project, Inc., 1917 Washtenaw Ave., Ann Arbor, MI 48104.

Abramson, Catherine. *Spouse Abuse: An Annotated Bibliography*. Center for Women Policy Studies, 2000 P Street, N.W., Suite 508, Washington, DC 20007, 1977. Free.
> *Comments*—Gives approximately sixty annotated entries and a list of suggested additional readings.

Center for Women Policy Studies. *Comprehensive Bibliography on Domestic Violence*. Center for Women Policy Studies, 2000 P Street, N.W., Suite 508, Washington, DC 20007, 1977. Free.
> *Comments*—Includes journal articles, books, handbooks, magazine and newspaper articles. Has a second part on crisis intervention.

Howard, Pamela F. *Wife Beating: Selected Annotated Bibliography*. Current Bibliography Series, Box 2709, San Diego, CA 92112, 1978. $3.00.
> *Comments*—30 books, 59 periodical articles, 14 newspaper articles. Also includes selected government publications, films, and agencies.

Johnson, Carolyn, Ferry, John; and Krovitz, Marjorie. *Spouse Abuse: A Selected Bibliography*. National Criminal Justice Reference Service. Box 6000 Rockville, Md. 20850, 1978. Free.
> Contains ninety-one entries, with semphosis on spouse abuse and the criminal-justice system.

Lystad, Mary. *Violence at Home: an Annotated Bibliography*. National Institute of Mental Health, 5600 Fishers Lane, Rockville, MD 20852, 1974. Free.

Comments—190 entries on theories of violence and aggression, child abuse, and family socialization, as well as on spouse abuse.

McShane, Claudette. *Annotated Bibliography on Woman Battering*. Center for Advanced Studies in Human Services, Midwest Parent-Child Welfare Resource Center, School of Social Welfare, University of Wisconsin-Milwaukee, P. O. Box 413, Milwaukee, WI 53201, 1977. Free.

Comments—Annotated books, articles, newsletters, guides, media, and more bibliographies (!) Over 130 entries.

Author's Note:

These bibliographies will refer you to a variety of publications, materials, and resources that will prove helpful in developing services for those living in violent families. Included is information on the following:

Fund raising
Police and court practices
Sources of aid for victims
Legal information
Psychology of victims, children, and abusers
Legislative change
Various research studies
Service provision

BOOKS

Carrington, Frank G. *The Victims*. New Rochelle, NY: Arlington House, 1975. $9.95.

Comments—Author contends that the criminal-justice system is a total failure. Conservative approach to problem. Victims are "unnamed and unrepresented."

Chapman, Jane R.; and Gates, M. *The Victimization of Women*. Beverly Hills, CA: Sage Publications, 1978. $18.50.

Comments—A book about violence, sex, and power. Eleven contributors—planners, practitioners, and policy-oriented professionals—all concerned with the ways in which women are collectively and individually abused in society.

Davidson, Terry. *Conjugal Crime*. New York: Hawthorn Books, 1978. $9.95.

Comments—Reviewed by Robert E. Gould in the New York *Times,* March 24, 1978: The ten chapters cover violence in the "best" families, the effects on children, the future, and the fastest-growing social movement in America. Appendixes include directory of fifty shelters and hotlines.

Gelles, Richard J. *The Violent Home: A Study of Physical Aggression Between Husbands and Wives*. Beverly Hills, CA: Sage Publications, 1972. $6.95.

Comments—Report of findings from interviews of eighty families. First major published research.

Langley, R. and Levy, R. *Wife-Beating: The Silent Crisis*. New York: E. P. Dutton, 1977. $9.95.

Comments—Introductory reference to the problem. Four case studies included. Cites sociologists, psychologists, criminologists, feminists, seven others.

Martin, Del. *Battered Wives*. San Francisco: New Glide Publications, 1976. $6.95.
    Comments—Ten chapters deal with violence in the home, the batterer, the victim, failure of the system, survival tactics, and remedial legislation. Author emphasizes the need to restructure the traditional family unit, giving women more power and control, to eliminate the inequities that exist.

McDonald, William, ed. *Criminal Justice and the Family*. Beverly Hills, CA: Sage Publications, 1976. $7.95.
    Comments—About relations between victim and criminal-justice system. Emphasizes victims as forgotten people in the system. Twenty-two contributors of articles.

Pascal, Harold. *Secret Scandal*. Canfield, OH: Alba House, 1977. $1.75.
    Comments—Written by a Catholic Vincentian priest and aimed at exposing the problem and encouraging others to come to the aid of battered women.

Pizzey, Erin. *Scream Quietly or the Neighbours Will Hear*. Ridlye Enslow, 60 Crescent Pl., Box 301, Short Hills, NJ 07078, 1974. $7.95.
    Comments—Author is founder of Chiswick Women's Aid, London, England. Experiences of the shelter are recorded in the book. Much success of the shelter is attributed to the willingness to accept all women, to respond quickly, and to provide a safe place for women to sort out their lives.

Roy, Maria. *Battered Women: A Psychosociological Study of Domestic Violence*. New York: Van Nostrand Reinhold, 1977. $10.95.
    Comments—Fourteen contributors, including Terry Davidson, Richard Gelles, Suzanne Steinmetz, Morton Bard, Darrel Stephens, Murray Straus, and others.

Steinmetz, Suzanne; and Straus, Murray, eds. *Violence in the Family*. New York: Dodd, Mead, 1974. $8.50.
    Comments—Over thirty contributors, including Morton Bard, Richard Gelles, Bruno Bettelheim, and other distinguished researchers.

Viano, Emilio, ed. *Victimology: An International Journal*. Washington, DC: Visage Press, 1977–78. $10.00.
    Comments—Contains book reviews, research and project notes, and over fifteen articles by Elaine Hilberman, Kit Munson, Lenore Walker, Elizabeth Waites, and others.

DOMESTIC-VIOLENCE NEWSLETTERS

Aegis: A Magazine on Organizing to Stop Violence Against Women, National Communications Network Feminist Alliance Against Rape, Box 21033, Washington, DC 20009. Send copy to: Denise Gamache, 4520 44th Ave. S., Minneapolis, MN 55406. $8.75 (indiv.); $20.00 (instit.).
    Comments—Purpose: "To generate a national network and facilitate a dialogue among feminists working to eliminate violence against women." Since April 1977.

Response: to Violence and Sexual Abuse in the Family, Center for Women Policy Studies, 2000 P Street, N.W., Suite 508, Washington, DC, 20036. Free.

> *Comments*—Since October 1976; expanded to monthly in October 1978. Will concentrate on problems of violence and sexual abuse in the family. LEAA-funded. Free

Monthly Memo on Family Violence, National Technical Assistance Center c/o Domestic Violence Project, Inc., 1917 Washtenaw Ave., Ann Arbor, MI 48104. Free.

SANEnews: (Spouse Abuse North East News), Domestic Violence Component of the Community Health Center, Inc. (CETA), P. O. Box 1076, Middletown, CT 06457.

> *Comments*—To date, four issues have been published to anyone wishing to be placed on the mailing list. They welcome information.

CONTRADICTING MASOCHISM THEORIES

Hiroto, D. S. "Locus of Control and Learned Helplessness," *Journal of Experimental Psychology,* 102, 1974.

Horney, Karen. *Feminine Psychology.* New York: W. W. Norton, 1967.

Kahneman, Daniel; and Tversky, Amos. *Prospect Theory: An Analysis of Decision Making Under Risk.* Technical Report PTR, Decision Research, 1977.

Klein, Melanie. *Envy and Gratitude and Other Works: 1946–1963.* New York: Delta Books, 1975.

Maier, N. R. F. *Frustration: The Study of Behavior Without a Goal.* Ann Arbor: University of Michigan Press, 1949.

Miller, W. P.; and Seligman, M. E. "Depression and Learned Helplessness in Man," *Journal of Abnormal Psychology,* 84(3), 1975.

INDEX

Abortion, 3

Abuse, 19–20, 21, 67, 78, 85, 227, 438; cause, 314–15; data, 332–34; legislation, 262ff.; love, 23; mandatory reporting, 441–42; "protection from" (law), 162–65; syndrome, 167; theories, 317. *See* Domestic violence

Abused Persons Program, 99, 311, 319

Abuser, *xvii, xix*, 12, 97, 125, 300, 314–15; characteristics, 66, 84, 92, 96, 97, 294–96, 331, 335 (*see* Chapter VI); convicted, 22; counseling, 12, 21–22, 285–96, 298ff., 303–9, 324; "identification with," 25; profile, 62, 287–96; programs, 296–309; rationalization, 294; role model, 25; staying with, 99, 100

Accompaniment, 442–46

ACTION (Agency for Volunteer Service), *xvi*, 419–21

Adultery, 34, 270

Advertising, 26

Advocacy, 11, 41, 146, 266, 359, 437, 442–46; groups, 58, 179, 181, 187, 200. *See* Advocates

Advocates, 48, 50–51, 97, 146, 198, 200ff., 438ff.; confidentiality, 226–27; criminal-justice system, 208–13; goals, 228ff.; guidelines, 442; prosecutors, difference, 196

Aegis, 263*n.,* 266, 515

Affirmative action, 384

Affluence, areas of, 330

AFSC (American Friends Service Committee), 213; clergy outreach, 441

Aged, the, 345

Akiko, Yosano, *xiv*

Alabama, 242, 420

Al-Anon, 56

Alaska, 242, 260, 421; shelters, 463

Alcohol (ics, ism), 37, 56, 104, 118, 130–31, 235, 290–92, 295, 314–15, 368, 376; abuse, 47–48, 91, 439; counseling, 367

Alcoholics Anonymous, 56

Alienation, 126

Aliens, 371. *See* Undocumented aliens

Alimony, 34, 91, 166, 440

Ambivalence, 88–92, 109, 120, 144

American Bar Association, 152*n.,* 202